Data Science and Big Data in Biology, Physical Science and Engineering

Data Science and Big Data in Biology, Physical Science and Engineering

Editor

Mohammed Mahmoud

 Basel • Beijing • Wuhan • Barcelona • Belgrade • Novi Sad • Cluj • Manchester

Editor
Mohammed Mahmoud
Department of Computer Science
University of Jamestown
Jamestown
United States

Editorial Office
MDPI
St. Alban-Anlage 66
4052 Basel, Switzerland

This is a reprint of articles from the Special Issue published online in the open access journal *Technologies* (ISSN 2227-7080) (available at: www.mdpi.com/journal/technologies/special_issues/ Data_Science_Biology).

For citation purposes, cite each article independently as indicated on the article page online and as indicated below:

Lastname, A.A.; Lastname, B.B. Article Title. *Journal Name* **Year**, *Volume Number*, Page Range.

ISBN 978-3-7258-0036-0 (Hbk)
ISBN 978-3-7258-0035-3 (PDF)
doi.org/10.3390/books978-3-7258-0035-3

© 2024 by the authors. Articles in this book are Open Access and distributed under the Creative Commons Attribution (CC BY) license. The book as a whole is distributed by MDPI under the terms and conditions of the Creative Commons Attribution-NonCommercial-NoDerivs (CC BY-NC-ND) license.

Contents

About the Editor vii

Mohammed Mahmoud
Editorial for the Special Issue "Data Science and Big Data in Biology, Physical Science and Engineering"
Reprinted from: *Technologies* 2024, *12*, 8, doi:10.3390/technologies12010008 1

Mehdi Imani and Hamid Reza Arabnia
Hyperparameter Optimization and Combined Data Sampling Techniques in Machine Learning for Customer Churn Prediction: A Comparative Analysis
Reprinted from: *Technologies* 2023, *11*, 167, doi:10.3390/technologies11060167 6

Jonathan Haase, Peter B. Walker, Olivia Berardi and Waldemar Karwowski
Get Real Get Better: A Framework for Developing Agile Program Management in the U.S. Navy Supported by the Application of Advanced Data Analytics and AI
Reprinted from: *Technologies* 2023, *11*, 165, doi:10.3390/technologies11060165 32

Abdu Salam, Faizan Ullah, Farhan Amin and Mohammad Abrar
Deep Learning Techniques for Web-Based Attack Detection in Industry 5.0: A Novel Approach
Reprinted from: *Technologies* 2023, *11*, 107, doi:10.3390/technologies11040107 48

Alireza Ebrahimi
Self-Directed and Self-Designed Learning: Integrating Imperative Topics in the Case of COVID-19
Reprinted from: *Technologies* 2023, *11*, 85, doi:10.3390/technologies11040085 66

Mohammadreza Iman, Hamid Reza Arabnia and Khaled Rasheed
A Review of Deep Transfer Learning and Recent Advancements
Reprinted from: *Technologies* 2023, *11*, 40, doi:10.3390/technologies11020040 76

Mohammad Arifuzzaman, Md. Rakibul Hasan, Tasnia Jahan Toma, Samia Binta Hassan and Anup Kumar Paul
An Advanced Decision Tree-Based Deep Neural Network in Nonlinear Data Classification
Reprinted from: *Technologies* 2023, *11*, 24, doi:10.3390/technologies11010024 90

Constantin Waubert de Puiseau, Dimitri Tegomo Nanfack, Hasan Tercan, Johannes Löbbert-Plattfaut and Tobias Meisen
Dynamic Storage Location Assignment in Warehouses Using Deep Reinforcement Learning
Reprinted from: *Technologies* 2022, *10*, 129, doi:10.3390/technologies10060129 114

Vittoria Biagi and Angela Russo
Data Model Design to Support Data-Driven IT Governance Implementation
Reprinted from: *Technologies* 2022, *10*, 106, doi:10.3390/technologies10050106 124

Jordina Orcajo Hernández and Pau Fonseca i Casas
Business Intelligence's Self-Service Tools Evaluation
Reprinted from: *Technologies* 2022, *10*, 92, doi:10.3390/technologies10040092 143

Teguh Handjojo Dwiputranto, Noor Akhmad Setiawan and Teguh Bharata Adji
Rough-Set-Theory-Based Classification with Optimized k-Means Discretization
Reprinted from: *Technologies* 2022, *10*, 51, doi:10.3390/technologies10020051 181

Tendai Musvuugwa, Muxe Gladmond Dlomu and Adekunle Adebowale
Big Data in Biodiversity Science: A Framework for Engagement
Reprinted from: *Technologies* **2021**, *9*, 60, doi:10.3390/technologies9030060 . . . . **194**

Evan Muzzall
A Novel Ensemble Machine Learning Approach for Bioarchaeological Sex Prediction
Reprinted from: *Technologies* **2021**, *9*, 23, doi:10.3390/technologies9020023 . . . . **214**

About the Editor

Mohammed Mahmoud

Dr. Mahmoud has occupied academic positions at several institutions, including Oakland University, Minnesota State University, and Bemidji State University, and is currently an Associate Professor of Computer Science at the University of Jamestown. Dr. Mahmoud is also a Topical Advisory Panel Member of both the *Sensors* and *Technologies* journals (MDPI). His research interests are Data Science, Big Data, Machine Learning, Deep Learning, Artificial Intelligence (AI), and Cybersecurity. In 2022, Dr. Mahmoud received the Outstanding Achievement Award in recognition and appreciation of his overall research leadership and contributions from the 2022 World Congress in Computer Science, Computer Engineering, and Applied Computing (CSCE 2022). He also received the Outstanding Achievement Award in recognition and appreciation of his research contributions to the fields of Cybersecurity and Machine Learning. In 2023, Dr. Mahmoud received the Outstanding Achievement Award in recognition and appreciation of his scholarly activities and undergraduate research leadership in Quantum Computing from the 2023 World Congress in Computer Science, Computer Engineering, and Applied Computing (CSCE 2023). He is also the recipient of the Outstanding Achievement Award in recognition and appreciation of his innovation and excellence in undergraduate teaching.

Dr. Mahmoud was the Editor-in-Chief for the 2022–2023 *Journal of Undergraduate and Graduate Student Research* as well as the Founder and Chair of the Computer Science Advisory Board at Bemidji State University. Dr. Mahmoud consistently attends different conferences, where he has chaired many sessions on varied topics in his areas of expertise. He also works on obtaining grants from several universities, in addition to research grants from academic journals.

Dr. Mahmoud established robust industry engagement and partnerships with various businesses in the industry. Additionally, he has obtained numerous industry certifications.

Editorial

Editorial for the Special Issue "Data Science and Big Data in Biology, Physical Science and Engineering"

Mohammed Mahmoud

Department of Computer Science, University of Jamestown, Jamestown, ND 58405, USA; prof.mahmoud@uj.edu

Citation: Mahmoud, M. Editorial for the Special Issue "Data Science and Big Data in Biology, Physical Science and Engineering". *Technologies* **2024**, *12*, 8. https://doi.org/10.3390/technologies12010008

Received: 18 December 2023
Revised: 27 December 2023
Accepted: 4 January 2024
Published: 8 January 2024

Copyright: © 2024 by the author. Licensee MDPI, Basel, Switzerland. This article is an open access article distributed under the terms and conditions of the Creative Commons Attribution (CC BY) license (https://creativecommons.org/licenses/by/4.0/).

Big Data analysis is one of the most contemporary areas of development and research in the present day. Tremendous amounts of data are generated every single day from digital technologies and modern information systems, such as cloud computing and Internet of Things (IoT) devices. Analysis of these enormous amounts of data became a essential and requires a large amount of effort in order to extract valuable knowledge for decision making which, in turn, will help in both academia and industry.

Big Data and Data Science have appeared due to the significant need for generating, storing, organizing and processing immense amounts of data. Data Scientists strive to use Artificial Intelligence (AI) and Machine Learning (ML) approaches and models to enable computers to detect and identify what the data represent and to detect patterns more quickly, efficiently and reliably than humans.

The goal behind this Special Issue is to explore and discuss various principles, tools and models in the context of Data Science, in addition to diverse and varied concepts and techniques regarding Big Data in Biology, Chemistry, Biomedical Engineering, Physics, Mathematics and other areas.

In this Special Issue, we present 12 papers that span a wide range of topics relating to Data Science, Big Data, machine learning, deep learning, Artificial Intelligence (AI) and cybersecurity.

In [1], the authors explored the application of various machine learning techniques for predicting customer churn in the telecommunications sector. They utilized a publicly accessible dataset and implemented several models, including Artificial Neural Networks, Decision Trees, Support Vector Machines, Random Forests, Logistic Regression and gradient boosting techniques (XGBoost, LightGBM and CatBoost). To mitigate the challenges posed by imbalanced datasets, the authors adopted different data sampling strategies, namely, SMOTE, SMOTE combined with Tomek Links and SMOTE combined with Edited Nearest Neighbors. Moreover, hyperparameter tuning was employed to enhance model performance. Their evaluation employed standard metrics, such as Precision, Recall, F1-score and the Receiver Operating Characteristic Area Under Curve (ROC AUC). In terms of the F1-score metric, CatBoost demonstrates superior performance compared to other machine learning models, achieving an outstanding 93% following the application of Optuna hyperparameter optimization. In the context of the ROC AUC metric, both XGBoost and CatBoost exhibit exceptional performance, recording remarkable scores of 91%. This achievement for XGBoost is attained after implementing a combination of SMOTE with Tomek Links, while CatBoost reaches this level of performance after the application of Optuna hyperparameter optimization.

In [2], the authors discussed the "Get Real Get Better" (GRGB) approach to implementing agile program management in the U.S. Navy, supported by advanced data analytics and Artificial Intelligence (AI). GRGB was designed as a set of foundational principles to advance Navy culture and support its core values. This article identifies a need for a more informed and efficient approach to program management by highlighting the benefits of implementing comprehensive data analytics that leverage recent advances in cloud computing and machine learning. The Jupiter enclave within Advana implemented by the

U.S. Navy is also discussed. The presented approach represents a practical framework that cultivates a "Get Real Get Better" mindset for implementing agile program management in the U.S. Navy.

As the manufacturing industry advances towards Industry 5.0, which heavily integrates advanced technologies such as cyber-physical systems, Artificial Intelligence, and the Internet of Things (IoT), the potential for web-based attacks increases. Cybersecurity concerns remain a crucial challenge for Industry 5.0 environments, where cyber attacks can cause devastating consequences, including production downtime, data breaches and even physical harm. To address this challenge, the third paper [3] proposed an innovative deep-learning methodology for detecting web-based attacks in Industry 5.0. Convolutional neural networks (CNNs), recurrent neural networks (RNNs) and transformer models are examples of deep learning techniques that are investigated in this study for their potential to effectively classify attacks and identify anomalous behavior. The proposed transformer-based system outperforms traditional machine learning methods and existing deep learning approaches in terms of accuracy, precision and recall, demonstrating the effectiveness of deep learning for intrusion detection in Industry 5.0. The study's findings highlighted the superiority of the proposed transformer-based system, outperforming previous approaches in accuracy, precision and recall. This highlights the significant contribution of deep learning in addressing cybersecurity challenges in Industry 5.0 environments, ensuring the protection of critical infrastructure and sensitive data.

Self-directed learning and self-design became unexpectedly popular and common during the COVID-19 era. Learners are encouraged to take charge of their learning and, often, the opportunity to independently design their learning experience. The fourth paper [4] illustrates the use of technology in teaching and learning technology with a central theme of promoting self-directed learning with engaging self-design for both educators and learners. The technology used includes existing tools such as web page design, Learning Management Systems (LMS), project management tools and basic programming foundations and concepts of Big Data and databases. In addition, end-users and developers can create their own tools with simple coding. Planning techniques, such as Visual Plan Construct Language with its embedded AI, are used to integrate course material and rubrics with time management. Educators may use project management tools instead. The research proposes a self-directed paradigm with self-designed resources using the existing technology with LMS modules, discussions and self-tests. The research establishes its criteria for ensuring the quality of content and design, known as 7x2C. Additionally, other criteria for analysis, such as Design Thinking, are included. The approach is examined for a technology-based business course in creating an experiential learning system for COVID-19 awareness. Likewise, among other projects, an environment for educating learners about diabetes and obesity has been designed. The project is known as Sunchoke, which has a theme of Grow, Eat and Heal. Educators can use their own content and rubrics to adapt this approach to their own customized teaching methods.

Deep neural networks (DNNs), the integration of neural networks (NNs) and deep learning (DL), have proven highly efficient in executing numerous complex tasks, such as data and image classification. Because the multilayer in a nonlinearly separable data structure is not transparent, it is critical to develop a specific data classification model from a new and unexpected dataset. In the fifth paper [5], the authors proposed a novel approach using the concepts of DNNs and decision trees (DTs) for classifying nonlinear data. They first developed a decision tree-based neural network (DTBNN) model. Next, they extended their model to a decision tree-based deep neural network (DTBDNN), in which the multiple hidden layers in a DNN are utilized. By using a DNN, the DTBDNN model achieved higher accuracy compared to the related and relevant approaches. Their proposal achieved the optimal trainable weights and bias to build an efficient model for nonlinear data classification by combining the benefits of DTs and NNs. By conducting in-depth performance evaluations, they demonstrated the effectiveness and feasibility of the proposal by achieving good accuracy over different datasets.

Organizations must quickly adapt their processes to understand the dynamic nature of modern business environments. As highlighted in the literature [6], centralized governance supports decision making and performance measurement processes in technology companies. For this reason, a reliable decision-making system with an integrated data model that enables the rapid collection and transformation of data stored in heterogeneous and different sources is needed. Therefore, the sixth paper [6] proposed the design of a data model to implement data-driven governance through a literature review of adopted approaches. The lack of a standardized procedure and a disconnection between theoretical frameworks and practical application has emerged. This paper documented the suggested approach following these steps: (i) mapping of monitoring requirements to the data structure, (ii) documentation of ER diagram design, and (iii) reporting dashboards used for monitoring and reporting. The paper helped fill the gaps highlighted in the literature by supporting the design and development of a DWH data model coupled with a BI system. The application prototype shows benefits for top management, particularly those responsible for governance and operations, especially risk monitoring, audit compliance, communication, knowledge sharing on strategic areas of the company, and identification and implementation of performance improvements and optimizations.

The discretization of continuous attributes in a dataset is an essential step before the Rough-Set-Theory (RST)-based classification process is applied. There are many methods for discretization, but few have linked RST instruments from the beginning of the discretization process. The objective of the seventh paper [7] was to propose a method to improve the accuracy and reliability of the RST-based classifier model by involving RST instruments at the beginning of the discretization process. In the proposed method, a k-means-based discretization method optimized with a genetic algorithm (GA) was introduced. Four datasets taken from UCI were selected to test the performance of the proposed method. The evaluation of the proposed discretization technique for RST-based classification was performed by comparing it to other discretization methods, i.e., equal frequency and entropy-based. The performance comparison among these methods was measured by the number of bins and rules generated and by their accuracy, precision and recall. A Friedman test, continued with post hoc analysis, was also applied to measure the significance of the difference in performance. The experimental results indicate that, in general, the performance of the proposed discretization method is significantly better than the other compared methods.

The eighth paper [8] presented a novel machine learning approach to predict sex in bioarchaeological records. Eighteen cranial interlandmark distances and five maxillary dental metric distances were recorded from n = 420 human skeletons from the necropolises at Alfedena (600–400 BCE) and Campovalano (750–200 BCE and 9–11th Centuries CE) in central Italy. A generalized low rank model (GLRM) was used to impute missing data and the Receiver Operating Characteristic Area Under Curve (AUC-ROC) with 20-fold stratified cross-validation was used to evaluate the predictive performance of eight machine learning algorithms on different subsets of the data. Additional perspectives such as this one show strong potential for sex prediction in bioarchaeological and forensic anthropological contexts. Furthermore, GLRMs have the potential to handle missing data in ways previously unexplored in the discipline. Although the results of this study look promising (highest AUC-ROC = 0.9722 for predicting binary male/female sex), the main limitation is that the sexes of the individuals included were not known but were estimated using standard macroscopic bioarchaeological methods. However, future research should apply this machine learning approach to known-sex reference samples in order to better understand its value, along with the more general contributions that machine learning can make to the reconstruction of past human lives.

Deep learning has been the answer to many machine learning problems during the past two decades. However, it comes with two significant constraints: dependency on extensive labeled data and training costs. Transfer learning in deep learning, known as Deep Transfer Learning (DTL), attempts to reduce such reliance and costs by reusing obtained knowledge from source data/task in training on a target data/task. Most applied DTL techniques are network/model-based approaches. These methods reduce the dependency of deep learning models on extensive training data and drastically decrease training costs. Moreover, the training cost reduction makes DTL viable on edge devices with limited resources. Like any new advancement, DTL methods have their own limitations, and a successful transfer depends on specific adjustments and strategies for different scenarios. The ninth paper [9] reviewed the concept, definition, and taxonomy of deep transfer learning and well-known methods. It investigated DTL approaches by reviewing applied DTL techniques of the past five years and a couple of experimental analyses of DTLs to discover the best practice for using DTL in different scenarios. Moreover, the limitations of DTLs (catastrophic forgetting dilemma and overly biased pre-trained models) were discussed, along with possible solutions and research trends.

Despite best efforts, the loss of biodiversity has continued at a pace that constitutes a major threat to the efficient functioning of ecosystems. Curbing the loss of biodiversity and assessing its local and global trends requires a vast amount of datasets from a variety of sources. Although the means for generating, aggregating and analyzing big datasets to inform policies are now within reach of the scientific community, the data-driven nature of a complex multidisciplinary field such as biodiversity science necessitates an overarching framework for engagement. In the tenth paper [10], the authors proposed such a schematic based on the life cycle of data to interrogate the science. The framework considers data generation and collection, storage and curation, access and analysis and, finally, communication as distinct yet interdependent themes for engaging biodiversity science for the purpose of making evidenced-based decisions. The authors summarized historical developments in each theme, including the challenges and prospects, and offered some recommendations based on best practices.

The warehousing industry is faced with increasing customer demands and growing global competition. A major factor in the efficient operation of warehouses is the strategic storage location assignment of arriving goods, termed the dynamic storage location assignment problem (DSLAP). The eleventh paper [11] presented a real-world case of the DSLAP, in which deep reinforcement learning (DRL) is used to derive a suitable storage location assignment strategy to decrease transportation costs within the warehouse. The DRL agent is trained on historic data of storage and retrieval operations gathered over one year of operation. An evaluation of the agent using new data of the past two months showed a 6.3% decrease in incurring costs compared to the currently utilized storage location assignment strategy, which is based on manual ABC classifications. Hence, DRL proves to be a competitive solution for the DSLAP and related problems in the warehousing industry.

The software selection process in the context of a big company is not an easy task. In the business intelligence area, this decision is critical since the resources needed to implement the tool are huge and necessitate the participation of all organization actors. In the twelfth paper [12], the authors proposed to adopt the systemic quality model to perform a neutral comparison between four business intelligence self-service tools. To assess the quality, they considered eight characteristics and eighty-two metrics. They built a methodology to evaluate self-service BI tools, adapting the systemic quality model. As an example, they evaluated four tools that were selected from all business intelligence platforms, following a rigorous methodology. Through the assessment, they obtained two tools with the maximum quality level. To acquire the differences between them, they were more restrictive increasing the level of satisfaction. Finally, they obtained a unique tool with the maximum quality level, while the other one was rejected according to the rules established in the methodology. The methodology works well for this type of software, helping in the detailed analysis and neutral selection of the final software to be used for the implementation.

Acknowledgments: I would like to take the opportunity to thank all the authors for submitting their work and contributing to the journal, as well as their passion for research. I would also like to extend a special thank you to the reviewers for their dedication in reading the submitted papers and providing useful comments that helped support their entry into the Special Issue. It was an absolute pleasure reviewing the submitted work for the Special Issue of the *Technologies* journal.

Conflicts of Interest: The authors declare no conflict of interest.

References

1. Imani, M.; Arabnia, H.R. Hyperparameter Optimization and Combined Data Sampling Techniques in Machine Learning for Customer Churn Prediction: A Comparative Analysis. *Technologies* **2023**, *11*, 167. [CrossRef]
2. Haase, J.; Walker, P.B.; Berardi, O.; Karwowski, W. Get Real Get Better: A Framework for Developing Agile Program Management in the U.S. Navy Supported by the Application of Advanced Data Analytics and AI. *Technologies* **2023**, *11*, 165. [CrossRef]
3. Salam, A.; Ullah, F.; Amin, F.; Abrar, M. Deep Learning Techniques for Web-Based Attack Detection in Industry 5.0: A Novel Approach. *Technologies* **2023**, *11*, 107. [CrossRef]
4. Ebrahimi, A. Self-Directed and Self-Designed Learning: Integrating Imperative Topics in the Case of COVID-19. *Technologies* **2023**, *11*, 85. [CrossRef]
5. Arifuzzaman, M.; Hasan, M.R.; Toma, T.J.; Hassan, S.B.; Paul, A.K. An Advanced Decision Tree-Based Deep Neural Network in Nonlinear Data Classification. *Technologies* **2023**, *11*, 24. [CrossRef]
6. Biagi, V.; Russo, A. Data Model Design to Support Data-Driven IT Governance Implementation. *Technologies* **2022**, *10*, 106. [CrossRef]
7. Dwiputranto, T.H.; Setiawan, N.A.; Adji, T.B. Rough-Set-Theory-Based Classification with Optimized *k*-Means Discretization. *Technologies* **2022**, *10*, 51. [CrossRef]
8. Muzzall, E. A Novel Ensemble Machine Learning Approach for Bioarchaeological Sex Prediction. *Technologies* **2021**, *9*, 23. [CrossRef]
9. Iman, M.; Arabnia, H.R.; Rasheed, K. A Review of Deep Transfer Learning and Recent Advancements. *Technologies* **2023**, *11*, 40. [CrossRef]
10. Musvuugwa, T.; Dlomu, M.G.; Adebowale, A. Big Data in Biodiversity Science: A Framework for Engagement. *Technologies* **2021**, *9*, 60. [CrossRef]
11. Waubert de Puiseau, C.; Nanfack, D.T.; Tercan, H.; Löbbert-Plattfaut, J.; Meisen, T. Dynamic Storage Location Assignment in Warehouses Using Deep Reinforcement Learning. *Technologies* **2022**, *10*, 129. [CrossRef]
12. Orcajo Hernández, J.; Fonseca i Casas, P. Business Intelligence's Self-Service Tools Evaluation. *Technologies* **2022**, *10*, 92. [CrossRef]

Disclaimer/Publisher's Note: The statements, opinions and data contained in all publications are solely those of the individual author(s) and contributor(s) and not of MDPI and/or the editor(s). MDPI and/or the editor(s) disclaim responsibility for any injury to people or property resulting from any ideas, methods, instructions or products referred to in the content.

Review

Hyperparameter Optimization and Combined Data Sampling Techniques in Machine Learning for Customer Churn Prediction: A Comparative Analysis

Mehdi Imani [1,*] and Hamid Reza Arabnia [2,*]

1. Department of Computer and System Sciences, Stockholm University, 10691 Stockholm, Sweden
2. School of Computing, University of Georgia, Athens, GA 30602, USA
* Correspondence: m.imani@gmail.com (M.I.); hra@uga.edu (H.R.A.)

Abstract: This paper explores the application of various machine learning techniques for predicting customer churn in the telecommunications sector. We utilized a publicly accessible dataset and implemented several models, including Artificial Neural Networks, Decision Trees, Support Vector Machines, Random Forests, Logistic Regression, and gradient boosting techniques (XGBoost, LightGBM, and CatBoost). To mitigate the challenges posed by imbalanced datasets, we adopted different data sampling strategies, namely SMOTE, SMOTE combined with Tomek Links, and SMOTE combined with Edited Nearest Neighbors. Moreover, hyperparameter tuning was employed to enhance model performance. Our evaluation employed standard metrics, such as Precision, Recall, F1-score, and the Receiver Operating Characteristic Area Under Curve (ROC AUC). In terms of the F1-score metric, CatBoost demonstrates superior performance compared to other machine learning models, achieving an outstanding 93% following the application of Optuna hyperparameter optimization. In the context of the ROC AUC metric, both XGBoost and CatBoost exhibit exceptional performance, recording remarkable scores of 91%. This achievement for XGBoost is attained after implementing a combination of SMOTE with Tomek Links, while CatBoost reaches this level of performance after the application of Optuna hyperparameter optimization.

Keywords: machine learning; churn prediction; imbalanced data; combined data sampling techniques; hyperparameter optimization

Citation: Imani, M.; Arabnia, H.R. Hyperparameter Optimization and Combined Data Sampling Techniques in Machine Learning for Customer Churn Prediction: A Comparative Analysis. *Technologies* **2023**, *11*, 167. https://doi.org/10.3390/technologies11060167

Academic Editors: Mohammed Mahmoud and Sikha Bagui

Received: 17 August 2023
Revised: 17 November 2023
Accepted: 21 November 2023
Published: 26 November 2023

Copyright: © 2023 by the authors. Licensee MDPI, Basel, Switzerland. This article is an open access article distributed under the terms and conditions of the Creative Commons Attribution (CC BY) license (https://creativecommons.org/licenses/by/4.0/).

1. Introduction

The implementation of Customer Relationship Management (CRM) is a strategic approach to managing and enhancing relationships between businesses and their customers. CRM is a tool employed to gain deeper insights into the requirements and behaviors of consumers, specifically end users, with the aim of fostering a more robust and meaningful relationship with them. Through the utilization of CRM, businesses can establish an infrastructure that fosters long-term and loyal customers. This concept is relevant across various industries, such as banking [1–4], insurance companies [5], and telecommunications [6–14], to name a few.

The telecommunications sector assumes a prominent role as a leading industry in revenue generation and a crucial driver of socioeconomic advancement in numerous countries globally. It is estimated that this sector incurs expenditures of approximately 4.7 trillion dollars annually [1,2]. Within the sector, there exists a high degree of competition among companies, driven by their pursuit of augmenting revenue streams and expanding the market influence through the acquisition of an expanded customer base. A key objective of CRM is customer retention, as studies have demonstrated that the cost of acquiring new customers can be 20 times higher than retaining existing ones [1]. Therefore, maintaining existing customers in the telecommunications industry is crucial for increasing revenue and reducing marketing and advertising costs.

The telecommunications sector is grappling with the substantial issue of customer attrition, commonly referred to as churn. This escalating issue has prompted service providers to shift their emphasis from acquiring new customers to retaining existing ones, considering the significant costs associated with customer acquisition. In recent years, service providers have been progressively emphasizing the establishment of enduring relationships with their customers. Consequently, these providers uphold CRM databases wherein every customer-specific interaction is systematically documented [5]. CRM databases serve as valuable resources for proactively predicting and addressing customer requirements by leveraging a combination of business processes and machine learning (ML) methodologies to analyze and understand customer behavior.

The primary goal of ML models is to predict and categorize customers into one of two groups: churn or non-churn, representing a binary classification problem. As a result, it is imperative for businesses to develop practical tools to achieve this goal. In recent years, various ML methods have been proposed for constructing a churn model, including Decision Trees (DTs) [8–16], Artificial Neural Networks (ANNs) [8,9,15–17], Random Forests (RFs) [18,19], Logistic Regression (LR) [9,12], Support Vector Machines (SVMs) [16], and a Rough Set Approach [20], among others.

In the following, an overview is provided of the most frequently utilized techniques for addressing the issue of churn prediction, including Artificial Neural Networks, Decision Trees, Support Vector Machines, Random Forests, Logistic Regression, and three advanced gradient boosting techniques, namely eXtreme Gradient Boosting (XGBoost), Categorical Boosting (CatBoost) and Light Gradient Boosting Machine (LightGBM).

Ensemble techniques [21], specifically boosting and bagging algorithms, have become the prevalent choice for addressing classification problems [22,23], particularly in the realm of churn prediction [24,25], due to their demonstrated high effectiveness. While many studies have explored the field of churn prediction, our research distinguishes itself by offering a comprehensive examination of how machine learning techniques, imbalanced data, and predictive accuracy intersect.

We carefully investigate a wide range of machine learning algorithms, along with innovative data sampling methods and precise hyperparameter optimization techniques. The objective is to offer subscription-based companies a comprehensive framework for effectively tackling the complex task of predicting customer churn. In the current data-centric business environment, the relevance of this study is not only significant but also imperative. It equips subscription-based businesses with the tools to retain customers, optimize revenue, and develop lasting relationships with their customers in the face of evolving industry dynamics. This study makes several significant contributions, including the following:

1. Providing a comprehensive definition of binary classification machine learning techniques tailored for imbalanced data.
2. Conducting an extensive review of diverse sampling techniques designed to address imbalanced data.
3. Offering a detailed account of the training and validation procedures within imbalanced domains.
4. Explaining the key evaluation metrics that are well-suited for imbalanced data scenarios.
5. Employing various machine learning models and conducting a thorough assessment, comparing their performance using commonly employed metrics across three distinct phases: after applying feature selection, after applying SMOTE, after applying SMOTE combined with Tomek Links, after applying SMOTE combined with ENN, and after applying Optuna hyperparameter tuning.

Table 1, below, shows a summary of the important acronyms used throughout this paper.

Table 1. Summary of important acronyms.

Acronym	Meaning
ANN	Artificial Neural Network
AUC	Area Under the Curve
BPN	Back-Propagation Network
CatBoost	Categorical Boosting
CNN	Condensed Nearest Neighbor
DT	Decision Tree
ENN	Edited Nearest Neighbor
LightGBM	Light Gradient Boosting Machine
LR	Logistic Regression
ML	Machine Learning
RF	Random Forest
ROC	Receiver Operating Characteristic
SMOTE	Synthetic Minority Over-Sampling Technique
SVM	Support Vector Machine
XGBoost	eXtreme Gradient Boosting

The remainder of the paper is organized as follows: Section 2 presents an introduction to classification machine learning techniques, Section 3 delves into the examination of sampling methods, Section 4 explains the training and validation process, Section 5 defines evaluation metrics, simulation results are presented in Section 6, and the paper concludes in Section 7.

2. Classification of Machine Learning Techniques

2.1. Artificial Neural Network

An Artificial Neural Network (ANN) is a widely employed technique for addressing complex issues, such as the churn-prediction problem [26]. ANNs are structures composed of interconnected units that are modeled after the human brain. They can be utilized with various learning algorithms to enhance the machine learning process and can take both hardware and software forms. One of the most widely utilized models is the Multi-Layer Perceptron, which is trained using the Back-Propagation Network (BPN) algorithm. Research has demonstrated that ANNs possess superior performance compared to Decision Trees (DTs) [26] and have been shown to exhibit improved performance when compared to Logistic Regression (LR) and DTs in the context of churn prediction [27].

2.2. Support Vector Machine

The technique of Support Vector Machine (SVM) was first introduced by the authors in [28]. It is classified as a supervised learning technique that utilizes learning algorithms to uncover latent patterns within data. A popular method for improving the performance of SVMs is the utilization of kernel functions [8]. In addressing customer churn problems, SVM may exhibit superior performance in comparison to Artificial Neural Networks (ANNs) and Decision Trees (DTs) based on the specific characteristics of the data [16,29].

For this study, we utilized both the Gaussian Radial Basis kernel function (RBF-SVM) and the Polynomial kernel function (Poly-SVM) for the Support Vector Machine (SVM) technique. These kernel functions are among the various options available for use with SVM.

For two samples x and x′, the RBF kernel is defined as follows:

$$K(x, x') = exp\left(-\frac{\|x - x'\|^2}{2\delta^2}\right) \quad (1)$$

where $\|x - x'\|^2$ can be the squared Euclidean distance, and δ is a free parameter.

For two samples x and x′, the d-degree polynomial kernel is defined as follows:

$$K(x.x') = \left(x^T x' + c\right)^d \qquad (2)$$

where $c \geq 0$ and $d \geq 1$ is the polynomial degree.

2.3. Decision Tree

A Decision Tree is a representation of all potential decision pathways in the form of a tree structure [30,31]. As Berry and Linoff stated, "a Decision Tree is a structure that can be used to divide up a large collection of records into successively smaller sets of records by applying a sequence of simple decision rules" [32]. Though they may not be as efficient in uncovering complex patterns or detecting intricate relationships within data, DTs may be used to address the customer churn problem, depending on the characteristics of the data. In DTs, class labels are indicated by leaves, and the conjunctions between various features are represented by branches.

2.4. Logistic Regression

Logistic Regression (LR) is a classification method that falls under the category of probabilistic statistics. It can be employed to address the churn-prediction problem by making predictions based on multiple predictor variables. In order to obtain high accuracy, which can sometimes be comparable to that of Decision Trees [9], it is often beneficial to apply pre-processing and transformation techniques to the original data prior to utilizing LR.

2.5. Ensemble Learning

Ensemble learning is one of the widely utilized techniques in machine learning for combining the outputs of multiple learning models (often referred to as base learners) into a single classifier [33]. In ensemble learning, it is possible to combine various weak machine learning models (base learners) to construct a stronger model with more accurate predictions [21,22]. Currently, ensemble learning methods are widely accepted as a standard choice for enhancing the accuracy of machine learning predictors [22]. Bagging and boosting are two distinct types of ensemble learning techniques that can be utilized to improve the accuracy of machine learning predictors [21].

2.5.1. Bagging

As depicted in Figure 1, in the bagging technique, the training data are partitioned into multiple subset sets, and the model is trained on each subset. The final prediction is then obtained by combining all individual outputs through majority voting (in classification problems) or average voting (in regression problems) [21,34–36].

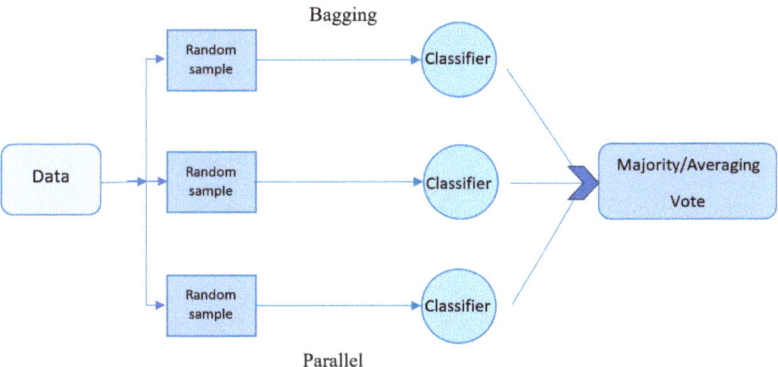

Figure 1. Visualization of the bagging approach.

Random Forest

The concept of Random Forest was first introduced by Ho in 1995 [18] and has been the subject of ongoing improvements by various researchers. One notable advancement in this field was made by Leo Breiman in 2001 [19]. Random Forests are an ensemble learning technique for classification tasks that employs a large number of Decision Trees in the training model. The output of Random Forests is a class that is selected by the majority of the trees, as shown in Figure 2. In general, Random Forests exhibit superior performance compared to Decision Trees. However, the performance can be influenced by the characteristics of the data.

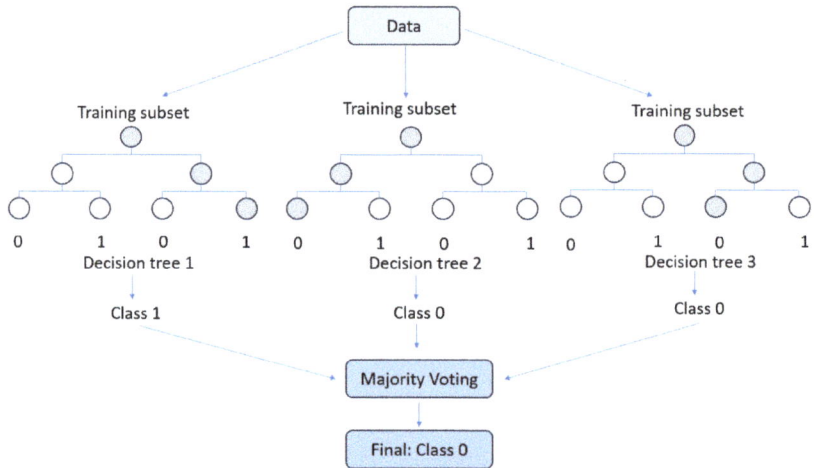

Figure 2. Visualization of the Random Forest classifier.

Random Forests utilize the bagging technique for their training algorithm. In greater detail, the Random Forests operate as follows: for a training set $TS_n = \{(x_1.y_1). \cdots .(x_n.y_n)\}$, bagging is repeated B times, and each iteration selects a random sample with a replacement from TS_n and fits trees to the samples:

1. Sample n training examples, $X_b.Y_b$.
2. Train a classification tree (in the case of churn problems) f_b on the samples $X_b.Y_b$.

After the training phase, Random Forests can predict unseen samples x' by taking the majority vote from all the individual classification trees x'.

$$\hat{f} = \frac{1}{B}\sum_{b=1}^{B} f_b(x') \quad (3)$$

2.5.2. Boosting

Boosting is another method for combining multiple base learners to construct a stronger model with more accurate predictions. The key distinction between bagging and boosting is that bagging uses a parallel approach to combine weak learners, while boosting methods utilize a sequential approach to combine weak learners and derive the final prediction, as shown in Figure 3. Like the bagging technique, boosting improves the performance of machine learning predictors, and in addition, it reduces the bias of the model [21].

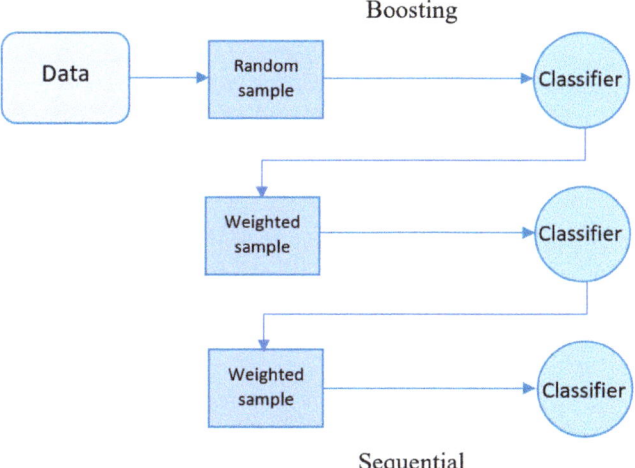

Figure 3. Visualization of the boosting approach.

The Famous Trio: XGBoost, LightGBM, and CatBoost

Recently, researchers have presented three effective gradient-based approaches using Decision Trees: CatBoost, LightGBM, and XGBoost. These new approaches have demonstrated successful applications in academia, industry, and competitive machine learning [37]. Utilizing gradient boosting techniques, solutions can be constructed in a stagewise manner, and the over-fitting problem can be addressed through the optimization of loss functions. For example, given a loss function $\psi(y, f(x))$ and a custom base-learner $h(x, \theta)$ (e.g., Decision Tree), the direct estimation of parameters can be challenging. Thus, an iterative model is proposed, which is updated at each iteration with the selection of a new base-learner function $h(x, \theta t)$, where the increment is directed by the following:

$$g_t(x) = E_y\left[\frac{\partial \psi(y, f(x))}{\partial f(x)}|x\right]_{f(x)=\hat{f}^{t-1}(x)} \quad (4)$$

Hence, the hard optimization problem is substituted with the typical least-squares optimization problem:

$$(p_t, \theta_t) = \arg\min_{p,\theta} \sum_{i=1}^{N}[-g_t(x_i) + ph(x_i, \theta)]^2 \quad (5)$$

Friedman's gradient boost algorithm is summarized by Algorithm 1.

Algorithm 1 Gradient Boost

1: *Let $\hat{f}_0$ be a constant*
2: *For i = 1 to M*
 a. Compute $g_i(x)$ using eq()
 b. Train the function $h(x, \theta_i)$
 c. Find p_i using eq()
 d. Update the function

$$\hat{f}_i = \hat{f}_{i-1} + p_i h(x, \theta_i)$$

3: *End*

After initiating the algorithm with a single leaf, the learning rate is optimized for each record and each node [38–40]. The XGBoost method is a highly flexible, versatile, and scalable tool that has been developed to effectively utilize resources and overcome the limitations of previous gradient boosting methods. The primary distinction between other gradient boosting methods and XGBoost is that XGBoost utilizes a new regularization approach for controlling overfitting, making it more robust and efficient when the model is fine-tuned. To regularize this approach, a new term is added to the loss function as follows:

$$L(f) = \sum_{i=1}^{n} L(\hat{y}_i, y_i) + \sum_{m=1}^{M} \Omega(\delta_m) \tag{6}$$

with

$$\Omega(\delta) = \alpha|\delta| + 0.5\beta||w||^2$$

where w represents the value of each leaf, Ω indicates the regularization function, and $|\delta|$ denotes the number of branches. A new gain function is used by XGBoost, as follows:

$$G_j = \sum_{i \in I_j} g_i \tag{7}$$

$$H_j = \sum_{i \in I_j} h_i$$

$$\text{Gain} = \frac{1}{2}\left[\frac{G_L^2}{H_L + \beta} + \frac{G_R^2}{H_R + \beta} - \frac{(G_R + G_L)^2}{H_R + H_L + \beta}\right] - \alpha$$

where

$$g_i = \partial_{\hat{y}_i} L(\hat{y}_i + y_i)$$

and

$$h_i = \partial_{\hat{y}_i}^2 L(\hat{y}_i + y_i)$$

The Gain represents the score of the no new child case, H indicates the score of the left child, and G denotes the score of the right child [41].

To decrease the implementation time, the LightGBM method was developed by a team from Microsoft in April 2017 [42]. The primary difference is that LightGBM Decision Trees are constructed in a leaf-wise manner, rather than evaluating all previous leaves for each new leaf (Figure 4a,b). The attributes are grouped and sorted into bins, known as the histogram implementation. LightGBM offers several benefits, including a faster training speed, higher accuracy, and the ability to handle large scale data and support GPU learning.

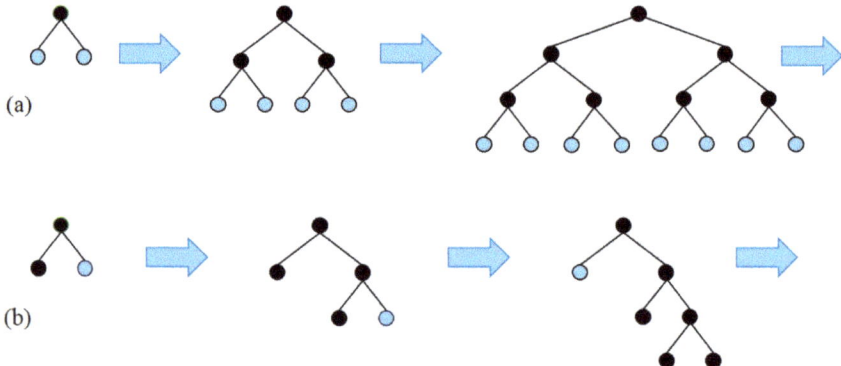

Figure 4. Comparison of tree growth methods. (a) XGBoost Level-wise tree growth. (b) LightGBM Leaf-wise tree growth.

The focus of CatBoost is on categorical columns through the use of permutation methods, target-based statistics, and one_hot_max_size (OHMS). By using a greedy technique at each new split of the current tree, CatBoost has the capability to address the exponential

growth of feature combinations. The steps described below are employed by CatBoost for each feature with more categories than the OHMS (an input parameter):
1. To randomly divide the records into subsets,
2. To convert the labels to integer numbers,
3. To transform the categorical features to numerical features, as follows:

$$\text{avgTarget} = \frac{\text{countInClass} + \text{prior}}{\text{totalCount} + 1} \qquad (8)$$

where totalCount denotes the number of previous objects, countInClass represents the number of ones in the target for a specific categorical feature, and the starting parameters specify prior [43].

3. Handling Imbalanced Data

Imbalanced data are a prevalent problem in data mining. For instance, in binary classifications, the number of instances in the majority class may be significantly higher than the number of instances in the minority class. As a result, the ratio of instances in the minority class to instances in the majority class (imbalanced ratio) may vary from 1:2 to 1:1000. The dataset used in this study is imbalanced, with the distribution of majority class (non-churned) instances being six times that of the minority class (churned) instances [44].

3.1. The Challenge of Imbalanced Data

While imbalanced datasets can skew overall model performance metrics towards the majority class, the more nuanced challenge lies in how specific algorithms inherently respond to this imbalance. For example, Support Vector Machines (SVMs) inherently aim to find a hyperplane that delineates classes by maximizing the margin. However, with imbalanced datasets, the sheer volume of majority class instances can push this hyperplane in a way that does not genuinely represent the optimal boundary, especially from the perspective of the minority class.

In a similar vein, Decision Tree algorithms, which seek to achieve node purity through recursive partitioning, can end up favoring the majority class. In imbalanced contexts, the tree's terminal nodes might predominantly represent the majority class, leading to compromised predictive accuracy for the minority instances.

Addressing these algorithmic biases necessitates approaches beyond mere accuracy metrics. Techniques, like sampling, which adaptively adjust the class distribution, emerge as pivotal to mitigate such biases, ensuring that algorithms do not just superficially perform well but genuinely understand and predict minority class instances.

3.2. Sampling Techniques

This characteristic of the imbalanced data leads to the construction of a biased classifier that has high accuracy for the majority class (non-churned) but low accuracy for the minority class (churned). Several sampling methods have been proposed to address this issue. Sampling techniques are applied to imbalanced data to alter the class distribution and create balanced data. Generally, sampling techniques are divided into two categories: undersampling, where instances from the majority class are removed, and oversampling, where instances from the minority class are artificially increased [45]. These methods aim to adjust the class distribution to enable the classifier to make better-informed decisions.

3.2.1. Synthetic Minority Over-Sampling Technique (SMOTE)

The Synthetic Minority Over-Sampling Technique (SMOTE) [46] is an oversampling technique that aims to balance the data by replicating instances of the minority class and is widely utilized to address this issue. Unlike simplistic methods that merely replicate minority instances, SMOTE innovatively crafts synthetic samples through an interpolation process between existing minority instances. This nuanced augmentation not only enhances the representation of the minority class but also fosters a more diverse and expansive decision boundary. Such an enriched decision space proves particularly beneficial for algorithms, like Support Vector Machines (SVMs), which are inherently sensitive to the distribution of instances in their modeling process.

3.2.2. Tomek Links

Tomek Links are an undersampling method and an extension to the Condensed Nearest Neighbor (CNN) method, proposed by Ivan Tomek (in his 1976 paper titled "Two modifications of CNN") [47]. The Tomek links method identifies pairs of examples (each from a different class) that have the minimum Euclidean distance from each other. By removing such instances, especially from the majority class, decision boundaries can become clearer and less prone to overlap. This enhanced delineation of decision spaces proves notably advantageous for classifiers, such as Decision Trees and k-Nearest Neighbors (k-NNs), which rely heavily on a clear distinction between classes for optimal performance.

3.2.3. Edited Nearest Neighbors (ENNs)

Edited Nearest Neighbors (ENN) are another undersampling method proposed by Wilson (in his 1972 paper titled "Asymptotic Properties of Nearest Neighbor Rules Using Edited Data") [48]. This method computes the three nearest neighbors for each instance in the dataset. If the instance belongs to the majority class and is misclassified by its three nearest neighbors, then it is removed from the dataset. Alternatively, if the instance belongs to the minority class and is misclassified by its three nearest neighbors, then the three majority-class instances are removed. This method often results in smoother decision boundaries, particularly benefiting algorithms sensitive to noisy data.

3.3. Combined Data Sampling Techniques

While individual sampling techniques can offer improvements, combining methods often yields superior results. This is because a combination captures the benefits of both oversampling and undersampling, refining decision boundaries and enhancing classifier robustness. In this study, to address imbalanced data, we use two of the most popular combinations of sampling techniques, such as the combination of SMOTE and Tomek Links and the combination of SMOTE and ENN.

4. Training and Validation Process

For evaluating our classifiers, we employ the k-fold cross-validation technique. However, there is a limitation when using this technique with imbalanced data. The issue is that, with this technique, the data are split into k-folds with a uniform probability distribution, and in imbalanced data, some folds may have no or few examples from the minority class. To address this issue, we can use a stratified sampling technique when performing train-test split or k-fold cross-validation. Using stratification ensures that each split of the data has an equal number of instances from the minority class.

We utilize an out-of-sample testing approach to evaluate the performance of the models. This approach demonstrates the performance of the models on unseen data that were not used to train the models.

When working with imbalanced data, it is essential to up-sample or down-sample only after splitting the data into train and test sets (and validate if desired). If the dataset is up-sampled prior to splitting it into test and train, it is likely that the model experiences data leakage. This way, we may wrongly assume that our machine learning model is performing well. After building a machine learning model, it is recommended to test the metric on the not-up-sampled train dataset. When the metric is tested on the not-up-sampled dataset, the model's performance can be more realistically estimated compared to when it is tested on the up-sampled dataset.

5. Evaluation Metrics

We employ two types of metrics to evaluate our models. (1) Threshold metrics: these metrics are designed to minimize the error rate and assist in calculating the exact number of predicted values that do not match the actual values. (2) Ranking metrics: these metrics are designed to evaluate the effectiveness of classifiers in separating classes. These metrics require classifiers to predict a probability or a score of class membership. By applying different thresholds, we can test the effectiveness of classifiers, and those classifiers that maintain a good score across a range of thresholds will have better class separation and, as a result, will have a higher rank.

5.1. Threshold Metrics

Normally, we use the standard accuracy metric (Equation (6)) for measuring the performance of ML models. However, for imbalanced data, classification ML models may achieve high accuracy, as this metric only considers the majority class. In an imbalanced dataset, instances of the minority class (churned) are rare, and thus, True Positives (TPs) do not have a significant impact on the standard accuracy metric. This metric, therefore, cannot accurately represent the performance of the models. For example, if the model correctly predicts all data points in the majority class (non-churned), it will result in high True Negatives (TNs) and a high standard of accuracy without accurately predicting anything about the minority class (churned). In the case of imbalanced data, this metric is not sufficient as a benchmark criterion measure [49]. Therefore, other metrics, such as recall, precision, and F1-score, are commonly used to evaluate the performance of ML models in minority classes and can be extracted from the confusion matrix, as shown in Table 2.

Table 2. The confusion matrix for evaluating methods.

		Predicted Class	
		Churners	Non-Churners
Actual Class	Churners	TP	FN
	Non-churners	FP	TN

The confusion matrix helps us to understand the performance of ML models by showing which class is being predicted correctly and which one is being predicted incorrectly.

In Table 2, TP and FP stand for True Positive and False Positive, and FN and TN stand for False Negative and True Negative, respectively. Precision, Recall, and Accuracy can be calculated using the following formulas:

$$\text{Precision} = \frac{TP}{TP + FP} \quad (9)$$

$$\text{Recall} = \frac{TP}{TP + FN} \quad (10)$$

$$\text{Accuracy} = \frac{\text{Correct Predictions}}{\text{Total Predictions}} = \frac{TP + TN}{TP + FP + TN + FN} \quad (11)$$

But Precision and Recall are not sufficient for evaluating the accuracy of the mentioned methods, since they do not provide enough information and can be misleading. Therefore, we usually use the F1-score metric as a single metric to evaluate the accuracy of our models. The F1-score is a combination of Precision and Recall metrics and balances both precision and recall and provides a single metric that represents the overall performance of the model. The F1-score is defined as follows:

$$F1 - \text{score} = \frac{2 \times \text{Precision} \times \text{Recall}}{\text{Precision} + \text{Recall}} \quad (12)$$

The more the value of the F1-score is closer to 1, the better combination of Precision and Recall is achieved by the model [50].

5.2. Ranking Metrics

In the field of churn prediction, the Receiver Operating Characteristic (ROC) Curve is widely recognized as a prominent ranking metric for evaluating the performance of classifiers. This metric enables the assessment of a classifier's ability to differentiate between classes by providing a visual representation of the True Positive rate and False Positive rate of predicted values, as calculated under various threshold values.

The True Positive rate (recall or sensitivity) is calculated as follows:

$$\text{TruePositiveRate} = \frac{\text{TP}}{\text{TP} + \text{FN}} \quad (13)$$

And the False Positive rate is calculated as follows:

$$\text{FalsePositiveRate} = \frac{\text{FP}}{\text{FP} + \text{TN}} \quad (14)$$

Each point on the plot represents a prediction made by the model, with the curve being formed by connecting all points. A line running diagonally from the bottom left to the top right on the plot represents a model with no skill, and any point located below this line represents a model that performs worse than one with no skill. Conversely, a point in the top left corner of the plot symbolizes a perfect model.

The Area Under the ROC curve can be calculated and utilized as a single score to evaluate the performance of models. A classifier with no skill has a score of 0.5, and a perfect classifier has a score of 1.0, as shown in Figure 5. However, it should be noted that the ROC curve can be effective for classification problems with a low imbalanced ratio and can be optimistic for classification problems with a high imbalanced ratio. In such cases, the Precision–Recall curve is a more appropriate metric because it focuses on the performance of the classifier on the minority class, as depicted in Figure 6.

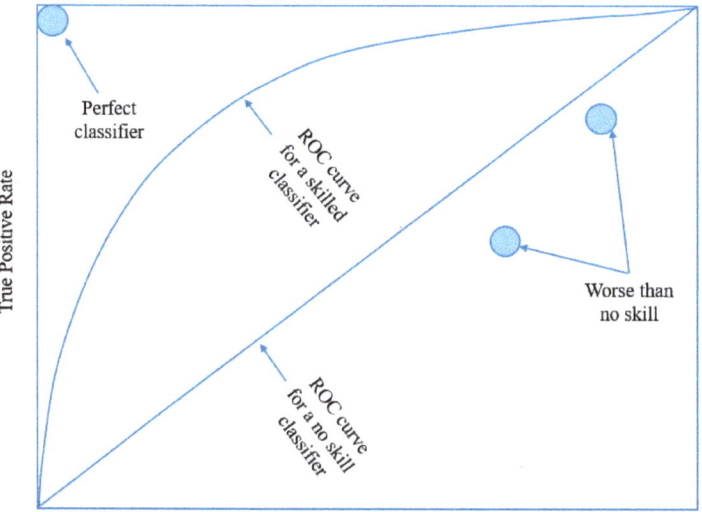

Figure 5. The ROC curve.

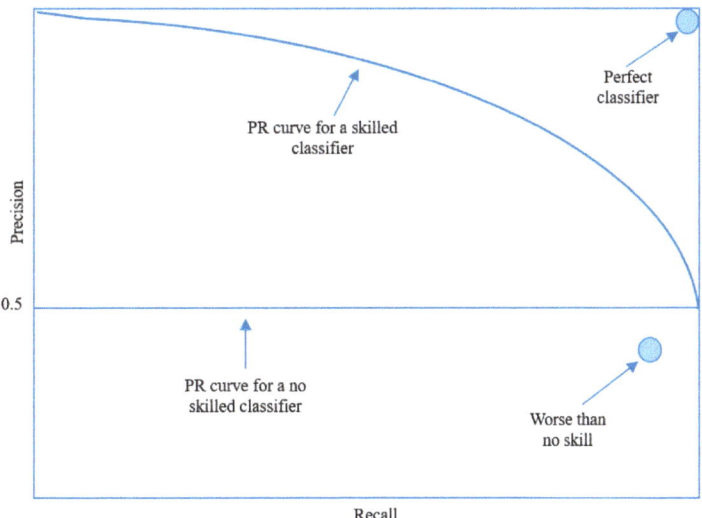

Figure 6. The Precision–Recall curve.

The ROC curve is a widely used method for evaluating the performance of machine learning models. The ROC curve plots the True Positive rate against the False Positive rate at various threshold settings, with each point on the curve representing a predicted value by the model.

A horizontal line on the plot signifies a model with no skill, while points below the diagonal line indicate a model that performs worse than random chance. Conversely, a point located in the top left quadrant of the plot represents a model with perfect performance.

In datasets with a balanced distribution of positive and negative examples, the horizontal line on the ROC plot is typically set at 0.5. However, when the dataset is imbalanced, such as with an imbalanced ratio of 1:10, the horizontal line is adjusted to 0.1 to reflect the imbalanced nature of the data.

In addition to the ROC curve, the Area Under the ROC curve (AUC) is also a commonly used metric for evaluating the performance of machine learning models. The AUC provides a single score for comparing the performance of different models. In cases where the dataset has a high imbalanced ratio, the Precision–Recall AUC (PR AUC) may be more informative as it specifically focuses on the performance of the minority class. However, if the imbalanced ratio of the dataset is not excessively high, such as the dataset utilized in this study, the use of PR AUC may not be necessary for the evaluation.

In this paper, we employ a comprehensive set of metrics to evaluate the performance of machine learning models, including Recall, Precision, F1-score, and Receiver Operating Characteristic (ROC) AUC. These metrics provide a comprehensive evaluation of the model's performance, including its ability to accurately identify positive examples, balance False Positives and False Negatives, and handle imbalanced datasets.

Among these four metrics, we primarily focused on the F1-score and ROC AUC metrics for the following reasons:

- ❖ F1-score: Given the imbalance in our dataset, the F1-score is particularly useful as it does not inflate the performance of the model due to the high number of True Negatives, which is a common issue with accuracy in such datasets.
- ❖ ROC AUC: Unlike the standard accuracy metric, ROC AUC places a particular emphasis on the performance of the minority class, and the accurate prediction of minority class instances is central to its calculation. This is particularly useful in situations where the dataset is imbalanced, as it ensures that the model's performance is evaluated fairly. This metric is less sensitive to class imbalance and provides insight into

the model's ability to distinguish between classes, making it a robust measure for comparing the performance of different models.

5.3. ROC AUC Benchmark

It is clear that an ROC Area Under the Curve (AUC) of 100% represents the optimal performance that a machine learning model can achieve, as it indicates that all instances of the positive class (e.g., churns in the case of customer retention) are ranked higher in risk than all instances of the negative class (e.g., non-churns). However, it is highly unlikely that any model will achieve this level of performance in real-world problems.

As such, when comparing the performance of different machine learning models using ROC AUC, it is necessary to have a benchmark to determine whether the model's performance is acceptable. The ROC AUC ranges from 50% to 100%, with 50% being equivalent to random guessing and 100% representing perfect performance. As can be seen in Table 3, the worst possible AUC is 50%, which is similar to the result of a coin flip for prediction. If the percentages are less than 50%, it indicates an issue with the model. Consider the worst-case scenario of obtaining a zero percent accuracy. While this might seem problematic, it actually means that the model ranked all non-churn customers as higher risk than churn customers. Surprisingly, this result could be considered good because it implies your model can perfectly predict customer retention. However, most likely, there was an error in your model setup causing it to predict in the opposite direction.

Table 3. ROC AUC benchmark for predicting churn.

ROC AUC Threshold	Description
ROC AUC < 50%	Something is wrong *
50% ≤ ROC AUC < 60%	Similar to flipping a coin
60% ≤ ROC AUC < 70%	Weak prediction
70% ≤ ROC AUC < 80%	Good Prediction
80% ≤ ROC AUC < 90%	Very Good Prediction
ROC AUC ≥ 90%	Excellent Prediction

* Check the data and the AUC calculation.

In Table 3, the categorization of the ROC AUC metric follows empirical norms and established methodologies within machine learning to yield a discernible evaluation of model efficacy. This discretization strategy is intended to furnish a pragmatic benchmark for evaluating churn-prediction models, facilitating a straightforward appraisal for both researchers and practitioners.

6. Simulation

6.1. Simulation Setup

The primary objective of this study is to evaluate and compare the performance of several popular classification techniques in solving the problem of customer churn prediction. The classifiers under examination include Decision Tree, Logistic Regression, Random Forest, Support Vector Machine, XGBoost, LightGBM, and CatBoost. To achieve this goal, simulations were conducted using the Python programming language and various libraries, such as Pandas, NumPy, and Scikit-learn.

A real-world dataset was used for this study, which was obtained from Kaggle and is outlined in Table 4 [44]. The training dataset consists of 20 attributes and 4250 instances, while the testing dataset has 20 attributes and 750 instances. The training dataset features a churn rate of 14.1% and an active subscriber rate of 85.9%. The performance of the models was evaluated using a variety of metrics, including the Precision, Recall, F1-score, and ROC AUC as defined previously. After undergoing pre-processing steps, such as handling categorical variables, feature selection, and removing outliers, these metrics were evaluated using both the training and testing datasets. Additionally, the SMOTE technique was used to handle imbalanced data, and the effect on the performance of the models was examined.

Table 4. The names and types of different variables in the churn dataset.

Variable Name	Type
state, (the US state of customers)	*string*
account_length (number of active months)	*numerical*
area_code, (area code of customers)	*string*
international_plan, (whether customers have international plans)	*yes/no*
voice_mail_plan, (whether customers have voice mail plans)	*yes/no*
number_vmail_messages, (number of voice-mail messages)	*numerical*
total_day_minutes, (total minutes of day calls)	*numerical*
total_day_calls, (total number of day calls)	*numerical*
total_day_charge, (total charge of day calls)	*numerical*
total_eve_minutes, (total minutes of evening calls)	*numerical*
total_eve_calls, (total number of evening calls)	*numerical*
total_eve_charge, (total charge of evening calls)	*numerical*
total_night_minutes, (total minutes of night calls)	*numerical*
total_night_calls, (total number of night calls)	*numerical*
total_night_charge, (total charge of night calls)	*numerical*
total_intl_minutes, (total minutes of international calls)	*numerical*
total_intl_calls, (total number of international calls)	*numerical*
total_intl_charge, (total charge of international calls)	*numerical*
number_customer_service_calls, (number of calls to customer service)	*numerical*
churn, (customer churn—the target variable)	*yes/no*

6.2. Simulation Results

In this study, we evaluate the performance of several machine learning models (Decision Tree, Logistic Regression, Artificial Neural Network, Support Vector Machine, Random Forest, XGBoost, LightGBM, and CatBoost) based on unseen data using a range of metrics, including the Precision, Recall, F1-score, Receiver Operating Characteristic (ROC) Area Under the Curve (AUC), and Precision–Recall (PR) AUC. The evaluation is carried out on the testing dataset to assess the generalization ability of the models and to determine their performance based on unseen data.

6.2.1. After Pre-Processing and Feature Selection

After undergoing several pre-processing steps, such as handling categorical features and feature selection, the aforementioned models were applied to the data, and their performance was evaluated. The results of this evaluation are presented in Table 5, with the highest values highlighted in bold and marked with an asterisk.

Table 5. Evaluation metrics for the different models after pre-processing and feature selection.

Models	Precision%	Recall%	F1-score%	ROC AUC%
DT	91	72	77	72
ANN	85	76	80	77
LR	61	70	62	70
SVM	81	57	59	57
RF	96	75	81	75
CatBoost	90	90	90	90
LightGBM	94	91	**92***	**91***
XGBoost	96	87	91	87

As depicted in Table 5, the boosting models demonstrate superior performance, particularly in relation to F1-score and ROC AUC metrics. Notably, LightGBM surpasses the performance of other methods, achieving an impressive F1-score of 92% and an ROC AUC of 91%. Figure 7 shows the diagram of the ROC curve for the different models after pre-processing and feature selection.

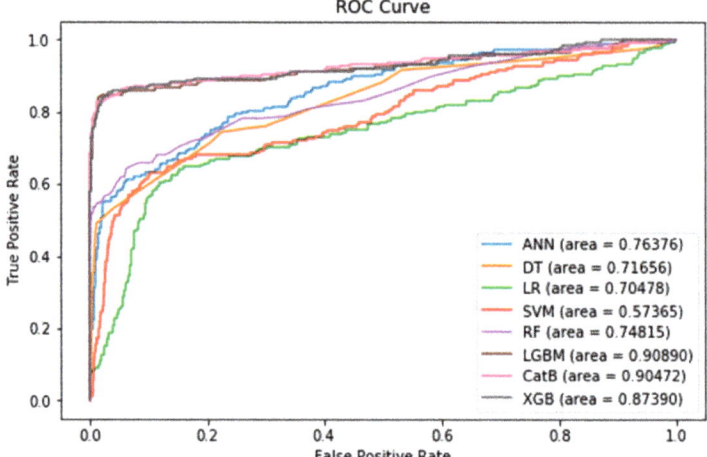

Figure 7. ROC curve after pre-processing and feature selection.

6.2.2. Applying SMOTE

To address the issue of class imbalance in the training data, where the number of instances of class-0 is 3652 and the number of instances of class-1 is 598, we have applied the SMOTE technique to the training dataset. This technique was used to create synthetic instances of the minority class in order to achieve a balanced training dataset. As a result of the application of SMOTE, the number of instances for both class-0 and class-1 is now equal to 2125.

As Table 6 shows, LightGBM and XGBoost outperform other ML techniques in all evaluation metrics. Notably, LightGBM and XGBoost surpass the performance of other methods, with both achieving an impressive ROC AUC of 90%, and XGBoost outperforms the other methods, achieving an impressive F1-score of 92%. Figure 8 shows the diagram of the ROC curve for the different models after applying SMOTE.

6.2.3. Applying SMOTE with Tomek Links

As previously discussed in Section IV, the Tomek Links method is an undersampling technique that is used to identify pairs of examples, where each example belongs to a different class that has the minimum Euclidean distance to each other. Additionally, as noted in the section, it is beneficial to utilize a combination of both oversampling and undersampling techniques to achieve optimal results. The results of the evaluation metrics for the various models after applying the SMOTE technique in conjunction with Tomek Links are presented in Table 7. Notably, LightGBM outperforms the other methods, achieving an impressive ROC AUC of 91%, and XGBoost surpasses the other methods, achieving an impressive F1-score of 91%. As indicated in Table 7, XGBoost demonstrates a marginal performance improvement, with a modest 2% enhancement in the ROC AUC compared to the pre-processing and feature selection stage (initial state), as shown in Table 6. Figure 9 shows the diagram of the ROC curve for the different models after applying SMOTE with Tomek Links.

Table 6. Evaluation metrics for the different models after applying SMOTE.

Models	Precision%	Recall%	F1-score%	ROC AUC%
DT	69	72	70	72
ANN	70	73	71	83
LR	61	71	61	70
SVM	65	73	68	73
RF	83	76	79	76
CatBoost	79	88	83	88
LightGBM	87	90	88	90*
XGBoost	95	90	92*	90*

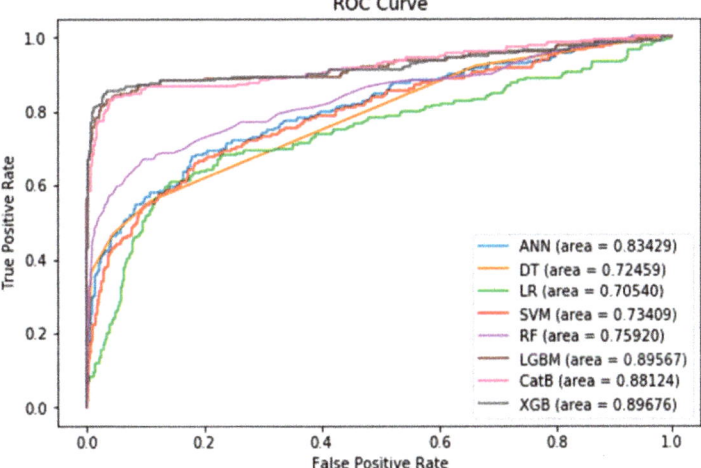

Figure 8. ROC curve after applying SMOTE.

Table 7. Evaluation metrics for the different models after applying SMOTE with Tomek Links.

Models	Precision%	Recall%	F1-score%	ROC AUC%
DT	74	74	74	74
ANN	69	75	71	75
LR	61	70	61	69
SVM	65	73	67	73
RF	85	78	81	78
CatBoost	80	88	83	88
LightGBM	89	91	90	91*
XGBoost	94	89	91*	89

6.2.4. Applying SMOTE with ENN

As previously discussed in Section 3 the ENN method is employed to compute the three nearest neighbors for each instance within the dataset. In instances where the sample belongs to the majority class and is misclassified by its three nearest neighbors, the instance is removed from the dataset. Conversely, if the instance belongs to the minority class and is misclassified by its three nearest neighbors, the three majority class instances are removed. Furthermore, as previously stated, it has been shown to be beneficial to utilize a combination of undersampling and oversampling techniques in order to achieve optimal results. Table 8 illustrates the evaluation metrics for the various models following the application of the SMOTE technique in conjunction with the ENN method. The results indicate that XGBoost outperforms the other machine learning techniques, achieving an F1-score of 88% and an ROC AUC of 89%. As indicated in Table 8, XGBoost exhibits a performance decline, experiencing a 3% reduction in F1-score compared to the preprocessing and feature selection stage (initial state), as shown in Table 6. Figure 10 shows the diagram of the ROC curve for the different models after applying SMOTE with ENN.

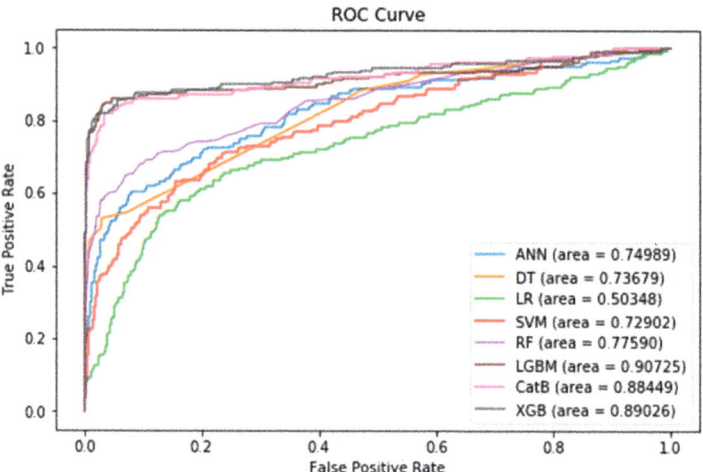

Figure 9. ROC curve after applying SMOTE with Tomek Links.

Table 8. Evaluation metrics for the different models after applying SMOTE with ENN.

Models	Precision%	Recall%	F1-Score%	ROC AUC%
DT	60	70	50	70
ANN	61	70	60	70
LR	52	50	50	50
SVM	60	70	58	70
RF	67	76	69	76
CatBoost	70	83	72	83
LightGBM	80	89	84	87
XGBoost	88	89	88*	89*

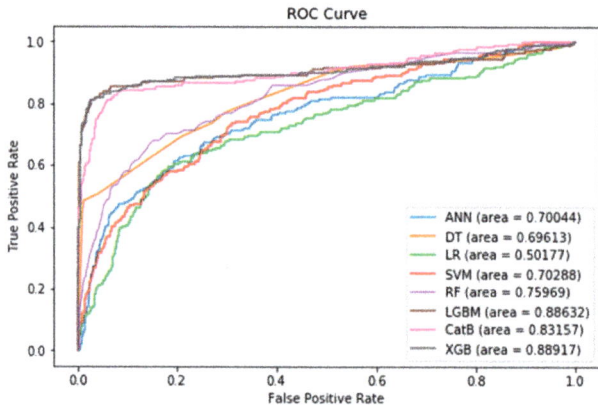

Figure 10. ROC curve after applying SMOTE with ENN.

6.2.5. The Impact of Sampling Techniques
F1-Score

Table 9 and Figure 11 show the impact of three distinct sampling techniques (SMOTE, SMOTE with Tomek Links, and SMOTE with ENN) on the F1-score metric of various machine learning models. These comparisons offer insights into the effectiveness of each technique in handling imbalanced datasets.

1. Impact of SMOTE Sampling Technique:
    - Most models saw a decrease in the F1-score after applying SMOTE compared to the pre-processing and feature selection stage (initial state).
    - CatBoost and LightGBM experienced a reduction in F1-scores, but XGBoost showed slight improvements.
    - Support Vector Machine (SVM) exhibits an enhanced F1-score.
2. Impact of SMOTE with Tomek Links Sampling Technique:
    - SMOTE with Tomek Links demonstrates further enhancements in F1-scores for several models compared to SMOTE alone.
    - Support Vector Machine (SVM) showed improvements.
    - CatBoost experienced a reduction in F1-scores compared to the pre-processing and feature selection stage (initial state).
    - LightGBM showed a slight reduction in F1-scores by 2%.
    - XGBoost remained consistent with an F1-score of 91.
3. Impact of SMOTE with ENN Sampling Technique:
    - SMOTE with ENN leads to varied impacts on F1-scores across models.
    - Some models, like the Decision Tree (DT), Logistic Regression (LR), and CatBoost, experience significant drops in F1 scores compared to the pre-processing and feature selection stage (initial state).
    - LightGBM maintains relatively high F1-scores, with LightGBM achieving 84%.
    - XGBoost remains strong with an F1-score of 88% despite the decline.
    - SMOTE with ENN may not consistently enhance performance and should be chosen carefully based on the specific model and dataset characteristics.

Table 9. F1-score of different ML models after applying different sampling techniques.

	DT	ANN	LR	SVM	RF	CatBoost	XGBoost	LightGBM
Initial	77*	80*	62*	59	81*	90*	92*	91
SMOTE	70	71	61	68 *	79	83	88	92*
SMOTE-TOMEK	74	71	61	67	81*	83	90	91
SMOTE-ENN	50	60	50	58	69	72	84	88

In summary, the impact of different sampling techniques on F1-scores varied across models. SMOTE generally led to reduced F1-scores, with CatBoost and LightGBM experiencing declines and XGBoost showing slight improvements. SMOTE with Tomek Links enhanced F1-scores for several models, particularly benefiting SVM, but CatBoost and LightGBM saw reductions. SMOTE with ENN had mixed effects on F1-scores, significantly decreasing scores for some models but maintaining higher scores for LightGBM and XGBoost. Among the sampling techniques, SMOTE-ENN yields the least favorable results for all machine learning models when contrasted with methods, such as SMOTE and SMOTE-TOMEK. Choosing the appropriate sampling technique should consider specific model and dataset characteristics.

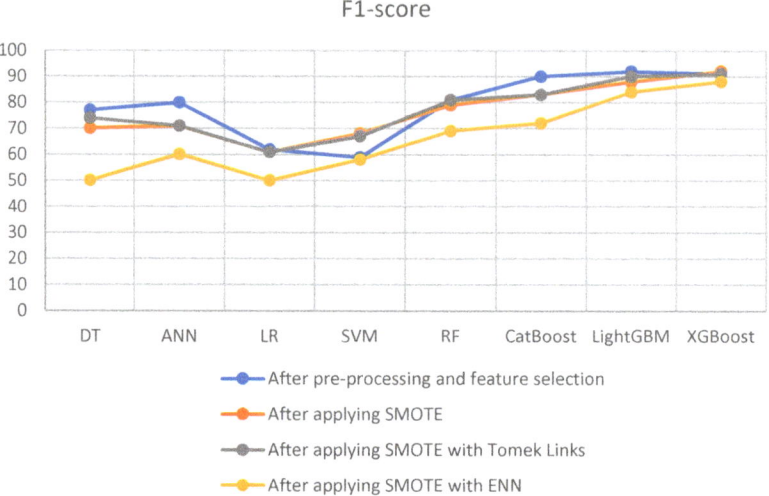

Figure 11. The impact of sampling techniques on the F1-score of different ML models.

ROC AUC

Table 10 and Figure 12 show the impact of three distinct sampling techniques (SMOTE, SMOTE with Tomek Links, and SMOTE with ENN) on the ROC AUC metric of various machine learning models. These comparisons offer insights into the effectiveness of each technique in handling imbalanced datasets.

1. Impact of SMOTE Sampling Technique:
   - After applying SMOTE, there are noticeable improvements in ROC AUC metrics for some models.
   - ANN, SVM, RF, and XGBoost experience ROC AUC enhancements, but CatBoost and LightGBM showed a slight reduction compared to the pre-processing and feature selection stage (initial state).
   - Models, like ANN and SVM, see substantial improvements, with ROC AUC scores reaching 83% and 73%, respectively.
2. Impact of SMOTE with Tomek Links Sampling Technique:
   - SMOTE combined with Tomek Links maintains or enhances ROC AUC metrics for most models.
   - DT, SVM, and RF observe improved ROC AUC metrics.
   - LightGBM and CatBoost maintain high ROC AUC scores of 91% and 88%, respectively.
   - This technique's combination of class balancing (SMOTE) and the removal of borderline instances (Tomek Links) continues to prove effective.
3. Impact of SMOTE with ENN Sampling Technique:
   - SMOTE with ENN produces mixed results for ROC AUC metrics.
   - While some models, like RF and XGBoost, and SVM showed improvements in ROC AUC metrics, others experienced drops.
   - Logistic Regression (LR) encounters a significant reduction in the ROC AUC.
   - LightGBM maintains a respectable ROC AUC metric of 87%.
   - Researchers should exercise caution when applying SMOTE with ENN, as its impact varies across models.

Table 10. ROC AUC of different ML models after applying different sampling techniques.

	DT	ANN	LR	SVM	RF	CatBoost	XGBoost	LightGBM
Initial	72	77	70*	57	75	90*	91*	87
SMOTE	72	83*	70*	73*	76	88	90	90*
SMOTE-TOMEK	74*	75	69	73*	78*	88	91*	89
SMOTE-ENN	70	70	50	70	76	83	87	89

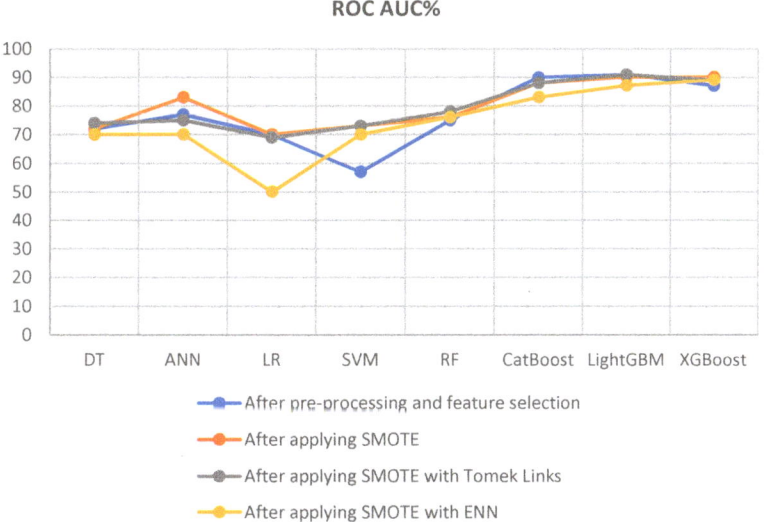

Figure 12. The impact of sampling techniques on ROC AUC of different ML models.

In summary, the impact of different sampling techniques on ROC AUC metrics varied among models. SMOTE led to improvements for ANN, SVM, RF, and XGBoost but slight reductions for CatBoost and LightGBM. Notably, ANN and SVM achieved substantial ROC AUC scores of 83% and 73%, respectively. SMOTE with Tomek Links generally maintained or improved ROC AUC metrics, benefiting models, like DT, SVM, RF, LightGBM, and CatBoost, with the latter two maintaining high scores. SMOTE with ENN produced mixed results, improving the ROC AUC for some models, such as RF, XGBoost, and SVM, while causing a significant reduction in Logistic Regression. LightGBM maintained a respectable ROC AUC of 87%. Similar to the F1-score metric, SMOTE-ENN demonstrates lower performance in terms of the ROC AUC for all machine learning models compared to techniques, such as SMOTE and SMOTE-TOMEK. Researchers should select the most appropriate sampling technique based on their dataset and model to achieve optimal ROC AUC results.

Sampling Techniques vs. Boosting Techniques

Several factors contribute to the relatively modest impact of sampling techniques on the performance of boosting algorithms:

- Iterative Nature: Boosting methods iteratively train a sequence of weak models, typically Decision Trees. Each subsequent model focuses on the errors made by the previous ones. Boosting is adaptive in the sense that it can adjust to the errors and potentially correct them in subsequent iterations.

- Adaptive Nature: While oversampling introduces more instances of the minority class, boosting models, given their adaptive nature, can sometimes already compensate for the imbalance to some degree. As a result, oversampling might not always result in significant performance improvements.
- Weighted Loss Function: Many boosting algorithms, like XGBoost, offer a weighted loss function where instances from different classes can be assigned different weights. This built-in mechanism can help in addressing class imbalance, reducing the need for external sampling methods.

In summary, while data sampling can rectify the decision boundary in models like SVM that are sensitive to class distributions, boosting techniques, due to their adaptive and iterative nature, might already have mechanisms to handle an imbalance to a certain extent. However, the actual impact of sampling can vary based on the dataset, the degree of imbalance, the specific boosting algorithm used, and its hyperparameters.

6.2.6. Applying Optuna Hyperparameter Optimizer

Hyperparameter optimization is pivotal in machine learning for enhancing the performance of models. While models come with default hyperparameters, fine-tuning them to a specific dataset can substantially boost their efficacy. One prominent tool in this space is Optuna. Takuya Akiba et al. (2019) [51] introduced Optuna, an open-source Python library for hyperparameter optimization. Optuna aims to balance the pruning and sampling algorithms through the execution of various techniques, such as the Tree-Structured Parzen Estimator (TPE) [52,53] for independent parameter sampling, Covariance Matrix Adaptation (CMA) [54], and Gaussian Processes (GPs) [53] for relational parameter sampling. The library also utilizes a variant of the Asynchronous Successive Halving (ASHA) algorithm [55] to prune search spaces.

TPE is a Bayesian optimization technique. Unlike grid or random search, which treats hyperparameters as isolated, TPE considers the relationship between hyperparameters and the objective function. The advantage of TPE over other methods lies in its efficiency. By constructing a probabilistic model of the objective function, it can suggest hyperparameters that are more likely to yield better results, hence reducing the number of trials [52,53].

Both CMA and GP are methodologies used in Optuna for relational parameter sampling. CMA captures the interdependencies between parameters, optimizing the sampling process, while GP uses the kernel trick to project data into higher dimensions, capturing complex relationships in the hyperparameter space [53,54].

The goal of ASHA is efficiency. It is an early stopping strategy to prune trials that do not show promise, which allows for a more efficient hyperparameter search. By identifying and halting unpromising trials early, computational resources are channeled more effectively [55].

In this study, we applied the Optuna library to the popular machine learning models, CatBoost, XGBoost, and LightGBM. The results, as presented in Table 11, indicate that CatBoost outperforms XGBoost and LightGBM when utilizing Optuna for hyperparameter optimization, achieving an impressive F1-score of 93% and an ROC AUC of 91%. The improved F1-score and ROC AUC results observed after employing Optuna hyperparameter tuning for CatBoost likely result from the enhanced hyperparameter settings. Optuna fine-tunes these settings more effectively for your specific data, reducing overfitting and enhancing the models' generalization to new data. This ultimately leads to improved overall model performance, as hyperparameters play a significant role in how effectively these algorithms operate with the dataset. Figure 13 shows the diagram of the ROC curve for the different models after applying Optunal hyperparameter tuning.

Table 12 includes all the parameters that were used in the XGBoost, LightGBM, and CatBoost models after applying Optuna hyperparameter tuning. The table provides a clear and concise summary of the parameter values that were selected for the models.

Table 11. Evaluation metrics for various models after applying Optuna hyperparameter optimization.

Models	Precision%	Recall%	F1-Score%	ROC AUC%
CatBoost	89	91	90	91*
CatBoost-Optuna	95	91	**93***	**91***
LightGBM	92	90	91	90
LightGBM-Optuna	93	89	90	89
XGBoost	93	88	90	88
XGBoost-Optuna	94	88	91	88

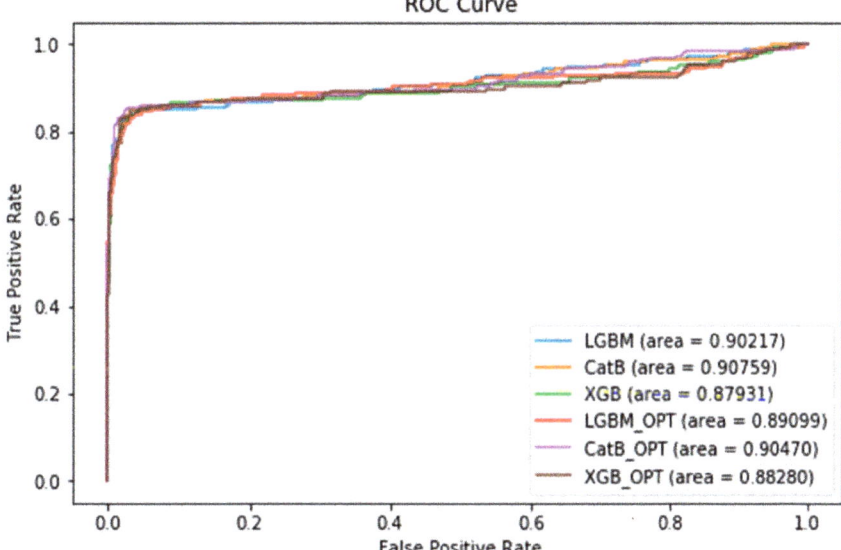

Figure 13. ROC curve after Optuna hyperparameter tuning.

Table 12. Optuna hyperparameter optimization parameters.

Parameter	Description	Value
XGBoost Tuning Parameters		
verbosity	Verbosity of printing messages	0
objective	Objective function	binary:logistic
tree_method	Tree construction method	exact
booster	Type of booster	dart
lambda	L2 regularization weight	0.010281489790562261
alpha	L1 regularization weight	0.0008440304772889829
subsample	Sampling ratio for training data	0.8298281841818362
colsample_bytree	Sampling according to each tree	0.9985902928710126
max_depth	Maximum depth of the tree	7
min_child_weight	Minimum child weight	2
eta	Learning rate	0.12406825365082062
gamma	Minimum loss reduction required to make a further partition on a leaf node of the tree	0.0004490383815764321
grow_policy	Controls the way new nodes are added to the tree	depthwise

Table 12. *Cont.*

Parameter	Description	Value
LightGBM Tuning Parameters		
objective	Objective function	binary
metric	Metric for binary classification	binary_logloss
verbosity	Verbosity of printing messages	-1
boosting_type	Type of booster	dart
num_leaves	Maximum number of leaves in one tree	1169
max_depth	Maximum depth of the tree	10
lambda_l1	L1 regularization weight	$2.689492421801289 \times 10^{-7}$
lambda_l2	L2 regularization weight	$7.2387875465462 \times 10^{-8}$
feature_fraction	LightGBM will randomly select part of features on each iteration	0.870805980078817
bagging_fraction	LightGBM will randomly select part of data without resampling	0.6280893693081118
bagging_freq	Frequency for bagging	7
min_child_samples	Minimum amount of data in one leaf	8
CatBoost Tuning Parameters		
Objective	Objective function	Logloss
colsample_bylevel	Subsampling rate per level for each tree	0.07760972009427407
depth	Depth of the tree	12
boosting_type	Type of booster	Ordered
bootstrap_type	Sampling method for bagging	Bayesian
bagging_temperature	Controls the similarity of samples in each bag	0.0

7. Conclusions

In this study, we employed various machine learning (ML) models, including Artificial Neural Networks, Decision Trees, Support Vector Machines, Random Forests, Logistic Regression, and three modern gradient boosting techniques, namely XGBoost, LightGBM, and CatBoost, to predict customer churn in the telecommunications industry using a real-world imbalanced dataset. We evaluated the impact of different sampling techniques, such as SMOTE, SMOTE with Tomek Links, and SMOTE with ENN, to handle the imbalanced data. We then assessed the performance of the ML models using various metrics, including the Precision, Recall, F1-score, and Receiver Operating Characteristic Area Under the Curve (ROC AUC). Finally, we utilized the Optuna hyperparameter optimization technique on CatBoost, LightGBM, and XGBoost to determine the effect of optimization on the performance of the models. We compared the results of all the steps and presented them in tabular form.

The simulation results demonstrate the performance of different models based on unseen data. LightGBM and XGBoost consistently exhibit superior performance across various evaluation metrics, including the Precision, Recall, F1-score, and ROC AUC. The performance of these models is further improved when applying techniques, such as SMOTE with Tomek Links or SMOTE with ENN, to handle imbalanced data. Additionally, the use of Optuna hyperparameter optimization for CatBoost, XGBoost, and LightGBM models shows further improvements in performance.

In summary, the key findings of the study are as follows:

❖ Impact of SMOTE: After applying SMOTE, both LightGBM and XGBoost achieved impressive ROC AUC scores of 90%. Additionally, XGBoost outperformed other methods with an impressive F1-score of 92%. SMOTE effectively balanced class distribution, leading to enhanced recall and ROC AUC for most models.

❖ SMOTE with Tomek Links: After applying SMOTE with Tomek Links, LightGBM excelled among the methods with an impressive ROC AUC of 91%. XGBoost also outperformed other methods with an impressive F1-score of 91%. LightGBM demonstrates a slight performance boost, with a modest 2% improvement in the F1-score and a 1% increase in ROC AUC compared to when using SMOTE alone. Conversely,

XGBoost showed a slight performance decline, experiencing a corresponding 1% reduction in the F1-score and ROC AUC compared to exclusive SMOTE utilization.
- ❖ SMOTE with ENN: After applying SMOTE with ENN, XGBoost surpassed other ML techniques, achieving an F1-score of 88% and an ROC AUC of 89%. However, XGBoost exhibited a performance decline, with a 4% reduction in the F1-score and a 1% decrease in ROC AUC compared to exclusive SMOTE utilization.

The best results for the F1-score and ROC AUC across different ML models after applying various sampling techniques are summarized in Table 13.

Table 13. The best result of the F1-score and ROC AUC for different ML models.

Metrics/ Methods	F1-Score	ROC AUC
DT	Initial = 77%	SMOTE-TOMEK = 74%
ANN	Initial = 80%	SMOTE = 83%
LR	Initial = 62%	Initial and SMOTE = 70%
SVM	SMOTE = 68%	SMOTE and SMOTE-TOMEK = 73%
RF	Initial and SMOTE-TOMEK = 81%	SMOTE-TOMEK = 78%
CatBoost	Initial = 90%	Initial = 90%
XGBoost	Initial = 92%	Initial and SMOTE-TOMEK = 91%
LightGBM	SMOTE = 92%	SMOTE = 90%

- ❖ Impact of Optuna Hyperparameter Tuning: After applying Optuna Hyperparameter Tuning, Cat-Boost outperformed XGBoost and LightGBM when Optuna was utilized for hyperparameter optimization, achieving an impressive F1-score of 93% and an ROC AUC of 91%. The enhanced F1-score and ROC AUC results observed after applying Optuna hyperparameter tuning to CatBoost, XGBoost, and LightGBM are likely attributable to improved hyperparameter configurations. Optuna fine-tuned these settings more effectively for the specific dataset, reducing overfitting and enhancing the models' capacity to generalize to new data. This ultimately resulted in improved overall model performance, as hyperparameters significantly influence the performance of these algorithms with your dataset.

In future work, several avenues can be explored. Firstly, other machine learning techniques, such as deep learning models, like Long Short-Term Memory (LSTM) or Transformer-based models, can be evaluated for churn prediction. These models have shown promise in various domains and may provide further insights into churn behavior. Secondly, we suggest exploring the use of the AdaSyn technique to handle imbalanced data and compare the results. Lastly, we recommend applying the above techniques to a highly imbalanced dataset to evaluate their performance in such conditions. Furthermore, employing the learning curve method to determine whether the models are overfitting could also be a valuable avenue of research.

Author Contributions: Writing and original draft preparation, subsequent revisions, coding, analysis, and interpretation of the results, M.I.; supervision, review, and editing, H.R.A. All authors have read and agreed to the published version of the manuscript.

Funding: This research received no external funding.

Institutional Review Board Statement: Not applicable.

Informed Consent Statement: Not applicable.

Data Availability Statement: This study makes use of a publicly accessible dataset sourced from Kaggle [44].

Conflicts of Interest: The authors declare no conflict of interest.

References

1. *Cost of Customer Acquisition versus Customer Retention*; The Chartered Institute of Marketing: Cookham, UK, 2010.
2. Eichinger, F.; Nauck, D.D.; Klawonn, F. Sequence mining for customer behaviour predictions in telecommunications. In Proceedings of the Workshop on Practical Data Mining at ECML/PKDD, Berlin, Germany, 18–22 September 2006; pp. 3–10.
3. Prasad, U.D.; Madhavi, S. Prediction of churn behaviour of bank customers using data mining tools. *Indian J. Market.* **2011**, *42*, 25–30.
4. Keramati, A.; Ghaneei, H.; Mirmohammadi, S.M. Developing a prediction model for customer churn from electronic banking services using data mining. *Financ. Innov.* **2016**, *2*, 10. [CrossRef]
5. Scriney, M.; Dongyun, N.; Mark, R. Predicting customer churn for insurance data. In *International Conference on Big Data Analytics and Knowledge Discovery*; Springer: Cham, Switzerland, 2020.
6. De Caigny, A.; Coussement, K.; De Bock, K.W. A new hybrid classification algorithm for customer churn prediction based on logistic regression and decision trees. *Eur. J. Oper. Res.* **2018**, *269*, 760–772. [CrossRef]
7. Kim, K.; Jun, C.-H.; Lee, J. Improved churn prediction in telecommunication industry by analyzing a large network. *Expert Syst. Appl.* **2014**, *41*, 6575–6584. [CrossRef]
8. Ahmad, A.K.; Jafar, A.; Aljoumaa, K. Customer churn prediction in telecom using machine learning in big data platform. *J. Big Data* **2019**, *6*, 28. [CrossRef]
9. Jadhav, R.J.; Pawar, U.T. Churn prediction in telecommunication using data mining technology. *IJACSA Edit.* **2011**, *2*, 17–19.
10. Radosavljevik, D.; van der Putten, P.; Larsen, K.K. The impact of experimental setup in prepaid churn prediction for mobile telecommunications: What to predict, for whom and does the customer experience matter? *Trans. Mach. Learn. Data Min.* **2010**, *3*, 80–99.
11. Richter, Y.; Yom-Tov, E.; Slonim, N. Predicting customer churn in mobile networks through analysis of social groups. In Proceedings of the 2010 SIAM International Conference on Data Mining, Columbus, OH, USA, 29 April–1 May 2010; Volume 2010, pp. 732–741.
12. Amin, A.; Shah, B.; Khattak, A.M.; Moreira, F.J.L.; Ali, G.; Rocha, A.; Anwar, S. Cross-company customer churn prediction in telecommunication: A comparison of data transformation methods. *Int. J. Inf. Manag.* **2018**, *46*, 304–319. [CrossRef]
13. Tsiptsis, K.; Chorianopoulos, A. *Data Mining Techniques in CRM: Inside Customer Segmentation*; John Wiley & Sons: Hoboken, NJ, USA, 2011.
14. Joudaki, M.; Imani, M.; Esmaeili, M.; Mahmoodi, M.; Mazhari, N. Presenting a New Approach for Predicting and Preventing Active/Deliberate Customer Churn in Tel-ecommunication Industry. In Proceedings of the International Conference on Security and Management (SAM), Las Vegas, NV, USA, 18–21 July 2011; The Steering Committee of the World Congress in Computer Science, Computer Engineering and Applied Computing (WorldComp): Athens, GA, USA, 2011.
15. Amin, A.; Al-Obeidat, F.; Shah, B.; Adnan, A.; Loo, J.; Anwar, S. Customer churn prediction in telecommunication industry using data certainty. *J. Bus. Res.* **2019**, *94*, 290–301. [CrossRef]
16. Shaaban, E.; Helmy, Y.; Khedr, A.; Nasr, M. A proposed churn prediction model. *J. Eng. Res. Appl.* **2012**, *2*, 693–697.
17. Khan, Y.; Shafiq, S.; Naeem, A.; Ahmed, S.; Safwan, N.; Hussain, S. Customers Churn Prediction using Artificial Neural Networks (ANN) in Telecom Industry. *Int. J. Adv. Comput. Sci. Appl.* **2019**, *10*. [CrossRef]
18. Ho, T.K. Random decision forests. In Proceedings of the 3rd International Conference on Document Analysis and Recognition, Montreal, QC, Canada, 14–16 August 1995; Volume 1.
19. Breiman, L. Random forests. *Mach. Learn.* **2001**, *45*, 5–32. [CrossRef]
20. Amin, A.; Shehzad, S.; Khan, C.; Ali, I.; Anwar, S. Churn Prediction in Telecommunication Industry Using Rough Set Approach. In *New Trends in Computational Collective Intelligence*; Springer: Berlin/Heidelberg, Germany, 2015; pp. 83–95.
21. Witten, I.H.; Frank, E.; Hall, M.A. *Data Mining: Practical Machine Learning Tools and Techniques*; Elsevier Science & Technology: San Francisco, CA, USA, 2016.
22. Alok, K.; Mayank, J. *Ensemble Learning for AI Developers*; BApress: Berkeley, CA, USA, 2020.
23. van Wezel, M.; Potharst, R. Improved customer choice predictions using ensemble methods. *Eur. J. Oper. Res.* **2007**, *181*, 436–452. [CrossRef]
24. Ullah, I.; Raza, B.; Malik, A.K.; Imran, M.; Islam, S.U.; Kim, S.W. A Churn Prediction Model Using Random Forest: Analysis of Machine Learning Techniques for Churn Prediction and Factor Identification in Telecom Sector. *IEEE Access* **2019**, *7*, 60134–60149. [CrossRef]
25. Lalwani, P.; Mishra, M.K.; Chadha, J.S.; Sethi, P. Customer churn prediction system: A machine learning approach. *Computing* **2021**, *104*, 271–294. [CrossRef]
26. Tarekegn, A.; Ricceri, F.; Costa, G.; Ferracin, E.; Giacobini, M. Predictive Modeling for Frailty Conditions in Elderly People: Machine Learning Approaches. *Psychopharmacol.* **2020**, *8*, e16678. [CrossRef] [PubMed]
27. Ahmed, M.; Afzal, H.; Siddiqi, I.; Amjad, M.F.; Khurshid, K. Exploring nested ensemble learners using overproduction and choose approach for churn prediction in telecom industry. *Neural Comput. Appl.* **2018**, *32*, 3237–3251. [CrossRef]
28. Boser, B.E.; Guyon, I.M.; Vapnik, V.N. A training algorithm for optimal margin classifiers. In Proceedings of the Fifth Annual Workshop on Computational Learning Theory, Pittsburgh, PA, USA, 27–29 July 1992; ACM: New York, NY, USA, 1992; pp. 144–152.

29. Hur, Y.; Lim, S. Customer churning prediction using support vector machines in online auto insurance service. In *Advances in Neural Networks, Proceedings of the ISNN 2005, Chongqing, China, 30 May–1 June 2005*; Springer: Berlin/Heidelberg, Germany, 2005; pp. 928–933.
30. Lee, S.J.; Siau, K. A review of data mining techniques. *Ind. Manag. Data Syst.* **2001**, *101*, 41–46. [CrossRef]
31. Mazhari, N.; Imani, M.; Joudaki, M.; Ghelichpour, A. An overview of classification and its algorithms. In Proceedings of the 3rd Data Mining Conference (IDMC'09), Tehran, Iran, 15–16 December 2009.
32. Linoff, G.S.; Berry, M.J. *Data Mining Techniques: For Marketing, Sales, and Customer Relationship Management*; John Wiley & Sons: Hoboken, NJ, USA, 2011.
33. Zhou, Z.-H. *Ensemble Methods—Foundations and Algorithms*; CRC press: Boca Raton, FL, USA, 2012.
34. Karlberg, J.; Axen, M. *Binary Classification for Predicting Customer Churn*; Umeå University: Umeå, Sweden, 2020.
35. Windridge, D.; Nagarajan, R. Quantum Bootstrap Aggregation. In Proceedings of the International Symposium on Quantum Interaction, San Francisco, CA, USA, 20–22 July 2016; Springer: Berlin/Heidelberg, Germany, 2017.
36. Wang, J.C.; Hastie, T. Boosted Varying-Coefficient Regression Models for Product Demand Prediction. *J. Comput. Graph. Stat.* **2014**, *23*, 361–382. [CrossRef]
37. Al Daoud, E. Intrusion Detection Using a New Particle Swarm Method and Support Vector Machines. *World Acad. Sci. Eng. Technol.* **2013**, *77*, 59–62.
38. Al Daoud, E.; Turabieh, H. New empirical nonparametric kernels for support vector machine classification. *Appl. Soft Comput.* **2013**, *13*, 1759–1765. [CrossRef]
39. Al Daoud, E. An Efficient Algorithm for Finding a Fuzzy Rough Set Reduct Using an Improved Harmony Search. *Int. J. Mod. Educ. Comput. Sci. (IJMECS)* **2015**, *7*, 16–23. [CrossRef]
40. Zhang, Y.; Haghani, A. A gradient boosting method to improve travel time prediction. *Transp. Res. Part C Emerg. Technol.* **2015**, *58*, 308–324. [CrossRef]
41. Dorogush, A.; Ershov, V.; Gulin, A. CatBoost: Gradient boosting with categorical features support. In Proceedings of the Thirty-first Conference on Neural Information Processing Systems, Long Beach, CA, USA, 4–9 December 2017; pp. 1–7.
42. Ke, G.; Meng, Q.; Finley, T.; Wang, T.; Chen, W.; Ma, W.; Ye, Q.; Liu, T.Y. Lightgbm: A highly efficient gradient boosting decision tree. In *Advances in Neural Information Processing Systems*; MIT Press: Cambridge, MA, USA, 2017; Volume 30.
43. Klein, A.; Falkner, S.; Bartels, S.; Hennig, P.; Hutter, F. Fast Bayesian optimization of machine learning hyperparameters on large datasets. In Proceedings of the Machine Learning Research PMLR, Sydney, NSW, Australia, 6–11 August 2017; Volume 54, pp. 528–536.
44. Christy, R. Customer Churn Prediction 2020, Version 1. 2020. Available online: https://www.kaggle.com/code/rinichristy/customer-churn-prediction-2020 (accessed on 20 January 2022).
45. Kubat, M.; Matwin, S. Addressing the curse of imbalanced training sets: One-sided selection. In Proceedings of the 14th International Conference on Machine Learning, Nashville, TN, USA, 8–12 July 1997; Volume 97, p. 179.
46. Chawla, N.V.; Bowyer, K.W.; Hall, L.O.; Kegelmeyer, W.P. SMOTE: Synthetic minority over-sampling technique. *J. Artif. Intell. Res.* **2002**, *16*, 321–357. [CrossRef]
47. Tomek, I. Two Modifications of CNN. *IEEE Trans. Syst. Man Cybern.* **1976**, *SMC-6*, 769–772. [CrossRef]
48. Wilson, D.L. Asymptotic Properties of Nearest Neighbor Rules Using Edited Data. *IEEE Trans. Syst. Man Cybern.* **1972**, *2*, 408–421. [CrossRef]
49. Tyagi, S.; Mittal, S. Sampling Approaches for Imbalanced Data Classification Problem in Machine Learning. In Proceedings of the ICRIC 2019: Recent Innovations in Computing, Jammu, India, 8–9 March 2019; Springer International Publishing: Berlin/Heidelberg, Germany, 2020; pp. 209–221.
50. Fawcett, T. An Introduction to ROC analysis. *Pattern Recogn. Lett.* **2006**, *27*, 861–874. [CrossRef]
51. Akiba, T.; Sano, S.; Yanase, T.; Ohta, T.; Koyama, M. Optuna: A next-generation hyperparameter optimization framework. In Proceedings of the 25th ACM SIGKDD International Conference on Knowledge Discovery & Data Mining, Anchorage, AK, USA, 4–8 August 2019.
52. Bergstra, J.; Yamins, D.; Cox, D. Making a science of model search: Hyperparameter optimization in hundreds of dimensions for vision architectures. In Proceedings of the 30th International Conference on Machine Learning, Atlanta, GA, USA, 17–19 June 2013.
53. Bergstra, J.; Bardenet, R.; Bengio, Y.; Kégl, B. Algorithms for hyper-parameter optimization. In *Advances in Neural Information Processing Systems*; MIT Press: Cambridge, MA, USA, 2011; Volume 24.
54. Hansen, N.; Ostermeier, A. Completely Derandomized Self-Adaptation in Evolution Strategies. *Evol. Comput.* **2001**, *9*, 159–195. [CrossRef]
55. Li, L.; Jamieson, K.; Rostamizadeh, A.; Gonina, E.; Ben-Tzur, J.; Hardt, M.; Recht, B.; Talwalkar, A. A system for massively parallel hyperparameter tuning. *Proc. Mach. Learn. Syst.* **2020**, *2*, 230–246.

Disclaimer/Publisher's Note: The statements, opinions and data contained in all publications are solely those of the individual author(s) and contributor(s) and not of MDPI and/or the editor(s). MDPI and/or the editor(s) disclaim responsibility for any injury to people or property resulting from any ideas, methods, instructions or products referred to in the content.

Article

Get Real Get Better: A Framework for Developing Agile Program Management in the U.S. Navy Supported by the Application of Advanced Data Analytics and AI

Jonathan Haase [1], Peter B. Walker [2,*], Olivia Berardi [3] and Waldemar Karwowski [4,*]

1. NAVSEA PEO USC, PMS 408, Expeditionary Warfare Office, Washington, DC 20376, USA; jonjhaase@gmail.com
2. PEO USC, PMS 408–Expeditionary Medicine, 1333 Isaac Hull Ave., Washington Navy Yard, DC 20376, USA
3. Cydecor, Inc., 251 18th St. S Ste 550, Arlington, VI 22202, USA; olivia.l.berardi.ctr@us.navy.mil
4. Department of Industrial Engineering and Management Systems, University of Central Florida, Orlando, FL 32816, USA
* Correspondence: peter.b.walker.mil@health.mil (P.B.W.); wkar@ucf.edu (W.K.)

Abstract: This paper discusses the *"Get Real Get Better"* (GRGB) approach to implementing agile program management in the U.S. Navy, supported by advanced data analytics and artificial intelligence (AI). GRGB was designed as a set of foundational principles to advance Navy culture and support its core values. This article identifies a need for a more informed and efficient approach to program management by highlighting the benefits of implementing comprehensive data analytics that leverage recent advances in cloud computing and machine learning. The Jupiter enclave within Advana implemented by the U.S. Navy, is also discussed. The presented approach represents a practical framework that cultivates a *"Get Real Get Better"* mindset for implementing agile program management in the U.S. Navy.

Keywords: program management; data analytics; machine learning; artificial intelligence; agile development

Citation: Haase, J.; Walker, P.B.; Berardi, O.; Karwowski, W. Get Real Get Better: A Framework for Developing Agile Program Management in the U.S. Navy Supported by the Application of Advanced Data Analytics and AI. *Technologies* **2023**, *11*, 165. https://doi.org/10.3390/technologies11060165

Academic Editors: Mohammed Mahmoud and Pedro Antonio Gutiérrez

Received: 26 August 2023
Revised: 12 November 2023
Accepted: 13 November 2023
Published: 20 November 2023

Copyright: © 2023 by the authors. Licensee MDPI, Basel, Switzerland. This article is an open access article distributed under the terms and conditions of the Creative Commons Attribution (CC BY) license (https://creativecommons.org/licenses/by/4.0/).

1. Introduction

Rapid advances in business applications of data analytics (DA) and artificial intelligence (AI) have great potential to transform and disrupt the current program-management capabilities and practices [1–3]. Many recently published studies have demonstrated the benefits of the effective implementation and integration of data analytics and AI in project management (see, for example, [4,5]). While most of these studies focused primarily on project management, Santos and de Carvalho [6] discussed the benefits of scaling agile project management to large projects. This paper introduces the requirements for leveraging data analytics and AI to enhance program management in the U.S. Navy environment.

In a fast-evolving world, the United States Navy military consistently strives to stay ahead by ensuring the efficient execution of complex programs while continuing to meet mission-critical objectives. To meet these continuing and changing demands, the Navy's Chief of Naval Operations established the foundations for a program known as *Get Real Get Better* (GRGB) in 2021. GRGB was designed as a set of foundational principles to advance Navy culture and support its core values. "Get Real" focuses on self-assessment and transparency. To stay ahead of its near-peer competition, the Navy needs to be continually self-aware and provide continued assessment regarding its performance. Similarly, "Get Better" attempts to utilize this self-assessment and commit to improvement. Here, the focus is on achieving the highest standards of performance.

This paper discusses the *Get Real Get Better* (GRGB) approach for developing agile program management in the U.S. Navy. Currently, the Navy seeks to apply advanced data analytics and artificial intelligence (AI) to transform program management by identifying and fixing the root causes of its current challenges. At its core, the proposed GRGB framework leverages data-driven decision making (Get Real) to build program management performance (PMP) and evaluation criteria to cultivate an environment of program management performance improvement (Get Better).

2. Background: Project and Program Management

2.1. Agile Project Management

The agile approach to project management has been extensively used within the software development sector and manufacturing settings due to the industry's dynamics and the need for rapid adaptation to unforeseen changes in business environments [7,8]. However, current agile project management is still limited by the absence of advanced analytical methods allowing for automated prediction, estimation, planning, resource and risk management, and decision-making in general [5]. For example, Cabrero-Daniel [9] conducted an extensive literature review and longitudinal meta-analysis of the retrieved studies, focusing on integrating artificial intelligence with agile software development methodologies and the role of artificial intelligence and its future applications within agile software development with a focus on continuous integration and delivery. Furthermore, Auth et al. [10] proposed a conceptual framework to speed up the potential applications of artificial intelligence in the project management area.

2.2. AI-Supported Agile Project Management

Many recent studies have pointed out that modern management faces the challenge created by potentially disruptive AI applications across entire organizations and their business processes [1,5], including, among others, organization-specific AI use cases [11], software engineering [12], healthcare [13], and medicine [14]. Most recently, Odeh [15] argued that project managers should take full advantage of AI to transform traditional project management processes to meet stakeholders' needs and deliver the desired project outcome. Furthermore, Bento et al. [16], based on a systematic literature review, pointed out that the field of project management still needs to fully embrace the benefits of AI technology, and more research and development is required in this direction.

As discussed by Dam et al. [17], the rapid developments in the field of artificial intelligence (AI) can transform the current practices in agile project management (APM) by accelerating productivity and increasing project success rates. Such a transformation can be achieved by assisting project managers through AI-based automation of repetitive and high-volume tasks, improving project analytics for estimation and risk prediction, and enabling AI-supported actionable decision-making. The most recent systematic literature review by Taboada et al. [18] concluded that AI and machine learning (ML) could be very useful in the management of IT and construction projects by enabling significant improvements in project planning [19], scheduling [20], cost and quality [21], forecasting [22], risk management [23], and decision-making competences [24–26].

2.3. Human–AI Collaboration in Project Management

According to Abedin et al. [27], AI systems are currently being implanted into various information systems, including medical diagnostics, health, layout design, human resources, arts, entertainment, financial/credit scoring, and autonomous vehicles. Shang et al. [28] suggested that AI technologies are underutilized in project management due to limited support from top management, the absence of organizational readiness, the high cost of AI implementation and maintenance, and the shortage of personnel trained in AI. Furthermore, a questionnaire study by Fridgeirsson et al. [29] suggested that the respondents did not consider artificial intelligence as a technology that could support the required human cognitive skills and leadership abilities. However, as pointed out by Puranam [30], effective human–AI collaborative decision making should be considered as a problem in organization design based on two different criteria, i.e., (1) specialization, where humans and AI systems perform tasks that they are best at, and (2) multiple learning configurations, which consider the ways that humans and AI systems may "learn together" and use the most relevant knowledge for collaboration.

Some recent studies have shown the success of human–AI teamwork [31] with hybrid decision making, where the individual strengths of the humans and the AI systems allow the optimization of the joint decision outcomes. Such collaborative efforts, where the human–AI team outperforms the individual agents acting separately, are also called hybrid intelligence [32,33]. Examples of such effective human–AI collaboration include knowledge work [34], data annotation [35], medical diagnosis [36], mental health [37], and computationally informed mission planning [38]. Furthermore, the new developments in the theory of organizational decision-making [39] also suggest effective ways in which the decisions of organizational members can be combined with AI-based decisions for successful human-AI teaming and collaboration in the project management area. Finally, it should be noted that, according to Smolensky et al. [40], the recent developments in neurocompositional computing [41] will allow us to overcome the limitations of current computing paradigms and enable building AI systems that exhibit a high level of cognitive abilities, which are required for the realization of AI-powered project management applications.

2.4. Program Management in the U.S. Navy

This paper describes a practical framework for developing agile program management in the U.S. Navy. It should be noted that most of the published literature on the applications of advanced data analytics and AI focuses on project management rather than program management. However, as pointed out by many studies [42–46], there are significant differences between project and program management. Notably, Lycett et al. [42] noted that program management is not just a scaled-up version of project management and that the "one size fits all" approach to program management is inappropriate in the dynamic business environment. They also pointed out that while project management is inward-focused and task-oriented, program management is strategy-focused and represents a wider organizational view. In that context, program management links the gap between project delivery and the organization's strategic planning [43]. For example, program management in the information technology sector should continually change to uphold effective alignment with organizational strategies and react to the external environment as needed to preserve its relevance [44]. On the other hand, managing specific projects in a given program requires making decisions to align them with the program goals.

Pellegrinelli [45] also contended that it is important to distinguish project management from program management, including the related concepts, approaches, and techniques relevant to each discipline. Concerning the role of managers, Walenta [46] outlined some key differences between project managers and program managers by noting that (1) project managers are inward-oriented, while program managers are focused on the outside environment; (2) the competencies of successful project managers significantly differ from the competencies of successful program managers; and (3) project managers do not possess the required knowledge and skills for program management. Furthermore, de Groth [47] noted that project-oriented organizations use program management to cope with learning challenges across teams at different organizational levels. To integrate the above concepts, Thiry [48] proposed a unified model for learning performance program management that combines value management with project management.

3. Data-Driven Organizations
3.1. The Power of Data-Driven Decision-Making

There are several recent studies on the benefits of data-driven decision-making, defined as the process of using data to inform decision-making and validate courses of action [7–9]. Stobierski [10] outlined the advantages of data-driven decision-making, arguing that data analytics can improve project management outcomes. From a program management perspective, data-driven decision-making could take many forms. For example, a program office might use spending plans to estimate obligations and expenditure rates. These estimates might then be used to make fiscal decisions regarding where to spend money in future years and how to break down procurement versus research expenditures or develop new contracts for execution. The important notion is that the data can drive the decision-making process and positively impact organizational performance. Indeed, as access to data and the ability to process these data in a more parallel manner become more accessible, it will become even easier for organizations to adopt a data-driven decision framework.

Data collection and analysis are key to the US Navy's *"Get Better, Get Real"* strategy. Specifically, the collection of authoritative data drives confidence in the decisions that are being made to drive programmatic change. Not only do the data help to baseline where certain program constraints exist, but they also provide traceability with respect to how changes may impact the organization. Data also reduces the need for intuitive decision-making, eliminating the influence of personal bias. By leveraging authoritative data, a program office can fully commit to a particular strategy by having confidence that this approach will have specific impacts in a particular area.

3.2. Becoming a Data-Driven Organization

Organizations seeking to become more data-driven need to foster a data-driven culture [7–10]. This requires the adoption of a mindset that values the insights and use of authoritative data. Program managers at the Navy can curate this by developing a culture of "data awareness" by encouraging behaviors that seek to leverage data to drive performance change. Program managers should also seek to eliminate barriers to accessing authoritative data as much as possible. As program offices seek to make this transition from an intuitive to a data-driven culture, there are several steps that can be taken to ensure this happens in a manner that facilitates programmatic success. These steps include the following:

<u>Establish an Authoritative Data Lake:</u> Create a centralized database to store and manage all project-related data, ensuring easy access for program managers (PMs) and other stakeholders. While there is a need to identify authoritative data sources, the data oftentimes may not exist or do not exist in the form that is needed for appropriate analyses. In this case, program managers should seek ways to develop new data pipelines that would allow for the collection of new and meaningful data;

<u>Develop Data Collection Standards:</u> One potential pitfall for organizations hoping to adopt a data-driven mindset is the inconsistency in which data are collected and reported. To avoid this, program managers should seek to implement uniform data collection standards across different departments, programs, and projects, making it easier to compare and analyze data. Developing data dictionaries or metadata repositories is critical here. A data dictionary is defined as a centralized repository of information about data, such as its meaning, relationships to other data, origin, usage, and format. By posting this information in an easily accessible location and ensuring the dictionary is available to users across all levels of the organization, the program office can ensure that data are being used in a reliable and consistent fashion. This also ensures that conclusions drawn from the use of those data are consistent and explainable to users;

<u>Invest in Data Management Tools:</u> The adoption of a data-driven culture begins with the consistent use of data management tools. Program managers should equip themselves and their professionals with data management tools, including machine learning and statistical modeling techniques, to enable them to derive valuable insights from the collected data. In addition, organizations should seek out new and meaningful ways to visualize their data. Data visualization is as critical a part of the data analytic process as any other. End users simply cannot derive any meaningful interpretation or action from raw data. Visual aids that emphasize the power of the data, the influence and impact of the raw data in drawing specific conclusions, and that demonstrate trends and patterns in the data are all critical pieces for data adoption. Visualization tools such as Qlik, Tableau, and even Excel allow users to convert raw data of any kind and make them more interpretable for stakeholders at all levels;

Encourage a Data-Driven Culture: Finally, organizations should seek to promote a culture that emphasizes the importance of data-driven decision-making at all levels of the organization. Organizational leaders should try to avoid situations that encourage intuitive decision-making and rely more on decision-making processes that allow them to trace those decisions back to authoritative data. In this case, leading by example will also create an environment within a program office that encourages analytical thinking. The inculcation of this framework begins by encouraging those behaviors that are consistent with data-driven values. This includes providing ongoing training, creating incentives, and recognizing achievements in data-driven program management.

4. Methodology

The adoption of a data-driven culture can be a key enabler for program managers willing to transform their organizations. By gathering and properly labeling data for future programs, the U.S. Navy can experience numerous benefits, including the following:

1. Enhanced Decision Making: access to well-structured data will allow PMs to gain a deeper understanding of their programs, helping them to identify potential risks and opportunities for improvement;
2. Optimized Resource Allocation: data-driven insights can guide PMs in making more informed decisions about resource allocation, ensuring that scarce resources are deployed effectively;
3. Fostered Collaboration: the availability of relevant data can promote information sharing and collaboration between different departments and stakeholders, resulting in more efficient project management and better outcomes;
4. Improved Accountability: data transparency will improve accountability by enabling PMs to track progress more accurately, making it easier to identify and address inefficiencies.

4.1. Business Analytics Use Case

In March 2023, the Expeditionary Missions Program Office (PMS 408) and Naval Sea Systems Command (NAVSEA) initiated a use case through Advana Jupiter of the Department of the Navy's (DoN) enterprise data environment [49,50]. Through a partnership with Advana that includes access to data mining and machine learning engineers, product managers, full-stack developers, and data visualization experts, PMS 408 sought to create a shared understanding of organizational metrics through historical, current, and forward-looking algorithms. The goal of this effort was two-fold: (1) to foster a data-driven decision culture that allows program managers and analysts at all levels to inform decisions through authoritative data, and (2) to simplify and automate existing reporting metrics.

To accomplish these goals, a need for reducing qualitative or intuitive decision-making processes was recognized. This was carried out to increase confidence in programmatic planning by developing a data-driven framework for planning and execution. This begins first by identifying authoritative data sources that drive programmatic execution. Once identified, it was important to understand how these data facilitate or inhibit organizational performance. At this stage, it was critical to engage with organizational leadership to understand their goals and how these authoritative data can serve as a proxy for assessment toward those goals. As with any data-driven environment, it was also important to focus on those features that aligned most with the strategic vision of organizational leadership. This should be carried out a priori rather than using a data exploration approach. Such an approach was encouraged to prevent the Navy from responding to artifacts that might exist within the data. Consequently, those features that were the true drivers of organizational performance were identified. It should be noted, however, that given the breadth and scope of data pipelines, this could potentially lead to "false positives" and other data artifacts.

4.2. Advana Jupiter

With the above-discussed goals in mind, the Navy initiated the creation of a data analytic dashboard sitting on top of the Advana Jupiter infrastructure [49,50]. Advana Jupiter serves as the DoN enterprise data hub. Through a tiered "Wisdom of Crowds" approach, DON Information Data Stewards create disparate data hubs across a variety of data domains. The integration of these data hubs allows for the aggregation of the most authoritative and comprehensive view of enterprise data.

It should be noted that the Advana Jupiter provides several inherent advantages over local or distributed cloud architectures. For example, Jupiter allows for more flexible cloud computing. Specifically, Jupiter provides both dedicated and "on-demand" computing and storage capacity. In addition, Jupiter and its licensed applications allow for a more robust data pipeline for more efficient data ingestion, processing, and visualization. A more attractive feature of Advana is the ability to develop specific queries on new or existing data. Metadata are stored on Advana and can be accessed via data discovery tools, technical documentation, and a data catalog. Lastly, Jupiter provides perhaps the most modern toolset for data analytics in the acquisition enterprise. Tools such as Apache Spark allow for large-scale data processing that is agnostic to programming languages. For data analytics, developers have access to tools such as PyTorch and TensorFlow, which allow for the development and deployment of machine learning algorithms such as deep learning.

PMS 408 has initiated several efforts that leverage the tools within Advana Jupiter to assist in programmatic development. These efforts are designed to leverage the tools and algorithms within this environment to provide more quantitative metrics to describe overall programmatic health in areas including contract performance, requirement traceability, and portfolio visualizations. For example, the PMS 408 team and its developers have developed visualizations surrounding portfolio investments using the Qlik business intelligence (BI) and visualization platform. This tool can be used in areas such as data integration to assist in importing and integrating portfolio investment data from data sources such as Navy Enterprise Resource Planning (ERP) data. Navy ERP captures and manages financial data related to the Navy's budgeting, accounting, and financial transactions. This includes data related to budget allocation, expenditure tracking, payroll, and financial reporting.

Some of the key data sources being integrated into this specific use case include procurement data. Here, the system maintains data related to the procurement of goods and services, including purchase orders, vendor information, contract details, and procurement history. In addition, models based on asset management data were developed. In this case, Navy ERP can track and manage assets such as equipment, vehicles, and facilities. This includes data on asset maintenance, depreciation, and utilization.

Similarly, a focused approach to analyzing data surrounding reporting and analytics has been adopted. The ERP generates various reports and analytics based on the data it collects. These reports help Navy leadership make informed decisions about resource allocation, budget planning, and operational efficiency. Taken together, the historical data were used to build predictive models of future performance. For example, Navy ERP accumulates historical data that can be used for trend analysis, forecasting, and performance evaluation. Finally, historical data can provide valuable insights into the Navy's financial and operational performance.

4.3. The Qlik Platform

For this business use case, data from ERP and other government data on the Qlik platform were used. This integration allowed the development of data models within Qlik to organize our portfolio data. These models help to define relationships between different data tables, such as investments, asset classes, and performance metrics. This step is crucial for building meaningful visualizations. A second advantage of the Qlik tool is that it allows for ease-of-dashboard creation and visualization. Qlik's drag-and-drop interface created interactive dashboards that can be updated in near real time. In addition, users could customize these dashboards to filter and drill down into the data. Analysts and programmatic leadership can select specific investments, time frames, or asset classes to focus on specific aspects of the portfolio.

Visualizations only represent a small fraction of the capability developed through the Advana Jupiter business use case. Using additional tools allowed through their secure government cloud brokerage enabled the Navy to build models that track key performance indicators (KPIs) to provide additional insights into portfolio performance. Examples include calculating contract performance deviations, long product delivery delays, and other hindrances to programmatic performance. Making further use of the Advana pipeline allowed implementing alerts and notifications within Advana to automatically alert users when investments failed to meet predefined criteria or required attention.

Overall, the tools within the Advana pipeline are a catalyst for developing quantifiable models to better understand portfolio performance. This study discussed how it was possible to use these tools and the Advana platform in the Navy for analysis and visualization purposes. Such tools provide flexibility and interactivity, making them well-suited for portfolio managers, financial analysts, and resource sponsors who want to gain deeper insights into their investment portfolios and make informed decisions.

5. Agile Program Development in the U.S. Navy

Several studies examined various aspects of agile project management [51–54]. For example, Koch and Schermuly [53] suggest that agile project management practices can significantly impact organizational culture. Coram and Bohner [55,56] discussed the impact of agile methods on software project management, arguing that agile methodologies improve project delivery and faster adaptation to changing market requirements. Conforto et al. [57] explored the feasibility of adopting agile project management methodologies outside the software industry.

To ensure the development of the present framework is both impactful and delivered at a pace that is consistent with the demands of the Navy's GRGB program, this project focused on developing an agile approach to project management [57]. Historically, much of the program and project management efforts have been focused on iterative and/or incremental approaches toward delivery. More recently, an emerging debate has arisen comparing more traditional "heavyweight" methods with more agile and fluid "lightweight" methods [58]. Heavyweight methods for project management are those that view the development process as more linear, leading to over-reliance on processes and milestones.

Beck et al. [59] proposed the *Manifesto for Agile Software Development*, which emphasizes the ability to respond to changing market conditions, customer collaboration, and meeting functional software requirements. The document addressed 12 universal principles designed to deliver products to customers much more efficiently and to directly address the needs and wants of the customer. The above principles are illustrated below in the context of program management responsibilities and their use by the Navy to drive the business analytics use case within the framework of *Advana* (see Table 1).

Table 1. Principles of agile software (v. 2001) development (modified after Beck et al., 2001).

Software delivery	Deliver working software frequently, from a couple of weeks to a couple of months, with a preference for a shorter timescale. Too often, projects are conducted in a manner where there may be an initial envisioning session. Beyond that, developers may fail to interact with either thought leaders or end users. This was carried out to avoid this through continuous and transparent communication with all stakeholders.
Collaboration	Businesspeople and developers must work together daily throughout the project. The development team must work directly with end users to better understand their problems and how algorithms should be designed to address those root problems.

Table 1. *Cont.*

Motivation	Build projects around motivated individuals. Give them the environment and support they need, and trust them to complete the job. This is carried out to empower the development teams by giving them the opportunity to build innovation. The teams' creativity was perceived as a key ingredient to ultimate success.
Communication	Face-to-face conversation continues to be the most efficient and effective method of conveying information to and within a development team. While the demands of a distributed world were recognized, as much face-to-face collaboration as possible was encouraged to facilitate the sharing of ideas and more open innovation.
Demonstrations	Working software is the primary measure of progress. The goal is to share the success via live demonstrations with the stakeholders.
Development	Agile processes promote sustainable development. The sponsors, developers, and users should be able to maintain a constant pace indefinitely. An emboldened collaborator will continue to seek ways to improve processes.
Promotion	Continuous attention to technical excellence and good design enhances agility. Strong technical achievements, as often as possible, are promoted.
Simplification	Simplicity, the art of maximizing the amount of work not completed, is essential to the developed development approach. The teams should not be burdened with administrative work that inhibits their ability to deliver new and innovative product lines.
Teams	The best architectures, requirements, and designs emerge from self-organizing teams. However, while collaboration across the effort is optional, it occurs organically.
Adaptation	The team regularly reflects on how to become more effective, then tunes and adjusts its behavior accordingly. In-progress reviews, ad hoc scrum teams, and other means for self-reflection have been used as the key facilitators.

5.1. Applications of Data Analytics and Machine Learning

The previous section described how the Advana Jupiter platform was harnessed to develop a pipeline that ingests, processes, and applies quantifiable models to inform analysts and program managers. This was carried out using the adoption of data mining and machine learning approaches. More explicitly and in the context of the presented BI use case, it was postulated that data mining and machine learning could address specific challenges in program management within the context of the U.S. Navy by leveraging data-driven insights to improve decision-making, optimize resource allocation, enhance operational efficiency, and reduce risks.

For example, machine learning models can analyze historical program data to improve the accuracy of cost estimates for new projects. They can help with budget planning and allocation. Similarly, these models can conduct real-time data analysis to identify cost overruns or anomalies, allowing program managers to promptly take corrective action. Similarly, data mining and machine learning can assist in resource allocation decision-making. Machine learning algorithms can allocate resources more efficiently by considering project complexity, resource availability, and historical performance data. In addition, data mining can identify potential bottlenecks or resource constraints that may impact program timelines. Furthermore, machine learning can be used to analyze historical scheduling data to optimize project timelines and reduce delays. These tools can also be applied to help predict maintenance needs for Navy equipment, reducing downtime and ensuring operational readiness.

Finally, the above tools have been utilized to assist in decision support. Specifically, the applied data mining and machine learning models have helped support predictive insights and allow program managers to make informed decisions about resource allocation and risk mitigation. Similarly, data mining can be applied to simulate different program scenarios to evaluate their potential impacts on outcomes. By leveraging data mining and machine learning in program management, the U.S. Navy can enhance its ability to plan, execute, and monitor programs effectively, improving mission success, cost control, and overall operational efficiency. However, the extent to which these tools can influence the discussed aspects of planning and execution depends on the quality of the iterative feedback on model development and deployment provided by the users. Therefore, it is critical in instances such as the use case presented here and others like it that program managers are motivated and able to adopt a more flexible framework for model acceptance and deployment.

5.2. How the Agile Approach Impacts Program Management in the U.S. Navy

In this paper, it has been postulated that a comprehensive data pipeline inspired by agile software development principles represents a realization of the "*Get Real Get Better*" initiative. The specific instances of how agile principles can be used to emphasize iterative development, collaboration, adaptability, and customer centricity, which can be highly beneficial in the context of Navy program management, are discussed below.

It is all too common for Navy programs to face issues such as changing requirements and operational environments. An agile-inspired data pipeline can be designed to accommodate changes gracefully. They allow for quick adjustments and additions to data sources, transformations, and analytics as program requirements evolve. Similarly, Navy program managers are consistently challenged with high-risk decisions without the time necessary to comprehensively weigh all options. Agile practices enable the rapid development of data analytics and visualizations. Program managers can access up-to-date information and quickly make informed decisions.

Program offices are also required to have continuous stakeholder collaboration. Simply put, without effective collaboration, programs are not able to deliver on their promised capabilities. However, agile frameworks emphasize continuous collaboration between data teams and program managers. Frequent check-ins and feedback loops ensure that data solutions align with program objectives. Identifying and mitigating risks is a key program management aspect. Agile's iterative approach allows for the continuous monitoring of program data. This helps in the early detection of risk factors and adapting strategies accordingly.

By embracing agile-inspired principles in the development and management of data pipelines for program management, the U.S. Navy has enhanced its ability to address dynamic challenges, make data-driven decisions, and achieve successful outcomes in a rapidly evolving operational environment. This framework promotes a culture of adaptability and continuous improvement that is well suited to the Navy's mission requirements and consistent with the vision that has been outlined by the "*Get Better Get Real Framework*".

6. AI and Data Science in Agile Project Management

Many recently published studies have demonstrated the effective implementation of data analytics and AI in project management [4,5]. Other studies [18,19] have discussed the challenges of incorporating AI and data analytics into agile project management to improve software development outcomes. Gil et al. [2] reviewed the recent approaches to incorporating AI in project management to optimize project processes. Crawford et al. [20] present a survey of AI applications in software engineering, specifically focusing on project management. Most recently, Hoda et al. [60–62] introduced the concept of human-centered AI-assisted agile project management that augments software management processes and human decision-making. The above studies presented the benefits of integrating the principles of agile project management, AI, and data science into various project management applications. The current paper introduces the requirements for leveraging data analytics and AI to enhance program management in the U.S. Navy environment.

6.1. Artificial Intelligence and Machine Learning Applications

Over the past 10 years, there has been exponential growth in the use and adoption of artificial intelligence tools, including machine learning [63]. Generally speaking, machine learning is typically categorized into one of three different categories: supervised, unsupervised, or reinforcement. Each of these approaches varies in the way it is trained, the outputs it provides, and the application of its algorithms to various data types. In a very general sense, artificial intelligence and machine learning represent sophisticated forms of data analysis. Using algorithms that continuously learn from data, these approaches allow machines to recognize hidden patterns in data sets that are often too subtle for humans to identify and/or explain. In addition, through repeated exposure to disparate data sets (training), machines can then extrapolate those patterns to new data to predict future states.

6.2. A Case for Deep Learning

Recent advances in computing power and architecture have allowed deep learning algorithms to reach performance levels unmatched by other machine learning approaches. Deep learning has been a key enabler in several key technology areas, including driverless cars, image recognition, and human–machine interaction [12,64]. In its most basic form, deep learning allows a computer model to perform classification tasks directly from images, text, or sound. Deep learning models can achieve state-of-the-art accuracy, sometimes exceeding human-level performance [65].

6.3. Generative AI

Within the past five years, there has been a resurgence of interest in the area of generative artificial intelligence. Generative AI describes algorithms (such as ChatGPT) [66] that can be used to create new content. In this case, content describes new material created by the algorithm. This might include content such as audio files, programming code, images, contract language, or videos. Recent advances in the field of large language models (LLMs) have dynamically changed the way artificial intelligence and its applications are being viewed today. Generative AI opens a plethora of potential use cases within the program management space. The primary reasoning for this is that users need not be experts in AI and machine learning (ML) to apply these machine learning approaches. Rather, they need to be experts in their respective domains. Indeed, a new and growing field in machine learning is known as "prompt engineering" [67]. Prompt engineering is a new concept within AI and machine learning where the description of the task that should be accomplished by the AI is embedded within the input. Rather than the algorithm attempting to extract those features based on the training data, prompt engineering allows the user to embed features based on the questions asked of the algorithm.

6.4. ChatGPT: Example

To demonstrate the power and ease of generative AI, a simple query using ChatGPT has been implemented. ChatGPT is an AI chatbot developed by OpenAI. ChatGPT is built on top of large language models (LLMs) and has been optimized using both supervised and reinforcement learning techniques. The primary use of traditional chatbots is to model human behavior. However, ChatGPT and this newer generation of generative AI are much more versatile. These models have been applied in various use cases, including reading and writing code, generating art, and other complex tasks (see Table 2).

While generative AI appears to be the most promising application of AI for program management, caution must be exercised as well. On the one hand, using and applying LLMs has seen exponential growth in the past half decade [68,69]. However, surrounding their use, there has been extensive hype, misunderstanding, and misrepresentation regarding their capabilities. For example, Bender et al. [4] pointed out that LLMs have been built on foundational work from Natural Language Processing (NLP) [70]. However, these models do not code for Natural Language Understanding (NLU).

Another issue with generative AI revolves around the poorly understood problem of latent concept learning. Specifically, these models are learning relationships within the training data that are so abstract that they are unlikely to be perceived by a human audience. It is believed that the issues revolving around concepts such as trust and fairness [71] will become more pronounced as these models are deployed more frequently going forward.

Table 2. Example of a ChatGPT query.

>>Provide Some Examples in Which Generative AI Can Be Used to Assist Program Managers.<<
ChatGPT Reply:
Generative AI, such as GPT-3, can be used to assist in program management in a variety of ways.
Here are some examples:
1. Requirement Gathering:
Program managers can use generative AI to help with requirement gathering. They can provide the AI with the project's scope and goals, and the AI can generate a list of requirements that need to be fulfilled to achieve those goals;
2. Risk Management:
AI can help in identifying potential risks in the program by analyzing data from past projects and identifying patterns that indicate potential problems. This can help the program manager take proactive measures to mitigate those risks;
3. Resource Allocation:
Program managers can use AI to assist in the allocation of resources such as personnel, equipment, and funding. AI can help in predicting future resource needs based on past performance data and other relevant information;
4. Schedule Optimization:
Generative AI can assist program managers in optimizing schedules by analyzing historical data to identify the best way to sequence tasks and allocate resources;
5. Decision-Making:
AI can assist program managers in making better decisions by providing them with data-driven insights and recommendations. This can help the program manager make informed decisions that are more likely to lead to successful outcomes;
Overall, generative AI can help program managers streamline their processes, improve decision-making, and increase the chances of program success. However, it is important to note that AI should be used as a tool to assist program managers rather than a replacement for human decision-making.
Department of Defense (DoD) program management involves complex and high-stakes projects, and machine learning can be used to support decision-making, risk management, resource allocation, and other aspects of program management. Here are some examples of machine learning techniques that can be used in DoD program management:
1. Predictive analytics:
Predictive analytics can be used to forecast future outcomes and identify trends based on historical data. This can be useful for predicting project completion dates, identifying potential cost overruns, and estimating resource needs;
2. Natural language processing (NLP):
NLP can be used to analyze unstructured data, such as emails, chat messages, and reports. This can help program managers identify potential risks and issues that may not be captured in structured data;

Table 2. *Cont.*

3. Computer vision:
Computer vision can be used for surveillance, image analysis, and other tasks that require processing large amounts of visual data. This can be particularly useful in the defense industry, where there is a need for situational awareness and real-time decision-making;
4. Reinforcement learning:
Reinforcement learning can be used to optimize resource allocation and scheduling. This approach involves using algorithms to learn from experience and improve over time based on feedback;
5. Deep learning:
Deep learning can be used for a variety of tasks, including image and speech recognition, natural language processing, and predictive analytics. This approach involves using neural networks to learn from data and make predictions or decisions based on that learning.
In addition to these techniques, there are also specialized machine learning algorithms and frameworks that have been developed specifically for defense applications, such as the Defense Advanced Research Projects Agency's (DARPA) Explainable Artificial Intelligence (XAI) program.
Ultimately, the choice of machine learning techniques will depend on the specific needs of the DoD program and the available data.

6.5. Implications of Generative AIs for Agile Program Management Development

Generative AI holds considerable promise for agile program management by potentially enhancing creativity, automating certain tasks, and introducing rapid prototyping capabilities. However, it also brings challenges related to quality assurance, complexity, the need for developing new skills among program managers, and many ethical considerations. As with any disruptive technology, the successful integration of generative AI into agile program management practices in the U.S. Navy will require thoughtful planning, continuous learning, and adaptability.

Generally, generative AI systems can create new content such as text, design concepts, and software code [70,71]. The applications of generative AI for developing agile program management have many theoretical and practical implications. The key theoretical considerations include complexity and uncertainty, continuous learning and adaptation, and redefining value. Generative AI can also introduce a new level of complexity to agile management programs due to the unpredictable and innovative nature of the generated content. This could affect program risk assessment and the required approaches when applying agile methodologies.

Furthermore, generative AI can constantly change its outputs based on knowledge feedback loops when applying the agile principle of iterative development. However, this also raises questions about achieving the successful completion of specific program objectives and related tasks. Finally, as agile management's traditional notion of "value" evolves, determining the desired value of AI-generated versus human-designed system solutions or components becomes critical to fulfilling the program management objectives.

The practical implications of agile program management in the U.S. Navy are significant and include (1) enhanced creativity, (2) automated task completion, (3) feedback integration, (4) rapid prototyping, (5) skill requirements, (6) resource allocation, (7) quality assurance and testing, and (8) ethical and governance concerns. These implications are described in Table 3 below.

Table 3. Practical implications of generative AI for agile program management.

Enhanced creativity	Program managers can leverage generative models to brainstorm and visualize multiple scenarios, designs, or solutions, which can then be refined based on specific stakeholder feedback.
Automated task completion	Generative AI can automate the generation of code, reports, or other outputs for specific repetitive or well-defined tasks, freeing program managers to focus on more complex or creative aspects.
Feedback integration	Generative models can be retrained or fine-tuned for program management purposes based on feedback, aligning with the agile practice of regular reflection and adaptation.
Rapid prototyping	The use of generative AI can quickly produce multiple prototypes or solutions to a variety of program management tasks, adhering to the agile principle of early and continuous delivery.
Skill requirements	The introduction of generative AI in agile program management will require new skill sets for program managers, including data analytics and AI training, which should be considered during the planning and execution phases of the program.
Resource allocation	The use of generative AI will require additional resources, such as high-performance computing and specialized AI-powered software tools, which should be accounted for during program development, planning, and execution.
Quality assurance and testing	The use of generative AI will require new testing and quality assurance procedures to ensure the accuracy and reliability of program management outputs.
Ethical and governance concerns	The use of generative AI in agile program management should be guided by ethical and governance considerations to ensure the responsible and ethical use of these technologies.

7. Conclusions

Focusing on the tenets within the *"Get Real Get Better"* framework, this paper has postulated that program managers at the U.S. Navy should leverage data-driven decision-making to build quantitative program assessment criteria [72,73]. An approach to achieving this has been demonstrated using a use case study implemented through the partnership with Advana to create a machine learning pipeline for data analytics that program offices can harness. Addressing advanced and intelligent data analytics capabilities in the U.S. Navy's program management is crucial to ensuring the sustained success of national security safeguarding [74,75]. By prioritizing data collection, labeling, and analysis, unlocking advanced data analytics and artificial intelligence's full potential becomes feasible, leading to better decision-making and improved program outcomes. The time has come for all stakeholders, ranging from program managers to top leadership, to collaborate in cultivating a culture of organizational excellence that is data-driven and empowered by artificial intelligence, thus fueling innovation, efficiency, and collaboration as the U.S. Navy progresses toward being a more adaptable and resilient organization.

Author Contributions: Conceptualization, J.H., P.B.W. and O.B.; validation, J.H., P.B.W., O.B. and W.K.; writing—original draft preparation, J.H., P.B.W., O.B. and W.K.; writing—review and editing, W.K. and P.B.W.; supervision, P.B.W.; project administration, J.H. All authors have read and agreed to the published version of the manuscript.

Funding: This research received no external funding.

Data Availability Statement: No new data were created or analyzed in this study. Data sharing is not applicable to this article.

Conflicts of Interest: Author Olivia Berardi is employed by the company Cydecor, Inc. The remaining authors declare that the research was conducted in the absence of any commercial or financial relationships that could be construed as a potential conflict of interest.

References

1. Niederman, F. Project management: Openings for disruption from AI and advanced analytics. *Inf. Technol. People* **2021**, *34*, 1570–1599. [CrossRef]
2. Gil, J.; Martinez Torres, J.; González-Crespo, R. The Application of Artificial Intelligence in Project Management Research: A review. *Int. J. Interact. Multimed. Artif. Intell.* **2021**, *6*, 54–66. [CrossRef]
3. Song, L.; Minku, L.L. Artificial Intelligence in Software Project Management. In *Optimising the Software Development Process with Artificial Intelligence*; Springer Nature: Singapore, 2023; pp. 19–65.
4. Bender, E.M.; Gebru, T.; McMillan-Major, A.; Shmitchell, S. On the Dangers of Stochastic Parrots: Can Language Models Be Too Big? In Proceedings of the 2021 ACM Conference on Fairness, Accountability, and Transparency, Virtual, 3–10 March 2021; pp. 610–623.
5. Ong, S.; Uddin, S. Data Science and Artificial Intelligence in Project Management: The Past, Present and Future. *J. Mod. Proj. Manag.* **2020**, *7*, 26–33.
6. Santos, P.D.O.; de Carvalho, M.M. Exploring the challenges and benefits for scaling agile project management to large projects: A review. *Requir. Eng.* **2022**, *27*, 117–134. [CrossRef]
7. Schrettenbrunner, M.B. Artificial-intelligence-driven management. *IEEE Eng. Manag. Rev.* **2020**, *48*, 15–19. [CrossRef]
8. Canals, J.; Heukamp, F. *The Future of Management in an AI World*; Palgrave Macmillan: London, UK, 2020.
9. Cabrero-Daniel, B. AI for Agile development: A Meta-Analysis. *arXiv* **2023**, arXiv:2305.08093.
10. Auth, G.; Jöhnk, J.; Wiecha, D.A. A Conceptual Framework for Applying Artificial Intelligence in Project Management. In Proceedings of the 2021 IEEE 23rd Conference on Business Informatics (CBI), Bolzano, Italy, 1–3 September 2021; Volume 1, pp. 161–170.
11. Hofmann, P.; Jöhnk, J.; Protschky, D.; Urbach, N. Developing Purposeful AI Use Cases-A Structured Method and Its Application in Project Management. In *Wirtschaftsinformatik (Zentrale Tracks)*; FIM Research Center: Fraunhofer, Stuttgart, 2020; pp. 33–49. Available online: https://www.fim-rc.de/Paperbibliothek/Veroeffentlicht/1025/wi-1025.pdf (accessed on 17 July 2023).
12. Crawford, T.; Duong, S.; Fueston, R.; Lawani, A.; Owoade, S.; Uzoka, A.; Parizi, R.M.; Yazdinejad, A. AI in Software Engineering: A Survey on Project Management Applications. *arXiv* **2023**, arXiv:2307.15224. Available online: https://arxiv.org/pdf/2307.152 24.pdf (accessed on 17 July 2023).
13. Wahl, B.; Cossy-Gantner, A.; Germann, S.; Schwalbe, N.R. Artificial intelligence (AI) and global health: How can AI contribute to health in resource-poor settings? *BMJ Glob. Health* **2018**, *3*, e00798. [CrossRef]
14. Lei, H.; Lai, W.; Feaster, W.; Chang, A.C. Artificial gence and agile project management. In *Intelligence-Based Cardiology and Cardiac Surgery*; Academic Press: Cambridge, MA, USA, 2024; pp. 401–405.
15. Odeh, M. The Role of Artificial Intelligence in Project Management. *IEEE Eng. Manag. Rev.* **2023**. [CrossRef]
16. Bento, S.; Pereira, L.; Gonçalves, R.; Dias, Á.; Costa, R.L.D. Artificial intelligence in project management: Systematic literature review. *Int. J. Technol. Intell. Plan.* **2022**, *13*, 143–163. [CrossRef]
17. Dam, H.K.; Tran, T.; Grundy, J.; Ghose, A.; Kamei, Y. Towards effective AI-powered agile project management. In Proceedings of the 2019 IEEE/ACM 41st International Conference On Software Engineering: New Ideas And Emerging Results (ICSE-NIER), Montreal, QC, Canada, 25–31 May 2019; pp. 41–44.
18. Taboada, I.; Daneshpajouh, A.; Toledo, N.; de Vass, T. Artificial Intelligence Enabled Project Management: A Systematic Literature Review. *Appl. Sci.* **2023**, *13*, 5014. [CrossRef]
19. Teslia, I.; Yehorchenkova, N.; Khlevna, I.; Yehorchenkov, O.; Kataieva, Y.; Klevanna, G. Development of reflex technology of action identification in project planning systems. In Proceedings of the 2022 International Conference on Smart Information Systems and Technologies (SIST), Nur-Sultan, Kazakhstan, 28–30 April 2022; pp. 1–6.
20. Bahroun, Z.; Tanash, M.; As'ad, R.; Alnajar, M. Artificial Intelligence Applications in Project Scheduling: A Systematic Review, Bibliometric Analysis, and Prospects for Future Research. *Manag. Syst. Prod. Eng.* **2023**, *31*, 144–161. [CrossRef]
21. Son, P.V.H.; Khoi, L.N.Q. Utilizing Artificial Intelligence to Solving Time–Cost–Quality Trade-Off Problem. *Sci. Rep.* **2022**, *12*, 20112. [CrossRef] [PubMed]
22. Morozov, V.; Kalnichenko, O.; Proskurin, M.; Mezentseva, O. Investigation of Forecasting Methods of the State of Complex IT-Projects with the Use of Deep Learning Neural Networks. *Adv. Intell. Syst. Comput.* **2020**, *1020*, 261–280.
23. Choetkiertikul, M.; Dam, H.K.; Tran, T.; Ghose, A. Predicting Delays in Software Projects Using Networked Classification. In Proceedings of the 2015 30th IEEE/ACM International Conference on Automated Software Engineering, Lincoln, NE, USA, 9–13 November 2015; pp. 353–364.
24. El Khatib, M.; Al Falasi, A. Effects of Artificial Intelligence on Decision Making in Project Management. *Am. J. Ind. Bus. Manag.* **2021**, *11*, 251–260. [CrossRef]

25. Münch, T. AI, Agile, and Organizations. In *System Architecture Design and Platform Development Strategies*; Springer: Cham, Switzerland, 2022; pp. 155–183.
26. Hassani, R.; El Bouzekri El Idriss, Y. Proposal of a Framework and Integration of Artificial Intelligence to Succeed IT Project Planning. *Int. J. Adv. Trends Comput. Sci. Eng.* **2019**, *8*, 3396–3404. [CrossRef]
27. Abedin, B.; Meske, C.; Junglas, I.; Rabhi, F.; Motahari-Nezhad, H.R. Designing and managing human-AI interactions. *Inf. Syst. Front.* **2022**, *24*, 691–697. [CrossRef]
28. Shang, G.; Low, S.P.; Lim, X.Y.V. Prospects, drivers of and barriers to artificial intelligence adoption in project management. *Built Environ. Proj. Asset Manag.* **2023**, *13*, 629–645. [CrossRef]
29. Fridgeirsson, T.V.; Ingason, H.T.; Jonasson, H.I.; Jonsdottir, H. An authoritative study on the near future effect of artificial intelligence on project management knowledge areas. *Sustainability* **2021**, *13*, 2345. [CrossRef]
30. Puranam, P. Human–AI collaborative decision-making as an organization design problem. *J. Organ. Des.* **2021**, *10*, 75–80.
31. National Academies of Sciences, Engineering, and Medicine. *Human-AI Teaming: State-of-the-Art and Research Needs*; The National Academies Press: Washington, DC, USA, 2022. [CrossRef]
32. Dellermann, D.; Ebel, P.; Söllner, M.; Leimeister, J.M. Hybrid intelligence. *Bus. Inf. Syst. Eng.* **2019**, *61*, 637–643. [CrossRef]
33. Akata, Z.; Balliet, D.; De Rijke, M.; Dignum, F.; Dignum, V.; Eiben, G.; Fokkens, A.; Grossi, D.; Hindriks, K.; Hoos, H.; et al. A research agenda for hybrid intelligence: Augmenting human intellect with collaborative, adaptive, responsible, and explainable artificial intelligence. *Computer* **2020**, *53*, 18–28. [CrossRef]
34. Sowa, K.; Przegalinska, A.; Ciechanowski, L. Cobots in knowledge work: Human–AI collaboration in managerial professions. *J. Bus. Res.* **2021**, *125*, 135–142. [CrossRef]
35. Zhang, H.; He, Y.; Wu, X.; Huang, P.; Qin, W.; Wang, F.; Ye, J.; Huang, X.; Luo, Y.; Chan, H.; et al. PathNarratives: Data annotation for pathological human-AI collaborative diagnosis. *Front. Med.* **2023**, *9*, 1070072. [CrossRef]
36. Reverberi, C.; Rigon, T.; Solari, A.; Hassan, C.; Cherubini, P.; Cherubini, A. Experimental evidence of effective human–AI collaboration in medical decision-making. *Sci. Rep.* **2022**, *12*, 14952. [CrossRef] [PubMed]
37. Creed, T.A.; Salama, L.; Slevin, R.; Tanana, M.; Imel, Z.; Narayanan, S.; Atkins, D.C. Enhancing the quality of cognitive behavioral therapy in community mental health through artificial intelligence generated fidelity feedback (Project AFFECT): A study protocol. *BMC Health Serv. Res.* **2022**, *22*, 1177. [CrossRef]
38. Kase, S.E.; Hung, C.P.; Krayzman, T.; Hare, J.Z.; Rinderspacher, B.C.; Su, S.M. The future of collaborative human-artificial intelligence decision-making for mission planning. *Front. Psychol.* **2022**, *13*, 850628. [CrossRef]
39. Shrestha, Y.R.; Ben-Menahem, S.M.; Von Krogh, G. Organizational decision-making structures in the age of artificial intelligence. *Calif. Manag. Rev.* **2019**, *61*, 66–83. [CrossRef]
40. Smolensky, P.; McCoy, R.; Fernandez, R.; Goldrick, M.; Gao, J. Neurocompositional computing: From the Central Paradox of Cognition to a new generation of AI systems. *AI Mag.* **2022**, *43*, 308–322. [CrossRef]
41. Zentner, M.; Stirm, C.; Gesing, S.; Quick, R.; Stubbs, J. The Impact of AI Computing Paradigms on Science Gateways and National Compute Resources. *PEARC23* **2023**. Available online: https://par.nsf.gov/biblio/10450536 (accessed on 21 August 2023).
42. Lycett, M.; Rassau, A.; Danson, J. Programme management: A critical review. *Int. J. Proj. Manag.* **2004**, *22*, 289–299. [CrossRef]
43. Gaddie, S. Enterprise programme management: Connecting strategic planning to project delivery. *J. Facil. Manag.* **2003**, *2*, 177–191. [CrossRef]
44. Jiang, J.J.; Klein, G.; Fernandez, W.D. From project management to program management: An invitation to investigate programs where IT plays a significant role. *J. Assoc. Inf. Syst.* **2018**, *19*, 1. [CrossRef]
45. Pellegrinelli, S. What's in a name: Project or programme? *Int. J. Proj. Manag.* **2011**, *29*, 232–240. [CrossRef]
46. Walenta, T. Projects & programs are two different animals, don't underestimate the gap. *Procedia Soc. Behav. Sci.* **2016**, *226*, 365–371.
47. de Groot, B.; Leendertse, W.; Arts, J. Learning across teams in project-oriented organisations: The role of programme management. *Learn. Organ.* **2022**, *29*, 6–20. [CrossRef]
48. Thiry, M. Combining value and project management into an effective programme management model. *Int. J. Proj. Manag.* **2002**, *20*, 221–227. [CrossRef]
49. Rorie, J.; Duclos, J.; Lee, D.; Michlin, B.; Sabater, A.; Williams, G.R. The DARTEBoard: Visualization of an Improved and Expanded DARTE. 2023. Available online: https://apps.dtic.mil/sti/trecms/pdf/AD1202414.pdf (accessed on 3 August 2023).
50. Whitlock, C.; Strickland, F. Leading the Technology. In *Winning the National Security AI Competition: A Practical Guide for Government and Industry Leaders*; Apress: Berkeley, CA, USA, 2022; pp. 195–225.
51. Pellegrinelli, S.; Murray-Webster, R.; Turner, N. Facilitating organizational ambidexterity through the complementary use of projects and programs. *Int. J. Proj. Manag.* **2015**, *33*, 153–164. [CrossRef]
52. Singh, H. *Project Management Analytics: A Data-Driven Approach to Making Rational and Effective Project Decisions*; FT Press: Upper Saddle River, NJ, USA, 2015.
53. Vanhoucke, M. The Data-Driven Project Manager. In *The Illusion of Control: Project Data, Computer Algorithms and Human Intuition for Project Management and Control*; Springer Nature: Berlin/Heidelberg, Germany, 2023; pp. 29–48.
54. Mahmood, A.; Al Marzooqi, A.; El Khatib, M.; AlAmeemi, H. How Artificial Intelligence can Leverage Project Management Information System (PMIS) and Data Driven Decision Making in Project Management. *Int. J. Bus. Anal. Secur. (IJBAS)* **2023**, *3*, 184–195. [CrossRef]

55. Koch, J.; Schermuly, C.C. Who is attracted and why? How agile project management influences employee's attraction and commitment. *Int. J. Manag. Proj. Bus.* **2020**, *14*, 699–720. [CrossRef]
56. Aponte, M. Modernization of Acquisition Planning and Communication. Doctoral Dissertation, Naval Postgraduate School, Monterey, CA, USA, 2021.
57. Joseph, B.B.; Pham, T.; Hastings, C. Topological Data Analysis in Conjunction with Traditional Machine Learning Techniques to Predict Future MDAP PM Ratings. Acquisition Research Program. 2021. Available online: https://dair.nps.edu/bitstream/123456789/4367/1/SYM-AM-21-060.pdf (accessed on 27 July 2023).
58. Coram, M.; Bohner, S. The impact of agile methods on software project management. In Proceedings of the 12th IEEE International Conference and Workshops on the Engineering of Computer-Based Systems (ECBS'05), Greenbelt, MD, USA, 4–7 April 2005; pp. 363–370.
59. Conforto, E.C.; Salum, F.; Amaral, D.C.; Da Silva, S.L.; De Almeida, L.F.M. Can agile project management be adopted by industries other than software development? *Proj. Manag. J.* **2014**, *45*, 21–34. [CrossRef]
60. Khan, A.I.; Qureshi, M.; Khan, U.A. A Comprehensive Study of Commonly Practiced Heavy & Light Weight Software Methodologies. *arXiv* **2012**, arXiv:1202.2514.
61. Beck, K.; Beedle, M.; Van Bennekum, A.; Cockburn, A.; Cunningham, W.; Fowler, M.; Grenning, J.; Highsmith, J.; Hunt, A.; Jeffries, R.; et al. Manifesto for agile software development. 2001. Available online: https://ai-learn.it/wp-content/uploads/2019/03/03_ManifestoofAgileSoftwareDevelopment-1.pdf (accessed on 30 July 2023).
62. Uysal, M.P. Machine learning and data science project management from an agile perspective: Methods and challenges. In *Contemporary Challenges for Agile Project Management*; IGI Global: Hershey, PA, USA, 2022; pp. 73–88.
63. Hoda, R.; Dam, H.; Tantithamthavorn, C.; Thongtanunam, P.; Storey, M.A. Augmented Agile: Human-Centered AI-Assisted Software Management. *IEEE Softw.* **2023**, *40*, 106–109. [CrossRef]
64. Jordan, M.I.; Mitchell, T.M. Machine learning: Trends, perspectives, and prospects. *Science* **2015**, *349*, 255–260. [CrossRef] [PubMed]
65. Xu, M.; Yoon, S.; Fuentes, A.; Park, D.S. A comprehensive survey of image augmentation techniques for deep learning. *Pattern Recognit.* **2023**, *137*, 109347. [CrossRef]
66. LeCun, Y.; Bengio, Y.; Hinton, G. Deep learning. *Nature* **2015**, *521*, 436–444. [CrossRef]
67. Deng, L.; Yu, D. Deep learning: Methods and applications. *Found. Trends®Signal Process.* **2014**, *7*, 197–387. [CrossRef]
68. George, A.S.; George, A.H. A review of ChatGPT AI's impact on several business sectors. *Partn. Univers. Int. Innov. J.* **2023**, *1*, 9–23.
69. Liu, V.; Chilton, L.B. Design guidelines for prompt engineering text-to-image generative models. In Proceedings of the 2022 CHI Conference on Human Factors in Computing Systems, New Orleans, LA, USA, 29 April–5 May 2022; pp. 1–23.
70. Bianchi, F.; Hovy, D. On the gap between adoption and understanding in NLP. In Proceedings of the Findings of the Association for Computational Linguistics: ACL-IJCNLP 2021, Online, 1–6 August 2021; pp. 3895–3901.
71. Glikson, E.; Woolley, A.W. Human trust in artificial intelligence: Review of empirical research. *Acad. Manag. Ann.* **2020**, *14*, 627–660. [CrossRef]
72. Lewis, L.; Vavrichek, D. Center for Naval Analyses. In *An AI Framework for the Department of the Navy*; Center for Naval Analysis: Arlington, VA, USA, 2019; p. 29.
73. Chief of Naval Operations, A Design for Maintaining Maritime Superiority—Version 2.0, December 2018. Available online: https://www.navy.mil/navydata/people/cno/Richardson/Resource/Design_2.0.pdf (accessed on 29 July 2023).
74. Department of Defense. *Summary of the Department of Defense Artificial Intelligence Strategy*; Department of Defense: Arlington, VA, USA, 2019.
75. Hull, A.D.; Liew, J.K.S.; Palaoro, K.T.; Grzegorzewski, M.; Klipstein, M.; Breuer, P.; Spencer, M. Why the United States Must Win the Artificial Intelligence (AI) Race. *Cyber Def. Rev.* **2022**, *7*, 143–158.

Disclaimer/Publisher's Note: The statements, opinions and data contained in all publications are solely those of the individual author(s) and contributor(s) and not of MDPI and/or the editor(s). MDPI and/or the editor(s) disclaim responsibility for any injury to people or property resulting from any ideas, methods, instructions or products referred to in the content.

Article

Deep Learning Techniques for Web-Based Attack Detection in Industry 5.0: A Novel Approach

Abdu Salam [1], Faizan Ullah [2], Farhan Amin [3,*] and Mohammad Abrar [4]

1. Department of Computer Science, Abdul Wali Khan University, Mardan 23200, Pakistan; abdusalam@awkum.edu.pk
2. Department of Computer Science, Bacha Khan University, Charsadda 24420, Pakistan; faizanullah@bkuc.edu.pk
3. Department of Information and Communication Engineering, Yeungnam University, Gyeongsan 38541, Republic of Korea
4. Faculty of Computer Studies, Arab Open University, P.O. Box 1596, Muscat 130, Oman; abrar.m@aou.edu.om
* Correspondence: farhanamin10@hotmail or farhan@ynu.ac.kr

Citation: Salam, A.; Ullah, F.; Amin, F.; Abrar, M. Deep Learning Techniques for Web-Based Attack Detection in Industry 5.0: A Novel Approach. *Technologies* 2023, 11, 107. https://doi.org/10.3390/technologies11040107

Academic Editors: Mohammed Mahmoud and Lipo Wang

Received: 21 May 2023
Revised: 25 June 2023
Accepted: 7 August 2023
Published: 8 August 2023

Copyright: © 2023 by the authors. Licensee MDPI, Basel, Switzerland. This article is an open access article distributed under the terms and conditions of the Creative Commons Attribution (CC BY) license (https://creativecommons.org/licenses/by/4.0/).

Abstract: As the manufacturing industry advances towards Industry 5.0, which heavily integrates advanced technologies such as cyber-physical systems, artificial intelligence, and the Internet of Things (IoT), the potential for web-based attacks increases. Cybersecurity concerns remain a crucial challenge for Industry 5.0 environments, where cyber-attacks can cause devastating consequences, including production downtime, data breaches, and even physical harm. To address this challenge, this research proposes an innovative deep-learning methodology for detecting web-based attacks in Industry 5.0. Convolutional neural networks (CNNs), recurrent neural networks (RNNs), and transformer models are examples of deep learning techniques that are investigated in this study for their potential to effectively classify attacks and identify anomalous behavior. The proposed transformer-based system outperforms traditional machine learning methods and existing deep learning approaches in terms of accuracy, precision, and recall, demonstrating the effectiveness of deep learning for intrusion detection in Industry 5.0. The study's findings showcased the superiority of the proposed transformer-based system, outperforming previous approaches in accuracy, precision, and recall. This highlights the significant contribution of deep learning in addressing cybersecurity challenges in Industry 5.0 environments. This study contributes to advancing cybersecurity in Industry 5.0, ensuring the protection of critical infrastructure and sensitive data.

Keywords: cyber-physical systems; CNN; Industry 5.0; transformer models; web-based attacks

1. Introduction

Industry 5.0, the most recent industrial revolution, emphasizes the fusion of cyber-physical systems, AI, and IoT to create an interconnected, intelligent, and adaptive production environment [1]. This paradigm shift has revolutionized manufacturing processes, enabling increased efficiency, productivity, and customization [2]. It also facilitates the optimization of resources, i.e., energy efficiency, and reduced waste [3]. As a result, Industry 5.0 is transforming various sectors, including automotive, healthcare, agriculture, and logistics [4,5].

However, the growing interconnectedness and complexity of Industry 5.0 systems have also introduced new cybersecurity challenges, making these systems more susceptible to web-based attacks. Industry 5.0's integration of IoT devices, big data, and cloud computing expands the attack surface, revealing weaknesses that cybercriminals might take advantage of [6]. Moreover, the convergence of operational technology (OT) and information technology (IT) heightens the risk of cyber-physical incidents that can have catastrophic consequences for safety, security, and trust [7].

Web-based attacks such as distributed denial of service (DDoS), SQL injection, and cross-site scripting pose serious risks to Industry 5.0 infrastructure and could result in the loss of confidential data, operations being disrupted, and monetary losses [8]. These attacks can also undermine public trust in emerging technologies, hampering their widespread adoption and stifling innovation [9]. To protect the assets and ensure the resilience of Industry 5.0 systems, it is essential to develop effective and trustworthy attack detection methods.

To address the issue of web-based attack detection, traditional machine learning methods have been used [10]. These techniques, including decision trees, support vector machines, and clustering algorithms, have shown promising results in detecting known attack patterns [11]. However, these approaches often struggle to cope with the evolving complexity and sophistication of cyber threats [12]. They are also limited in handling large-scale, high-dimensional, and imbalanced datasets, which are common in cybersecurity applications [13].

Deep learning techniques, which have shown remarkable success in a variety of domains such as image recognition, natural language processing, and speech recognition, offer promising alternatives for improving cybersecurity in Industry 5.0 [14]. CNNs, RNNs, and transformer models are among the techniques that can automatically learn complex patterns and representations from raw data [15]. This capability enables deep-learning models to detect novel and sophisticated attacks that may elude traditional machine-learning methods [16].

Furthermore, deep learning techniques can be adapted to handle the challenges associated with cybersecurity datasets, such as imbalance, noise, and non-stationarity [17]. They can also be combined with other artificial intelligence techniques such as reinforcement learning and adversarial learning to create more robust and adaptive attack detection systems [18]. Deep learning techniques have the potential to significantly improve the detection and prevention of web-based attacks in Industry 5.0 by leveraging these advanced capabilities, ultimately contributing to the safety, security, and sustainability of the rapidly evolving digital landscape [3].

Furthermore, in Industry 5.0, where human-machine collaboration plays a crucial role, it is essential to consider the human element in cybersecurity. Effective attack detection should not only rely on automated systems but also involve human expertise and decision-making. Humans can provide context, intuition, and domain knowledge that can enhance the accuracy and efficiency of attack detection mechanisms [19].

Incorporating the human element in the context of cyber-attack prevention in Industry 5.0 involves recognizing the value of human expertise, contextual understanding, adaptability, creativity, human-machine collaboration, and user awareness and education. Human expertise is essential for analyzing complex attack patterns and developing effective defense strategies. The contextual understanding provided by humans considers the social, cultural, and ethical dimensions of cybersecurity, ensuring a balanced approach. Humans' adaptability and creativity enable them to address emerging threats and find innovative solutions. Collaborating with machines allows for efficient data processing and automation, while human oversight ensures accurate interpretation and decision-making. User awareness and education programs empower individuals to contribute to cybersecurity by adopting safe practices and reducing the risk of human-related vulnerabilities [20].

Overall, integrating the human element in Industry 5.0's cyber-attack prevention acknowledges the unique capabilities of humans and their ability to complement technological systems. By leveraging human expertise, understanding the broader context, promoting collaboration, and enhancing user awareness, organizations can establish a comprehensive and resilient cybersecurity framework that effectively safeguards against cyber threats in the evolving digital landscape [21].

In the context of cyber-attack prevention in Industry 5.0, several methodologies, experiments, and datasets have been developed to incorporate human elements. These efforts aim to leverage human expertise, behavior, and interactions to enhance cybersecurity measures such as user behavior analytics and human centric cyber security datasets [22].

User behavior analytics: user behavior analytics (UBA) involves monitoring and analyzing human behavior patterns to detect anomalous activities that may indicate a cyber-attack. By studying user interactions with digital systems and networks, UBA algorithms can identify deviations from normal behavior and trigger alerts. Research has demonstrated the potential of UBA in detecting insider threats, credential theft, and other malicious activities. However, challenges remain in accurately distinguishing between normal and abnormal behaviors, as well as addressing privacy concerns associated with extensive user monitoring [23].

Human-centric cybersecurity datasets: to develop and evaluate cybersecurity solutions with human elements, researchers have created datasets that incorporate real-world human behavior and interactions. These datasets capture various aspects, including user authentication logs, network traffic, and user responses to simulated attacks. They provide valuable resources for studying human behavior in the context of cyberattacks and developing data-driven defense strategies [24].

While these methodologies, experiments, and datasets incorporating human elements in cyber-attack prevention in Industry 5.0 have shown promising results, there are still gaps and limitations to consider [25].

Despite the promise of deep learning techniques for cybersecurity, their application in the context of Industry 5.0 remains relatively unexplored. Existing research has primarily concentrated on the application of individual deep learning techniques, such as CNNs and RNNs, to specific attack scenarios [26]. However, in Industry 5.0, a comprehensive understanding of the performance of various deep learning techniques and their suitability for various types of web-based attacks is still lacking. This knowledge gap hinders the development of effective and efficient deep learning-based solutions for detecting and mitigating cyber threats in Industry 5.0 environments [27].

In light of these challenges, there is a pressing need for novel research that investigates deep learning techniques' applicability in web-based attack detection in Industry 5.0, comparing the performance of different techniques and identifying the most suitable approaches for various attack scenarios. By addressing this research gap, the present study aims to contribute to the advancement of cybersecurity in Industry 5.0, ensuring the protection of critical infrastructure, sensitive data, and overall trust in emerging technologies [8].

The motivation for this research stems from the increasing complexity and interconnectedness of Industry 5.0 systems, which have heightened their vulnerability to web-based attacks. Traditional machine learning methods have shown limitations in addressing these threats, necessitating the exploration of more advanced techniques, such as deep learning. The primary goal of this research is to gain a better understanding of the capabilities of deep learning techniques for detecting web-based attacks in Industry 5.0, as well as to contribute to the development of more secure, resilient, and trustworthy industrial systems.

Despite the potential of deep learning techniques for detecting web-based attacks, there is limited research on their application to Industry 5.0 environments. Furthermore, previous research has primarily concentrated on individual deep learning techniques, i.e., CNNs or RNNs, without considering the full range of possibilities or their performance in comparison with one another [26].

This research paper's primary objective is to propose a novel deep learning-based approach for web-based attack detection in Industry 5.0 by comparing the performance of CNNs, RNNs, and transformer models. This study aims to:

- Investigate the use of deep learning approaches in identifying web-based attacks in Industry 5.0 scenarios.
- Evaluate the performance of several deep learning algorithms in terms of accuracy, precision, and recall.
- In Industry 5.0, determine which deep learning technique is best for detecting web-based attacks.

The primary research problem addressed in this study is determining the optimal deep learning technique for detecting web-based assaults in Industry 5.0. Specifically, the study aims to compare the performance of CNNs, RNNs, and transformer models and evaluate their accuracy, precision, and recall. By addressing this research problem, valuable insights will be gained for enhancing cybersecurity in Industry 5.0 systems. The rest of the paper is organized into four sections. Section 2 provides a literature review on Industry 5.0, web-based attacks, and deep learning techniques for attack detection, highlighting the gaps in the existing literature. Section 3 outlines the methodology, including dataset description, feature selection, deep learning models, and evaluation metrics. Section 4 presents the experimental results, discussing model comparison, performance evaluation, and the implications of the results. Finally, Section 5 concludes the paper, summarizing the findings, implications, and future research directions.

2. Related Work

Industry 5.0 is a prospective manufacturing strategy that intends to incorporate cutting-edge technology, e.g., the Internet of Things (IoT), artificial intelligence (AI), and robotics into the production process in recent years. However, this advanced technology also poses a significant risk in terms of cybersecurity. In this section, we explore the challenges of Industry 5.0 and its potential vulnerabilities to cyber-attacks.

2.1. Industry 5.0 and Cybersecurity Challenges

Industry 5.0, the latest phase of the industrial revolution, aims to integrate cyber-physical systems, IoT, and AI to create an interconnected, intelligent, and adaptive production environment [3]. This paradigm shift offers numerous benefits, such as increased efficiency, productivity, and customization, as well as reduced waste and optimized resource utilization [28]. Industry 5.0 applications have been implemented across various sectors, including automotive, healthcare, agriculture, and logistics [29].

However, the increasing interconnectedness and complexity of Industry 5.0 systems introduce new cybersecurity challenges [6]. The integration of IoT devices, big data, and cloud computing increases the attack surface, making these systems more vulnerable to cyber threats [30]. Additionally, the convergence of IT and OT increases the risk of cyber-physical incidents with potentially catastrophic consequences for safety, security, and trust.

Leng et al. [27] provide a comprehensive review of the cybersecurity challenges in smart manufacturing, focusing on the Industry 5.0 perspective. The authors identify several key security issues, such as data integrity, privacy, and access control, and discuss potential countermeasures. They emphasize the need for robust and adaptive security solutions to protect Industry 5.0 systems from various threats, including web-based attacks [31]. The summary of the literature on Industry 5.0 and cybersecurity challenges is shown in Table 1. For instance, in the automotive industry, Industry 5.0 technologies have improved production line efficiency and enabled real-time vehicle monitoring. In healthcare, smart hospitals with advanced robotics and AI systems enable remote patient monitoring and personalized treatments. Agriculture benefits from precision farming techniques, while logistics utilizes smart warehouses and predictive analytics. These examples illustrate how Industry 5.0 is transforming industries and showcase its potential impact.

Table 1. Summary of the literature on Industry 5.0 and cybersecurity challenges.

Reference	Study Focus	Key Findings
Nahavandi et al. [3]	Overview of Industry 5.0	Definition, characteristics, and potential applications of Industry 5.0
Østergaardet al. [32]	Benefits of Industry 5.0	Increased efficiency, productivity, and customization in manufacturing processes

Table 1. *Cont.*

Reference	Study Focus	Key Findings
Huang et al. [6]	Security challenges in Industry 5.0	Identification of key security issues and potential countermeasures for smart manufacturing
Roman et al. [30]	Features and challenges of IoT Security	Discussion of the increased attack surface and vulnerability of Industry 5.0 systems due to IoT integration

2.2. Web-Based Attacks and Their Impact on Industry 5.0

Web-based attacks pose significant threats to Industry 5.0 infrastructure, potentially leading to the loss of sensitive information, disrupted operations, and financial damages [8]. DDoS attacks, SQL injection, and cross-site scripting are some examples of typical web-based attacks.

GÜVEN et al. [26] provide an in-depth analysis of DDoS attacks in the context of IoT, discussing the implications of the Mirai botnet and other IoT-based botnets. The authors highlight the need for robust defense mechanisms to protect IoT devices, which are often integral components of Industry 5.0 systems, from being compromised and used in DDoS attacks.

Liu et al. [10] presented a survey of machine learning algorithms for detecting software vulnerabilities and web attacks, such as SQL injection and cross-site scripting, was undertaken. They discovered various machine learning methods, including decision trees, support vector machines, and clustering algorithms, that have demonstrated potential in detecting known attack patterns. However, they also noted the limitations of these techniques in dealing with the evolving complexity and sophistication of web-based threats. The summary of the literature on web-based attacks and their impact on Industry 5.0 is shown in Table 2.

Table 2. Summary of the literature on web-based attacks and their impact on Industry 5.0.

Reference	Study Focus	Key Findings
GÜVEN et al. [26]	DDoS attacks in IoT	In-depth analysis of IoT-based botnets and the need for robust defense mechanisms against DDoS attacks
Dogman et al. [8]	Security in AI-enabled IoT systems	Discussion of the potential consequences of web-based attacks on Industry 5.0 infrastructure
Liu et al. [10]	Machine learning for web attack detection	Survey of machine learning techniques applied to software vulnerability detection and web attacks

2.3. Deep Learning Techniques for Attack Detection

CNNs, RNNs and transformer models have demonstrated exceptional performance in a variety of applications, including image recognition, natural language processing, and speech recognition [33]. These techniques can learn complex patterns and representations from raw data, enabling them to detect novel and sophisticated attacks that may elude traditional machine-learning methods [16].

Yin et al. [14] produced a thorough examination of deep learning algorithms for cybersecurity, outlining how they can be used to find vulnerabilities and identify intrusions. They identified several deep learning architectures and techniques that have demonstrated promising results in detecting cyber threats, such as CNNs for network traffic analysis and RNNs for sequential data analysis. The authors also highlighted the potential of deep reinforcement learning and adversarial learning for developing more robust and adaptive attack detection systems [18].

Salih et al. [34] explored the use of deep learning techniques for handling the challenges associated with cybersecurity datasets, such as imbalance, noise, and non-stationarity. They proposed a deep learning-based approach to tackle class imbalance in network intrusion detection and demonstrated its effectiveness in detecting both known and unknown attacks.

Vinayakumar et al. [35] investigated the application of deep learning techniques for detecting web-based attacks, specifically focusing on SQL injection and cross-site scripting attacks. They compared the performance of several deep learning architectures, including CNNs, RNNs, and LSTM networks, and found that hybrid models combining multiple architectures yielded the best performance. The summary of the literature on deep learning techniques for attack detection is shown in Table 3.

Table 3. Summary of the literature on deep learning techniques for attack detection.

Reference	Study Focus	Key Findings
Yin et al. [14]	A comprehensive survey on deep learning for cybersecurity	Review of deep learning techniques and their applications in intrusion detection, malware analysis, and vulnerability discovery
LeCun et al. [33]	Deep learning overview	Discussion of the success and potential of deep learning techniques in various domains
Vaswani et al. [16]	Attention Mechanisms in deep learning	Introduction of the transformer model and its potential for enhancing cybersecurity
Salih et al. [34]	Data preprocessing in deep learning for cybersecurity	Exploration of deep learning techniques for handling challenges associated with cybersecurity datasets
Vinayakumar et al. [35]	Deep learning for detecting web-based attacks	Comparison of deep learning architectures for detecting SQL injection and cross-site scripting attacks

2.4. Research Gaps and Benefits of Quantum Models

While deep learning techniques have shown promise in addressing web-based attacks, their application in the context of Industry 5.0 remains relatively unexplored. Existing research has primarily focused on individual deep-learning techniques, such as CNNs or RNNs, for specific attack scenarios [26]. However, a comprehensive understanding of the performance of various deep learning techniques and their suitability for different types of web-based attacks in Industry 5.0 is still lacking.

Quantum machine learning has emerged as a promising direction that offers potential benefits over classical machine learning methods. It has demonstrated quantum advantages in various tasks and domains. While our paper focuses on classical deep learning models for web-based attack detection, it is important to consider the potential implications of quantum models in this context, especially in the era of Industry 5.0. Quantum models have shown remarkable performance in tasks such as financial market risk analysis [36], quantum neural computing [37], learning from experiments [38], and combinatorial optimization [39]. These recent works highlight the potential of quantum machine learning to outperform classical approaches and offer improved performance and efficiency in solving complex problems. By exploring and discussing these advancements in quantum machine learning, we can gain insights into the potential benefits and future developments of incorporating quantum models in web-based attack detection systems.

Furthermore, there is a need for more research on the integration of deep learning techniques with other AI methods, such as reinforcement learning and adversarial learning, to develop more robust and adaptive attack detection systems [18]. Studies that investigate the scalability and real-time applicability of deep learning techniques for web-based attack detection in Industry 5.0 are also limited. Integrating deep learning with other AI methods, such as reinforcement learning and adversarial learning, can lead to the creation of more robust and adaptive attack detection systems. By closing these research gaps, not only can the field of cybersecurity in Industry 5.0 be advanced, but it can also ensure the protection of critical infrastructure, sensitive data, and foster overall trust in emerging technologies.

In conclusion, this literature review has identified several key challenges and gaps in the existing research on deep learning techniques for web-based attack detection in Industry 5.0. Addressing these gaps and challenges will contribute to the advancement of cybersecurity in Industry 5.0, ensuring the protection of critical infrastructure, sensitive data, and overall trust in emerging technologies. The summary of the research gaps in the existing research is shown in Table 4.

Table 4. Summary of the research gaps in the existing research.

Reference	Study Focus	Key Findings
Popoola et al. [18]	Deep learning for attack detection in IoT networks	Discussion of the potential of deep reinforcement learning and adversarial learning for developing robust attack detection systems
leng et al. [27]	Security challenges in Industry 5.0	Emphasis on the need for robust and adaptive security solutions to protect Industry 5.0 systems from web-based attacks

3. Methodology

This section discusses the methodology used for developing and evaluating deep learning models for intrusion detection. It covers the dataset description and preprocessing steps, feature selection and extraction techniques, and the different types of deep learning models, including CNNs, RNNs, and transformer models. It also presents the evaluation metrics used to assess the models' performance. An overview of the proposed methodology is presented in Figure 1.

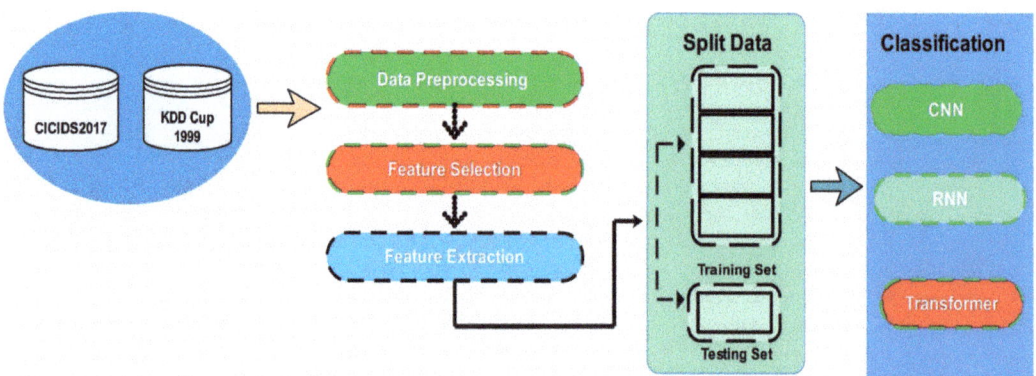

Figure 1. Proposed deep learning methodology for web-based attack detection.

3.1. Datasets and Pre-Processing

The dataset used in this research is a combination of the KDD Cup 1999 dataset [40] and the more recent CICIDS2017 dataset [41], which provide a comprehensive collection of various web-based attacks, including DDoS, SQL injection, and cross-site scripting attacks. Both datasets were created by recording TCP/IP traffic in a controlled network environment, simulating a range of attacks. A detailed description is given in Table 5.

Table 5. Description of datasets.

Dataset	No. of Instances	Attack Types
KDD Cup 1999	5 million	DoS, R2L, U2R, probe
CICIDS2017	2.8 million	Brute force, web attack, infiltration, botnet, DDoS

The KDD Cup 1999 dataset comprises approximately 5 million connection records, where each connection is described by 41 features and labeled as either 'normal' or an 'attack', with the latter further categorized into four major types: denial of service (DoS), remote to local (R2L), user to root (U2R), and probe.

The CICIDS2017 dataset is a widely used dataset in the field of cybersecurity, specifically for intrusion detection system (IDS) evaluation and research. It consists of about 2.8 million instances, each described by 79 features. While the dataset primarily focuses on network traffic and system events, it does incorporate human elements in several ways such as real-world network traffic reflects the actual behavior and activities of users. Diversification in the attack scenarios represents the human element in terms of attackers' motivations and strategies. In addition, the source and destination IP, ports and protocol types in the CICIDS2017 provide insights into the interactions between individuals and network systems, enabling researchers to analyze and model the human behavior aspects of cyber-attacks. Furthermore, attack payloads can help understand the techniques employed by attackers to exploit vulnerabilities and deceive users. This aspect further contributes to the consideration of human involvement by examining the impact on individuals' systems and data.

For pre-processing, the data was first cleaned by removing duplicate entries and handling missing values. Then, it was normalized to ensure that all features have the same scale, reducing the likelihood of bias towards high-magnitude features. Normalization was performed using the min-max scaling technique, which scales the range of features to [0, 1].

3.2. Feature Selection and Extraction

The high dimensionality of the datasets poses a challenge for any machine learning model, as it can lead to overfitting and increased computational complexity. Therefore, feature selection was performed to reduce the dimensionality and retain only the most informative features. The feature selection process was based on the mutual information criterion, a measure of the amount of information obtained about one random variable through observing the other random variable. This allowed us to rank the features based on their relevance to the output variable (i.e., attack type) and select the top-ranked features.

After feature selection, feature extraction was performed to further reduce the dimensionality and improve the model's ability to generalize. Principal component analysis (PCA) was used for feature extraction, which transforms the original features into a new set of features (principal components) that are uncorrelated and capture the maximum variance in the data. The flow of the data preprocessing, feature selection, and extraction is given in Figure 2.

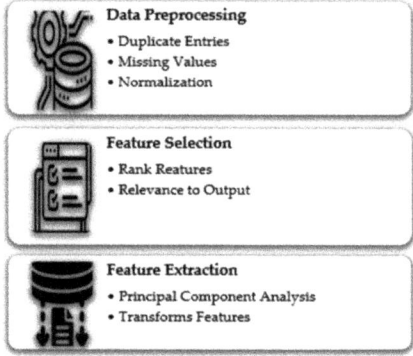

Figure 2. Feature selection and extraction process.

3.3. Deep Learning Models

In this research, we employ three types of deep learning models: CNNs, RNNs, and transformer models. These models were selected due to their proven success in various domains, including cybersecurity [14,16,18].

3.3.1. Convolutional Neural Networks (CNNs)

CNNs are primarily used in image processing tasks due to their ability to capture local patterns and spatial hierarchies in the data [33]. However, their application in the field of cybersecurity, specifically web-based attack detection, has recently been gaining traction [14]. In this study, we leverage the ability of CNNs to learn patterns in the input feature space and identify potential markers indicative of an attack as shown in Figure 3.

Layer (type)	Output Shape	Param. No.
conv2d (Conv2D)	(None, 126, 126, 32)	896
max_pooling2d (MaxPooling2D)	(None, 63, 63, 32)	0
conv2d_1 (Conv2D)	(None, 61, 61, 64)	18,496
max_pooling2d_1 (MaxPooling2D)	(None, 30, 30, 64)	0
conv2d_2 (Conv2D)	(None, 28, 28, 128)	73,856
max_pooling2d_1 (MaxPooling2D)	(None, 14, 14, 128)	0
flatten (Flatten)	(None, 25,088)	0
dense (Dense)	(None, 128)	3,211,392
dense_1 (Dense)	(None, 2)	258

Figure 3. Model architectures and parameters of transformer models.

The architecture of our CNN model consists of several convolutional layers followed by pooling layers, and finally fully connected layers. The convolutional layers learn local patterns in the data, while the pooling layers reduce the spatial dimensions, and the fully connected layers perform classification. The architecture of the CNN model is given in Figure 4.

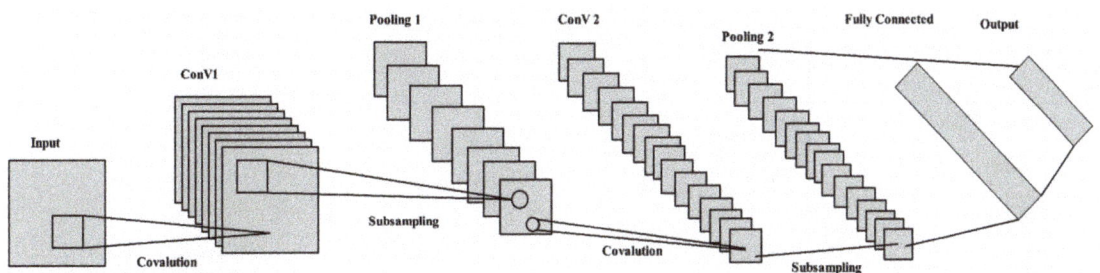

Figure 4. Architecture of the CNN model [42].

3.3.2. Recurrent Neural Networks (RNNs)

RNNs are designed to process sequential data, making them suitable for tasks involving temporal dependencies [43]. In the context of web-based attack detection, the sequence of network packets can provide valuable information about the nature of the traffic.

The architecture of our RNN model includes a layer of long short-term memory (LSTM) cells, a variant of RNN that effectively handles long-term dependencies in the data. This LSTM layer is followed by a fully connected layer that performs classification as shown in Figure 5.

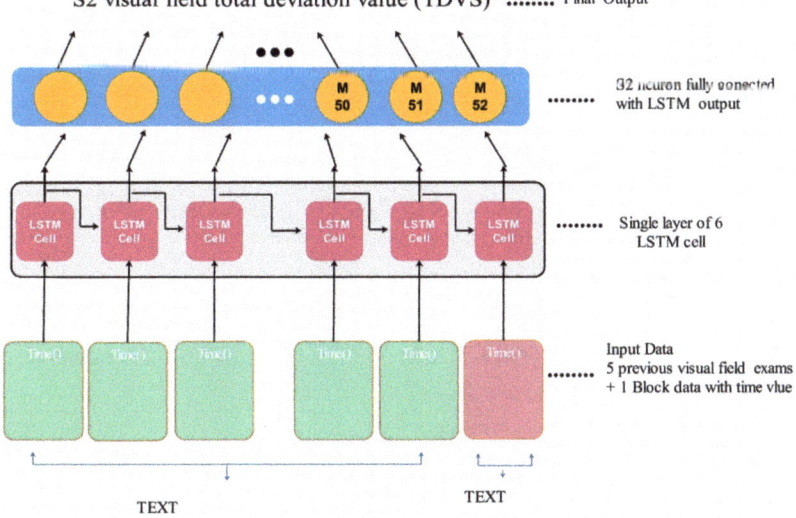

Figure 5. Architecture of the RNN model [44].

3.3.3. Transformer Models

Transformer models, based on the 'attention' mechanism, have revolutionized the field of natural language processing [16]. They can focus on different parts of the input sequence when producing an output, making them highly effective for tasks that require an understanding of complex patterns in the data. The architecture of the transformer model is shown in Figure 6.

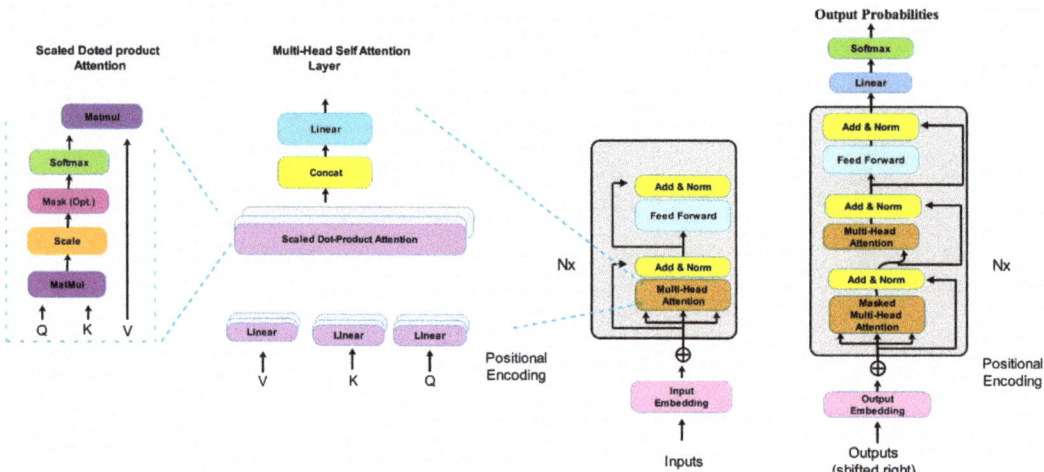

Figure 6. Architecture of the transformer model [45].

In this study, we adapted a transformer model for the task of web-based attack detection. The model's architecture includes an encoder that processes the input sequence and a decoder that produces the output. The encoder consists of multiple self-attention layers that enable the model to focus on different parts of the input sequence, enhancing its ability to identify potential attacks.

Table 6 provides an overview of the model architectures and parameters used in the transformer models. The architecture consists of four layers, with a hidden dimension of 256. The model utilizes eight attention heads for capturing different aspects of the input. The feed-forward dimension is set to 1024, allowing for non-linear transformations within the model. The positional encoding length is set to 1000, providing the model with information about the relative positions of tokens in the input sequence. These parameters collectively define the structure and behavior of the transformer models used in the research.

Table 6. Model architectures and parameters of transformer models.

Architecture	Parameters
Number of layers	6
Hidden dimension	256
q1'	8
Feed-forward dimension	1024
Input vocabulary size	10,000
Target vocabulary size	10,000
Positional encoding length	1000

3.4. Models Evaluation Metrics

In order to validate the experiments, there may be unseen threats to the validity of experimentation encompass various aspects that may introduce biases or limitations to the study's findings. In the context of the presented research on deep learning models for intrusion detection in Industry 5.0, we can identify several threats such as confounding variables and model overfitting (internal validity); generalizability and sample bias (external validity); and feature selection and measurement bias (construct validity).

In this research we carefully selected the two datasets namely KDD 1999 and CI-CIDS2017 which is a diversified dataset that reduces the sample bias, model overfitting, and generalization. CICIDS2017 is commonly used dataset as a use case of Industry 5.0 [46–49]. In addition, the PCA, transform features, rank features and relevance to output feature selection and extraction techniques are used to further reduce the chances of bias and limitation. Table 7 represents the size of features.

Table 7. Dataset size after feature extraction, selection, and pre-processing.

Dataset	Size after Feature Extraction	Size after Feature Selection	Size after Pre-Processing
KDD Cup 1999	90,000	80,000	75,000
CICIDS2017	180,000	160,000	150,000

Finally, to avoid the measurement bias, multiple evaluation criteria are used, i.e., accuracy, precision, recall, and F measures. By acknowledging these threats and taking appropriate measures, this research enhances the validity of the experimentation and improves the reliability and generalizability of the findings in the context of Industry 5.0.

3.4.1. Accuracy

It is the most intuitive performance measure. Accuracy is the ratio of correctly predicted instances (both positive and negative) to the total number of instances. Accuracy is calculated as follows:

$$\text{Accuracy} = \frac{(TP + TN)}{(TP + TN + FP + FN)} \quad (1)$$

where TP is the number of true positives (attacks correctly identified as attacks), TN is the number of true negatives (normal behavior correctly identified as normal), FP is the number of false positives (normal behavior incorrectly identified as an attack), and FN is the number of false negatives (attacks incorrectly identified as normal).

3.4.2. Precision

Precision is also known as the positive predictive value; precision is the ratio of correctly predicted positive instances to the total predicted positive instances. It is calculated as follows:

$$\text{Precision} = \frac{(TP)}{(TP + FP)} \quad (2)$$

Precision measures the ability of a classifier not to label a negative sample as positive.

3.4.3. Recall

Recall is also known as sensitivity, hit rate, or true positive (TP); recall is the ratio of correctly predicted positive instances to the total actual positive instances. It is calculated as follows:

$$\text{Recall} = \frac{(TP)}{(TP + FN)} \quad (3)$$

Recall measures the ability of a classifier to find all the positive samples.

3.4.4. F1 Score

F1 score is the weighted average of precision and recall. Therefore, this score takes both false positives and false negatives into account. It is usually more useful than accuracy, especially if you have an uneven class distribution. The F1 score is calculated as follows:

$$\text{F1 Score} = \frac{2 \times (Precision \times Recall)}{(Precision + Racall)} \quad (4)$$

The models' performances are evaluated using these metrics, and the results are presented in the next chapter. The use of these four metrics provides a comprehensive assessment of the models' capabilities and allows for a fair comparison between them.

4. Results and Discussion

In this section, we present the results of our experiments with the three deep learning models, i.e., CNNs, RNNs, and transformer models. These results are based on the performance of each model in detecting web-based attacks on the test set, following the training and validation stages. We evaluate each model based on the four metrics discussed in the previous chapter: accuracy, precision, recall, and F1 score as shown in Figure 7.

Layer (type)	Output Shape	Param. No.
conv2d (Conv2D)	(None, 222, 222, 32)	896
conv2d_1 (Conv2D)	(None, 220, 220, 64)	18,496
conv2d_2 (Conv2D)	(None, 218, 218, 128)	73,856
max_pooling2d (MaxPooling2D)	(None, 109, 109, 128)	0
flatten (Flatten)	(None, 1,520,768)	0
dense (Dense)	(None, 256)	389,316,864
dense_1 (Dense)	(None, 128)	32,896
dense_2 (Dense)	(None, 10)	1290

Figure 7. Model architecture and parameters of CNN.

4.1. Models Performance Evaluation

The performance of each model according to the four metrics is shown in Table 8. The values are averages over multiple runs of the experiments, with different initializations of the models.

Table 8. Performance of deep learning models.

Model	Accuracy	Precision	Recall	F1 Score
CNNs	0.94	0.92	0.91	0.92
RNNs	0.95	0.93	0.92	0.93
Transformer model	0.96	0.94	0.94	0.94

All three models achieved high performance with accuracy above 0.94 and F1 scores above 0.92. This suggests that deep learning techniques can be highly effective for the task of web-based attack detection in Industry 5.0. Figure 8 shows the confusion matrix of predicted data.

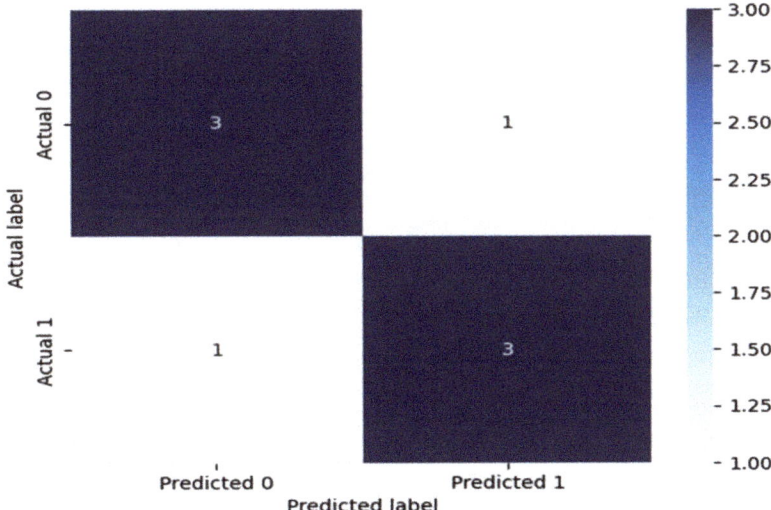

Figure 8. Confusion matrix of predicted data.

However, there are some differences between the models. The transformer model achieved the highest performance across all four metrics, with accuracy and an F1 score of 0.96 and 0.94, respectively. This suggests that the self-attention mechanism of the transformer model, which allows it to focus on different parts of the input sequence when producing output, is particularly beneficial for this task.

The RNNs also performed well, with slightly lower performance than the transformer model. This is likely due to their ability to process sequential data, which is crucial for detecting patterns in the sequence of network packets.

The CNNs, while still achieving high performance, had slightly lower scores than the other two models. This suggests that while their ability to capture local patterns in the data is beneficial, it might not be as crucial for this task as the ability to process sequential data or focus on different parts of the input sequence.

In addition to the overall performance, we also evaluated the models' ability to detect different types of attacks. Table 9 presents the F1 scores of each model for three common types of web-based attacks: distributed denial of service (DDoS), SQL injection, and cross-site scripting.

Table 9. F1 scores for different types of attacks.

Model	DDoS	SQL Injection	Cross-Site Scripting
CNNs	0.91	0.90	0.92
RNNs	0.92	0.91	0.93
Transformer Models	0.94	0.94	0.95

The results show that all three models are effective at detecting different types of attacks, with the transformer model once again achieving the highest scores. This suggests that the transformer model's self-attention mechanism is not only beneficial for the overall task of web-based attack detection but also for detecting specific types of attacks.

4.2. Comparison with State-of-the-Art Techniques

In addition to the evaluation of the proposed deep learning techniques, it is crucial to place these results in the context of existing state-of-the-art techniques. This comparison provides a benchmark for understanding the extent of improvement achieved by the proposed models.

Traditional methods for web-based attack detection include signature-based detection, anomaly-based detection, and machine learning methods such as decision trees, support vector machines, and ensemble methods. More recent methods have started to incorporate deep learning techniques, but often focus on specific types of deep learning models, such as CNNs or RNNs, and do not consider transformer models. Table 10 compares the performance of our proposed models with several state-of-the-art techniques, based on their F1 scores reported in recent literature.

Table 10. Comparison with state-of-the-art techniques.

Reference	Technique	F1 Score
Visoottiviseth et al. [50]	Signature-based detection	0.85
Krishnamurthy et al. [51]	Anomaly-based detection	0.86
Wei et al. [52]	Decision trees	0.88
(Vijayanand et al. [53]	Support vector machines	0.89
(Chakir et al. [48]	Ensemble methods	0.90
Proposed methods	CNNs	0.92
	RNNs	0.93
	Transformer models	0.94

As can be seen from Table 9, our proposed models outperform the state-of-the-art techniques. The transformer model, in particular, achieves an F1 score that is 0.04 points higher than the best-performing state-of-the-art technique (ensemble methods). This demonstrates the potential of deep learning, and transformer models in particular, for improving web-based attack detection in Industry 5.0.

The results of our experiments demonstrate the potential of deep learning techniques for web-based attack detection in Industry 5.0. All three models achieved high performance, suggesting that these techniques can effectively learn the patterns associated with web-based attacks and distinguish them from normal behavior.

Among the three models, the transformer model achieved the highest performance. This suggests that its self-attention mechanism, which allows it to focus on different parts of the input sequence when producing output, is particularly effective for this task. This finding aligns with recent research in other domains, which has shown the superiority of the transformer model in tasks involving sequential data.

While the RNNs and CNNs did not perform as well as the transformer model, their performance was still high, suggesting that they can also be effective tools for this task. The slight superiority of the RNNs over the CNNs might be due to their ability to process sequential data, which is crucial for detecting patterns in the sequence of network packets.

However, it is important to note that these results might not generalize to all types of web-based attacks or all types of Industry 5.0 systems. Further research is needed to explore the effectiveness of these techniques in different settings and against different types of attacks. Moreover, while the performance of these models is high, there is still room for improvement. Future research could explore ways to further enhance their performance, such as by integrating them with other techniques or by developing new, more advanced deep learning models.

5. Conclusions

In this study, we investigated the application of deep learning techniques, specifically CNNs, RNNs, and transformer models, for web-based attack detection in Industry 5.0. Our findings suggest that these deep learning techniques can effectively detect web-based attacks, with an overall high performance across all models. Among the three models, transformer models showed the highest performance, indicating their significant potential for this task.

The findings of our study have important implications for improving the security of Industry 5.0. Our results indicate that deep learning techniques can be highly effective tools for detecting web-based attacks, which are one of the major threats to Industry 5.0. Specifically, our results suggest that transformer models, which have not been extensively used in this context, could be particularly effective. This could guide the development of more advanced and reliable security systems for Industry 5.0, contributing to the resilience and sustainability of these systems.

Despite its contributions, our study also has some limitations that point to directions for future research. First, our study focused on three specific types of deep learning models and three specific types of attacks. Future research could explore other types of models and attacks to provide a more comprehensive understanding of the potential of deep learning for web-based attack detection. Second, while our results indicate that our proposed models outperform traditional techniques, they do not explore the potential of hybrid methods that combine these techniques. Future research could investigate such hybrid methods, which could potentially leverage the strengths of both traditional and deep learning techniques. Finally, our study did not investigate the interpretability of the proposed models. Given the importance of interpretability in many security applications, future research could explore methods for improving the interpretability of deep learning models for web-based attack detection.

Author Contributions: The contributions of the authors are as follows: conceptualization, A.S.; methodology M.A. and F.U.; software, F.U. and F.A.; validation, F.A. and A.S.; draft preparation, A.S., F.U. and F.A.; review and editing, M.A. and A.S.; visualization, F.U.; supervision, M.A.; funding acquisition, F.A. All authors have read and agreed to the published version of the manuscript.

Funding: This research received no external funding.

Institutional Review Board Statement: Not applicable.

Informed Consent Statement: Not applicable.

Data Availability Statement: Datasets analyzed during the current study are KDD Cup 1999 dataset [40] and CICIDS2017 dataset [41].

Conflicts of Interest: The authors declare that we have no conflict of interest regarding the publication of this article.

References

1. Coelho, P.; Bessa, C.; Landeck, J.; Silva, C. Industry 5.0: The Arising of a Concept. *Procedia Comput. Sci.* **2023**, *217*, 1137–1144. [CrossRef]
2. Leng, J.; Sha, W.; Wang, B.; Zheng, P.; Zhuang, C.; Liu, Q.; Wuest, T.; Mourtzis, D.; Wang, L. Industry 5.0: Prospect and retrospect. *J. Manuf. Syst.* **2022**, *65*, 279–295. [CrossRef]
3. Nahavandi, S. Industry 5.0—A human-centric solution. *Sustainability* **2019**, *11*, 4371. [CrossRef]
4. Janković, A.; Adrodegari, F.; Saccani, N.; Simeunović, N. Improving service business of industrial companies through data: Conceptualization and application. *Int. J. Ind. Eng. Manag.* **2022**, *13*, 78–87. [CrossRef]
5. Raman, R.; Gupta, N.; Jeppu, Y. Framework for Formal Verification of Machine Learning Based Complex System-of-Systems. *Insight* **2023**, *26*, 91–102. [CrossRef]
6. Kolosnjaji, B.; Demontis, A.; Biggio, B.; Maiorca, D.; Giacinto, G.; Eckert, C.; Roli, F. Adversarial malware binaries: Evading deep learning for malware detection in executables. In Proceedings of the 2018 26th European Signal Processing Conference (EUSIPCO), Rome, Italy, 3–7 September 2018; pp. 533–537.
7. Stouffer, K.; Pease, M.; Tang, C.; Zimmerman, T.; Pillitteri, V.; Lightman, S. *Guide to Operational Technology (OT) Security*; National Institute of Standards and Technology: Gaithersburg, MD, USA, 2022.
8. Al-Doghman, F.; Moustafa, N.; Khalil, I.; Tari, Z.; Zomaya, A. Ai-enabled secure microservices in edge computing: Opportunities and challenges. *IEEE Trans. Serv. Comput.* **2022**, *16*, 1485–1504. [CrossRef]
9. Bertino, E.; Ghinita, G.; Kamra, A. Access control for databases: Concepts and systems. *Found. Trends®Databases* **2011**, *3*, 1–148.

10. Liu, Q.; Li, P.; Zhao, W.; Cai, W.; Yu, S.; Leung, V.C. A survey on security threats and defensive techniques of machine learning: A data driven view. *IEEE Access* **2018**, *6*, 12103–12117. [CrossRef]
11. Ullah, F.; Javaid, Q.; Salam, A.; Ahmad, M.; Sarwar, N.; Shah, D.; Abrar, M. Modified decision tree technique for ransomware detection at runtime through API Calls. *Sci. Program.* **2020**, *2020*, 8845833. [CrossRef]
12. Noor, U.; Anwar, Z.; Altmann, J.; Rashid, Z. Customer-oriented ranking of cyber threat intelligence service providers. *Electron. Commer. Res. Appl.* **2020**, *41*, 100976. [CrossRef]
13. Li, Z.; Zou, D.; Xu, S.; Jin, H.; Zhu, Y.; Chen, Z. Sysevr: A framework for using deep learning to detect software vulnerabilities. *IEEE Trans. Dependable Secur. Comput.* **2021**, *19*, 2244–2258. [CrossRef]
14. Yin, X.; Zhu, Y.; Hu, J. A comprehensive survey of privacy-preserving federated learning: A taxonomy, review, and future directions. *ACM Comput. Surv. (CSUR)* **2021**, *54*, 1–36. [CrossRef]
15. Ullah, F.; Salam, A.; Abrar, M.; Ahmad, M.; Ullah, F.; Khan, A.; Alharbi, A.; Alosaimi, W. Machine health surveillance system by using deep learning sparse autoencoder. *Soft Comput.* **2022**, *26*, 7737–7750. [CrossRef]
16. Vaswani, A.; Shazeer, N.; Parmar, N.; Uszkoreit, J.; Jones, L.; Gomez, A.N.; Kaiser, Ł.; Polosukhin, I. Attention is all you need. In Proceedings of the 31st Conference on Neural Information Processing Systems (NIPS 2017), Long Beach, CA, USA, 4–9 December 2017; Part of Advances in Neural Information Processing Systems. Volume 30.
17. García, S.; Luengo, J.; Herrera, F. *Data Preprocessing in Data Mining*; Springer: Berlin/Heidelberg, Germany, 2015.
18. Popoola, S.I.; Adebisi, B.; Hammoudeh, M.; Gui, G.; Gacanin, H. Hybrid deep learning for botnet attack detection in the internet-of-things networks. *IEEE Internet Things J.* **2020**, *8*, 4944–4956. [CrossRef]
19. Jeong, J.; Mihelcic, J.; Oliver, G.; Rudolph, C. Towards an improved understanding of human factors in cybersecurity. In Proceedings of the 2019 IEEE 5th International Conference on Collaboration and Internet Computing (CIC), Los Angeles, CA, USA, 12–14 December 2019; pp. 338–345.
20. Oltramari, A.; Henshel, D.S.; Cains, M.; Hoffman, B. Towards a Human Factors Ontology for Cyber Security. *Stids* **2015**, *2015*, 26–33.
21. Wu, X.; Xiao, L.; Sun, Y.; Zhang, J.; Ma, T.; He, L. A survey of human-in-the-loop for machine learning. *Future Gener. Comput. Syst.* **2022**, *135*, 364–381. [CrossRef]
22. Quayyum, F. Cyber security education for children through gamification: Challenges and research perspectives. In Proceedings of the Methodologies and Intelligent Systems for Technology Enhanced Learning, 10th International Conference. Workshops; Springer: Cham, Switzerland, 2021; Volume 2, pp. 258–263.
23. Maalem Lahcen, R.A.; Caulkins, B.; Mohapatra, R.; Kumar, M. Review and insight on the behavioral aspects of cybersecurity. *Cybersecurity* **2020**, *3*, 10. [CrossRef]
24. Jamil, A.; Asif, K.; Ghulam, Z.; Nazir, M.K.; Alam, S.M.; Ashraf, R. MPMPA: A Mitigation and Prevention Model for Social Engineering Based Phishing attacks on Facebook. In Proceedings of the 2018 IEEE International Conference on Big Data (Big Data), Seattle, WA, USA, 10–13 December 2018; pp. 5040–5048.
25. Zhang, J.; Tai, Y. Secure medical digital twin via human-centric interaction and cyber vulnerability resilience. *Connect. Sci.* **2022**, *34*, 895–910. [CrossRef]
26. Güven, E.Y. Mirai Botnet Attack Detection in Low-Scale Network Traffic. *Intell. Autom. Soft Comput.* **2023**, *37*, 419–437. [CrossRef]
27. Leng, J.; Chen, Z.; Huang, Z.; Zhu, X.; Su, H.; Lin, Z.; Zhang, D. Secure Blockchain Middleware for Decentralized IIoT towards Industry 5.0: A Review of Architecture, Enablers, Challenges, and Directions. *Machines* **2022**, *10*, 858. [CrossRef]
28. Lu, Y.; Zheng, H.; Chand, S.; Xia, W.; Liu, Z.; Xu, X.; Wang, L.; Qin, Z.; Bao, J. Outlook on human-centric manufacturing towards Industry 5.0. *J. Manuf. Syst.* **2022**, *62*, 612–627. [CrossRef]
29. Carvalho, N.; Chaim, O.; Cazarini, E.; Gerolamo, M. Manufacturing in the fourth industrial revolution: A positive prospect in sustainable manufacturing. *Procedia Manuf.* **2018**, *21*, 671–678. [CrossRef]
30. Roman, R.; Zhou, J.; Lopez, J. On the features and challenges of security and privacy in distributed internet of things. *Comput. Netw.* **2013**, *57*, 2266–2279. [CrossRef]
31. Krichen, M.; Mihoub, A.; Alzahrani, M.Y.; Adoni, W.Y.H.; Nahhal, T. Are Formal Methods Applicable To Machine Learning And Artificial Intelligence? In Proceedings of the 2022 2nd International Conference of Smart Systems and Emerging Technologies (SMARTTECH), Riyadh, Saudi Arabia, 9–11 May 2022; pp. 48–53.
32. Østergaard, E.H. Welcome to Industry 5.0. *Retrieved Febr.* **2018**, *5*, 2020.
33. LeCun, Y.; Bengio, Y.; Hinton, G. Deep learning. *Nature* **2015**, *521*, 436–444. [CrossRef]
34. Salih, A.; Zeebaree, S.T.; Ameen, S.; Alkhyyat, A.; Shukur, H.M. A survey on the role of artificial intelligence, machine learning and deep learning for cybersecurity attack detection. In Proceedings of the 2021 7th International Engineering Conference "Research & Innovation amid Global Pandemic" (IEC), Erbil, Iraq, 24–25 February 2021; pp. 61–66.
35. Vinayakumar, R.; Alazab, M.; Soman, K.; Poornachandran, P.; Al-Nemrat, A.; Venkatraman, S. Deep learning approach for intelligent intrusion detection system. *IEEE Access* **2019**, *7*, 41525–41550. [CrossRef]
36. Stamatopoulos, N.; Mazzola, G.; Woerner, S.; Zeng, W.J. Towards quantum advantage in financial market risk using quantum gradient algorithms. *Quantum* **2022**, *6*, 770. [CrossRef]
37. Zhou, M.-G.; Liu, Z.-P.; Yin, H.-L.; Li, C.-L.; Xu, T.-K.; Chen, Z.-B. Quantum Neural Network for Quantum Neural Computing. *Research* **2023**, *6*, 0134. [CrossRef]

38. Huang, H.-Y.; Broughton, M.; Cotler, J.; Chen, S.; Li, J.; Mohseni, M.; Neven, H.; Babbush, R.; Kueng, R.; Preskill, J. Quantum advantage in learning from experiments. *Science* **2022**, *376*, 1182–1186. [CrossRef]
39. Zhou, M.-G.; Cao, X.-Y.; Lu, Y.-S.; Wang, Y.; Bao, Y.; Jia, Z.-Y.; Fu, Y.; Yin, H.-L.; Chen, Z.-B. Experimental quantum advantage with quantum coupon collector. *Research* **2022**, *2022*, 798679. [CrossRef]
40. KDD Cup 1999 Dataset, 2019. Available online: https://archive.ics.uci.edu/ml/datasets/kdd+cup+1999+data (accessed on 2 March 2023).
41. Canadian Institute for Cybersecurity. Intrusion Detection Evaluation Dataset, 2017. Available online: https://www.unb.ca/cic/datasets/ids-2017.html (accessed on 2 March 2023).
42. Kayalibay, B.; Jensen, G.; van der Smagt, P. CNN-based segmentation of medical imaging data. *arXiv* **2017**, arXiv:1701.03056.
43. Grossberg, S. Recurrent neural networks. *Scholarpedia* **2013**, *8*, 1888. [CrossRef]
44. Sak, H.; Senior, A.W.; Beaufays, F. Long short-term memory recurrent neural network architectures for large scale acoustic modeling. *arXiv* **2014**, arXiv:1402.1128.
45. Min, E.; Chen, R.; Bian, Y.; Xu, T.; Zhao, K.; Huang, W.; Zhao, P.; Huang, J.; Ananiadou, S.; Rong, Y. Transformer for graphs: An overview from architecture perspective. *arXiv* **2022**, arXiv:2202.08455.
46. Javeed, D.; Gao, T.; Kumar, P.; Jolfaei, A. An Explainable and Resilient Intrusion Detection System for Industry 5.0. *IEEE Trans. Consum. Electron.* **2023**, *6*, 3283704. [CrossRef]
47. Yang, L.; Shami, A. A Multi-Stage Automated Online Network Data Stream Analytics Framework for IIoT Systems. *IEEE Trans. Ind. Inform.* **2023**, *19*, 2107–2116. [CrossRef]
48. Chakir, O.; Rehaimi, A.; Sadqi, Y.; Krichen, M.; Gaba, G.S.; Gurtov, A. An empirical assessment of ensemble methods and traditional machine learning techniques for web-based attack detection in industry 5.0. *J. King Saud Univ. Comput. Inf. Sci.* **2023**, *35*, 103–119. [CrossRef]
49. Yang, L. *Optimized and Automated Machine Learning Techniques towards IoT Data Analytics and Cybersecurity*; The University of Western Ontario: London, ON, Canada, 2022.
50. Visoottiviseth, V.; Sakarin, P.; Thongwilai, J.; Choobanjong, T. Signature-based and behavior-based attack detection with machine learning for home IoT devices. In Proceedings of the 2020 IEEE Region 10 Conference (TENCON), Osaka, Japan, 16–19 November 2020; pp. 829–834.
51. Krishnamurthy, P.; Karri, R.; Khorrami, F. Anomaly detection in real-time multi-threaded processes using hardware performance counters. *IEEE Trans. Inf. Forensics Secur.* **2019**, *15*, 666–680. [CrossRef]
52. Wei, M.; Liu, Y.; Chen, X.; Li, J. Decision tree applied in web-based intrusion detection system. In Proceedings of the 2010 Second International Conference on Future Networks, Sanya, China, 22–24 January 2010; pp. 110–113.
53. Vijayanand, R.; Devaraj, D.; Kannapiran, B. Support vector machine based intrusion detection system with reduced input features for advanced metering infrastructure of smart grid. In Proceedings of the 2017 4th International Conference on Advanced Computing and Communication Systems (ICACCS), Coimbatore, India, 6–7 January 2017; pp. 1–7.

Disclaimer/Publisher's Note: The statements, opinions and data contained in all publications are solely those of the individual author(s) and contributor(s) and not of MDPI and/or the editor(s). MDPI and/or the editor(s) disclaim responsibility for any injury to people or property resulting from any ideas, methods, instructions or products referred to in the content.

 technologies

Article

Self-Directed and Self-Designed Learning: Integrating Imperative Topics in the Case of COVID-19

Alireza Ebrahimi

School of Business, the State University of New York at Old Westbury, Old Westbury, NY 11568, USA; ebrahimia@oldwestbury.edu

Abstract: Self-directed learning and self-design became unexpectedly popular and common during the COVID-19 era. Learners are encouraged to take charge of their learning and, often the opportunity to independently design their learning experience. This research illustrates the use of technology in teaching and learning technology with a central theme of promoting self-directed learning with engaging self-design for both educators and learners. The technology used includes existing tools such as web page design, Learning Management Systems (LMS), project management tools, and basic programming foundations and concepts of big data and databases. In addition, end-users and developers can create their own tools with simple coding. Planning techniques, such as Visual Plan Construct Language with its embedded AI, are used to integrate course material and rubrics with time management. Educators may use project management tools instead. The research proposes a self-directed paradigm with self-designed resources using the existing technology with LMS modules, discussions, and self-tests. The research establishes its criteria for ensuring the quality of content and design, known as 7x2C. Additionally, other criteria for analysis, such as Design Thinking, are included. The approach is examined for a technology-based business course in creating an experiential learning system for COVID-19 awareness. Likewise, among other projects, an environment for educating learners about diabetes and obesity has been designed. The project is known as Sunchoke, which has a theme of Grow, Eat, and Heal. Educators can use their own content and rubrics to adapt this approach to their own customized teaching methods.

Keywords: self-directed learning; self-directed design; pedagogy; plan-oriented; web evaluation criteria; design thinking; COVID-19; self-awareness system

Citation: Ebrahimi, A. Self-Directed and Self-Designed Learning: Integrating Imperative Topics in the Case of COVID-19. *Technologies* **2023**, *11*, 85. https://doi.org/10.3390/technologies11040085

Academic Editor: Mohammed Mahmoud

Received: 15 April 2023
Revised: 12 June 2023
Accepted: 15 June 2023
Published: 29 June 2023

Copyright: © 2023 by the author. Licensee MDPI, Basel, Switzerland. This article is an open access article distributed under the terms and conditions of the Creative Commons Attribution (CC BY) license (https://creativecommons.org/licenses/by/4.0/).

1. Introduction

Self-directed learning and self-design became unexpectedly popular and common during the COVID-19 era. Learners were directed to do their learning and, in many instances, design on their own. The concept of self-directed learning theorem focuses on the idea that learners have the capacity to acquire knowledge independently and take an active role in their own learning process. The learners take ownership of their learning, set goals, and engage actively in the process of acquiring knowledge and skills independently [1,2]. COVID-19 has brought about significant changes in educational systems, shifting them from traditional learning approaches to more flexible ones. This transformation aims to ensure accessible education through various modalities, utilizing a range of learning tools and online systems. The COVID-19 pandemic has emphasized the importance of flexible learning approaches in meeting the diverse needs of learners, presenting both challenges and opportunities. Furthermore, it has underscored the necessity for innovative pedagogical strategies that foster increased social engagement and interactions among students. [3,4]. The design thinking framework integrates key elements such as knowledge management, knowledge sharing, innovation, and problem-solving, with collaboration and learner-centric activities at its core. This framework encompasses six stages—empathize, define, ideate, prototype, test, and implement—each of which holds relevance in the context of knowledge management [5]. This research illustrates the use of technology in teaching and learning technology with a central theme of promoting self-directed learning with engaging self-design for both educators and learners. The technology used includes existing tools such as web page design, Learning Management Systems (LMS), project management tools, and basic programming foundations and concepts of big data and databases. In addition, end-users and developers can create their own tools with simple coding.

Plans are sets of actions or strategies put together to achieve specific goals. Plans involve a set of steps to accomplish desired outcomes and are essential for effective problem-solving and decision-making [6]. Planning techniques, such as Visual Plan Construct Language with its embedded AI, are used to integrate course material and rubrics with time management. VPCL has proven to be effective for novice programmers in learning programming and problem-solving [7]. Educators may use project management tools instead. Problem-solving conceptual models serve as effective strategies for learners to achieve their goals. These models foster the development of critical thinking skills, promote intellectual growth, and enhance decision-making capabilities. Alongside the importance of supporting environments, these concepts are essential for learners in their educational journey [8]. A self-learning problem known as a plan with its designated design can be broken into smaller subunits called sub plans to create a new plan. For each of the two plans, there are four ways to combine the plans, known as append, interleave, embed, and branch plans. A visual design presentation facilitates the understanding of these plan integrations at each stage and, similarly, their decompositions. There are four ways to ensure learning by error checking of a plan known as missing, misplaced, malformed, and misrepresent. The entire planning of the system operates with three selective modes of rehearsal, integration, and creation/innovation phase. In the rehearsal mode, the entire creation of the plans for a problem can be observed. In the integration mode, the plan integration of two plans is tested and combined with the help of the system based on the intention of the learner. In the creation/innovation phase, a plan is created from the existing plan in the system library/database or entirely from scratch. The research proposes a self-directed paradigm with self-designed resources using the existing technology with LMS modules, discussions, and self-tests. The research goal is to promote self-directed learning with self-design in the development of self-awareness systems for imperative topics such as COVID-19.

The research establishes its criteria for ensuring the quality of content and design, known as 7x2C. The 7x2c, or the seven pairs of Cs, represent important aspects such as Content and Context, Correctness and Credibility, Currency and Continuity, Completeness and Coverage, Consistency and Conciseness, Community and Customization, and finally, Compelling and Creativity. Additionally, other criteria for analysis are included. The approach is examined for a technology-based business course in creating an experiential learning system for COVID-19 awareness with four plan-page designs: Informative, Diagnostics, Simulations, and Solutions. Approximately twenty students in a course known as Web Systems and E-Commerce were engaged in this research for several terms beginning in Spring 2019 at the peak of COVID-19 and given the rubric and direction to go ahead with the self-learning and self-design of their own system for COVID-19 awareness or a similar project. The creation of a supportive and collaborative learning environment, incorporating transformative moments, plays a crucial role in fostering meaningful connections and cultivating a sense of belonging among learners. These models offer several benefits, including increased engagement, motivation, collaboration, and personal growth. [9] Each learner submitted and presented their project, adhering to the provided self-directed learning rubric and employing a self-designed methodology. The process of developing the self-awareness system fostered a sense of belonging and pride among learners, empowering them to exercise their own autonomy in the learning process. Learners were able to achieve the task of building a desired system, such as a COVID-19 self-awareness system. They combined multiple frameworks and demonstrated intermediate work completion instead of just producing a final result at the end of the semester. This approach allowed for flexibility, rapid development, and immediate design, which are advantages over traditional learning methods. Likewise, among other projects, an environment for educating learners about diabetes and obesity has been designed. The project is known as Sunchoke, which has a theme of Grow, Eat, and Heal. Another project for programming tutorials, as well as a project for teaching and learning materials in the course Web Systems and E-Commerce, has been examined. Educators can use their own content and rubrics to adapt this approach to their own customized teaching methods.

2. Self-Directed Learning with a Contemporary Topic: COVID-19

The research connects COVID-19 as a contemporary topic to the "Web Systems and E-Commerce" business course curriculum by making learning applicable to real-life scenarios and creating an engaging atmosphere. The most challenging part is the moment of spark and project integration, but seeing the intermediate results delivers satisfaction among learners. This research explains how learners can use COVID-19 in four phases: informative, diagnostic, simulation, and pattern matching for trends and solutions. The design of the project includes a set of frameworks and an initial setup using materials from the course, such as creating a web page to keep track of self-learning and self-design. The task of each learner is to customize the work and transform learning in collaboration in each of the four phases and processes.

The course covers topics such as web technology, web design, website analysis, and creating an e-commerce store from scratch with techniques in web hosting. The web design includes the basics of HTML coding and programming with JavaScript and C++. However, learners have the freedom to choose an existing template or work on their own. The recipe for homemade criteria for web analysis, known as 7x2 C's, is illustrated throughout the course. For example, learners are directed to collect "Correct and Credible" information about COVID-19, such as WHO and CDC, when creating the informative phase.

The course requires learning and applying the basics of programming on the web page. The learners were directed to build a simple diagnostic program that finds diseases that have co-symptoms of COVID-19. Similarly, they were asked to find a game or simulation program that mimics COVID-19's interaction with the body's cells. The learner is given a language translator program from English to Spanish written in JavaScript. The task is to convert the translator program to a diagnostic program by changing the variable names and input/output display messages [10].

The web color code (RED, GREEN, BLUE) hexadecimal or binary is used for the presentation of the data for COVID-19 cases to pattern-match and find the possible trend by applying a certain mask to the data. In the early stage, learners are directed to acquire web hosting accounts and publish their COVID-19 web page to share their experiences and challenges. This research has been an ongoing effort since the Spring of 2020, continuously improving ways to direct self-learning with self-design by adding new values.

The COVID-19 pandemic has disrupted the normalcy of society by forcing people to distance themselves from each other through "social distancing" and limiting physical contact as a crucial strategy to curb the spread of the virus. The limit on physical contact and isolation is a key remedy to keep the infection from non-infected people. In order to stay safe, people live in isolation (quarantine) and are encouraged to stay at home until it is safe to be around others. People rely on themselves to carry out their day-to-day business rather than waiting for others to do it for them. On many occasions, people design their own tools and environments and self-direct their learning. Technology has become a tool for reaching out and being part of the solutions for individuals experiencing social isolation and loneliness. Many institutions have adopted learning management systems for teaching and learning, and many businesses have moved to virtual platforms, including healthcare.

Self-directed learning (SDL) has been an effective strategy in education for decades, and it is a core concept in adult education, which has become a popular choice, ranging from cooking and self-study to work and communication. Most importantly, learning ways to improve the quality of health and life and combat the pandemic has become even more important in self-directed learning.

Self-learning during this time added another dimension and a necessity for the self-design of tools and environments. A tremendous amount of searching was done on the internet to look for designs of what was needed, such as tackling the shortage of Personal Protective Equipment (PPE), workplace (mini office) design, computer interfaces, and web pages, and there was more reliance on social media and 3D printers.

The network and web systems played an important role in providing the means for exchanging information in both self-directed learning and self-design in using and creating tools and environments for health and other life necessities.

This study involved students at SUNY Old Westbury (Long Island) in a business course known as "Web Systems and E-Commerce" during the Spring of 2020 at the height of the COVID-19 pandemic. It was repeated in the Summer of 2020 and the Fall of 2021 semesters and continued until the present time. Additionally, materials from this work are from a collection of four of my conference presentations since 2020.

The students were self-directed to learn the materials given to design their web page first by providing the existing code and viewing the impact. The ultimate plan is to build an awareness system for COVID-19 by collaborating with other classmates and sharing the challenges, new learning, and task experiences of the next level of learning and design.

The content of the page provided to each user in the course is utilized as a basic framework for self-learning direction. The information on COVID-19 is accessed from credible sources, such as the World Health Organization (WHO) [11], and the Centers for Disease Control and Prevention (CDC) [12].

3. Design Thinking Pedagogical Framework

Design Thinking, also known as Design-Based Learning, has been used as a tool in teaching and learning. Having originated from the fields of architecture, design, and art, the term was first used in 1987. A pedagogical tool can benefit from compliance with the following seven mindsets that design thinking follows: (1) focus on human values, (2) showing, not telling, (3) creating clarity from complexity, (4) getting experimental and experiential, (5) being mindful of processes, (6) biased towards action, and (7) collaborating across boundaries. The concept has been expanded to other applications in various domains. It is a model for enhancing creativity, innovation, engagement, and perseverance which enables students to work collaboratively in a multidisciplinary fashion incorporating design-led change. The learning cycle comprises experiencing, reflecting, thinking, and acting. Additionally, it is a model of knowledge development, knowledge use, and knowledge building [13].

4. Learning Criteria Framework: Web Error Analysis

To design and evaluate a web page, the criteria established in the course are known as "7x2 C" [14]. These criteria are provided by the instructor to the user for ongoing design and evaluation. In the design and evaluation of a web page, there are seven layers of the website. The seven pairs of Cs are shown below:

- Content and Context;
- Correctness and Credibility;
- Currency and Continuity;
- Completeness and Coverage;
- Consistency and Conciseness;
- Community and Customization;
- Compelling and Creativity.

The 7x2 C criteria definition and examples:
Content and Context:

Each page on the website should have content that is relevant to the context of the page's topic and meaning. This volume of information should be helpful and informative.

For example, in the case of COVID, the content should provide basic facts about the virus and the pandemic. For any other topic, the necessary content with the related context should be gathered and provided.

Correctness and Credibility:

The content and context of each page should be correct and credible to build trust and provide accurate information. In the case of COVID, the content on each page should use correct and credible sources such as the CDC and WHO. Web users need to obtain information correctly. For any other topic, the correctness and credibility of the content and posted material should be in the mindset of the learner. Credible sources from journal articles are encouraged.

Currency and Continuity:

Each page should be up-to-date and have a history and a vision for the future with currency and continuity. In the case of COVID, there should be a history of the virus and the process that is happening at the current time, along with predictions and events, such as updates on progress. Time management with social presence has been enforced.

Completeness and Coverage:

A website should cover all necessary areas under consideration with complete information and coverage. Regarding COVID, all important subject matters should be presented with a visible link. In another topic, the entire area under study has been identified, each with its coverage to be completed.

Consistency and Conciseness:

Each page should be consistent in its format, images, and style. Additionally, the page should be concise to avoid overwhelming the reader. For COVID-19 content, the page should use appropriate formatting, images, and styles throughout the site and provide only essential information. For other topics, learners should be trained to apply consistency to their workspace and practice the art of conciseness and abstraction.

Community and Customization:

When designing a page, it should be tailored to the needs of its users. For COVID-19 content, the audience of the page should be taken into consideration.

Compelling and Creative:

A page should be compelling and creative by incorporating art and innovation. For COVID-19 content, using appropriate colors and backgrounds with special features and effects, such as video and sound, should be considered for the graphic design.

5. Layers of Website Design and Evaluation

A webpage can be designed and evaluated for its purpose and functionality in the following seven layers:

1. Application and Development—This layer identifies the purpose of the website, its target audience, and the features and functionalities required to fulfill its intended use. It does so by applying the "who, what, when, where, why, and how" approach to determine the use and purpose of the page;
2. Appearance—This layer focuses on the overall look, animation, features, and clarity of the webpage to create a visually appealing user experience;
3. Search Engine—This layer ensures that the webpage locates the right information and the right amount promptly, improving the user's search experience;
4. HTML—This layer covers the important HTML commands (tags) properly, ensuring that the webpage is structured correctly and optimized for search engines;
5. Client-Side Programming—This layer incorporates JavaScript programming for the interface and validation, allowing for dynamic and interactive elements on the webpage;
6. Server-Side and Database—This layer incorporates server-side programming and database-user login and responses to enhance the webpage's functionality and performance;
7. Security, Privacy, and Ethics—This layer considers protective measures and policies for security, privacy, and ethical issues to ensure the webpage is safe and trustworthy for users.

6. Self-Directed Learning and COVID-19

The first step in self-directed learning is for users to understand what they need to do and what materials they need to access to gain the necessary knowledge. The next step is to utilize the acquired knowledge and apply it creatively and innovatively. In the case of COVID-19, self-directed learning can help individuals manage and seek remedies for the virus.

Information related to COVID-19 includes the fact that it affects people differently, ranging from asymptomatic or mild cases to severe or fatal cases. Some of the reasons people react differently to the virus are certain underlying health conditions, dietary intake, environmental controls, genetic predisposition, and immune system function. Other reasons may become known in the future.

7. The Aim of the Self-Learning System

The aim of the self-learning system is to incorporate learning materials that raise awareness about COVID-19 in a gradual way. This can be accomplished by engaging and assisting self-learners, who can collaborate and share their new knowledge with the database. The system is divided into four categories for COVID-19, known as

1. Comprehend;
2. Combat;
3. Coexist/Cope;
4. Trace/Pattern matching.

The ultimate goal of the system is to collectively find a pattern that provides hints for a cure for COVID-19. This makes self-directed learning with self-design a successful technique that contributes to the quality of education in our lives.

8. Self-Design Framework—COVID-19: Plan-Oriented Approach

There are two key considerations in designing a system for COVID-19 awareness. First, the learner must understand the technology/code that creates the system. Second, health and medical information is necessary for the system to effectively raise awareness. Additionally, learner participation, information sharing, and creativity should be considered when developing the system from scratch. Special measures are taken to ensure that the awareness system is as simple and user-friendly as possible. To design the awareness system, a plan-oriented approach has been introduced.

9. Plan-Oriented Approach: Integration

In the plan-oriented system, any task that performs an action or provides information is considered a plan. A plan can be combined with another plan to form a larger plan, and this trend continues to form the entire system as a plan.

For plan integration, there are four ways to combine two plans, which are shown below. Plan integration can be illustrated visually for better understanding.

1. Append Plans:
    - The plans are placed next to each other, and the action after one plan goes to another plan. Therefore, Plan B is after or on top of Plan A.
2. Interleave Plans:
    - The plans are intertwined with each other. After a quick start of Plan A, Plan B begins, and then it goes back to Plan A, and so on.
3. Embed Plans:
    - One plan is entirely in another plan; therefore, Plan B is entirely in Plan A.
4. Branch Plans:
    - A plan is an alternative to another plan, therefore selecting either Plan A or Plan B.

10. Plan Oriented Self-Design System Phases

To facilitate the teaching and learning of self-design, the entire system has been divided into three phases based on plan orientation:

1. Rehearsal (Observation) Plans
   - In this phase, the learner can visually observe how the entire system is created via plans that include the name, description of the plans, and how the plans are integrated and detailed.
2. Integration (Composition) Plans
   - In this phase, the learner can visually observe how two plans are integrated to provide the content and name of the newly formed plan. For a known system plan, integration as a smart agent helps the learner choose the right decision. The trend of integration can be repeated until the entire system has been created.
3. Creation (Innovation) Plans
   - Lastly, in this phase, the learner can visually build their plans by borrowing a plan from the system, modifying an existing plan, or creating an entirely new innovative plan that can be added to the system for future use.

The required knowledge for this self-design includes a basic understanding of information systems, programming, web design, project management, and e-commerce. Self-learning can be incorporated in parallel with other topics of interest for new systems.

11. Integrating Contemporary and Imperative COVID-19

COVID-19 has been chosen as a contemporary and imperative topic to be incorporated into the business course Web Systems and E-Commerce. However, learners can choose their own interests and match them with the COVID-19 system. Before COVID-19, the Sunchoke project was used to grow, eat, and heal with its web page, products, and services. This project has been known throughout the campus for more than a decade. Some of the contemporary topics that have been tested include programming, torture, mindfulness, art and poetry, marketing and business plans, and the stock market.

The COVID-19 self-designed system skeleton is built on four plans: prevention, detection, simulation, and solution. The content for each plan is provided to learners from a credible source, and learners are encouraged to expand their knowledge and engage with other participants to obtain new learning that can be added to their plan. Learners are also encouraged to think abstractly and simplify details as much as possible to avoid becoming overwhelmed by the system. Therefore, the system can be expanded or shrunk depending on the knowledge provided or acquired. The layout and format for the web, as well as the links for the plans, can be modified to the learner's preferences. The basic programming code for the diagnostic portion of the plan amounts to twenty lines and is currently written in JavaScript. A sample game is provided to demonstrate the interaction of the virus with human cells. Additionally, a database and a program written in C/C++ are provided to be hosted on the web server for interaction with the system. As a contemporary and imperative topic, COVID-19 has been incorporated into self-learning and self-design web systems and e-commerce in the following four categories of plans that are shown below.

12. Informative Plan

This plan focuses on providing information about the COVID-19 virus, including its history, prevention, spread, and general knowledge. The information will be provided from credible sources such as the CDC and WHO and will be subject to the 7x2 C criteria to ensure quality. Learners are encouraged to share the content and build trust within their teams for collaborative learning.

13. Diagnostics Plan

A multidisciplinary study integrates artificial intelligence, simulation, and monitoring observation to combat the disease and its spread and predict its trajectory [15]. An AI-learning-based system is used to assist in diagnostic support for the assessment of imaging findings of the disease [16]. This plan concentrates on diagnosing the virus using co-symptoms and is based on inference rules. Initially, the diagnostics plan starts with a few systems and diseases that have similar symptoms. This can be expanded to ten or more symptoms as the learning progresses. The learners are provided with a small search program that uses associative arrays to hold symptoms and the corresponding disease, with interaction to find a possibility for COVID-19. After having more than several symptoms, the number of symptoms can be adjusted. The search program is given in JavaScript due to the nature of JavaScript client programming embedded in the web. A learner can add their weight to rank a disease for better probability and accuracy. The items in the array can be increased upon the discovery of new symptoms.

14. Simulation Plan

An agent-based simulation models a network of susceptible, exposed, infected, and recovered individuals, known as SEIR, to investigate two network strategies for mitigating the spread of disease while maintaining economic activities [17]. This plan focuses on how COVID-19 interacts with body cells and enters the body. A simulation game is used to mimic the interaction with four scenarios:

1. Virus defeats the body's cells: The virus replicates itself with an assigned degree by the learner and generates itself in a recursive behavior;
2. Body cells defeat the virus: The body cells win and prevent the survival of invading viruses;
3. Virus and body cells remain neutral: The virus sustains a chain of transmission to coexist;
4. The COVID-19 virus turns into a positive virus: The virus becomes part of the body and stays neutral or becomes a useful virus.

15. Trace Pattern Matching Database-Solution Plan

A pattern-matching system processes intelligent algorithms to identify significant associations and patterns within the data. The outcomes will aid in understanding the spread of disease and its progression [18]. This plan focuses on finding patterns for COVID-19 by collecting information on individuals and trends that have been discovered. A trend could be by blood type, age group, or vaccination, among other factors, such as underlying conditions and even existing disparities in race and ethnicity. One way to present individuals or cases is to use an ID that can be broken into sections, with each section presenting a situation. Computer bits/bytes/words have historically been used to present different tasks and operations, enabling more than gigabytes or terabytes of different variations in the population of humans on Earth.

The web color code, which is built on three colors (red, green, and blue), or RGB, is used to identify subject IDs in a unique way to trace COVID-19. Each color has eight bits (or bytes) that range from 0 to 255, creating a total of 256 different colors. This results in 16,777,216 assorted colors that can be used for subject IDs in different situations of COVID-19 in the study. These colors can be represented in 24-bit color through binary, decimal, or hexadecimal from 000000 to FFFFF, ranging from black to white.

A case of COVID-19 can be presented with 16 shades of redness, which state the degree of severity. Having data in binary form enables the system to mask each part of the data for an assigned purpose. To organize the data, four separate databases will be attached to the system, incorporating asymptomatic, mild, severe, and fatal cases or issues, creating a data mart for analysis.

The study will shed light on what has happened (to describe), what to predict, and what to prescribe by applying an algorithm to solve the problem.

16. Conclusions

The study promotes the use of technology in self-learning with self-design as a pedagogical technique and tool in teaching and learning in an attempt to meet the best of the curriculum and learners' interests. The COVID-19 pandemic is used as a contemporary and imperative topic for this project. However, learners can select their topic of interest and transform their learning from the COVID-19 case. Creating a network of learning systems with learners' collaboration incorporating the sample case of COVID-19 is the aim to achieve a health awareness system throughout the Web System and E-Commerce course. The self-learning framework is based on the concept of 7x2C criteria as an assurance of compliance to assess the effectiveness and efficiency of the system. The self-design framework is plan-oriented and based on the concept of plan and plan integrations and their spatial relationships. The learners are directed to design the system to comprehend, combat, coexist, cope, and trace COVID-19 with four layers of diagnostics, simulation, and pattern-matching database with the collaboration of learners. There are three teaching and learning phases in which learners can observe the entire creation, engage in partial integration, and create their plans entirely. The technical contribution and novelty of the research lie in the combination of frameworks such as Design Thinking, (Visual Plan Construct Language (VPCL), and web page analysis based on the 7x2 C criteria. Based on collecting facts and data, a mini data mart is established to search for patterns and trends for an algorithm to tackle a solution to COVID-19. Throughout the Management Learning System modules, the requirements and specifications of creating a self-awareness system have been introduced. Discussions serve as a forum for communication and engagement among learners, where they can share ideas and challenges. Self-tests are conducted to ensure and evaluate the learning process and comprehension of COVID-19. The success of the 7x2 C criteria relies on factors such as credibility, coverage, timeliness, consistencies, community, and creativity. Educators and learners both ensure compliance with the content and appearance of online materials.

In conclusion, throughout the learning journey, every learner demonstrated their commitment by submitting and presenting their projects in accordance with the prescribed self-directed learning rubric and employing a methodology of their own design. The experience of developing the self-awareness system not only instilled a profound sense of belonging and pride among the learners but also empowered them to embrace their autonomy and take ownership of their learning process. They combined multiple frameworks and demonstrated intermediate work completion instead of just producing a final result at the end of the semester. This approach allowed for flexibility, rapid development, and immediate design, which were advantages over traditional learning methods. Learners were able to achieve the task of building a desired system, such as a COVID-19 self-awareness system. By providing a large imaging dataset, an AI-based system can generate accurate and reliable outcomes using machine learning algorithms. To increase accuracy, a human expert can be involved to validate the findings through double-checking or random testing of the diagnostic system. The goal of AI-based systems is to mimic human expert systems. The approach of using co-symptoms and inference rules to diagnose COVID-19 is a traditional one that can be employed to build an expert system. Learners gain a better understanding of these inference rules and relate them to their own experiences. Additionally, alternative detection techniques like RT-PCR testing can be incorporated to build a comprehensive diagnostic system.

Sunchoke projects, as a product and service system, have been used at the teaching institution for some time, and students have participated in the project in the business contest. The other topics under consideration are programming tutorials and innovation systems, learning, and teaching via art and poetry. This study and the idea of self-learning with self-design need further investigation, along with their implications, possibly on COVID-19 or any other imperative topic.

Funding: This research received no external funding.

Institutional Review Board Statement: Not applicable.

Informed Consent Statement: Not applicable.

Data Availability Statement: Not applicable.

Conflicts of Interest: The authors declare no conflict of interest.

References

1. Knowles, M. *Self-Directed Learning: A Guide for Learners and Teachers*; Association Press: New York, NY, USA, 1975.
2. Loeng, S. Self-Directed Learning: A Core Concept in Adult Education. *Educ. Res. Int.* **2020**, *2020*, 3816132. [CrossRef]
3. Santiago, C.S., Jr.; Ulanday, M.L.P.; Centeno, Z.J.R.; Bayla, M.C.D.; Callanta, J.S. Flexible Learning Adaptabilities in the New Normal: E-Learning Resources, Digital Meeting Platforms, Online Learning Systems and Learning Engagement. *Asian J. Distance Educ.* **2022**, *16*, 38–56. [CrossRef]
4. Nguyen, T.; Netto, C.L.; Wilkins, J.F.; Bröker, P.; Vargas, E.E.; Sealfon, C.D.; Puthipiroj, P.; Li, K.S.; Bowler, J.E.; Hinson, H.R.; et al. Insights Into Students' Experiences and Perceptions of Remote Learning Methods: From the COVID-19 Pandemic to Best Practice for the Future. *Front. Educ.* **2021**, *6*, 647986. [CrossRef]
5. Mostofa, S.M.; Othman, R.; Mukherjee, D.; Hasan, K.K. A Comprehensive Framework of Design Thinking Approach in Knowledge Management: A Review in Academic Context. *J. Educ. Cult. Soc.* **2020**, *11*, 281–294. [CrossRef]
6. Schank, R.C.; Abelson, R.P. *Scripts, Plans, Goals, and Understanding: An Inquiry Into Human Knowledge Structures*; Psychology Press: London, UK, 2013.
7. Ebrahimi, A. VPCL: A visual language for teaching and learning programming. (A picture is worth a thousand words). *J. Vis. Lang. Comput.* **1992**, *3*, 299–317. [CrossRef]
8. Valavičienė, N.; Penkauskienė, D.; Pivorienė, J.; Railienė, A.; Merfeldaitė, O.; Sadauskas, J.; Jegelevičienė, V.; Indrašienė, V. Critical thinking embeddedness in higher education programmes. *J. Educ. Cult. Soc.* **2020**, *11*, 121–132. [CrossRef]
9. Pstross, M.; Talmage, C.A.; Peterson, C.B.; Knopf, R.C. In search of transformative moments: Blending community building pursuits into lifelong learning experiences. *J. Educ. Cult. Soc.* **2017**, *8*, 62–78. [CrossRef]
10. Ebrahimi, A. *C++ Programming EasyWays*; American Press: Boston, MA, USA, 2002.
11. World Health Organization. Available online: https://www.who.int (accessed on 1 October 2021).
12. Centers for Disease Control and Prevention. Available online: https://www.cdc.gov/coronavirus/2019-ncov/your-health (accessed on 1 October 2021).
13. Luka, I. Design Thinking in Pedagogy. *J. Educ. Cult. Soc.* **2020**, *5*, 63–74. [CrossRef]
14. Ebrahimi, A.; Schweikert, C.; Sayeed, S.; Parham, S.; Akibu, H.; Saeed, A.; Parris, W. Website Error Analysis of Colleges and Universities on Long Island in New York. *ACM SIGCSE Bull.* **2007**, *39*, 2. [CrossRef]
15. Allam, M.; Cai, S.; Ganesh, S.; Venkatesan, M.; Doodhwala, S.; Song, Z.; Hu, T.; Kumar, A.; Heit, J.; Coskun, A.F. COVID-19 diagnostics, tools, and prevention. *Diagnostics* **2020**, *10*, 409. [CrossRef] [PubMed]
16. Harmon, S.; Sanford, T.; Xu, S.; Turkbey, E.; Roth, H.; Xu, Z.; Yang, D.; Myronenko, A.; Anderson, V. Artificial intelligence for the detection of COVID-19 pneumonia on chest CT using multinational datasets. *Nat. Commun.* **2020**, *11*, 4080. [CrossRef] [PubMed]
17. Barak, O.; Gavish, N.; Hari, L.P.; Shohat, T. Simulator of Interventions for COVID-19. 2020. Available online: https://applied-math.net.technion.ac.il/files/2020/06/Covid_simulator.pdf (accessed on 1 October 2021).
18. Wasiq, K.; Hussain, A.; Khan, S.A.; Al-Jumailey, M.; Nawaz, R.; Liatsis, P. Association learning between the COVID-19 infections and global demographic Characteristics using the class rule mining and pattern matching. *arXiv* **2020**. [CrossRef]

Disclaimer/Publisher's Note: The statements, opinions and data contained in all publications are solely those of the individual author(s) and contributor(s) and not of MDPI and/or the editor(s). MDPI and/or the editor(s) disclaim responsibility for any injury to people or property resulting from any ideas, methods, instructions or products referred to in the content.

Review

A Review of Deep Transfer Learning and Recent Advancements

Mohammadreza Iman [1,*], Hamid Reza Arabnia [1] and Khaled Rasheed [2]

[1] School of Computing, University of Georgia, Athens, GA 30602, USA; hra@uga.edu
[2] Institute for Artificial Intelligence, Franklin College of Arts and Sciences, University of Georgia, Athens, GA 30602, USA; khaled@uga.edu
* Correspondence: m.iman@uga.edu

Abstract: Deep learning has been the answer to many machine learning problems during the past two decades. However, it comes with two significant constraints: dependency on extensive labeled data and training costs. Transfer learning in deep learning, known as Deep Transfer Learning (DTL), attempts to reduce such reliance and costs by reusing obtained knowledge from a source data/task in training on a target data/task. Most applied DTL techniques are network/model-based approaches. These methods reduce the dependency of deep learning models on extensive training data and drastically decrease training costs. Moreover, the training cost reduction makes DTL viable on edge devices with limited resources. Like any new advancement, DTL methods have their own limitations, and a successful transfer depends on specific adjustments and strategies for different scenarios. This paper reviews the concept, definition, and taxonomy of deep transfer learning and well-known methods. It investigates the DTL approaches by reviewing applied DTL techniques in the past five years and a couple of experimental analyses of DTLs to discover the best practice for using DTL in different scenarios. Moreover, the limitations of DTLs (catastrophic forgetting dilemma and overly biased pre-trained models) are discussed, along with possible solutions and research trends.

Keywords: machine learning; deep learning; transfer learning; deep transfer learning; progressive learning

Citation: Iman, M.; Arabnia, H.R.; Rasheed, K. A Review of Deep Transfer Learning and Recent Advancements. *Technologies* 2023, 11, 40. https://doi.org/10.3390/technologies11020040

Academic Editor: Mohammed Mahmoud

Received: 2 February 2023
Revised: 6 March 2023
Accepted: 13 March 2023
Published: 14 March 2023

Copyright: © 2023 by the authors. Licensee MDPI, Basel, Switzerland. This article is an open access article distributed under the terms and conditions of the Creative Commons Attribution (CC BY) license (https://creativecommons.org/licenses/by/4.0/).

1. Introduction

In recent years, Deep Learning (DL) has successfully addressed a number of challenging and interesting applications; in particular, problems that involved non-linearity of datasets. Recent advancements in deep learning methods deliver various usages and applications in extremely different areas such as image processing, natural language processing (NLP), numerical data analysis and predictions, and voice recognition. However, deep learning comes with restrictions, such as expensive training processes (time and processing) and the requirement of extensive training data (labeled data) [1].

Since the start of the Machine Learning (ML) era, transfer learning has been a neat exploration for scientists. Before the rise of deep learning models, transfer learning was known as domain adaptation and focused on homogeneous data sets and how to relate such sets to each other because of the nature of ML algorithms [2,3]. Traditional ML models have less dependency on the dataset size, and usually, their training is less costly than deep learning models since they have been mostly designed for linear problems. Therefore, the motivation for using transfer learning in deep learning is higher than ever in the AI (Artificial Intelligence) and ML fields since it can address the two restraints of extensive training data and training costs.

Recent transfer learning methods on deep learning aim to reduce the training process time and cost, and the necessity of extensive training datasets which can be hard to harvest in some areas such as medical images. Moreover, a pre-trained model for a specific job can be run on a simple edge device such as a cellphone with limited processing capacity and limited training time [4]. Moreover, developments in DTL are opening the door to more intuitive and sophisticated AI systems since it considers learning a continuous task. A great example of this idea is Google's deep mind project and advancements such as progressive learning [5]. All this is bringing DTL to the forefront of research in artificial intelligence and machine learning.

This review aims to answer the following research questions: (i) What is DTL, and how does it differ from semi-supervised, multiview, and multitask learning? (ii) What are different transfer learning methods and their taxonomy? (iii) What are the most applied DTL methods, and how are they effective? (iv) What is the best practice of DTL model-based approaches in practice? (v) What are the limitations of DTL and possible solutions/research trends?

In this paper, first, the definition of DTL is reviewed, followed by the taxonomy of DTL. Then, the selected recent practical studies of DTL are listed, categorized, and summarized. Moreover, two experimental evaluations of DTL and their conclusions are reviewed. Last but not least, we discuss the limitations of today's DTL techniques and possible ways to tackle them.

2. Deep Learning

Deep learning (DL) or deep neural network (DNN) is a machine learning subcategory, which can deal with nonlinear datasets. DNNs consist of layers of stacked nodes, with activation function and associated weights, (fully/partially) connected and usually trained (weight adjustments) by back-propagation and optimization algorithms. During the past two decades, DNNs were developed rapidly and are used in many aspects of our daily lives today. For instance, Convolutional Neural Network (CNN) layers have improved deep learning models for visual-related tasks since 2011, and as of today, most DLs use CNN layers [1]. For more details about machine learning and deep learning, please refer to [1], since this paper is focused on deep transfer learning, and we assume that the reader should have a thorough understanding of machine learning and deep learning.

3. Deep Transfer Learning (DTL)

Deep transfer learning is about using the obtained knowledge from another task and dataset (even one not strongly related to the source task or dataset) to reduce learning costs. In many ML problems, arranging a large amount of labeled data is impossible, which is mandatory for most DL models. For instance, at the beginning of the COVID-19 pandemic or even a year into it, providing enough chest X-ray-labeled data for training a deep learning model was still challenging, while when using deep transfer learning, the AI succeeded in detecting the disease with a very high accuracy with a limited training set [6,7]. Another application is applying machine learning on edge devices such as phones for variant tasks by taking advantage of deep transfer learning to reduce the need for processing power.

An untrained DL uses a random initializing weight for nodes, and during the expensive training process, those weights adjust to the most optimized values by applying an optimization algorithm for a specific task (dataset). Remarkably, Ref. [8] proved that initializing those weights based on a trained network with even a very distant dataset improves the training performance compared to the random initialization.

Deep transfer learning differs from semi-supervised learning since, in DTL, the source and target datasets can have a different distribution and just be related to each other, while in semi-supervised learning, the source and target data are from the same dataset, only the target set does not have the labels [2]. DTL is also not the same as Multiview learning, since Multiview learning uses two or more distinct datasets to improve the quality of one task, e.g., video datasets can be separated into image and audio datasets [2]. Last but not least, DTL differs from Multitask learning despite many shared similarities. The most fundamental difference is that in Multitask learning, the tasks use interconnections to boost each other, and knowledge transfer happens concurrently between related tasks. In contrast in DTL, the target domain is the focus, and the knowledge has already been obtained for target data from source data, and they do not need to be related or function simultaneously [2].

4. From Transfer Learning to Deep Transfer Learning, Taxonomy

It is possible to categorize Deep Transfer Learnings (DTLs) in different ways by various criteria, similar to Transfer Learnings. DTLs can be divided into two categories of homogeneous and heterogenous based on the homogeneity of source and target data [2]. However, this categorization can be conducted differently because it is subjective and relative. For example, a dataset of X-ray photos can be considered heterogeneous to a dataset of tree species photos when the comparison domain is limited to only image data. In contrast, it can be considered homogeneous to the same tree species photo dataset when the domain consists of audio and text datasets.

Moreover, DTLs can be categorized into three groups based on label-setting aspects: (i) transductive, (ii) inductive, and (iii) unsupervised [2]. Briefly, transductive is when only the source data is labeled; if both source and target data are labeled it is inductive; if none of the data are labeled, it is unsupervised deep transfer learning [2].

Refs. [2,9] mention and define another categorization of DTLs through the aspect of applied approaches. They similarly categorized DTLs into four groups of: (i) instance-based, (ii) feature-based/mapping-based, (iii) parameter-based/model-based, and (iv) relational-based/adversarial-based approaches. Instance-based transfer learning approaches are based on using the selected parts of instances (or all) in source data and applying different weighting strategies to be used with target data. Feature-based approaches map instances (or some features) from both source and target data into more homogeneous data. Further, the [2] survey divides the feature-based category into asymmetric and symmetric feature-based transfer learning subcategories. "Asymmetric approaches transform the source features to match the target ones. In contrast, symmetric approaches attempt to find a common latent feature space and then transform both the source and the target features into a new feature representation" [2]. The model-based (parameter-based) methods are about using the obtained knowledge in the model (network) with different combinations of pre-trained layers: freezing some and/or finetuning some and/or adding some fresh layers. Relational/adversarial-based approaches focus on extracting transferable features from both source and target data either using the logical relationship or rules learned in the source domain or by applying methods inspired by generative adversarial networks (GAN) [2,9]. Figure 1 shows the taxonomy of the above-mentioned categories [2].

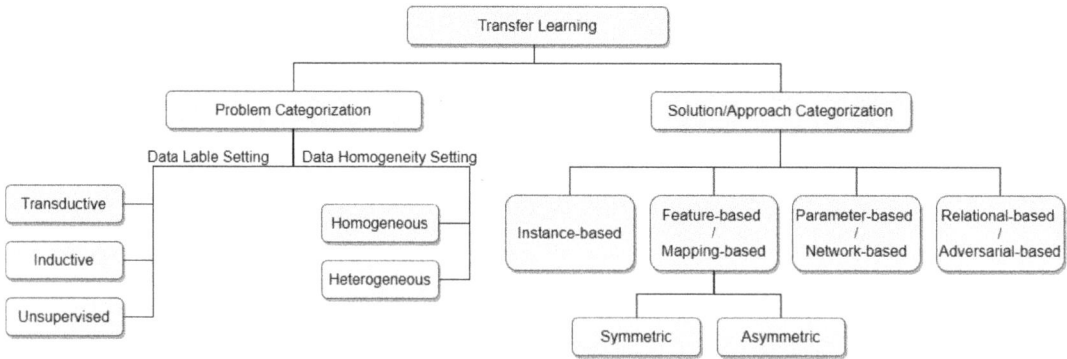

Figure 1. Taxonomy of Transfer Learning which is extendable to Deep Transfer Learning as well.

Other than the model-based and adversarial-based approaches, all other categories have been explored deeply during the last couple of decades for different ML techniques known as domain adaptation or transfer learning [2,3]. However, most of those techniques are still applicable to deep transfer learning (DTL) as well. Model-based (parameter-based) approaches are the most applied techniques in DTL since they can tackle the domain adaptation between the source and target data by adjusting the network (model). In other words, deep transfer learning is mainly focused on model-based approaches. Remarkably, model-based approaches in deep learning models can even tackle the adaptation of a very distant source and target data [2,9].

In deep transfer learning (DTL), different techniques are applied for model-based approaches, although generally, they are combinations of pre-training, freezing, finetuning, and/or adding a fresh layer(s). A deep learning network (DL model) trained on source data is called a pre-trained model consisting of pre-trained layers. Freezing and finetuning are techniques using some or all layers of pre-trained models to train the model on target data. Freezing some layers means the parameters/weights will not change and are constant values for frozen layers from a pre-trained model. Finetuning means the parameters/weights are initialized with the pre-trained values instead of random initialization for the whole network or some selected layers. Another recent DTL technique is based on freezing a pre-trained model and adding new layers to that model for training on target data; Google's deep mind project introduces this technique in 2016 as Progressive Learning/progressive neural networks (PNNs) [5,10].

The concept of progressive learning mimics human skill learning, which is adding a new skill on top of previously learned skills as a foundation to learn a new one. E.g., a child learns how to run after learning to crawl and walk and using all the skills obtained in the process. Similarly, PNNs prevent catastrophic forgetting in DTL versus finetuning techniques by freezing the whole pre-trained model and learning (adjusting to) the new task by training the newly added layers on top of the previously trained layers [5,10].

In deep learning models, usually, the earlier layers conduct the feature extraction at a high level of detail, further layers towards the end extract the information and conceptualize the given data, and lateral layers conduct the classifications or predictions. For instance, in the image-related model, the earlier layers of CNN extract the edges, corners, and tiny patches of a given image. Further layers put those details together to detect objects or faces, and the lateral layers, usually fully connected layers, conduct the classification [11]. Given this process, the most effective and efficient approach for DTL, to our knowledge, is to freeze the earlier and middle layers from a related pre-trained model and finetune the lateral layers for the new task/dataset [12]. Similarly, the new layers are added to the last part of a pre-trained model in progressive learning.

Nonetheless, some other research in this area use combinational and sophisticated methods to tackle transfer learning in deep learning such as ensembled networks, weighting strategies, etc. [2]. However, to our knowledge, the search for recent advancements in DTL for practical tasks ends up with methods based on mostly the model-based and limited number of adversarial-based approaches.

5. Review of Recent Advancements in DTL

We limited our selection to the last five years of published studies on deep transfer learning for various tasks and data types. Table 1 shows the list of selected works from hundreds of reviewed literature sorted by their DTL approaches. We used the systematic literature review (SLR) technique [13] for the process of finding and selecting these thirty-eight publications. The inclusion criteria that we used for our selection process are as follows: (a) published in the past five years, (b) reproducible (detailed implementation and models), (c) applied to practical ML problems, and (d) generalizable. We found that all reviewed studies mostly fall into three categories of model-based approaches and some into the adversarial-based approach, which are explained in the previous section. We name these approaches as (i) Finetuning: finetuning a pre-trained model on target data; (ii) freezing CNN layers: the earlier CNN layers are frozen, and only the lateral fully connected layers are finetuned; (iii) progressive learning: some or all layers of a pre-trained model are selected and used frozen, and some fresh layers will be added to the model to be trained on target data; and (iv) adversarial-based: extracting transferable features from both source and target data using adversarial or relational methods, as shown in Figure 2.

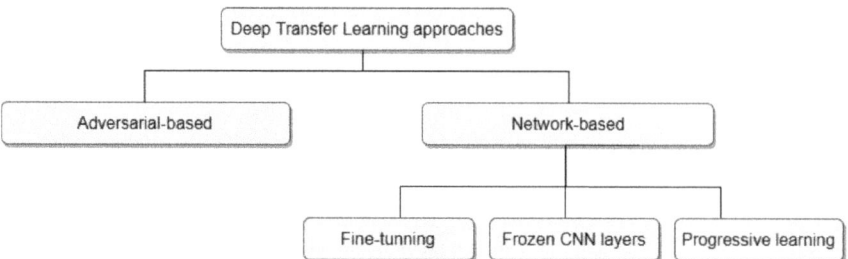

Figure 2. Most common Deep Transfer Learning approaches.

The most common DTL method is using a trained model on a highly related dataset to target data and finetune it on target data (finetuning). The simplicity of applying this technique makes it the most popular DTL method in our selection; 21 of 38 selected works have used this method. This method can improve training on target data in various ways, such as reducing training costs and tackling the need for an extensive target dataset. However, it is still prone to catastrophic forgetting. Needless to say, it is a very effective DTL method for many tasks and datasets in various fields such as medical, mechanics, art, physics, security, etc. Moreover, it has been applied for both image datasets and tabular (numerical) datasets as listed in Table 1.

The second popular approach in DTL is freezing CNN layers in a pre-trained model and finetuning only lateral fully connected layers (Freezing CNN layers). CNN layers extract features from the given dataset, and the fully connected layers are responsible for classification, which in this method will be finetuned to the new task for target data.

Table 1. List of selected recent deep transfer learning (DTL) publications.

Ref.	Year	Title	Data Type	Time Series	Approach	CNN	Known Models Used	Dataset Field
[14]	2022	UAV swarm-based radar signal sorting via multi-source data fusion: A deep transfer learning framework	Image	No	Finetuning	Yes	Yolo, Faster-RCNN, and Cascade-RCNN	Radar image
[15]	2022	Classification of analyzable metaphase images using transfer learning and fine tuning	Image	No	Finetuning	Yes	VGG16, Inception V3	Medical image
[16]	2021	Multiclassification of Endoscopic Colonoscopy Images Based on Deep Transfer Learning	Image	no	Finetuning	yes	AlexNet, VGG, and Res-Net	Medical Image
[17]	2021	MCFT-CNN: Malware classification with fine-tune convolution neural networks using traditional and transfer learning in Internet of Things	Image	No	Finetuning	yes	Res-Net50	Malware classification

Table 1. Cont.

Ref.	Year	Title	Data Type	Time Series	Approach	CNN	Known Models Used	Dataset Field
[18]	2021	Facial Emotion Recognition Using Transfer Learning in the Deep CNN	Image	no	Finetuning	yes	VGGs, Res-Nets, Inception-v3, DenseNet-161	Facial emotion recognition (FER)
[6]	2020	Automated Deep Transfer Learning-Based Approach for Detection of COVID-19 Infection in Chest X-rays	Image	no	Finetuning	yes	Inception-Xception	Medical image
[7]	2020	Classification of the COVID-19 infected patients using DenseNet201 based deep transfer learning	Image	no	Finetuning	yes	ImageNet, Dense-Net	Medical image
[19]	2019	Enhancing materials property prediction by leveraging computational and experimental data using deep transfer learning	Tabular/bigdata	yes	Finetuning	no	none	Quantum mechanics
[20]	2019	Application of deep transfer learning for automated brain abnormality classification using MR images	Image	no	Finetuning	yes	Res-Net	Medical image
[21]	2019	An adaptive deep transfer learning method for bearing fault diagnosis	Tabular/bigdata	Yes	Finetuning	No	LSTM RNN	Mechanic
[22]	2019	Online detection for bearing incipient fault based on deep transfer learning	Image	Yes	Finetuning	Yes	VGG-16	Mechanic
[23]	2019	Towards More Accurate Automatic Sleep Staging via Deep Transfer Learning	Tabular/bigdata	Yes	Finetuning	Yes	None	Medical data
[24]	2019	Deep Transfer Learning for Multiple Class Novelty Detection	Image	No	Finetuning	Yes	Alex-Net, VGG-Net	Vision
[25]	2019	A Digital-Twin-Assisted Fault Diagnosis Using Deep Transfer Learning	Tabular/bigdata	No	Finetuning	No	None	Mechanic
[26]	2019	Learning to Discover Novel Visual Categories via Deep Transfer Clustering	Image	No	Finetuning	Yes	None	Vision
[27]	2018	Deep Transfer Learning for Person Re-identification	Image	No	Finetuning	Yes	None	Identification/security
[28]	2018	Deep Transfer Learning for Art Classification Problems	Image	No	Finetuning	Yes	None	Art
[29]	2018	Classification and unsupervised clustering of LIGO data with Deep Transfer Learning	Image	No	Finetuning	Yes	None	Physics/Astrophysics

Table 1. *Cont.*

Ref.	Year	Title	Data Type	Time Series	Approach	CNN	Known Models Used	Dataset Field
[30]	2018	Empirical Study and Improvement on Deep Transfer Learning for Human Activity Recognition	Tabular/bigdata	Yes	Finetuning	Yes	None	Human Activity Recognition
[31]	2018	Automatic ICD-9 coding via deep transfer learning	Tabular/bigdata	No	Finetuning	Yes	None	Medical
[32]	2017	Video-based emotion recognition in the wild using deep transfer learning and score fusion	Video (audio and visual)	Yes	Finetuning	Yes	VGG-Face	Human science/psychology
[33]	2022	Deep transfer learning-based visual classification of pressure injuries stages	Image	No	Freezing CNN layers	Yes	Dense-Net 121, Inception V3, MobilNet V2, Res-Nets, VGG16	Medical image
[34]	2021	Deep Transfer Learning for WiFi Localization	Tabular/bigdata	No	Freezing CNN layers	Yes	None	WiFi Localization
[35]	2020	Automated invasive ductal carcinoma detection based using deep transfer learning with whole-slide images	Image	No	Freezing CNN layers	Yes	Res-Net, Dense-Net	Medical image
[36]	2019	Deep Transfer Learning for Signal Detection in Ambient Backscatter Communications	Tabular/bigdata	No	Freezing CNN layers	Yes	None	Tele-communication
[37]	2019	Brain tumor classification using deep CNN features via transfer learning	Image	No	Freezing CNN layers	Yes	Google-Net	Medical image
[38]	2018	Comparison of Deep Transfer Learning Strategies for Digital Pathology	Image	No	Freezing CNN layers	Yes	None	Medical image
[39]	2018	Deep transfer learning for military object recognition under small training set condition	Image	No	Freezing CNN layers	Yes	None	Military
[40]	2018	Deep Transfer Learning for Image-Based Structural Damage Recognition	Image	No	Freezing CNN layers	Yes	VGG-Net	Civil engineering
[41]	2017	Deep Transfer Learning for Modality Classification of Medical Images	Image	No	Freezing CNN layers	Yes	VGG-Net, Res-Net	Medical image
[42]	2017	Folding Membrane Proteins by Deep Transfer Learning	Tabular/bigdata	No	Freezing CNN layers	Yes	Res-Net	Chemistry
[43]	2021	Progressive Transfer Learning Approach for Identifying the Leaf Type by Optimizing Network Parameters	Image	No	Progressive learning	Yes	Res-Net50	Plant science

Table 1. Cont.

Ref.	Year	Title	Data Type	Time Series	Approach	CNN	Known Models Used	Dataset Field
[44]	2020	An Evaluation of Progressive Neural Networks for Transfer Learning in Natural Language Processing	NLP/text	No	Progressive learning	No	None	NLP
[45]	2020	Progressive Transfer Learning and Adversarial Domain Adaptation for Cross-Domain Skin Disease Classification	Image	No	Progressive learning	Yes	None	Medical image
[46]	2017	Progressive Neural Networks for Transfer Learning in Emotion Recognition	Image and audio	Yes	Progressive learning	No	None	Para-linguistic
[47]	2020	A deep transfer learning model with classical data augmentation and CGAN to detect COVID-19 from chest CT radiography digital images	Image	No	Adversarial-based	Yes	Alex-Net, VGG-Net16, VGG-Net19, Google-Net, Res-Net50	Medical image
[48]	2019	Diagnosing Rotating Machines with Weakly Supervised Data Using Deep Transfer Learning	Tabular/bigdata	Yes	Adversarial-based	Yes	None	Mechanic
[49]	2017	A New Deep Transfer Learning Based on Sparse Auto-Encoder for Fault Diagnosis	Tabular/bigdata	Yes	Sparse Auto-Encoder	No	None	Mechanic

Refs. [33–42] are the sample research publications, which have used this method for different data types such as image and tabular data as listed in Table 1. This technique is specific to the models consisting of CNN layers; however, it can be extended to other deep learning models by assuming that the earlier and middle layers are acting similarly to CNN layers for feature extraction.

Using well-known models such as VGG-Net, Alex-Net, and Res-Net, which have already been trained on ImageNet datasets [50], is a general approach for both of the techniques mentioned above, since they are easily accessible, and they are pre-trained to the highest possible accuracy. It is worth mentioning that such training can take days of processing time even with clusters of GPUs/TPUs, and the mentioned methods are skipping the pre-training step by simply downloading a publicly available pre-trained model. Refs. [43–46] are based on the progressive learning method, also known as progressive neural networks (PNNs), described earlier. Ref. [44] evaluates the progressive learning effectiveness for common natural language processing (NLP) tasks: sequence labeling and text classification. Through the evaluation and comparison of applying PNNs to various models, datasets, and tasks, they show how PNNs improve DL models' accuracy by avoiding the catastrophic forgetting in finetuning techniques. Refs. [43,45,46] use PNNs for image and audio datasets and similarly finds tangible improvements in comparison to other DTL techniques. Refs. [47,48] are examples of adversarial-based approaches that we found in the literature. In [47], they used conditional generative adversarial networks (CGAN) to expand the limited target data of chest X-ray images for detecting the COVID-19 DTL model. Ref. [48] applies the domain adversarial training to obtain the shared features between multiple source datasets.

Moreover, we found some tailored DTL methods for specific tasks and datasets such as [49]. The proposed method in [49], as they describe it, is based on the "three-layer sparse auto-encoder to extract the features of raw data, and applies the maximum mean discrepancy term to minimizing the discrepancy penalty between the features from training data and target data." They tailor that method for smart industry fault diagnosis problems and achieve a 99.82% accuracy which is better than other approaches such as the deep belief network, sparse filter, deep learning, and support vector machine. Such tailored DTL approaches are not usually easy to generalize for different tasks or datasets. Nonetheless, they can open the door to interesting and new techniques in deep transfer learning's future.

6. Experimental Analyzations of Deep Transfer Learning

In this section, we review two remarkable experimental evaluations of DTL techniques. The tests' setup, analysis, and conclusions are noteworthy for applying DTL techniques in different scenarios.

"What is being transferred in transfer learning?" [51] is a recent experimental study which uses a series of tests on visual domain and deep learning models and tries to investigate what makes a successful transfer and which part of the network is responsible for that. To do so, they analyze networks in four different cases: (i) pre-trained network, (ii) random initialized network, (iii) finetuned network on target domain after pretraining on source domain, and (iv) trained network from random initialization [51]. Moreover, to characterize the role of the feature reuse, they use a source (pre-train) domain containing natural images (IMAGENET), and a few target (downstream) domains with decreasing visual similarities from natural images: DOMAINNET real, DOMAINNET clipart, CHEXPERT (medical chest X-rays) and DOMAINNET quickdraw [51].

The study demonstrates that feature reuse plays a key role in deep transfer learning as a pre-trained model on IMAGENET, and shows the largest performance improvement on the real domain, which shares similar visual features (natural images) with IMAGENET in comparison to randomly initialized models. Moreover, they run a series of experiments by shuffling the image blocks (different block sizes). These experiments prove that feature reuse plays a very important role in transfer learning, particularly when the target domain shares visual features with the source domain. However, they realize that feature reuse is not the only reason for deep transfer learning success, since even for distant targets such as CHEXPERT and quickdraw, they still observe performance boosts from deep transfer learning. Additionally, in all cases pre-trained models converge way faster than random initialized models [51].

Further, they manually analyze common and uncommon mistakes in the training of randomly initialized versus pre-trained models. They observe that data samples marked incorrect in the pre-trained model and correct in the randomly initialized model are mostly ambiguous samples. On the other hand, the majority of the samples that a pre-trained model marked correct and a randomly initialized model marked incorrect are straightforward samples. This means that a pre-trained model has a stronger prior, and it is harder to adapt to the target domain. Moreover, using the centered kernel alignment to measure feature similarities, they conclude that the initialization point drastically impacts feature similarity, and two networks with a high accuracy can have a different feature space. Moreover, they discover similar results for distance in the parameter space, in which two random-initialized models are farther from each other compared to two pre-trained models [51].

In regards to performance barriers and basins in the loss landscape, they have concluded that the network stays in the same basin of the solution when finetuning a pretrained network. They reached this conclusion by training pre-trained models from two random runs as well as training random initialized models twice and comparing. Even when training a random initialized model two times with the same random values, the models end up in different basins [51].

Module criticality is an interesting analysis of deep learning models. Usually, in a deep CNN model, each layer of CNN considers a module, while in some models a component of the network can be considered as a module. To measure the criticality of a module, it is possible to take a trained model and re-initialize each module at once and compare the amount of model accuracy drop. Adopting this technique, the authors of [51] discovered: (i) fully connected layers (near to the model output) become critical for the P-T model, and the (ii) module criticality increases moving from the input side of the model towards the output, which is consistent with the concept of earlier layers (near the input), extracting more general features, while lateral layers have features that are more specialized for the target domain. Ref. [52] is another experimental analysis of transfer learning in visual tasks with the title of "Factors of Influence for Transfer Learning across Diverse Appearance Domains and Task Types". Three factors of influence are investigated in this study: (i) image domain, the difference in image domain between source and target tasks, (ii) task type, the difference in task type, and (iii) dataset size, the size of the source, and target training sets. They perform over 1200 transfer learning experiments on 20 datasets spanning seven diverse image domains (consumer, driving, aerial, underwater, indoor, synthetic, and closeups) and four task types (semantic segmentation, object detection, depth estimation, and keypoint detection) [52].

They use data normalization (e.g., Illumination normalization) and augmentation techniques to improve the models' accuracy. They adopt recent high-resolution backbone HRNetV2, which consists of 69M parameters. This backbone is easily adjustable for different datasets by simply replacing the head of the backbone. To make a fair comparison, they pre-trained (to be used for transfer learning) their models from scratch and evaluated their performance using a top-1 accuracy on the ILSVRC'12 validation set [52].

The transfer learning experiments are mainly divided into two settings of the (i) transfer learning with a small target training set and (ii) with the full target set. The evaluation of transfer learning models is based on the gain obtained from finetuning from a specific source model compared to finetuning from ILSVRC'12 image classification with the main question of "are additional gains possible, by picking a good source?". Furthermore, they added a series of experiments for multi-source training to investigate the impact of using multi-source training for a specific task [52].

Such an exhaustive experimental analysis resulted in following observations: (i) all experiments proved that transfer learning outperforms training from scratch (random initialization); (ii) for 85% of target tasks there exists a source task which tops ILSVCR'12 pre-training; (iii) the most transfer gain happens when the source and target tasks are in the same image domain (within-domain), which is even more important than the source size; (iv) positive transfer gain is possible when the source image domain includes the target domain; (v) although multisource models bring good transfer, they are outperformed by the largest within-domain source; (vi) "for 65% of the targets within the same image domain as the source, cross-task-type transfer results in positive transfer gains"; (vii) as naturally expected, the larger datasets positively transfer towards the smaller datasets; (viii) transfer effects are stronger for a small target training set, which helps the process of choosing the transfer learning model by testing several models with a small section of target data [52].

7. Discussion

The Deep Transfer Learning (DTL) research field is thriving because of the motivation to handle the limitations of Deep Learning (DL) models, which are the dependency on extensive labeled data and training costs. The main idea is to use the obtained knowledge from source data in the training process on target data. Another possible impactful outcome of the DTL research line is to achieve continual learning, which brings the Artificial General Intelligence [1] a step closer to reality. Continual learning can be achieved simply through a chain of transfer learning processes, while the end model is still valid on all previous training sources.

As we reviewed in previous sections, model-based approaches are the most commonly used approaches in DTL, since deep learning models have the capacity to be adjusted to transfer knowledge. However, there are two main constraints in such approaches—the catastrophic forgetting dilemma and an overly biased pre-trained model.

In the case of finetuning a pre-trained model, there is a high chance of the drastic changes of weights through the whole model resulting in the catastrophic forgetting dilemma. Therefore, the obtained knowledge could be partially or even completely wiped out, resulting in unsuccessful training and no possibility of continual learning. This constraint limits the success of the finetuning approach to the tightly related source and target data. Moreover, a very well-known technique to reduce the forgetting effect is to add a limited number of source samples to the target training data.

Freezing the pre-trained CNN layers technique tries to tackle the catastrophic forgetting by freezing the obtained knowledge on earlier layers and finetuning the fully-connected lateral layers to achieve transfer learning for target data. Given the fact that earlier layers in DL models extract detailed features and move towards the output, more abstract knowledge is extracted [11]; freezing the earlier layers limits the ability of the model to learn any new features from target data, which is known as an overly biased pre-trained model. Having extensive source data or access to a pre-trained model on a large dataset is critical for a successful transfer using this technique. In this way, there is a high chance that the pre-trained model has already learned any possible detailed features, and simply by finetuning, the lateral layers can perform on target data. However, even tackling the first obstacle, this solution is still imperiled by the catastrophic forgetting in lateral layers. This technique is still successful in the case of the related source and target data and tasks despite the limitations mentioned above.

Progressive learning tries to find a middle ground between catastrophic forgetting and a biased model by adding a new layer(s) to the end of a frozen pre-trained model. This technique is successful in the case of a task transfer for the related source and target data. It cannot deal with the distant source and target data since the earlier layers are frozen and cannot learn new features; however, the new lateral layer helps the model adjust to a new task.

A possible solution to address both catastrophic forgetting and an overly biased pre-trained model in DTL is to increase the learning capacity of a pre-trained model by vertically expanding it. In another research paper, we propose expanding the model vertically in training on target data, adding new nodes on frozen pre-trained layers throughout the model instead of adding a new layer(s) to the end of the model [53]. The vertical expansion increases the model learning capacity while keeping the previously obtained knowledge intact. Therefore, not only do we achieve successful transfer learning, our final model is still valid on the source data, opening the door to deep continual learning [53].

8. Conclusions

This paper reviews the taxonomy of deep transfer learning (DTL) and the definitions of different approaches. Moreover, we review, list, categorize and analyze over thirty recently applied DTL research studies. Then, we investigate the methodology and limitations of the three most common model-based deep transfer learning methods: (i) Finetuning, (ii) Freezing CNN Layers, and (iii) Progressive Learning. These techniques have proven their ability and effectiveness for various machine learning problems. The simplicity of finetuning publicly available pre-trained models on extensive datasets is the reason for it being the most common transfer learning technique. Moreover, two thorough experimental studies in DTL are summarized; their discoveries clarify the details of a successful deep transfer learning approach for different scenarios. Last but not least, the limitations of current DTLs, catastrophic forgetting dilemma, and overly biased pre-trained models are discussed, along with possible solutions.

Author Contributions: Writing and original draft preparation, M.I.; supervision, review, and editing, H.R.A. and K.R. All authors have read and agreed to the published version of the manuscript.

Funding: This research received no external funding.

Institutional Review Board Statement: Not applicable.

Informed Consent Statement: Not applicable.

Data Availability Statement: Not applicable.

Conflicts of Interest: The authors declare no conflict of interest.

References

1. Iman, M.; Arabnia, H.R.; Branchinst, R.M. *Pathways to Artificial General Intelligence: A Brief Overview of Developments and Ethical Issues via Artificial Intelligence, Machine Learning, Deep Learning, and Data Science*; Springer: Cham, Switzerland, 2021; pp. 73–87.
2. Zhuang, F.; Qi, Z.; Duan, K.; Xi, D.; Zhu, Y.; Zhu, H.; Xiong, H.; He, Q. A comprehensive survey on transfer learning. *Proc. IEEE* **2020**, *109*, 43–76. [CrossRef]
3. Farahani, A.; Voghoei, S.; Rasheed, K.; Arabnia, H.R. A brief review of domain adaptation. In *Advances in Data Science and Information Engineering*; Springer: Cham, Switzerland, 2021; pp. 877–894.
4. Voghoei, S.; Tonekaboni, N.H.; Wallace, J.G.; Arabnia, H.R. Deep learning at the edge. In Proceedings of the 2018 International Conference on Computational Science and Computational Intelligence (CSCI), Las Vegas, NV, USA, 12–14 December 2018; pp. 895–901.
5. Chang, H.S.; Fu, M.C.; Hu, J.; Marcus, S.I. Google Deep Mind's AlphaGo. *Or/Ms Today* **2016**, *43*, 24–29.
6. Das, N.N.; Kumar, N.; Kaur, M.; Kumar, V.; Singh, D. Automated Deep Transfer Learning-Based Approach for Detection of COVID-19 Infection in Chest X-rays. *Irbm* **2022**, *43*, 114–119.
7. Jaiswal, A.; Gianchandani, N.; Singh, D.; Kumar, V.; Kaur, M. Classification of the COVID-19 infected patients using DenseNet201 based deep transfer learning. *J. Biomol. Struct. Dyn.* **2020**, *39*, 5682–5689. [CrossRef] [PubMed]
8. Yosinski, J.; Clune, J.; Bengio, Y.; Lipson, H. How transferable are features in deep neural networks? *Adv. Neural Inf. Process. Syst.* **2014**, *4*, 3320–3328.
9. Tan, C.; Sun, F.; Kong, T.; Zhang, W.; Yang, C.; Liu, C. A survey on deep transfer learning. *Lect. Notes Comput. Sci. (Incl. Subser. Lect. Notes Artif. Intell. Lect. Notes Bioinform.)* **2018**, *11141*, 270–279.
10. Rusu, A.A.; Rabinowitz, N.C.; Desjardins, G.; Soyer, H.; Kirkpatrick, J.; Kavukcuoglu, K.; Pascanu, R.; Hadsell, R. Progressive neural networks. *arXiv* **2016**, arXiv:1606.04671. [CrossRef]
11. Yosinski, J.; Clune, J.; Nguyen, A.; Fuchs, T.; Lipson, H. Understanding neural networks through deep visualization. *arXiv* **2015**, arXiv1506.06579. [CrossRef]
12. Hariharan, R.; Sudhakar, P.; Venkataramani, R.; Thiruvenkadam, S.; Annangi, P.; Babu, N.; Vaidya, V. Understanding the mechanisms of deep transfer learning for medical images. In *Deep Learning and Data Labeling for Medical Applications*; Springer: Cham, Switzerland, 2016; pp. 188–196.
13. Kitchenham, B.; Pearlbrereton, O.; Budgen, D.; Turner, M.; Bailey, J.; Linkman, S. Systematic literature reviews in software engineering—A systematic literature review. *Inf. Softw. Technol.* **2009**, *51*, 7–15. [CrossRef]
14. Wan, L.; Liu, R.; Sun, L.; Nie, H.; Wang, X. UAV swarm based radar signal sorting via multi-source data fusion: A deep transfer learning framework. *Inf. Fusion* **2022**, *78*, 90–101. [CrossRef]
15. Albayrak, A. Classification of analyzable metaphase images using transfer learning and fine tuning. *Med. Biol. Eng. Comput.* **2022**, *60*, 239–248. [CrossRef] [PubMed]
16. Kumar, S. MCFT-CNN: Malware classification with fine-tune convolution neural networks using traditional and transfer learning in internet of things. *Future Gener. Comput. Syst.* **2021**, *125*, 334–351.
17. Wang, Y.; Feng, Z.; Song, L.; Liu, X.; Liu, S. Multiclassification of endoscopic colonoscopy images based on deep transfer learning. *Comput. Math. Methods Med.* **2021**, *2021*, 2485934. [CrossRef] [PubMed]
18. Akh, M.A.H.; Roy, S.; Siddique, N.; Kamal, M.A.S.; Shimamura, T. Facial Emotion Recognition Using Transfer Learning in the Deep CNN. *Electronics* **2021**, *10*, 1036.
19. Dipendra, J.; Choudhary, K.; Tavazza, F.; Liao, W.; Choudhary, A.; Campbell, C.; Agrawal, A. Enhancing materials property prediction by leveraging computational and experimental data using deep transfer learning. *Nat. Commun.* **2019**, *10*, 1–12.
20. Talo, M.; Baloglu, U.B.; Yıldırım, Ö.; Acharya, U.R. Application of deep transfer learning for automated brain abnormality classification using MR images. *Cogn. Syst. Res.* **2019**, *54*, 176–188. [CrossRef]
21. Wu, Z.; Jiang, H.; Zhao, K.; Li, X. An adaptive deep transfer learning method for bearing fault diagnosis. *Measurement* **2020**, *151*, 107227. [CrossRef]
22. Mao, W.; Ding, L.; Tian, S.; Liang, X. Online detection for bearing incipient fault based on deep transfer learning. *Meas. J. Int. Meas. Confed.* **2020**, *152*, 107278. [CrossRef]
23. Huy, P.; Chén, O.Y.; Koch, P.; Lu, Z.; McLoughlin, I.; Mertins, A.; Vos, M.D. Towards more accurate automatic sleep staging via deep transfer learning. *IEEE Trans. Biomed. Eng.* **2020**, *68*, 1787–1798.

24. Perera, P.; Patel, V.M. Deep Transfer Learning for Multiple Class Novelty Detection. In Proceedings of the IEEE/CVF Conference on Computer Vision and Pattern Recognition, Long Beach, CA, USA, 15–20 June 2019; pp. 11544–11552.
25. Xu, Y.; Sun, Y.; Liu, X.; Zheng, Y. A Digital-Twin-Assisted Fault Diagnosis Using Deep Transfer Learning. *IEEE Access* **2019**, *7*, 19990–19999. [CrossRef]
26. Han, K.; Vedaldi, A.; Zisserman, A. Learning to Discover Novel Visual Categories via Deep Transfer Clustering. In Proceedings of the IEEE/CVF International Conference on Computer Vision, Seoul, Republic of Korea, 27 October–2 November 2019; pp. 8401–8409.
27. Geng, M.; Wang, Y.; Xiang, T.; Tian, Y. Deep Transfer Learning for Person Re-identification. *arXiv* **2016**, arXiv:1611.05244.
28. Sabatelli, M.; Kestemont, M.; Daelemans, W.; Geurts, P. Deep Transfer Learning for Art Classification Problems. In Proceedings of the European Conference on Computer Vision (ECCV) Workshops, Munich, Germany, 8–14 September 2018.
29. George, D.; Shen, H.; Huerta, E.A. Deep transfer learning: A new deep learning glitch classification method for advanced ligo. *arXiv* **2017**, arXiv:1706.07446. [CrossRef]
30. Ding, R.; Li, X.; Nie, L.; Li, J.; Si, X.; Chu, D.; Liu, G.; Zhan, D. Empirical study and improvement on deep transfer learning for human activity recognition. *Sensors* **2019**, *19*, 57. [CrossRef]
31. Zeng, M.; Li, M.; Fei, Z.; Yu, Y.; Pan, Y.; Wang, J. Automatic ICD-9 coding via deep transfer learning. *Neurocomputing* **2019**, *324*, 43–50. [CrossRef]
32. Kaya, H.; Gürpınar, F.; Salah, A.A. Video-Based emotion recognition in the wild using deep transfer learning and score fusion. *Image Vis. Comput.* **2017**, *65*, 66–75. [CrossRef]
33. Ay, B.; Tasar, B.; Utlu, Z.; Ay, K.; Aydin, G. Deep transfer learning-based visual classification of pressure injuries stages. *Neural Comput. Appl.* **2022**, *4*, 16157–16168. [CrossRef]
34. Li, P.; Cui, H.; Khan, A.; Raza, U.; Piechocki, R.; Doufexi, A.; Farnham, T.M. Deep transfer learning for WiFi localization. In Proceedings of the 2021 IEEE Radar Conference (RadarConf21), Atlanta, GA, USA, 8–14 May 2021; IEEE: Piscataway, NJ, USA, 2021.
35. Celik, Y.; Talo, M.; Yildirim, O.; Karabatak, M.; Acharya, U.R. Automated invasive ductal carcinoma detection based using deep transfer learning with whole-slide images. *Pattern Recognit. Lett.* **2020**, *133*, 232–239. [CrossRef]
36. Liu, C.; Wei, Z.; Ng, D.W.K.; Yuan, J.; Liang, Y.C. Deep Transfer Learning for Signal Detection in Ambient Backscatter Communications. *IEEE Trans. Wirel. Commun.* **2020**, *20*, 1624–1638. [CrossRef]
37. Deepak, S.; Ameer, P.M. Brain tumor classification using deep CNN features via transfer learning. *Comput. Biol. Med.* **2019**, *111*, 103345. [CrossRef] [PubMed]
38. Mormont, R.; Geurts, P.; Marée, R. Comparison of Deep Transfer Learning Strategies for Digital Pathology. In Proceedings of the IEEE Conference on Computer Vision and Pattern Recognition Workshops, Salt Lake City, UT, USA, 18–22 June 2018; pp. 2262–2271.
39. Zhi, Y.; Yu, W.; Liang, P.; Guo, H.; Xia, L.; Zhang, F.; Ma, Y.; Ma, J. Deep transfer learning for military object recognition under small training set condition. *Neural Comput. Appl.* **2019**, *31*, 6469–6478.
40. Gao, Y.; Mosalam, K.M. Deep Transfer Learning for Image-Based Structural Damage Recognition. *Comput. Civ. Infrastruct. Eng.* **2018**, *33*, 748–768. [CrossRef]
41. Yu, Y.; Lin, H.; Meng, J.; Wei, X.; Guo, H.; Zhao, Z. Deep Transfer Learning for Modality Classification of Medical Images. *Information* **2017**, *8*, 91. [CrossRef]
42. Wang, S.; Li, Z.; Yu, Y.; Xu, J. Folding Membrane Proteins by Deep Transfer Learning. *Cell Syst.* **2017**, *5*, 202–211.e3. [CrossRef] [PubMed]
43. Joshi, D.; Mishra, V.; Srivastav, H.; Goel, D. Progressive Transfer Learning Approach for Identifying the Leaf Type by Optimizing Network Parameters. *Neural Process. Lett.* **2021**, *53*, 3653–3676. [CrossRef]
44. Abdul, M.; Hagerer, G.; Dugar, S.; Gupta, S.; Ghosh, M.; Danner, H.; Mitevski, O.; Nawroth, A.; Groh, G. An evaluation of progressive neural networks for transfer learning in natural language processing. In Proceedings of the 12th Language Resources and Evaluation Conference, Marseille, France, 11–16 May 2020; pp. 1376–1381.
45. Gu, Y.; Ge, Z.; Bonnington, C.P.; Zhou, J. Progressive Transfer Learning and Adversarial Domain Adaptation for Cross-Domain Skin Disease Classification. *IEEE Biomed. Health Informa.* **2020**, *24*, 1379–1393. [CrossRef] [PubMed]
46. Gideon, J.; Khorram, S.; Aldeneh, Z.; Dimitriadis, D.; Provost, E.M. Progressive Neural Networks for Transfer Learning in Emotion Recognition. *Proc. Annu. Conf. Int. Speech Commun. Assoc. Interspeech* **2017**, *2017*, 1098–1102.
47. Loey, M.; Manogaran, G.; Khalifa, N.E.M. A deep transfer learning model with classical data augmentation and CGAN to detect COVID-19 from chest CT radiography digital images. *Neural Comput. Appl.* **2020**, 1–13. [CrossRef]
48. Li, X.; Zhang, W.; Ding, Q.; Li, X. Diagnosing Rotating Machines with Weakly Supervised Data Using Deep Transfer Learning. *IEEE Trans. Ind. Inform.* **2020**, *16*, 1688–1697. [CrossRef]
49. Wen, L.; Gao, L.; Li, X. A new deep transfer learning based on sparse auto-encoder for fault diagnosis. *IEEE Trans. Syst. Man, Cybern. Syst.* **2019**, *49*, 136–144. [CrossRef]
50. Simon, M.; Rodner, E.; Denzler, J. ImageNet Pre-Trained Models with Batch Normalization; *arXiv* **2016**, arXiv:1612.01452. [CrossRef]
51. Neyshabur, B.; Sedghi, H.; Zhang, C. What is being transferred in transfer learning? *Adv. Neural Inf. Process. Syst.* **2020**, *33*, 512–523.

52. Mensink, T.; Uijlings, J.; Kuznetsova, A.; Gygli, M.; Ferrari, V. Factors of Influence for Transfer Learning across Diverse Appearance Domains and Task Types. *IEEE Trans. Pattern Anal. Mach. Intell.* **2021**, *44*, 9298–9314. [CrossRef] [PubMed]
53. Iman, M.; Miller, J.A.; Rasheed, K.; Branch, R.M.; Arabnia, H.R. EXPANSE: A Continual and Progressive Learning System for Deep Transfer Learning. In Proceedings of the 2022 International Conference on Computational Science and Computational Intelligence (CSCI), Las Vegas, NV, USA, 14–16 December 2022; IEEE: Piscataway, NJ, USA, 2022.

Disclaimer/Publisher's Note: The statements, opinions and data contained in all publications are solely those of the individual author(s) and contributor(s) and not of MDPI and/or the editor(s). MDPI and/or the editor(s) disclaim responsibility for any injury to people or property resulting from any ideas, methods, instructions or products referred to in the content.

Article

An Advanced Decision Tree-Based Deep Neural Network in Nonlinear Data Classification

Mohammad Arifuzzaman [1], Md. Rakibul Hasan [1], Tasnia Jahan Toma [2], Samia Binta Hassan [2] and Anup Kumar Paul [1,*]

[1] Department of Electronics and Communications Engineering, East West University, Dhaka 1212, Bangladesh
[2] Department of Computer Science and Engineering, East West University, Dhaka 1212, Bangladesh
* Correspondence: anuppaul@ewubd.edu

Abstract: Deep neural networks (DNNs), the integration of neural networks (NNs) and deep learning (DL), have proven highly efficient in executing numerous complex tasks, such as data and image classification. Because the multilayer in a nonlinearly separable data structure is not transparent, it is critical to develop a specific data classification model from a new and unexpected dataset. In this paper, we propose a novel approach using the concepts of DNN and decision tree (DT) for classifying nonlinear data. We first developed a decision tree-based neural network (DTBNN) model. Next, we extend our model to a decision tree-based deep neural network (DTBDNN), in which the multiple hidden layers in DNN are utilized. Using DNN, the DTBDNN model achieved higher accuracy compared to the related and relevant approaches. Our proposal achieves the optimal trainable weights and bias to build an efficient model for nonlinear data classification by combining the benefits of DT and NN. By conducting in-depth performance evaluations, we demonstrate the effectiveness and feasibility of the proposal by achieving good accuracy over different datasets.

Keywords: neural network; deep neural network; decision tree; nonlinear data classification; back propagation; gradient descent

Citation: Arifuzzaman, M.; Hasan, M.R.; Toma, T.J.; Hassan, S.B.; Paul, A.K. An Advanced Decision Tree-Based Deep Neural Network in Nonlinear Data Classification. Technologies 2023, 11, 24. https://doi.org/10.3390/technologies11010024

Academic Editor: Mohammed Mahmoud

Received: 31 December 2022
Revised: 28 January 2023
Accepted: 30 January 2023
Published: 1 February 2023

Copyright: © 2023 by the authors. Licensee MDPI, Basel, Switzerland. This article is an open access article distributed under the terms and conditions of the Creative Commons Attribution (CC BY) license (https://creativecommons.org/licenses/by/4.0/).

1. Introduction

When sufficient training data and computing power are available, one of the consolidated findings of contemporary (very) deep-learning approaches [1–4] is that their joint and unified method of learning feature representations together with their classifiers significantly outperforms traditional feature descriptors and classifier pipelines.

Learning from large datasets is now a necessity in many sectors, including machine learning, pattern identification, medical diagnosis, speech recognition, localization, cybersecurity, and image processing, thanks to advancements in science and technology [5–11]. Decision tree learning benefits from easy implementation, few parameters, low calculation, and the ability to adapt to different huge data types. In decision trees, the scale of the tree somewhat reflects the degree of generalizability. The rules retrieved from the tree become more complex as the tree's scale increases. Overfitting issues will result from overly complex rules [12]. Making the optimum decision tree as compact as feasible is crucial without compromising classification accuracy. Neural networks have been demonstrated to be a successful learning technique for carrying out classification tasks, particularly when high-dimensional data are input and the relationship between the input and output is complex [13]. According to studies, the depth of neural network models improves the classification or prediction accuracy by exponentially increasing their ability to represent data. However, a lot of training time will be needed for this process.

Numerous ensemble learning techniques about neural networks and decision trees have been put out by academics in recent years. The author of [14] suggested using a neural network to preprocess each attribute's relationship with the target attribute and then create a derivative relationship between each attribute and the classification outcome to create a tree. However, the algorithm's time complexity is significant. The author of [15] proposed a hybrid learning model of the BP algorithm based on the C4.5 algorithm and optimization to address the issue of difficult input parameter selection for the BP neural network and hidden layer nodes. However, because the model is a binary tree, it is unable to address the multi-classification issue. An extreme learning machine tree (ELM-Tree) model was proposed in [16], although the technique leverages information gain in node splitting, which has a tendency to be biased towards the attributes of picking more branches and results in overfitting.

In recent years, deep learning has become one of the breakthroughs in the field of machine learning [17]. In deep learning, deep neural network (DNN), developed from the neural network (NN), is a machine learning technique imitating the human nervous system and the brain's structure [18–21]. In general, NN consists of the input layer, hidden layer, and output layer [22,23], where each node or unit is interconnected to its peer entities in the adjacent layer, and the corresponding weight values are introduced in every connection [5]. DNNs are widely used to solve various problems, including automated image classification, data classification, data clustering, data approximation, data optimization, computer vision application, natural language processing, and predictive analysis [7,21,24–30]. DNN is also proven to be a cogent method for solving large-scale real-world problems [31].

Moreover, decision tree (DT) models are widely used for classification, where they perform a recursive partition for the input data and assign a weight to the final node. One of the critical advantages of DT models is that they are simple to decipher. Further, DT-based models are comparatively similar and, in some cases, better than NNs at predicting or classifying when using tabular data [32].

Nonlinear data classification, namely planar data classification, which involves multiple classes in the real-world [33–35], is a crucial research theme in the data classification field. In this context, classification is one of the most important aspects in a variety of practice scenarios where it plays an important role, such as environmental monitoring, multi-colored classification of space data, including stars, mars, the moon, or any complex data pattern, urbanization, disaster-affected areas, and traffic supervision [36]. Different neural network models have been proposed to segment or cluster a dataset [37]. In general, logistic regression is mostly used for linearly separable data since it gives a lower classification error [38]. In this paper, we use nonlinear separable complex data to address various practical scenarios where a single decision tree or logistic regression demonstrates a relatively high classification error rate. The NN model can automatically learn from complex data, which may contain millions of data points or thousands of parameters in a dataset [22].

To enable a considerable performance enhancement in nonlinear data classification, we propose the integrated models of DT and DNN for nonlinear data classification; namely decision tree-based deep neural network (DTBDNN). The proposal then realizes a better solution to the problem of nonlinear data with complex and low-contrast objects. While it would be quite difficult for the traditional algorithm to classify nonlinearly separable data [38], our proposal can effectively resolve the speculation and decipher capacity. Better still, the proposed DTBDNN model is developed using DT, in which we used a back propagation algorithm along with a gradient descent optimizer to optimize the trainable parameters. Second, we do not restrict the decision tree split to being binary; rather, we used a differentiable soft-binning [39] function to split nodes into multiple (>2) leaves that further improve the performance of the DTBDNN model.

The rest of the paper is organized as follows: We start with related work in Section 2. Section 3 describes the materials and methods of our proposed model. Section 4 depicts the results of our proposed model, where we made an analysis of the results, and finally, we conclude in Section 5.

2. Related Work

2.1. Background on Decision Tree

J. Ross Quinlan, a machine learning researcher, created the ID3 (Iterative Dichotomiser) decision tree method in the late 1970s and early 1980s. E. B. Hunt, J. Marin, and P. T. Stone's earlier study on concept learning systems were expanded upon in this paper. Later, Quinlan presented C4.5 (a replacement for ID3), which went on to serve as a standard by which newer supervised learning algorithms are frequently measured. The creation of binary decision trees was covered in the 1984 book Classification and Regression Trees (CART), written by a team of statisticians that included L. Breiman, J. Friedman, R. Olshen, and C. Stone. Though they were developed independently at about the same time, ID3 and CART use a similar method to learn decision trees from training tuples. An explosion of research on decision tree induction was spurred by these two cornerstone techniques [40].

The way the attributes are chosen when building the tree is one of the differences between decision tree algorithms. A heuristic for choosing the splitting criterion that "best" divides a given data partition, D, of class-labeled training tuples into distinct classes is known as an attribute selection measure. The ideal partition would be pure (i.e., all the tuples that fall into a given partition would belong to the same class) if we were to divide D into smaller partitions based on the results of the splitting criterion. The splitting criterion that yields the closest results in such a case is conceptually the "best" splitting criterion. Because they specify how the tuples at a specific node are to be split, attribute selection measures are also known as splitting rules.

Each attribute describing the given training tuples is ranked using the attribute selection measure (The best result is determined by the measure's highest or lowest score (i.e., some measures strive to maximize while others strive to minimize)). For the provided tuples, the attribute with the highest score for the measure is selected as the dividing attribute. A split point or a splitting subset must also be defined as part of the splitting criterion if the splitting attribute has continuous values or if binary trees are our only option. The splitting criterion is marked on the tree node made for partition D, branches are developed for each result of the criterion, and the tuples are partitioned as necessary. Three widely used attribute selection metrics are information gain, gain ratio, and Gini index.

Information gain: Information gain is the criterion used by ID3 to choose attributes. This measurement is based on Claude Shannon's ground-breaking information theory research, which examined the "information content" of signals. Let node N stand in for or contain the partition D tuples. The splitting attribute for node N is determined to be the one with the greatest information gain. This feature represents the least randomness or "impurity" in the generated partitions and reduces the amount of information required to categorize the tuples in those partitions. Such a method reduces the anticipated number of tests required to categorize a given tuple and ensures the discovery of a simple (but not necessarily the simplest) tree.

The expected information required to categorize a tuple in D is provided by

$$Info(D) = -\sum_{i=1}^{m} P_i log_2 P_i \quad (1)$$

where P_i is calculated as $|C_{i,D}|/|D|$ and represents the non-zero likelihood that each given tuple in D belongs to class C_i. The average amount of information required to determine a tuple's class label in D is called Info(D) or entropy of D.

Now, to categorize the tuples in D based on an attribute A that had v different values, such as $a_1, a_2, \cdots, a_v$, as seen in the training data. These values precisely equate to the v results of a test on A if A has discrete values. D can be divided into v divisions or subsets, $D_1, D_2, \cdots, D_v$, depending on the value of attribute A, where D_j includes the tuples in

D that match the outcome a_j of A. These divisions would line up with the branches that emerged from node N. This amount is measured by

$$Info_A(D) = \sum_{j=1}^{v} \frac{|D_j|}{|D|} \times Info(D_j) \qquad (2)$$

The difference between the initial information requirement (i.e., based solely on the proportion of classes) and the new requirement (i.e., as determined after partitioning on A) is known as the information gain. That is,

$$Gain(A) = Info(D) - Info_A(D) \qquad (3)$$

Gain(A) thus informs us of the gain that would result from branching on A. It is the anticipated decrease in the information needed to be brought on by understanding the value of A. The splitting attribute at node N is determined to be attribute A with the biggest information gain, Gain(A).

Gain ratio: The information gain metric favors tests with a wide range of results. In other words, it favors choosing qualities with a lot of possible values. Consider a property that serves as a distinctive identifier, such as a product ID. With a split based on product ID, there would be as many partitions as there are values, each carrying a single tuple. Each partition is pure; hence, the only data needed to categorize data set D using this partitioning would be $Info_{product_{ID}}(D) = 0$. As a result, partitioning on this attribute yields the most information. It is obvious that such a split is not useful for categorization.

In order to combat this prejudice, C4.5, the successor to ID3, introduces an addition to information gain known as a gain ratio. It uses a "split information" value defined analogously to Info(D) as a type of normalization to apply to information gain and is defined as

$$SplitInfo_A(D) = -\sum_{j=1}^{v} \frac{|D_j|}{|D|} \times log_2\left(\frac{|D_j|}{|D|}\right) \qquad (4)$$

This value shows the potential information that might be produced by partitioning the training data set, D, into v groups, each grouping the results of a test on attribute A. Notably, it takes into account the proportion of tuples that have each outcome relative to the total number of tuples in D for each outcome. It is distinct from information gain, which evaluates the classification of newly acquired information based on the same partitioning. A definition of the gain ratio is

$$GainRatio(A) = \frac{Gain(A)}{SplitInfo_A(D)} \qquad (5)$$

The attribute chosen as the splitting attribute is the one with the highest gain ratio.

Gini Index: In CART, the Gini index is employed. The Gini index calculates the impurity of D, a data partition or collection of training tuples as

$$Gini(D) = 1 - \sum_{i=1}^{m} P_i^2 \qquad (6)$$

where P_i is the probability that a tuple in D belongs to class C_i and is estimated by $|C_{i,D}|/|D|$. The sum is computed over m classes.

For each attribute, the Gini index takes a binary split into account. We calculate a weighted total of the impurity of each resulting partition while considering a binary split. As an illustration, if D is partitioned into D1 and D2 by a binary split on A, D's Gini index after that partitioning is

$$Gini_A(D) = \frac{|D_1|}{|D|}Gini(D_1) + \frac{|D_2|}{|D|}Gini(D_2) \qquad (7)$$

Each of the potential binary splits is taken into consideration for each attribute. The subset that has the lowest Gini index for a discrete-valued property is chosen as the subset's splitting subset.

Each potential split-point must be taken into account for continuous-valued attributes. Similar to the information gain approach previously discussed, the midpoint between each pair of (sorted) neighboring values is taken into consideration as a potential split-point. The split-point for a particular (continuous-valued) attribute is taken to be the point producing the smallest Gini index for that attribute. Remember that D_1 is the set of tuples in D satisfying the $A \leqslant SplitPoint$, and D_2 is the set of tuples in D satisfying the $A > splitPoint$, given a potential split-point of A.

The reduction in impurity that would result from a binary split on an attribute A with discrete or continuous values is

$$\Delta Gini(A) = Gini(D) - Gini_A(D) \tag{8}$$

The splitting attribute is chosen to optimize impurity reduction (or, equivalently, to have the lowest Gini index). The splitting criterion is the combination of this characteristic plus either its splitting subset (for a discrete-valued splitting attribute) or split-point (for a continuous-valued splitting attribute).

2.2. Neural Networks and Hybrid Models

Deep learning has surpassed human-level performance and capability in many areas, such as data classification, prediction and forecasting, the decision to approve loan applications, the time taken to deliver any object, etc. [41,42]. A decision tree creates a model that predicts the value of the targeted data or variable through the learning of simple decision rules from the data features. The DT algorithm is an easy one, as it is understandable and interpretable. DT works better for both categorical and numerical data and is able to handle multi-output data. In [43], the authors review several optimization methods with deep learning design, such as deep convolutional neural networks, recurrent neural networks, reinforcement learning, and autoencoders, to improve the accuracy of the training and show how we could reduce the training time with iterations.

Despite the enormous success of neural networks over the past decade, several industries, including health and security, have not adopted them widely or in a way that makes them more dependable. Researchers started looking into approaches to explain neural network decisions as a result of this fact. Saliency maps, approximation via interpretable methods, and joint models are some of the methodologies used to explain neural network judgments [44].

Saliency maps are a means to draw attention to the parts of the input that a neural network uses most frequently while making predictions. To show an input-specific linearization of the entire network, an earlier study [45] uses the gradient of the neural network output with respect to the input. Another piece of work [46] uses a deconvnet to return to decisions' features. These methods frequently produce noisy saliency maps that make it difficult to understand the choices that were made. The derivative of a neural network's output with respect to an activation, often the one just before completely connected layers, is used in another track of approaches [47–50]. These approaches lack a thorough logical justification for the decision while being beneficial for tasks such as determining whether the decision's backing is solid.

The conversion of interpretable by-design models, such as decision trees, to neural networks, has attracted attention. A technique for initializing neural networks with decision trees was developed in [51]. Decision tree equivalents for neural networks are also provided by [32,52,53]. These works' neural networks have particular topologies; hence, there is no generalization to any model. In [54], neural networks were trained so that trees could reasonably approximate their decision limits. Decision trees are only used as a regularization in this work; they are not provided as a correlation between neural networks and decision trees. In [55], a decision tree was trained using a neural network. This tree distillation performs badly on the tasks that the neural network was trained on since it approximates a neural network rather than performing a direct conversion.

Joint neural network and decision tree models [56–62] typically employ deep learning to support some trees or to create a neural network structure that mimics a tree. In a recent paper [63], a decision tree is used in place of a neural network's final fully connected layer. Since neural networks' fundamental characteristics remain the same, an explanation is sought through the provision of a method for people to judge if a decision is good or bad rather than through a thorough, logical analysis of it.

In [64], the authors discuss the characteristics of DNN for image processing, and they provide two typical algorithms for saliency detection by using DNN. They then analyze three future robust developments of deep learning. The authors in [65] present a deep learning method for the machine identification of traffic signals. First, various stochastic gradient optimization algorithms, such as SGD (Stochastic Gradient Descent), nesterov accelerated gradient (NAG), RMSprop, and Adam, are tested. Subsequently, several configurations of spatial transformer networks are studied. A model with feature extraction and a learning algorithm of DNN is proposed in [66] to classify and recognize the patterns in Antarctica with hydrological features and is compared with some existing classification methods. The study in [67] proposed a two-stage deep feature fusion for scene classification, where the authors showed the advantage of using lower-layer features compared to exploiting fully connected layers.

Some commonly used deep learning architectures and their practical implementations are addressed in [41]. The authors surveyed four deep learning architectures, namely autoencoder, convolutional neural network, deep belief network, and restricted Boltzmann system, to provide an up-to-date overview. In this context, the authors in [32] proposed a deep neural decision tree (DNDT) by using the NN toolkit, and they evaluated the model's performance on various tabular datasets. In many datasets, they have proved that a decision tree-based neural network can achieve better accuracy compared to only a decision tree-based approach or only an NN-based approach. Another notable recent approach to constructing a deep forward neural network using a decision tree is introduced in [51], where the authors used their model to classify iris, digits, wine, and breast cancer data. However, their proposed model does not work for classifying non-planar data.

An extreme learning machine tree (ELM-Tree) model was proposed in [16]. The model tree provided in [68] and the ELM-Tree is comparable. A model tree and an ELM-Tree differ in that an ELM-Tree has each leaf node be an ELM, whereas a model tree is a decision tree with linear regression functions as leaf nodes. Single-hidden layer feedforward neural networks can be trained using ELMs or emergent learning methods. In an ELM, the output weights are calculated analytically using the pseudoinverse of the hidden layer output matrix, whereas the input weights are allocated at random [69–71]. In the ELM-Tree approach, a threshold is provided to decide whether or not to divide a node further. According to the class of impurity, if the learner chooses to stop splitting a node, it will either turn into a conventional leaf node or an ELM leaf node. Then, a parallel ELM-Tree model for big-data classification is created by parallelizing computation across five ELM-Tree components. Although the technique leverages information gain in node splitting, which has a tendency to be biased towards the attributes of picking more branches and results in overfitting.

3. Materials and Methods

The research methods and proposed models, along with their algorithms, have been discussed in this section as follows:

3.1. The Proposed DTBDNN Model

The relation between input and output data gets more complicated in the case of high-dimensional input data and a large number of training samples [36]. For a particular data classification test case, it is difficult to find how a single neural network predicts a particular classification decision due to their dependency on distributed hierarchical representations [72]. Hence, in this research, we aim to build an efficient solution that acquires knowledge using a DNN model. This acquired knowledge is then expressed in another model that exploits the hierarchical decision tree structure to predict a particular classification decision efficiently and with good accuracy.

This section represents the proposed model, namely the decision tree-based deep neural network (DTBDNN) for nonlinear data classification that considers DNN with multiple hidden layers. In our model, we can route the input examples to leaf nodes of the neural network (the output layer) and classify them. Thus, training the neural network becomes training the soft bin cut points, and finally, leaf node classifiers perform the final computation for the classification decision. Then, we demonstrate a considerable difference between our proposed model and other state-of-the-art models when classifying nonlinear data. Further, the performance evaluations of the proposed DTBDNN in terms of accuracy and loss error are presented. The architectural overview of the methodology for building the proposed DTBDNN models is shown in Figure 1.

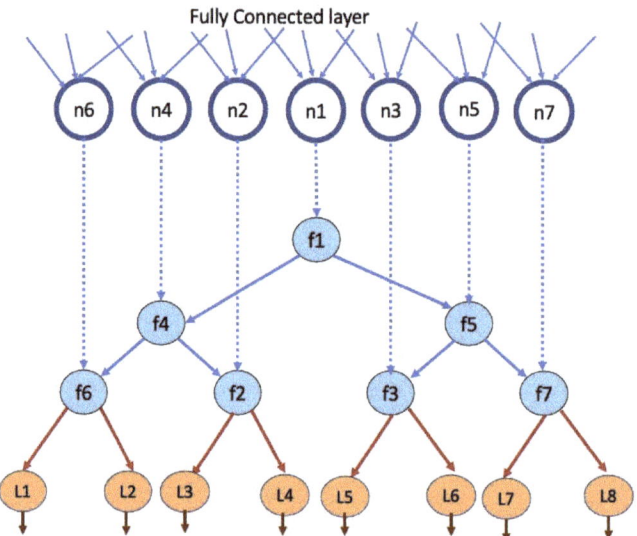

Figure 1. Architectural overview of the proposed model. Illustration of how to implement a decision tree-based neural network. The routing (split) decisions are created when each output of f_n is brought into correspondence with a split node in a tree. The assignment of output units to decision nodes can be performed in any order (the one we show allows a simple visualization). As a result of resolving the convex optimization issue, the circles at the bottom are leaf nodes containing probability distributions over the multiclass classification problem.

We defined decision functions f_n in terms of real-valued functions $f_n = tanh(W^T X + b)$, which are related but not necessarily independent due to the shared parametrization. By embedding functions f_n within a deep neural network with parameter W, we hope to give the trees the ability to learn new features. In particular, each function f_n can be viewed as a linear output unit of a deep network that will be converted into a routing choice by the action of f_n, which uses hyperbolic tangent activation to provide a response in the $[-1, 1]$ range. A schematic illustration of this concept is shown in Figure 1, which demonstrates how decision nodes can be built using commonly available fully connected (or inner-product) and tanh layers in DNN frameworks. It is clear that the number of output nodes in the fully connected layer above determines the number of split nodes. Because of this, the output units of the deep network under the proposed structure do not directly offer the final predictions, such as through a Softmax layer, but rather, each unit is in charge of influencing a node's decision inside the tree. In fact, a data sample x causes soft activations of the tree's routing decisions during the forward run through the deep network, which causes the routing function to generate a variety of leaf predictions that make up the final output.

The approach for determining if the datasets are linearly separable is depicted in the next section by using the data visualization technique. A dataset would be linearly separated if a linear function could separate the features of the dataset completely. In contrast, a nonlinear dataset is defined if no hyperplane lies on the pre-assigned side of the plane. For the DTBDNN models, we implemented a two-class NN classification with one hidden layer and a two-class DNN classification with multiple hidden layers, respectively. In the hidden layer(s) of NN and DNN, we use a nonlinear activation function unit, which is the tanh function for the forward propagation, whereas another activation function unit is used in a single node output layer, which is the sigmoid function. The reason for this is that deep neural networks' excellent speculation capacity is based on their use of conveyed representations in their hidden layers [73]. After tuning the performance of the NN and DNN models, we also found out and verified that the tanh activation function unit for every hidden layer would be best when we used the sigmoid activation function in the output layer. Further, we demonstrate that these nonlinear activation function combinations would be better than any other activation function combinations for any type of planar data classification.

3.1.1. System Model Overview

We design our decision tree-based deep neural network model by initially identifying the number of input, hidden, and output layers in the defined network structure. The main function that we used to make split decisions in our model is the soft-binning function. Typically, a soft-binning function takes the input features and produces an index of the bin to which the input features belong. Instead of using a hard-binning function, we have used a soft-binning function so that it can be differentiable during the back propagation phase of the neural network training. Then we construct multiple hidden layers. After that, we update the weights of the parameters and bias of the structure, where inputs are multiplied with the respective weights, adding a bias at each hidden node or unit, as shown in Figure 2. Typically, in each hidden unit, we have applied a nonlinear activation function "tanh", while in the output layer, the activation function undergoes a transformation based on another activation function, which is a sigmoid function. The input is squashed into a narrow output range from 0 to 1 and from -1 to 1 for the "sigmoid" and "tanh" functions, respectively. The acquired knowledge from the DNN model is expressed in another model that relies on the hierarchical decision tree algorithm to predict planar data classification with high accuracy. Then the prediction result of the final output layer is used as the solution to the problem of nonlinear data classification. For better presentation and exploration, we selected a nonlinear multi-colored flower dataset [74].

Figure 2 depicts the output of a given node as $H_i^{[L]}$, where "L" denotes the hidden layer numbers and "i" represents the specific units in that hidden layer. The output is calculated as the dot products of the input vector with the initialized pseudo-random weight (W) and adding the results with the bias (b). This intermediate result is then passed on to the nonlinear activation function g, which could be tanh, sigmoid, RELU, or Leaky RELU. We chose "tanh" as the activation function in a unit of the hidden layer because, by tuning the parameters, we found that it would gain better performance for the nonlinear data classification than using any other activation functions.

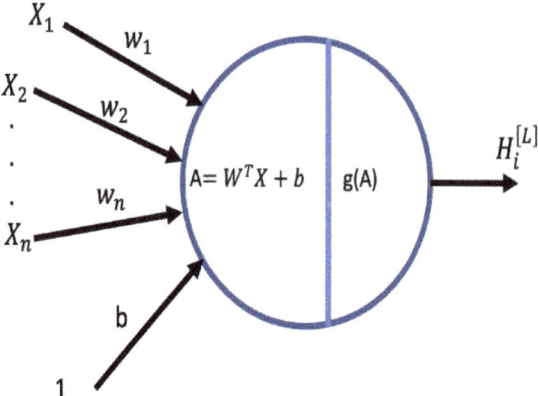

Figure 2. Hidden node in a hidden layer.

Figure 3 shows the general architecture of a deep neural network, where each node's functionality is depicted in Figure 2. The input to the network is an n-dimensional vector. The network contains L-1 hidden layers (two in this case) having n neurons each. Finally, there is one output layer containing k neurons (say, corresponding to k classes). Each neuron in the hidden layer and output layer can be split into two parts: preactivation and activation (a_i and h_i are vectors). The input layer can be called the 0-th layer, and the output layer can be called the L-th layer. $W_i \in \mathbb{R}^{n \times n}$ and $b_i \in \mathbb{R}^n$ are the weight matrix and bias vectors between layers $i-1$ and i ($0 < i < L$). $W_L \in \mathbb{R}^{n \times k}$ and $b_L \in \mathbb{R}^k$ are the weight matrix and bias vectors between the last hidden layer and the output layer (L = 3 in this case). The preactivation at layer i is given by

$$a_i(x) = W_i h_{i-1}(x) + b_i \tag{9}$$

The activation at layer i is given by

$$h_i(x) = g(a_i(x)) \tag{10}$$

where g is called the activation function. The activation at the output layer is given by

$$h_L(x) = O(a_L(x)) \tag{11}$$

where O is the output activation function (softmax, linear, etc.). Therefore, for this three-layer network, as shown in Figure 3, the predicted output $\hat{y}$ is a linear combination of weights, inputs, and biases:

$$\hat{y}_i = O(W_3 g(W_2 g(W_1 x + b_1) + b_2) + b_3) \tag{12}$$

If the actual output is y, then we can calculate the loss/cost function depending on whether we want to solve the regression problem or a classification problem. For regression types of problems, the cost function is a mean square error and is defined as

$$J(\Theta) = \min \frac{1}{N} \sum_{i=1}^{N} \sum_{j=1}^{k} (\hat{y}_{ij} - y_{ij})^2 \tag{13}$$

For classification types of problems, the cost function is a cross-entropy function and is defined as

$$J(\Theta) = -\frac{1}{N}(y_i \log(\hat{y}_i) + (1 - y_i) \log(1 - \hat{y}_i)) \tag{14}$$

where $\Theta = W_1, W_2, \cdots W_L, b_1, b_2, \cdots b_L$. In order to train the neural network, we have to minimize the cost function with respect to the parameters θ as follows

$$\Theta_{t+1} \leftarrow \Theta_t - \eta \nabla \Theta_t \qquad (15)$$

where $\nabla \Theta_t = \left[\frac{\delta J(\Theta)}{\delta W_t}, \frac{\delta J(\Theta)}{\delta b_t}\right]^T$, t is the iteration index, and η is the learning rate. The complete algorithm for training a deep neural network is given in Algorithm 1.

Algorithm 1 Deep Learning Algorithm Forward Propagation Along With Gradient Descent.

Require: Network depth, L
Require: $W_i, i \in 1 \cdots L$, the weight matrices of the model
Require: $b_i, i \in 1 \cdots L$, the bias parameters of the model
Require: X, the input to process
Require: y, the target output
  $h_0 \leftarrow x$
  $t \leftarrow 0$
  $maxIterations \leftarrow 1000$
  $\Theta_0 = [w_0, b_0]$
  while $t++ < maxIterations$ **do**
    $k = 1$
    while $k \leq L$ **do**
      $a_k = W_k h_{k-1} + b_k$
      $h_k = g(a_k)$
      $k = k + 1$
    end while
    $\hat{y} = h_L$
    $J(\Theta) = \mathcal{L}(y, \hat{y})$ ▷ $\mathcal{L}$ is the loss function
    $\Theta_{t+1} \leftarrow \Theta_t - \eta \nabla \Theta_t$ ▷ $\nabla \Theta_t = \left[\frac{\delta J(\Theta)}{\delta W_t}, \frac{\delta J(\Theta)}{\delta b_t}\right]^T$
  end while

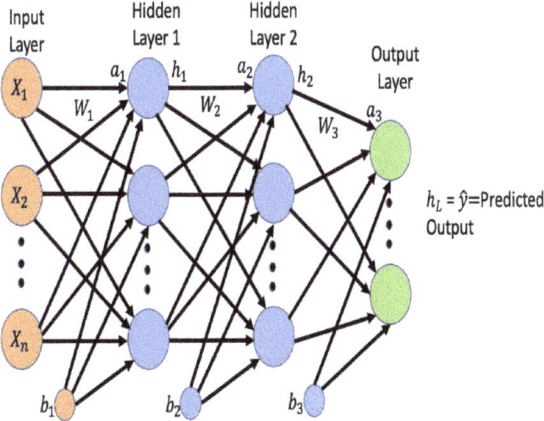

Figure 3. A Multilayer Deep Neural Network Architecture.

3.1.2. Decision Tree-Based Deep Neural Network (DTBDNN) Algorithm

In Algorithm 2, we introduce the algorithms for the DTBDNN model (number of hidden layers > 1). The main goal of this algorithm is to build a decision tree-based neural network framework in which the weight and bias are initialized and fed into the proposed DT with the optimized values from the DNN models. We set the parameter n_x as the input layer size, n_h as the hidden layer size, and n_p as the output layer size. Here, the parameters, the weight matrix of the hidden layer (W_1), and the weight matrix of the output layer (W_2) are initialized randomly to ensure that the initial weight cannot be large. Then, we initialize the bias vectors b_1 and b_2.

Algorithm 2 Decision Tree-Based Deep Neural Network (DTBDNN) Algorithm.

Require: X,W,b, Input, Weight, bias of the model
Require: y, the target output (Binary or Multiclass)
Require: Initialization: $h_0 \leftarrow X$; $g_1 \leftarrow tanh$; $g_2 \leftarrow sigmoid$; Cutpoints = $[c_1, c_2, \cdots, c_n] \leftarrow$ SoftBinning(X,n); bias vector $b = [0, -c_1, -c_1 - c_2, \cdots, -c_1 - c_2 - \cdots - c_n]$
  function ForwardPropagation
  $i \leftarrow 1$
  while $i \leq L$ **do**   ▷ L is the total number of layers, here L = 2
    $a_i = W_i h_{i-1} + b_i$
    $h_i = g_i(a_i)$
    $i = i + 1$
    Cache $\leftarrow a_i, h_i$
  end while
  $\hat{y} \leftarrow h_L$
  Return $\hat{y}$, Cache
  End ForwardPropagation
  function ComputeLoss
  $J(W,b) = -\frac{1}{N}(y_i log(\hat{y}_i) + (1 - y_i) log(1 - \hat{y}_i))$
  Return $J(W,b)$
  End ComputeLoss
  function BackPropagation
  Import a_1, h_1, a_2, h_2 from Cache
  $g_1' \leftarrow 1 - g_1^2$
  $\delta a_2 \leftarrow h_2 - y$
  $\delta W_2 \leftarrow \frac{1}{m} \times (\delta W_2 \times h_1^T)$
  $\delta b_2 \leftarrow \frac{1}{m} \times \sum \delta a_2$
  $\delta a_1 \leftarrow W_2^T \times \delta a_2 \times g_1' \times a_1$
  $\delta W_1 \leftarrow \frac{1}{m} \times \delta a_1 \times X^T$
  $\delta b_1 \leftarrow \frac{1}{m} \times \sum \delta a_1$
  grads $\leftarrow [\delta W_1, \delta W_2, \delta b_1, \delta b_2]$
  Return grads
  End BackPropagation
  function UpdateParameters
  $i \leftarrow 1$
  while $i \leq L$ **do**
    $W_i \leftarrow W_i - \eta \times \delta W_i$
    $b_i \leftarrow b_i - \eta \times \delta b_i$
  end while
  Parameters$\leftarrow W_i, b_i$
  Return Parameters
  End UpdateParameter

Then we apply the "soft-binning" function [39] on the input x to split nodes into multiple (>2) leaves. Assume we have an input x that we want to categorize into n cut points ($c_1, c_2, \ldots, c_n$) that are trainable variables in this context. Then, we calculate the output predictions by applying the forward propagation algorithm of a neural network and comparing those predictions with the actual output values. This helps us reveal and interpret the difference between the predicted and actual ones using a cross-entropy cost function. Based on this predicted probability, we can decide if the output is either red or green. For instance, the output is green when the value is 1 and red when the value is 0.

We used the cross-entropy loss [75–77] to verify the difference between our prediction and the actual values in Algorithm 2. The cost function defined in Equation (14) is computed. After implementing forward propagation through the NN model, we used back propagation along with the gradient descent algorithm for training our model to determine the derivatives of the loss function with respect to the parameters and updating our parameters (W_1, b_1, and W_2, b_2). These steps are repeated until we find the lowest cost or global optimal point.

If we only use the decision tree model, the performance would not be very efficient. However, when the DT learning is integrated with the DNN models, the proposed approach acts as a recursive partitioning for the nonlinearly separable training samples. Particularly in the DTBDNN model, before performing the prediction phase, each node is added to the tree depending on the input samples, which are used to select the logical test at every node. Then, the proposal will decide which model will be used for the data classification. We used TensorFlow to implement our DTBDNN model because it supports "out-of-the-box" GPU acceleration.

4. Experimental Results, Performance Evaluations and Discussion

In this section, we present the results of the traditional logistic regression model classification and those of the DTBDNN model (number of hidden layers >= 1) classifications using the datasets in [78]. Then, we validate the efficiency of our proposed model in conjunction with the complex dataset through a subjective test in which we demonstrate that our model would be more stable to learn in the presence of outliers in the dataset with a large number of training samples. By comparing our proposed model to conventional nonlinear data classification, we find that the prediction and classification procedure in our model can converge quickly because it is based on fewer sequences of decisions, with each decision directly dependent on the training samples of the input data.

4.1. Dataset and Visualization

We have taken a nonlinearly separable dataset [78], which generates two-class classification. After visualization of the dataset, as depicted in Figure 4a, we demonstrate that it has two classes, represented by the red and green points, in the form of a flower with a color pattern. Specifically, if p = 0, then the data are labeled as red, and if p = 1, then they are labeled as green. The plot shows that the data are not linearly separable. Hence, our goal is to apply DNN classifiers, which are driven by DT, to predict the correct class of data with high accuracy and classify those data using our proposed model.

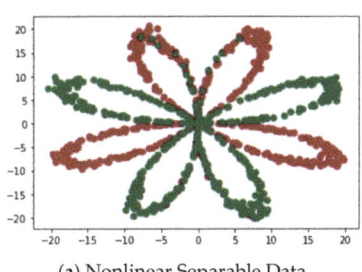
(a) Nonlinear Separable Data

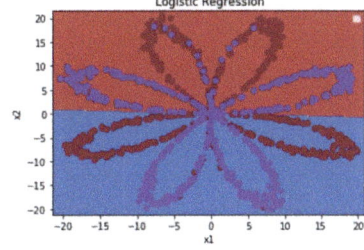
(b) Classification using Logistic Regression

Figure 4. Classification of nonlinear data using logistic regression model.

4.2. Context-Based Logistic Regression Model's Result

Because the obtained training samples in the dataset are not linearly separable, logistic regression (LR) simply draws a straight line to separate the data into two classes, as shown in Figure 4b. Here, we can see that the LR model classifier can only classify 19% of data points correctly. The result validates that when the data points are not linearly separable, the LR classifier model will not be able to classify these types of data accurately.

We then take another dataset that contains only a linearly separable training sample and visualize the linearly separable data, as illustrated in Figure 5a. When we use these linearly separable data points, as expected, the LR classifier performs the data classification well with much higher accuracy. The decision boundary classification of the linearly separable data for the LR classifier is shown in Figure 5b, where the LR classifier can classify 99% of data points accurately.

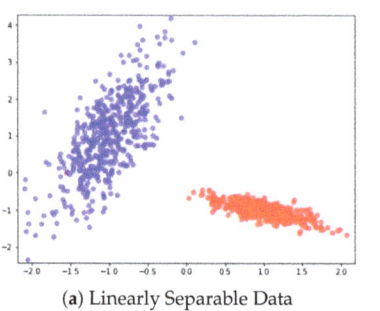
(a) Linearly Separable Data

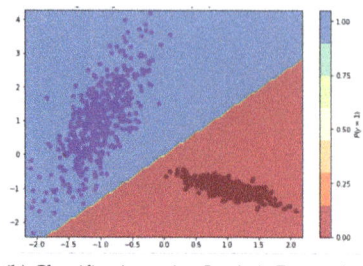
(b) Classification using Logistic Regression

Figure 5. Classification of linear data using the Logistic Regression model.

Hence, we can deduce that the LR classifier would be the best-fit model for linearly separable data or training samples, while it performs very poorly in the case of nonlinearly separable or complex data classifications.

4.3. The Proposed DTBDNN Model's Result

As described in the previous section, the selected parameters are used to predict the classification of the nonlinearly separable planar data group.

For all the training samples (m), we perform 10,000 epochs or iterations, i.e., 10,000 rounds of forward propagation and back propagation, to get the minimum cost. If the cost value is close to zero, then the model performance is said to be converged. We observed that the cost values after every 1000 iterations are decreasing to a close-to-zero value over the iterations, especially when the number of iterations surpasses 1000.

Since the imported dataset input contains nonlinear or planar training samples, we select the NN model using one hidden layer with multiple hidden nodes so that the acquired knowledge from the NN model is expressed and utilized in the DT model. The classification report of the NN model with its performance measurement parameters is shown in Table 1.

Table 1. Performance Measurement Parameters of the NN Model.

Attributes	Precision	Recall	F1-Score	Support
0	0.93	0.92	0.93	500
1	0.94	0.94	0.92	500
Micro Avg	0.94	0.93	0.93	500
Macro Avg	0.46	0.46	0.46	500
Weighted Avg	0.93	0.93	0.93	500
Sample Avg	0.94	0.93	0.93	500
Total	0.93	0.94	0.93	1000

When tuning the hidden layer size, we observe the interesting behavior of the proposed model. Specifically, by increasing the size of the hidden layer (i.e., the number of hidden nodes), we can measure the accuracy of the model and demonstrate its performance in terms of classifying any complex planar data. The accuracy over different numbers of hidden units in a hidden layer is shown in Table 2. The evaluation results show that the NN model achieves 93% accuracy for nonlinear data classification for hidden node sizes of 4 and above.

Table 2. Accuracy over different numbers of hidden nodes in the hidden layer.

Hidden Layer Size	Accuracy (%)
Accuracy for NN Model (No hidden layers)	93
Accuracy for 1 hidden unit	71.30
Accuracy for 2 hidden units	70.899
Accuracy for 3 hidden units	70.8
Accuracy for 4 hidden units	93.10
Accuracy for 5 hidden units	92.10
Accuracy for 20 hidden units	93.30

We now integrate our NN model into the proposed DT classifier. Specifically, the obtained update parameters from the NN model are fed into a set of rules given by the DT algorithm to predict the nonlinear data classification. The nonlinear classified data of our DTBDNN model is plotted in Figure 6a. The DTBDNN model achieves 95% accuracy for nonlinear and linear data classification when the hidden layer size is 4 (Figure 6b). The result shows that DTBDNN can classify the nonlinear or linear dataset's data with much higher accuracy compared to the traditional logistic regression method.

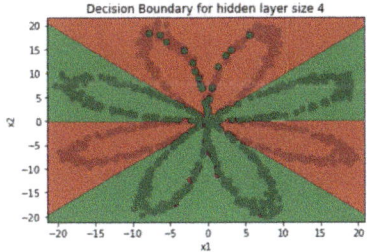
(a) Nonlinear data classification (DTBDNN)

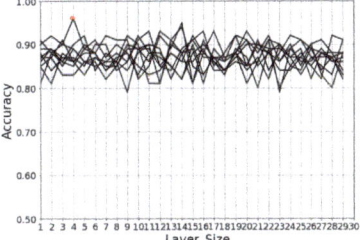
(b) Accuracy over hidden layer sizes

Figure 6. Accuracies of the DTBDNN model to classify nonlinear data.

Figure 7 depicts the convergence of accuracy in the DTBDNN model. The results show that the accuracy in DTBDNN tends to converge when the hidden layer reaches a threshold number, whereas, in the conventional NN model, the accuracy level does not converge for any particular hidden layer size. In fact, accuracy improves when the number of hidden nodes is increased. Typically, in the NN model, when the layer size of a hidden layer is 4, we get 93.1%, and we also get 93.3% accuracy in the case of 20 hidden units. In contrast, in the DTBDNN model, an increase in the size of a hidden layer results in an increase in accuracy, as shown in Figure 7. Furthermore, when the hidden layer size in the DTBDNN model reaches 19, accuracy convergence and maximum accuracy can be achieved, implying that the proposed model achieves 100% accuracy.

The linear/nonlinear data classification for different hidden units in a hidden layer is plotted in Figure 8. Moreover, the confusion matrix for the measurement of the accuracy of the DTBNN model is shown in Figure 9.

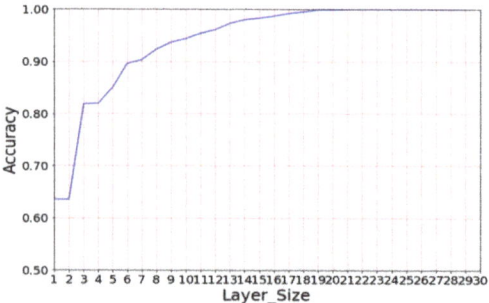

Figure 7. Convergence of accuracy over the different layer sizes of the DTBDNN model.

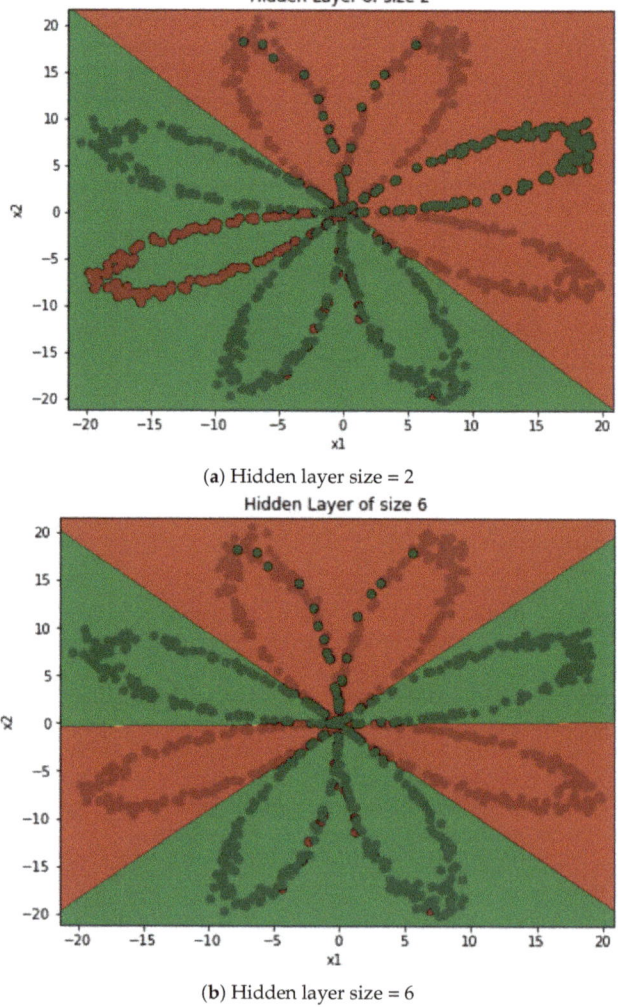

(**a**) Hidden layer size = 2

(**b**) Hidden layer size = 6

Figure 8. Decision boundary over different hidden layer sizes of the DTBNN model.

Then, we developed a DTBDNN model with multiple hidden layers and a higher number of hidden units at each layer to classify planar data with maximum accuracy. The accuracy, precision, recall, f1-score, and confusion matrix of the DTBDNN model are shown in Figure 9a. We observe that the DTBDNN model achieves 98% accuracy, and the precision, recall, and f1-score values are higher as well. The reason for the near-maximum accuracy in DTBDNN is the computation of the optimized cost value. Different from the DTBDNN model with only one hidden layer, in which the loss error values are decreased to near zero over iterations to reach the global minimum point for the classification of the planar data, the loss error value in the DTBDNN model is very close to zero after the predefined number of iterations. As a result, the accuracy of the DTBDNN model converges to the peak value quickly, as shown in Figure 9b.

Further, the computation of the cost-effective function and prediction accuracy are shown in Figure 10. The results show that the loss error decreases linearly from nearly 0.6 to 0.1 when the number of iterations is 1600, and the increase in the number of iterations leads to a small value of the loss error, which is almost zero. Hence, the proposed DTBDNN model can achieve a maximum of 100% accuracy in classifying the nonlinear data. The figure shows the computational cost in terms of loss calculation after each epoch, which demonstrates how well our model helps to reach the global minimum point for the classification of the nonlinear data with high accuracy in the DTBDNN model. From this figure, we see that after 1000 iterations, the value of the cost for different numbers of samples does not change.

Next, we take different numbers of training samples and compare the accuracy of the DTBDNN models (number of hidden layers = 1 (DTBNN) vs. number of hidden layers >1 (DTBDNN)), as plotted in Figure 11a. It can be seen that the DTBDNN model has a maximum accuracy of 100%. Moreover, the comparison between the loss error or cost values between DTBNN and DTBDNN over the different numbers of training samples is shown in Figure 11b. The result validates that the loss error values of the DTBNN model are decreasing to nearly zero over iterations but not to zero. For the iterations ranging from 0 to 1000, the loss error decreased linearly from 0.6 to 0.2, and afterward, irrespective of increasing the number of iterations, the loss error values did not decrease much. On the other hand, the loss error values for the DTBDNN model decrease significantly over the iterations, and they are close to zero after the first 1000 iterations. Hence, the DTBDNN model can achieve 100% accuracy, whereas the DTBNN model can only obtain up to 95% accuracy.

The noisy moon nonlinear dataset [78] was then used, as shown in Figure 12a. When fitting this dataset into our DTBDNN model, we achieve 97% accuracy where the cost value is only 0.077227, and the decision boundary for the hidden layer size is depicted in Figure 12b.

Then, we evaluate the application of the DTBDNN model on the noisy Gaussian dataset [78]. The result shows that after fitting the dataset in the DTBDNN model, we achieve 98% accuracy, and the loss error of our model value is minimized at 0.070100 after a pre-specified number of iterations. The corresponding dataset is plotted in Figure 13a, and the decision boundary after fitting the data with the proposed model is shown in Figure 13b.

```
Accuracy : 0.9566666666666667
Precision : 0.9444444444444444
recall : 0.9645390070921985
f1 Score : 0.9543859649122806

[[136    8]
 [  5  151]]
```

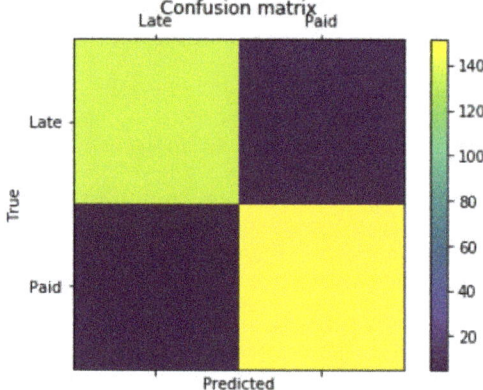

(a) Confusion matrix of the DTBNN model

```
Accuracy : 0.98
Precision : 0.9794520547945206
recall : 0.9794520547945206
f1 Score : 0.9794520547945206

[[143    3]
 [  3  151]]
```

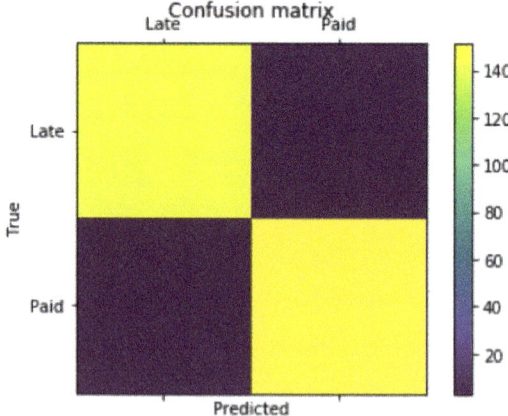

(b) Confusion matrix of the DTBDNN model

Figure 9. Confusion matrix with accuracy of the DTBNN model and DTBDNN model.

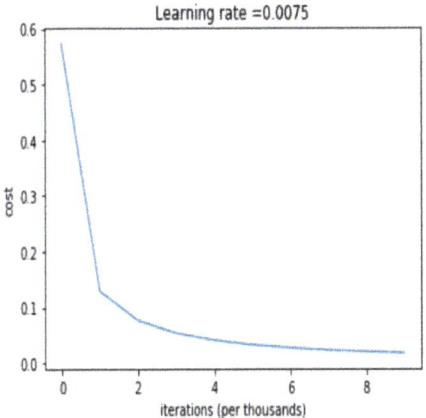

Figure 10. Accuracy of the DTBDNN model.

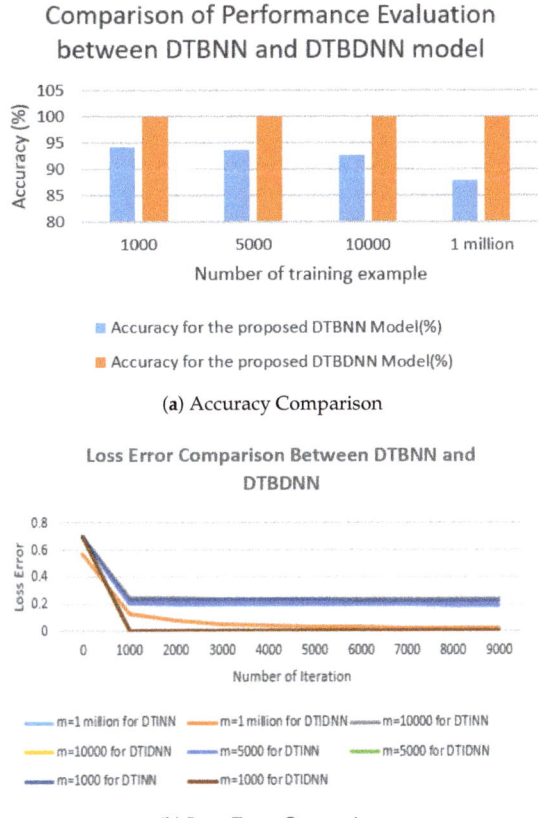

(a) Accuracy Comparison

(b) Loss Error Comparison

Figure 11. Comparison of performance evaluation between DTBNN and DTBDNN models.

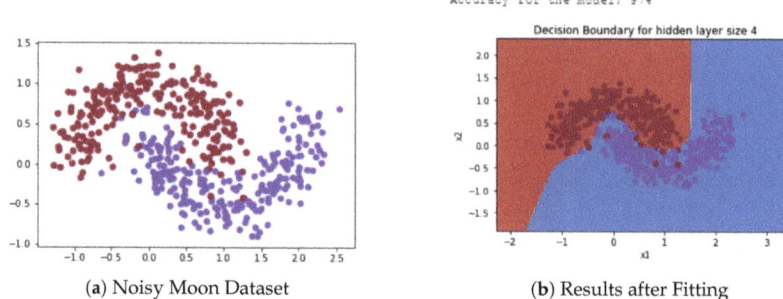

Figure 12. Visualization of the noisy moon dataset and results after fitting the DTBDNN model into the noisy moon dataset.

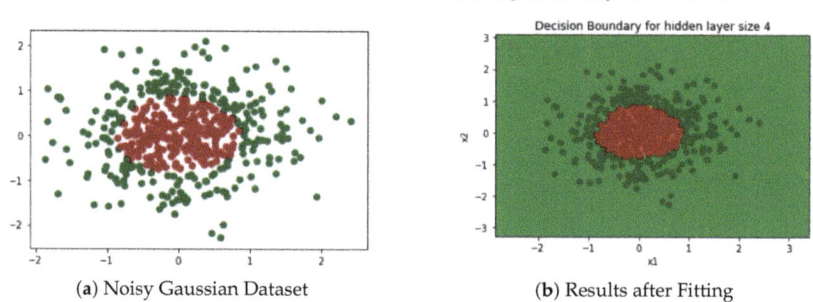

Figure 13. Visualization of the noisy Gaussian dataset and results after fitting the DTBDNN model into the noisy Gaussian dataset.

The blobs dataset [78] is another meaningful dataset where multiple circles are plotted on the same surface with different radii. This dataset is also a sample of a nonlinear dataset, and it can be solved by our proposed DTBDNN model with a high accuracy rate of 91%. The training samples of the blobs dataset are shown in Figure 14a, and the decision boundary for the DTBDNN model to classify the blobs dataset's training samples is shown in Figure 14b.

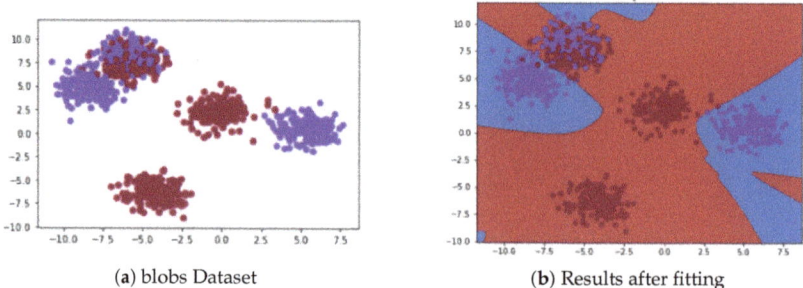

Figure 14. Visualization of the blobs dataset and results after fitting the DTBDNN model into the blobs dataset.

Further, Table 2 reveals that our proposed models achieve a maximum accuracy above 90% in different contexts compared to other related and relevant models. The DTBNN and DTBDNN models can then improve the performance of NN and DNN, respectively, by analyzing the loss error function and tuning the hidden layers and output activation functions to optimize the data classification of the separable datasets, especially the nonlinear ones. This proposed framework then enables a feasible and highly efficient approach to training the predictive models for nonlinear data classifications with a wide range of complex nonlinear datasets.

Finally, we have conducted an experiment to evaluate our proposed approach and DT-based algorithm on different datasets collected from UCI. On 10 different datasets gathered from UCI, we evaluate our suggested approach, DTBDNN, versus DT (C4.5 algorithm) versus another state-of-the-art algorithm, ELM-Tree. Table 3 shows the dataset's specifics as well as the test accuracies of DTBDNN, DT, and ELM-Tree. Two of the critical hyperparameter criteria were set to "gini" and "best" for the DT baseline. For the neural network (DTBDNN), we employ a two-hidden-layer architecture with 40 neurons per layer for all datasets. The number of cut points for each feature (also known as the branching factor) is another hyper-parameter in DTBDNN that we set to 1 for all features and datasets. We employ an ensemble of DTBDNN for datasets with more than 12 features, with a total of 10 trees, each of which randomly selects 10 features. The ultimate forecast is provided by majority voting. The DTBDNN is the model that performs the best overall. It is not unexpected that DT performed well, given that these datasets are primarily tabular and have a small feature dimension. Because the hyperparameters in each of these models are adjustable, this is simply an indicative result. It's intriguing that neither model has a clear advantage, though.

Scalability is a problem for induction using decision trees. In other words, the training set of class-labeled tuples stored on disk does not fit in the memory. Or, to put it another way, how scalable is decision tree induction? For comparatively small datasets, the effectiveness of current decision tree algorithms, such as ID3, C4.5, and CART, has been well demonstrated. When these algorithms are used to mine very large real-world databases, efficiency becomes a concern. The limitation of the ground-breaking decision tree algorithms that we have so far covered is that the training tuples must be stored in memory. Very large training sets with millions of tuples are typical in data mining applications. The training data will frequently be too large to fit in memory!

As a result, switching training tuples between main and cache memories makes decision tree construction inefficient. There is a need for more scalable methods that can handle training data that are too big to fit in the memory. Earlier methods of "saving space" included sampling data at each node and discretizing continuous-valued features. However, these methods continue to rely on the notion that the training set may be stored in memory.

Due to mini-batch training in the style of a neural network, DTBDNN scales well with the number of instances. The design, however, has a significant flaw in that it cannot accommodate an increase in the number of features. To avoid this problem with "large" datasets by training a forest with random subspace at the cost of interpretability [52]. Adding numerous trees, each trained on a random subset of characteristics, is what this means. Utilizing the sparsity of the final binning during learning, where the number of non-empty leaves grows far more slowly than the total number of leaves, is a preferable option that avoids the need for an unintelligible forest. However, this makes the otherwise straightforward implementation of DTBDNN a little more complex.

Table 3. Testing accuracies of DTBDNN and decision tree (C4.5 algorithm) and ELM-Tree models.

Dataset	No. of Instances	No. of Features	No. of Classes	DTBDNN	DT	ELM-Tree
Wireless Indoor Localization	2000	7	4	87.21	86.79	86.4
OBS-Network	1075	22	4	96.76	95.87	96.12
Gime-Me-Some-Credit	201,669	10	2	97.78	91.89	95.56
SARS B-cell Epitope Prediction	14,387	13	2	85.34	68.93	81.1
Pima Indian Diabetes	768	8	2	67.23	71.56	74.48
MAGIC Gamma Telescope	19,020	11	2	83.56	80.76	82.58
Waveform Noise	5000	40	3	75.21	69.76	75.2
Credit Approval	690	15	2	81.35	83.32	81.23
Healthy Older People	75,128	9	4	97.35	95.34	96.67
Flight Delay	1,100,000	9	2	77.89	66.67	75.34

5. Conclusions

We created the DTBDNN models in this paper to obtain the most relevant parameters for processing nonlinear data classification by combining the benefits of DT and DNN. In particular, DT extracts the knowledge from the trained DNN models, which are generated from the input data for nonlinear data classification, instead of performing this classification directly from the input data or training samples. A full set of induction algorithms is developed to build and train the DNN model. As a result, the in-depth performance evaluations demonstrate that for classifying any nonlinear data, the proposed models demonstrate a substantial performance improvement compared to the widely used techniques, including decision tree. We then conclude that the proposed model outperformed the relevant state-of-the-art approaches in terms of predicting the nonlinear data classification with the stability of the model and can be used for the realization of efficient prediction to classify any nonlinear or planar data with higher accuracy.

Future employment opportunities are numerous. We want to find out what caused the self-regularization we saw, investigate adding DTBDNN as a module to a traditional convolutional neural network (CNN) feature learner for end-to-end learning of image data, determine whether DTBDNN's whole-tree ADAM-based learning can be used as postprocessing to improve the performance of conventionally greedily trained DTs, and determine whether the various neural-network-based transfer learning approaches can be used to enable transfer learning.

Author Contributions: Conceptualization, M.A.; Data curation, T.J.T.; Formal analysis, A.K.P.; Software, M.R.H.; Writing—original draft, T.J.T. and S.B.H.; Writing—review and editing, A.K.P. All authors have read and agreed to the published version of the manuscript.

Funding: This research received no external funding.

Data Availability Statement: The data used in this study are available upon request.

Conflicts of Interest: The authors declare no conflict of interest.

References

1. Krizhevsky, A.; Sutskever, I.; Hinton, G.E. ImageNet Classification with Deep Convolutional Neural Networks. *Commun. ACM* **2017**, *60*, 84–90. [CrossRef]
2. Hu, Z.; Bodyanskiy, Y.V.; Kulishova, N.Y.; Tyshchenko, O.K. A multidimensional extended neo-fuzzy neuron for facial expression recognition. *Int. J. Intell. Syst. Appl.* **2017**, *9*, 29. [CrossRef]
3. Hu, Z.; Ivashchenko, M.; Lyushenko, L.; Klyushnyk, D. Artificial Neural Network Training Criterion Formulation Using Error Continuous Domain. *Int. J. Mod. Educ. Comput. Sci.* **2021**, *3*, 13–22. [CrossRef]
4. Hu, Z.; Tereykovskiy, I.A.; Tereykovska, L.O.; Pogorelov, V.V. Determination of structural parameters of multilayer perceptron designed to estimate parameters of technical systems. *Int. J. Intell. Syst. Appl.* **2017**, *9*, 57. [CrossRef]
5. Ng, A. Machine Learning Yearning. 2017. Available online: https://www.mlyearning.org/ (accessed on 1 September 2022).
6. Paul, A.K.; Das, D.; Kamal, M.M. Bangla Speech Recognition System Using LPC and ANN. In Proceedings of the 2009 Seventh International Conference on Advances in Pattern Recognition, Kolkata, India, 4–6 February 2009; pp. 171–174. [CrossRef]
7. Muhammad, K.; Ahmad, J.; Mehmood, I.; Rho, S.; Baik, S.W. Convolutional Neural Networks Based Fire Detection in Surveillance Videos. *IEEE Access* **2018**, *6*, 18174–18183. [CrossRef]

8. Paul, A.K.; Sato, T. Localization in Wireless Sensor Networks: A Survey on Algorithms, Measurement Techniques, Applications and Challenges. *J. Sens. Actuator Netw.* **2017**, *6*, 24. [CrossRef]
9. Paul, A.K.; Yanwei, L.; Sato, T. A Distributed Range Free Sensor Localization with Friendly Anchor Selection Strategy in Anisotropic Wireless Sensor Network. *Trans. Jpn. Soc. Simul. Technol.* **2013**, *4*, 96–106.
10. Paul, A.K.; Qu, X.; Wen, Z. Blockchain—A promising solution to internet of things: A comprehensive analysis, opportunities, challenges and future research issues. *Peer-to-Peer Netw. Appl.* **2021**, *14*, 2926–2951. [CrossRef]
11. Asghar, M.A.; Khan, M.J.; Fawad; Amin, Y.; Rizwan, M.; Rahman, M.; Badnava, S.; Mirjavadi, S.S. EEG-Based Multi-Modal Emotion Recognition using Bag of Deep Features: An Optimal Feature Selection Approach. *Sensors* **2019**, *19*, 5218. [CrossRef]
12. Zhai, J.; Wang, X.; Zhang, S.; Hou, S. Tolerance Rough Fuzzy Decision Tree. *Inf. Sci.* **2018**, *465*, 425–438. [CrossRef]
13. Kolsbjerg, E.L.; Peterson, A.A.; Hammer, B. Neural-network-enhanced evolutionary algorithm applied to supported metal nanoparticles. *Phys. Rev. B* **2018**, *97*, 195424. [CrossRef]
14. Fubao, Z.; Mengmeng, T.; Lijie, X.; Haodong, Z. A Classification Algorithm of CART Decision Tree based on MapReduce Attribute Weights. *Int. J. Perform. Eng.* **2018**, *14*, 17. [CrossRef]
15. OrShea, J.; Crockett, K.; Khan, W.; Bandar, Z.; Bandar, Z. A hybrid model combining neural networks and decision tree for comprehension detection. In Proceedings of the 2018 International Joint Conference on Neural Networks (IJCNN), Rio de Janeiro, Brazil, 8–13 July 2018; pp. 1–7. [CrossRef]
16. Wang, R.; He, Y.L.; Chow, C.Y.; Ou, F.F.; Zhang, J. Learning ELM-Tree from Big Data Based on Uncertainty Reduction. *Fuzzy Sets Syst.* **2015**, *258*, 79–100. [CrossRef]
17. Zhang, J.; Yu, K.; Wen, Z.; Qi, X.; Paul, A.K. 3D Reconstruction for Motion Blurred Images Using Deep Learning-Based Intelligent Systems. *Comput. Mater. Contin.* **2021**, *66*, 2087–2104. [CrossRef]
18. Peng, X.; Feng, J.; Xiao, S.; Yau, W.Y.; Zhou, J.T.; Yang, S. Structured AutoEncoders for Subspace Clustering. *IEEE Trans. Image Process.* **2018**, *27*, 5076–5086. [CrossRef]
19. Raissi, M.; Wang, Z.; Triantafyllou, M.S.; Karniadakis, G.E. Deep learning of vortex-induced vibrations. *J. Fluid Mech.* **2018**, *861*, 119–137. [CrossRef]
20. Ma, T.; Benon, K.; Arnold, B.; Yu, K.; Yang, Y.; Hua, Q.; Wen, Z.; Paul, A.K. Bottleneck Feature Extraction-Based Deep Neural Network Model for Facial Emotion Recognition. In *Proceedings of the Mobile Networks and Management*; Loke, S.W., Liu, Z., Nguyen, K., Tang, G., Ling, Z., Eds.; Springer International Publishing: Cham, Switzerland, 2020; pp. 30–46.
21. Chhowa, T.T.; Rahman, M.A.; Paul, A.K.; Ahmmed, R. A Narrative Analysis on Deep Learning in IoT based Medical Big Data Analysis with Future Perspectives. In Proceedings of the 2019 International Conference on Electrical, Computer and Communication Engineering (ECCE), Cox's Bazar, Bangladesh, 7–9 February 2019; pp. 1–6. [CrossRef]
22. Canziani, A.; Paszke, A.; Culurciello, E. An Analysis of Deep Neural Network Models for Practical Applications. *arXiv* **2016**, arXiv:1605.07678. [CrossRef]
23. Bianco, S.; Cadene, R.; Celona, L.; Napoletano, P. Benchmark Analysis of Representative Deep Neural Network Architectures. *IEEE Access* **2018**, *6*, 64270–64277. [CrossRef]
24. Cheng, G.; Li, Z.; Yao, X.; Guo, L.; Wei, Z. Remote Sensing Image Scene Classification Using Bag of Convolutional Features. *IEEE Geosci. Remote Sens. Lett.* **2017**, *14*, 1735–1739. [CrossRef]
25. Zhang, Y.D.; Zhang, Y.; Hou, X.X.; Chen, H.; Wang, S.H. Seven-Layer Deep Neural Network Based on Sparse Autoencoder for Voxelwise Detection of Cerebral Microbleed. *Multimed. Tools Appl.* **2018**, *77*, 10521–10538. [CrossRef]
26. Tang, B.; Tu, Y.; Zhang, Z.; Lin, Y. Digital Signal Modulation Classification With Data Augmentation Using Generative Adversarial Nets in Cognitive Radio Networks. *IEEE Access* **2018**, *6*, 15713–15722. [CrossRef]
27. Yao, X.; Guo, J.; Hu, J.; Cao, Q. Using Deep Learning in Semantic Classification for Point Cloud Data. *IEEE Access* **2019**, *7*, 37121–37130. [CrossRef]
28. Miikkulainen, R.; Liang, J.; Meyerson, E.; Rawal, A.; Fink, D.; Francon, O.; Raju, B.; Shahrzad, H.; Navruzyan, A.; Duffy, N.; et al. Evolving Deep Neural Networks. *arXiv* **2017**, arXiv:1703.00548. [CrossRef]
29. Wang, J.; Ding, Y.; Bian, S.; Peng, Y.; Liu, M.; Gui, G. UL-CSI Data Driven Deep Learning for Predicting DL-CSI in Cellular FDD Systems. *IEEE Access* **2019**, *7*, 96105–96112. [CrossRef]
30. Paul, A.K.; Khan, J.M.; Parvin, T.T. Convolutional Neural Network Based Real Time Pneumonia Detection Using Transfer Learning and Image Augmentation. In Proceedings of the ICSTEM4IR 2022, Khulna, Bangladesh, 1–3 July 2022; pp. 28–39.
31. Goodfellow, I.J.; Bengio, Y.; Courville, A. *Deep Learning*; MIT Press: Cambridge, MA, USA, 2016. Available online: http://www.deeplearningbook.org (accessed on 1 September 2022).
32. Yang, Y.; Morillo, I.G.; Hospedales, T.M. Deep Neural Decision Trees. *arXiv* **2018**, arXiv:1806.06988. [CrossRef]
33. Song, Q.; Xu, F.; Jin, Y.Q. Reconstruction of Full-Pol SAR Data from Partialpol Data Using Deep Neural Networks. In Proceedings of the IGARSS 2018—2018 IEEE International Geoscience and Remote Sensing Symposium, Valencia, Spain, 22–27 July 2018; pp. 4383–4386. [CrossRef]
34. Guan, J.; Lai, R.; Xiong, A. Wavelet Deep Neural Network for Stripe Noise Removal. *IEEE Access* **2019**, *7*, 44544–44554. [CrossRef]
35. Xu, G.; Su, X.; Liu, W.; Xiu, C. Target Detection Method Based on Improved Particle Search and Convolution Neural Network. *IEEE Access* **2019**, *7*, 25972–25979. [CrossRef]
36. Hatcher, W.G.; Yu, W. A Survey of Deep Learning: Platforms, Applications and Emerging Research Trends. *IEEE Access* **2018**, *6*, 24411–24432. [CrossRef]

37. Min, E.; Guo, X.; Liu, Q.; Zhang, G.; Cui, J.; Long, J. A Survey of Clustering With Deep Learning: From the Perspective of Network Architecture. *IEEE Access* **2018**, *6*, 39501–39514. [CrossRef]
38. Wang, W.; Gao, Z.; Zhao, M.; Li, Y.; Liu, J.; Zhang, X. DroidEnsemble: Detecting Android Malicious Applications With Ensemble of String and Structural Static Features. *IEEE Access* **2018**, *6*, 31798–31807. [CrossRef]
39. Dougherty, J.; Kohavi, R.; Sahami, M. Supervised and Unsupervised Discretization of Continuous Features. In *Machine Learning Proceedings 1995*; Prieditis, A., Russell, S., Eds.; Morgan Kaufmann: San Francisco, CA, USA, 1995; pp. 194–202.
40. Han, J.; Kamber, M.; Pei, J. *Data Mining Concepts and Techniques*, 3rd ed.; Morgan Kaufmann Publishers: Waltham, MA, USA, 2012.
41. Liu, W.; Wang, Z.; Liu, X.; Zeng, N.; Liu, Y.; Alsaadi, F.E. A survey of deep neural network architectures and their applications. *Neurocomputing* **2017**, *234*, 11–26. [CrossRef]
42. Shin, H.C.; Roth, H.R.; Gao, M.; Lu, L.; Xu, Z.; Nogues, I.; Yao, J.; Mollura, D.; Summers, R.M. Deep Convolutional Neural Networks for Computer-Aided Detection: CNN Architectures, Dataset Characteristics and Transfer Learning. *arXiv* **2016**, arXiv:1602.03409. [CrossRef]
43. Shrestha, A.; Mahmood, A. Review of Deep Learning Algorithms and Architectures. *IEEE Access* **2019**, *7*, 53040–53065. [CrossRef]
44. Aytekin, C. Neural Networks are Decision Trees. *arXiv* **2022**, arXiv:2210.05189. [CrossRef]
45. Simonyan, K.; Vedaldi, A.; Zisserman, A. Deep Inside Convolutional Networks: Visualising Image Classification Models and Saliency Maps. *arXiv* **2013**, arXiv:1312.6034. [CrossRef]
46. Zeiler, M.D.; Fergus, R. Visualizing and Understanding Convolutional Networks. *arXiv* **2013**, arXiv:1311.2901. [CrossRef]
47. Zhou, B.; Khosla, A.; Lapedriza, A.; Oliva, A.; Torralba, A. Learning Deep Features for Discriminative Localization. *arXiv* **2015**, arXiv:1512.04150. [CrossRef]
48. Selvaraju, R.R.; Cogswell, M.; Das, A.; Vedantam, R.; Parikh, D.; Batra, D. Grad-CAM: Visual Explanations from Deep Networks via Gradient-Based Localization. In Proceedings of the 2017 IEEE International Conference on Computer Vision (ICCV), Venice, Italy, 22–29 October 2017; pp. 618–626. [CrossRef]
49. Chattopadhay, A.; Sarkar, A.; Howlader, P.; Balasubramanian, V.N. Grad-CAM++: Generalized Gradient-Based Visual Explanations for Deep Convolutional Networks. In Proceedings of the 2018 IEEE Winter Conference on Applications of Computer Vision (WACV), Lake Tahoe, NV, USA, 12–15 March 2018; pp. 839–847. [CrossRef]
50. Draelos, R.L.; Carin, L. Use HiResCAM instead of Grad-CAM for faithful explanations of convolutional neural networks. *arXiv* **2020**, arXiv:2011.08891. [CrossRef]
51. Humbird, K.D.; Peterson, J.L.; Mcclarren, R.G. Deep Neural Network Initialization With Decision Trees. *IEEE Trans. Neural Netw. Learn. Syst.* **2019**, *30*, 1286–1295. [CrossRef]
52. Kontschieder, P.; Fiterau, M.; Criminisi, A.; Bulo, S.R. Deep Neural Decision Forests. In Proceedings of the 2015 IEEE International Conference on Computer Vision (ICCV), Santiago, Chile, 7–13 December 2015; pp. 1467–1475. [CrossRef]
53. Sethi, I. Entropy nets: From decision trees to neural networks. *Proc. IEEE* **1990**, *78*, 1605–1613. [CrossRef]
54. Wu, M.; Hughes, M.C.; Parbhoo, S.; Zazzi, M.; Roth, V.; Doshi-Velez, F. Beyond Sparsity: Tree Regularization of Deep Models for Interpretability. In Proceedings of the Thirty-Second AAAI Conference on Artificial Intelligence, New Orleans, LA, USA, 2–7 February 2018.
55. Frosst, N.; Hinton, G. Distilling a Neural Network Into a Soft Decision Tree. *arXiv* **2017**, arXiv:1711.09784. [CrossRef]
56. Shazeer, N.; Fatahalian, K.; Mark, W.R.; Mullapudi, R.T. HydraNets: Specialized Dynamic Architectures for Efficient Inference. In Proceedings of the 2018 IEEE/CVF Conference on Computer Vision and Pattern Recognition, Salt Lake City, UT, USA, 18–23 June 2018; pp. 8080–8089. [CrossRef]
57. Redmon, J.; Farhadi, A. YOLO9000: Better, Faster, Stronger. *arXiv* **2016**, arXiv:1612.08242. [CrossRef]
58. Murdock, C.; Li, Z.; Zhou, H.; Duerig, T. Blockout: Dynamic Model Selection for Hierarchical Deep Networks. In Proceedings of the 2016 IEEE Conference on Computer Vision and Pattern Recognition (CVPR), Las Vegas, NV, USA, 27–30 June 2016; pp. 2583–2591. [CrossRef]
59. Murthy, V.N.; Singh, V.; Chen, T.; Manmatha, R.; Comaniciu, D. Deep Decision Network for Multi-class Image Classification. In Proceedings of the 2016 IEEE Conference on Computer Vision and Pattern Recognition (CVPR), Las Vegas, NV, USA, 27–30 June 2016; pp. 2240–2248. [CrossRef]
60. Roy, A.; Todorovic, S. Monocular Depth Estimation Using Neural Regression Forest. In Proceedings of the 2016 IEEE Conference on Computer Vision and Pattern Recognition (CVPR), Las Vegas, NV, USA, 27–30 June 2016; pp. 5506–5514. [CrossRef]
61. McGill, M.; Perona, P. Deciding How to Decide: Dynamic Routing in Artificial Neural Networks. *arXiv* **2017**, arXiv:1703.06217. [CrossRef]
62. Veit, A.; Belongie, S. Convolutional Networks with Adaptive Inference Graphs. *arXiv* **2017**, arXiv:1711.11503. [CrossRef]
63. Wan, A.; Dunlap, L.; Ho, D.; Yin, J.; Lee, S.; Jin, H.; Petryk, S.; Bargal, S.A.; Gonzalez, J.E. NBDT: Neural-Backed Decision Trees. *arXiv* **2020**, arXiv:2004.00221. [CrossRef]
64. Zhao, R.; Ouyang, W.; Li, H.; Wang, X. Saliency detection by multi-context deep learning. In Proceedings of the 2015 IEEE Conference on Computer Vision and Pattern Recognition (CVPR), Boston, MA, USA, 7–12 June 2015; pp. 1265–1274. [CrossRef]
65. García, Á.A.; Álvarez, J.A.; Soria-Morillo, L.M. Deep neural network for traffic sign recognition systems: An analysis of spatial transformers and stochastic optimisation methods. *Neural Netw.* **2018**, *99*, 158–165. [CrossRef]
66. Wu, Q.; Fan, C.; Chen, H.; Gu, D. Construction of a Neural Network and its Application on Target Classification. *IEEE Access* **2019**, *7*, 29709–29721. [CrossRef]

67. Liu, Y.; Liu, Y.; Ding, L. Scene Classification Based on Two-Stage Deep Feature Fusion. *IEEE Geosci. Remote Sens. Lett.* **2018**, *15*, 183–186. [CrossRef]
68. Frank, E.; Wang, Y.; Inglis, S.; Holmes, G.; Witten, I.H. Using Model Trees for Classification. *Mach. Learn.* **1998**, *32*, 63–76. [CrossRef]
69. Huang, G.B.; Wang, D.H.; Lan, Y. Extreme learning machines: A survey. *Int. J. Mach. Learn. Cybern.* **2011**, *2*, 107–122. [CrossRef]
70. Huang, G.B.; Zhou, H.; Ding, X.; Zhang, R. Extreme Learning Machine for Regression and Multiclass Classification. *IEEE Trans. Syst. Man, Cybern. Part B* **2012**, *42*, 513–529. [CrossRef] [PubMed]
71. Huang, G.B.; Zhu, Q.Y.; Siew, C.K. Extreme learning machine: Theory and applications. *Neurocomputing* **2006**, *70*, 489–501. [CrossRef]
72. Vinayakumar, R.; Alazab, M.; Soman, K.P.; Poornachandran, P.; Al-Nemrat, A.; Venkatraman, S. Deep Learning Approach for Intelligent Intrusion Detection System. *IEEE Access* **2019**, *7*, 41525–41550. [CrossRef]
73. LeCun, Y.; Bengio, Y.; Hinton, G. Deep learning. *Nature* **2015**, *521*, 436. [CrossRef]
74. Reyes-Nava, A.; Sánchez, J.; Alejo, R.; Flores-Fuentes, A.; Rendón, E. Performance Analysis of Deep Neural Networks for Classification of Gene-Expression Microarrays. In *Pattern Recognition*; Springer: Berlin/Heidelberg, Germany, 2018; pp. 105–115. [CrossRef]
75. Bosman, A.S.; Engelbrecht, A.; Helbig, M. Visualising basins of attraction for the cross-entropy and the squared error neural network loss functions. *Neurocomputing* **2020**, *400*, 113–136. [CrossRef]
76. Rusiecki, A. Trimmed Robust Loss Function for Training Deep Neural Networks with Label Noise. In Proceedings of the ICAISC, Zakopane, Poland, 16–20 June 2019.
77. Wang, S.; Liu, W.; Wu, J.; Cao, L.; Meng, Q.; Kennedy, P.J. Training deep neural networks on imbalanced data sets. In Proceedings of the 2016 International Joint Conference on Neural Networks (IJCNN), Vancouver, BC, Canada, 24–29 July 2016; pp. 4368–4374. [CrossRef]
78. UCI Machine Learning Repository. Available online: http://archive.ics.uci.edu/ml/index.php (accessed on 25 October 2022).

Disclaimer/Publisher's Note: The statements, opinions and data contained in all publications are solely those of the individual author(s) and contributor(s) and not of MDPI and/or the editor(s). MDPI and/or the editor(s) disclaim responsibility for any injury to people or property resulting from any ideas, methods, instructions or products referred to in the content.

Case Report

Dynamic Storage Location Assignment in Warehouses Using Deep Reinforcement Learning

Constantin Waubert de Puiseau [1,*], Dimitri Tegomo Nanfack [2], Hasan Tercan [1], Johannes Löbbert-Plattfaut [2] and Tobias Meisen [1]

1. Institute for Technologies and Management of Digital Transformation, Lise-Meitner-Strasse 27, 42119 Wuppertal, Germany
2. Ingstep GmbH, Ferdinand-Thun-Straße 52B, 42289 Wuppertal, Germany
* Correspondence: waubert@uni-wuppertal.de

Abstract: The warehousing industry is faced with increasing customer demands and growing global competition. A major factor in the efficient operation of warehouses is the strategic storage location assignment of arriving goods, termed the dynamic storage location assignment problem (DSLAP). This paper presents a real-world use case of the DSLAP, in which deep reinforcement learning (DRL) is used to derive a suitable storage location assignment strategy to decrease transportation costs within the warehouse. The DRL agent is trained on historic data of storage and retrieval operations gathered over one year of operation. The evaluation of the agent on new data of two months shows a 6.3% decrease in incurring costs compared to the currently utilized storage location assignment strategy which is based on manual ABC-classifications. Hence, DRL proves to be a competitive solution alternative for the DSLAP and related problems in the warehousing industry.

Keywords: warehouse management; logistics; dynamic storage location assignment; reinforcement learning; deep learning; artificial intelligence

Citation: Waubert de Puiseau, C.; Nanfack, D.T.; Tercan, H.; Löbbert-Plattfaut, J.; Meisen, T. Dynamic Storage Location Assignment in Warehouses Using Deep Reinforcement Learning. *Technologies* **2022**, *10*, 129. https://doi.org/10.3390/technologies10060129

Academic Editor: Mohammed Mahmoud

Received: 28 October 2022
Accepted: 9 December 2022
Published: 11 December 2022

Publisher's Note: MDPI stays neutral with regard to jurisdictional claims in published maps and institutional affiliations.

Copyright: © 2022 by the authors. Licensee MDPI, Basel, Switzerland. This article is an open access article distributed under the terms and conditions of the Creative Commons Attribution (CC BY) license (https://creativecommons.org/licenses/by/4.0/).

1. Introduction

The increasing market share of e-commerce and shorter delivery time promises require more flexible and optimized warehouses so that goods are stored and retrieved efficiently. One of the main objectives of operating warehouses lies in the reduction of transport times of pallets from one location to another within the warehouse [1]. The problem of determining where to optimally store goods in a warehouse upon entry or reentry into the system is commonly defined as the Dynamic Storage Location Assignment Problem (DSLAP). The combinatorial nature of the problem as well as uncertainties about the timing of future demands for different goods renders the problem inherently challenging to solve. In other words, whenever a single storage location assignment is needed, the effect of the decision depends on future decisions and required storage operations that may only be predicted to a certain extent a priori. In practice, the storage location assignment task is often handled manually and relies on the expertise of human workers. This expertise predominantly lies in knowledge about the frequency, seasonality, and timing of storage and retrieval operations of goods in warehouses. In the current state of research, more advanced approaches for tackling DSLAP problems exist. They are typically based on a statistical analysis of historical data and warehouse simulations for the derivation of heuristic, metaheuristic, and storage policy-based solution methods [2].

In recent years, machine learning algorithms have increasingly been utilized for the derivation of powerful statistical models in many application domains. For planning problems, deep reinforcement learning (DRL) has emerged as a promising alternative solution approach. It is a machine learning paradigm in which a reinforcement learning agent (RL agent) autonomously derives solution strategies from trial-and-error experiences by updating neural network parameters based on a feedback signal (reward) [3]. DRL is applicable to sequential decision problems that can be formulated as Markov Decision Processes, i.e., processes in which any next decision can be inferred from the cur-rent situation alone and is independent of previous states of the process [3]. A formal introduction to DRL is presented in Section 4.1. Most famously, DRL has been applied to board and video games, where it resulted in superhuman performance without the supervision and input of experts [4,5]. Driven by these successes, the adaption to use cases in industrial planning problems, such as scheduling problems, has also recently been carried out [6–11]. Since the DSLAP can be formulated as a Markov Decision Process, DRL is theoretically also applicable to the DSLAP and related problems.

In this paper we report a practical case study on a new problem setting in the young field of DRL-based DSLAP solutions. The case study is based on a real-world warehouse from which operational data was stored over the course of 14 months. A DRL agent is trained in simulated re-runs to dynamically assign storage locations with the data of the first twelve months and then evaluated in simulations with data of the last two months. The main contributions of this paper are:

- The empirical proof-of-concept that a real-world DSLAP may be solved end-to-end using DRL.
- Practical design choices for solving the presented DSLAP using DRL.

The remainder of this paper is structured as follows: in Section 2, we discuss related work addressing the DSLAP with machine learning methods. The real-world use case defining the object of study is described in Section 3. Our DRL solution approach is detailed in Section 4. Section 5 covers the experimental setup and used benchmarks. The results are presented in Section 6, followed by a critical discussion of the results in Section 7 and conclusive remarks in Section 8.

2. Related Work

The DSLAP has attracted research interest for a long time and many algorithmic solution methods have been proposed. Most recent methods are metaheuristic algorithms [12,13], but tailored solutions based on statistical analysis and manually defined rules [14] or integer linear programming models [15] also continue to be developed. For a survey of solution methods for the DSLAP, we refer the interested reader to Ref. [2].

The capability of machine learning models to derive useful information from warehouse operation data has been investigated in several research works. For example, Li et al. [16] trained a deep learning model to predict the duration-of-stay (DoS), i.e., the time a pallet is going to stay at the assigned location within the warehouse. This prediction is then leveraged in a constraint optimization algorithm to reach the final allocation decision. To obtain a more direct strategy using machine learning, Rimélé et al. [17] proposed a deep learning model to predict the probabilities with which a Monte-Carlo-Tree-Search (MCTS) algorithm would have assigned a particular storage location. To generate a suitably labeled dataset, extensive MCTS runs are required before training. Berns et al. [18], used decision trees to predict zones A, B, or C for pallets entering a simulated warehouse, where each class represents a zone in the warehouse to which the pallet is then transported. All approaches mentioned above have shown performance increases compared to previous methods used in each respective scenario. However, they rely on time-consuming manual labeling by experts or expert systems of historic operations because they are supervised learning methods. In contrast, the method we propose in this case study is based on DRL and therefore does not rely on manual labels.

The general feasibility of DRL for variations of the DSLAP has also been explored recent years. Kim et al. [19] addressed a DSLAP in a ship block stockyard to minimize the rearrangement of ship blocks. In the described setting, ship blocks are assigned a storage location and often must be rearranged due to new unforeseen circumstances. The authors trained two DRL agents, one that assigns the primary location and one that performs all relocations. Another DSLAP variation was studied by Rimélé et al. [20]. Here, a DRL agent was trained to assign pallets to one of six different zones upon new arrival at the warehouse.

The pallet was then transported to the chosen zone by a robot, which picks up a retrieval order on the way back to the entrance. Both publications report substantial improvements of the DRL-based methods over the existing method.

In this paper, we describe a real-world use case of the DLSAP and a methodology to tackle it effectively using DRL. Similarly to the works in Refs. [19,20], we exclusively use DRL for the solution generation, but we address a generally different warehouse logic and layout. In addition, compared to prior publications, no information about future demand is available as a basis for each new storage location assignment. Therefore, the DRL agent, similarly to experts in the warehouse, must learn when and how often certain products are moved solely from historic data and then act accordingly.

3. Use Case

In the following we describe the outline, logic and simulation of the studied warehouse, the used data and the implementation details of the reinforcement learning approach.

3.1. Warehouse Outline, Logic and Simulation

The object of study is a real-world semi-automatic high-bay warehouse. It has a single point of entry for all arriving and departing goods, where the distribution onto a part of the first rack is carried out manually. The warehouse further consists of twelve lines of high-bay racks which are handled by two automatic storage and retrieval systems (ASTS) which can move freely along guide rails on corridors between racks (see Figure 1). In addition, goods can be moved via conveyor belts between rack 2 and 3, facilitating storage and retrieval from and on racks 3 and 4.

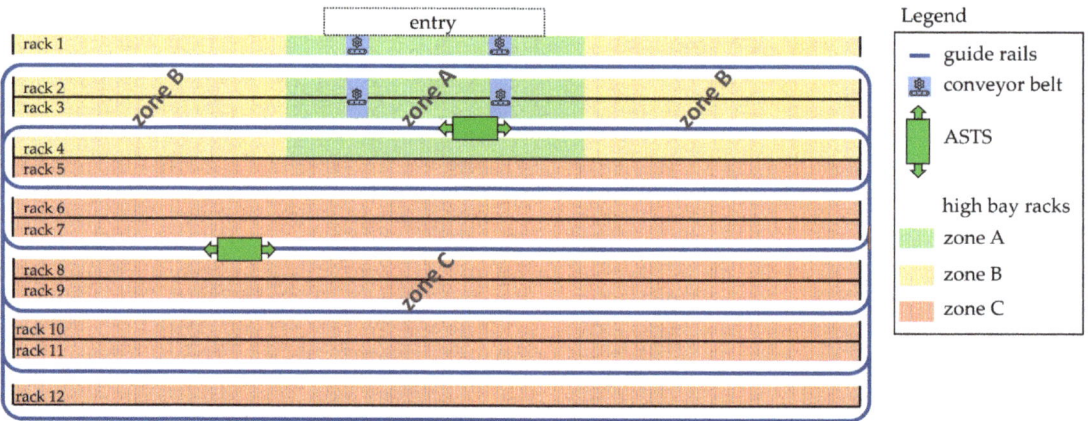

Figure 1. Schematic layout of the warehouse.

Operations in the warehouse follow a strict logic: When new goods arrive at the entry point, they are first assigned a storage location in the warehouse. All goods arrive on pallets containing varying amounts of multiple good types. The pallet is manually moved to the first rack and, depending on the assigned storage location, picked up by an ASTS that carries the pallet to the assigned destination. In the afternoon, pallets are often stored in a two-step process: they are first brought to a temporary location close to the entry and then moved to their final location during nighttime. Small conveyor belts installed in racks 1–3 can move pallets between two racks. Usually, one of the ASTS remains in the corridor between racks 3 and 4, because entering this corridor takes a particularly long time. In addition to newly arriving pallets, pallets may be brought to the entry point to retrieve some or all goods on them. If goods remain, a new storage location is determined. Otherwise, the pallet leaves the warehouse. The transport time between storage location assignment and arrival is roughly proportional to the cost of the storage process and therefore constitutes the objective to be globally minimized. In practice, the storage location assignment takes the form of a manual classification into class A, B or C for each pallet and is based on the experience of the worker. The three classes correspond to zones within the warehouse, for which the transportation time and cost are roughly the same. The zones are distributed as depicted in Figure 1.

The simulation that we used for conducting the experiments represents the described warehouse structure. It stores the current capacity utilization of the racks and keeps track of all transportation costs which arise from conducted storage and retrieval operations. The cost is represented by a unitless metric which corresponds to the mean relative transportation times measured in reality. Correspondingly, transportation operations to zone A take one cost unit, to zone B two cost units and to zone C ten cost units. The capacities of each zone are 9%, 25% and 66% of 9000 total storage locations for zone A, B and C, respectively. As a simplification, we did not consider the two-stage storing process which occurs in the afternoon but treat all pallets as if they were moved to their final location directly. We implemented the simulation logic in Python and follow the OpenAI Gym API guidelines [21], which present a common API for simulations used in reinforcement learning research and practice.

3.2. Real-World Data

The used data basis for training and testing of the DRL agent comprises of 12,100 items of historical information on storage and retrieval operations. The data contain all such operations of 500 different goods types collected between January 2021 and April 2022. The information for each operation consists of:

- A timestamp [YYYY-MM-DD hh-mm-ss] when the location assignment took place.
- The loaded good type identification number.
- The number of articles on the pallet.
- The date on which the pallet was first packed and entered the warehouse system.
- The type of storage location assignment (first entry or re-entry after partial retrieval of articles).
- The class (A, B or C), assigned to the pallet based on subjective experience by human workers.

4. Reinforcement Learning Approach

In this section, an introduction to DRL and the design choices of the proposed approach are presented regarding the action design of the agent, the observation space, the reward formulation, and the learning algorithm along with its hyperparameters. Unless stated otherwise, they were obtained through preliminary experiments.

4.1. Introduction to Deep Reinforcement Learning

Reinforcement learning (RL) can roughly be categorized into value-based and policy-based methods. Value-based methods update Q-values representing the expected discounted cumulative reward given the current state s for all available actions a:

$$Q^\pi(s,a) = \mathbb{E}_\pi \left[\sum_{k=0}^{\infty} \gamma^k R(s_t|a_t) | s_0 = s, a_0 = a \right] \quad (1)$$

The policy of the RL agent during inference is obtained by choosing the action with the maximal corresponding Q-value for each state. Since the number of different states in scheduling problems is very large, the function representing the Q-values is approximated with a deep neural network and updated using the gathered data during training [3]. A popular representative of value-based methods is DQN [22]. Policy-based methods optimize the policy π more directly by learning a function mapping a state s to an action.

This function, in DRL, is also approximated using a deep neural network parameterized with parameters θ. The updates to the policy function follow the gradient

$$\nabla_\theta J(\theta|s) = \mathbb{E}_{\pi_\theta}[Q^\pi(s,a) \cdot \nabla_\theta \log \pi_\theta(s,a)] \quad (2)$$

which was first proposed in Ref. [23]. A popular modern representative is Proximal Policy Optimization (PPO) [24].

4.2. Action Space and Interaction with the Simulation

A storage location assignment is required whenever a pallet is in the front of the warehouse (entry) and not empty. The actions the DRL agent may take mirrors the timing and possible choices of the decision-making process that is currently conducted by human workers in the warehouse: the DRL agent may assign a pallet to zone A, B or C. Hence, the action space of the DRL agent is discrete and of size three. The simulation automatically interprets the action and executes the process: changing the location status of the zone and adding the transport cost to the total cost. In the hypothetical situation in which a zone is full, the agent may not choose that zone. This exception is handled by the DRL algorithm and explained in Section 4.5.

4.3. Observation Space

In each step, the action should be based on the state of the warehouse, the characteristics of goods on the pallet for which the storage location must be assigned, the storage location assignment and the date. The necessary information on the state of the warehouse is the current capacity utilization in each of the zones. Therefore, the capacity CAP of the warehouse is represented as a three-dimensional vector

$$CAP = \left[\frac{\text{items in } A}{\text{total capacity of } A}, \frac{\text{items in } B}{\text{total capacity of } B}, \frac{\text{items in } C}{\text{total capacity of } C} \right]. \quad (3)$$

The goods information is represented by a vector containing the multi-hot encoded goods type (vector of zeros with length 500). The type of storage location assignment is binary: a 0 indicates that the pallet is entering the warehouse for the first time, whereas a 1 indicates a re-entry. The date is encoded as a single value representing the day of the year. It is scaled through division by 365. From these three features, the agent is supposed to learn, when and how often particular good types are moved in the warehouse. The aggregated resulting observation vector is of length 505.

4.4. Reward Design

The chosen reward is directly proportional to the resulting cost of each operation and was scaled such that a stable learning was reached in preliminary experiments. Accordingly, the assignment to zone A is rewarded (or rather punished) with -0.01, the assignment to zone B with -0.02 and to zone C with -0.1 (confer Equation (2)). Note that the sum of all rewards over an observed period will be proportional to the total transportation cost in that time. The agent is supposed to learn to accept temporarily larger punishments for the sake of maintaining enough capacity in less expensive zones for more frequently moved pallets.

$$reward = \begin{cases} -0.01 & if\ action = Zone\ A \\ -0.02 & if\ action = Zone\ B \\ -0.1 & if\ action = Zone\ C \end{cases} \quad (4)$$

4.5. Learning Algorithm and Hyperparameters

The chosen DRL-algorithm is PPO [24]. PPO is a popular DRL-algorithm for its stable learning behavior, and it is applicable to the chosen discrete action space design. We compared the performance of PPO with that of DQN [22] in preliminary experiments and observed far superior performance and learning behavior by PPO. Specifically, we deployed the action-masked version of PPO from the StableBaselines3 implementation [25]. Action masking ensures that no invalid actions, such as assigning a pallet to a full zone, may be taken by the agent during both training and deployment. Although the DRL agent could theoretically learn not to suggest invalid actions through the reward signal, our experiments showed much better learning behavior for the masked version. Suitable hyperparameters were obtained through trial and error. The ones that differ from the defaults of Ref. [25] are listed in Table 1.

Table 1. Used hyperparameters for PPO.

Hyperparameter	Value
alpha	0.0001
steps	19500
gamma	0.99
ent_coef	0.00
gae_lambda	1
vf_coef	0.5
n_epochs	10
batch_size	256
policy_kwargs: net_arch	[256, 256, 256]

All Code was implemented in Python and executed on an AMD Ryzen 7 4700U (8 MB Cache, 2 GHz) hardware. This relatively limited hardware configuration led to real-world applicable training times of about four hours and inference times for a single storage location allocation decision of 0.7 ms.

5. Experimental Setup

5.1. Train-Test Split

The division of all historic data into a training dataset and testing dataset is non-trivial, since more training data generally lead to a better generalization to unseen data but more testing data leads to more meaningful evaluations. In this study, the training data includes all data from February 2021 to January 2022. Accordingly, the testing data includes data from February 2022 and March 2022. This way, a seasonality in the frequency of storage and retrieval operations of certain goods, could be learned by the DRL agent from the training data and could be evaluated on the test data.

The training was performed with five different random seeds used for the random initialization of the neural network parameters.

5.2. Benchmarks

To evaluate the performance of the DRL agent, four rule-based benchmark storage location assignment methods were implemented:

1. *RANDOM:* The easiest benchmark method samples actions (A, B or C) randomly from a uniform distribution.
2. *Just-in-Order:* This method follows the intuition that the cheapest zones should be used to the limit. Therefore, as long as the capacity utilization of zone A is not 100%, pallets are assigned to zone A. When it is full, pallets are assigned to zone B and so on.
3. *ABC:* This method represents the currently running system in the warehouse. For this benchmark, we use those classes that were assigned by experts and executed in reality.
4. *DoS-Quantiles:* This method is engineered from historic data and serves as the strongest baseline, which can be created only in retrospective. It is based on the duration of stay (DoS) of a certain good type. Two quantiles $q1$ and $q2$ of the DoS are defined. When the historic average DoS of a good type on a pallet is smaller than or equal to $q1$, the pallet is assigned to zone A. If it is between $q1$ and $q2$, it is assigned to zone B. The rest is assigned to zone C. In a preliminary grid-search of quantile values

$q1 \in [0.35, 0.40, 0.45 \ldots 0.95]$ and $q2 \in [0.40, 0.45, 0.50 \ldots 1.00]$, $q1 = 0.70$ and $q2 = 0.90$ achieved the best results on the whole dataset.

In contrast to all rule-based benchmarks, the DRL agent incorporates knowledge about the current zone capacity utilization, which gives it a theoretical advantage. If one of the benchmark methods assigns a pallet to a full zone, the action is overwritten with the next cheapest zone for an assignment to zones B and C, and with B in case of an invalid assignment to A.

6. Results

The learning curve of the DRL agent over training steps on the x-axis is depicted in Figure 2. The solid black line indicates the cumulative reward of the DRL agent after each training episode, i.e., after all storage location assignment decisions of one year. It is averaged across the five random seeds. Minimum and maximum values across the random seeds are indicated by the gray shaded area. The horizontal lines depict the cumulative rewards of the benchmarks on the same training data: *DoS-Quantile* (orange), *ABC* (green), *RANDOM* (red) and *Just-in-Order* (blue) from top to bottom in that order. After around 2.5 Mio. executed actions (steps), the DRL agent already performs better than *Just-in-Order* on the training dataset. After 5 Mio. training steps, it consistently beats *RANDOM* and *ABC*. Around 20 Mio. steps into training it converges towards a value between *ABC* and *DoS-Quantile*. Note that, as previously mentioned, *DoS-Quantile* is an artificial benchmark created posteriori that represents an upper limit. It is noteworthy that all five DRL agents train very consistently and differ only marginally in their performance across training.

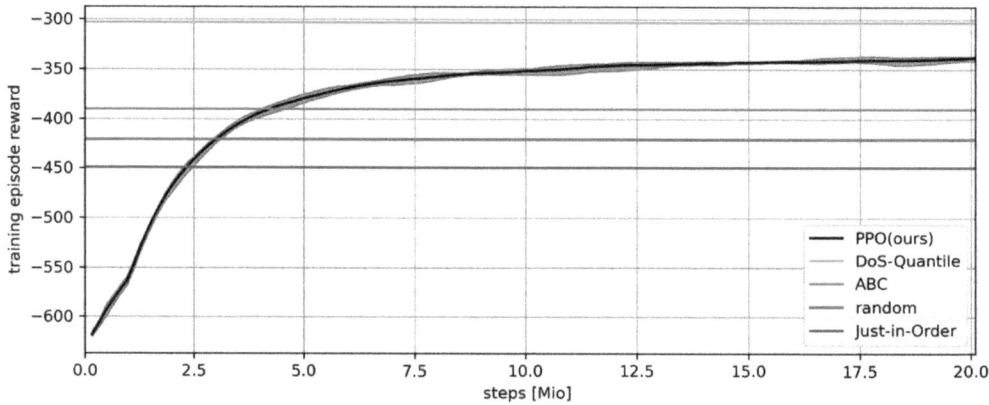

Figure 2. Learning curve of the DRL agent displaying the average and standard deviation of the cumulative reward on each training episode over training progress in million steps.

The results on the testing data are summarized in Table 2. The *Total Cost* column lists the unitless cost achieved by the DRL agent (PPO) and all five benchmarks. Thus, lower values represent better performances. The results are qualitatively similarly to the results on the training data: the DRL agent outperforms all realistic benchmark methods, including the reality-based *ABC* method, which it outperforms with 6.3% lower transportation costs.

Table 2. Results on the test data. DRL results are boldfaced.

Agent	Total Cost	Number of Assignments per Zone				Mean DoS per Zone		
		Total	A	B	C	A	B	C
PPO (Ours)	**37.78**	**1088**	**214**	**647**	**227**	**2.16**	**4.12**	**9.12**
DoS-Quantile	35.99	1088	257	621	210	2.58	3.83	16.12
ABC	40.34	1088	262	561	265	2.25	4.45	7.54
RANDOM	45.43	1088	369	377	342	4.41	4.95	4.29
Just-in-Order	45.70	1088	110	665	313	4.87	3.87	6.08

The *Number of Assignments per Zone* and *Mean DoS per Zone* columns give insights into the strategy learned by the DRL agent. Since *DoS-Quantile* is the best solution found on the data and *Just-in-Order* the worst, it is helpful to compare the results of PPO to those two. PPO assigns fewer pallets to zone A than *DoS-Quantile*, but more than *Just-in-Order*. One explanation is that PPO is pushed towards the *Just-in-Order* strategy at the beginning of training, because assigning most pallets to zone A gives the largest immediate reward. Over the course of training, the agent learns to move away from that short-sighted strategy for the sake of optimizing the cumulative reward across the whole learning episode. Yet, the number of assignments to zone A falls below the optimal number, indicating a potential remaining bias towards zone A.

The mean DoS per zone indicates that the DRL agent has successfully learned to classify goods into shorter and longer mean DoS in an assigned location. Pallets in zone A have the smallest mean DoS when assigned by the DRL agent compared to all benchmarks. However, the best strategy (*DoS-Quantile*) successfully lowers the mean DoS in zone B, which seems to be a better strategy, and realizes a very large DoS for zone C. This could be an artifact of changing DoS times throughout over time, which can lead to a difference between the training and test data.

7. Discussion and Future Work

A reliable reduction of 6.3% in transportation cost is a significant improvement. At the scale of modern warehouses, this brings a substantial competitive advantage. It is worth noting that the presented reinforcement learning approach is easily transferable to warehouses of other industries by modifying only use-case specific details (e.g., goods types and reward signals).

Moreover, we believe that further improvements of the results may be possible but exceed the scope of this case study. In the future we plan to analyze whether the potential bias towards zone A mentioned above can be addressed by means of different reward functions. Furthermore, as we have shown in Section 6, the solution strategy found by PPO does not lead to perfect mean DoS for zone C. We expect that the gap between mean DoS times per zone between *DoS-Quantile* and PPO would become narrower with more available training data. This data is constantly gathered in the warehouse and will be used in future studies. Lastly, the results could possibly be further improved through an extended hyperparameter optimization.

Despite the success, there are limitations to the provided methodology, currently still hindering its deployment. The first is a certain difference between the logic implemented in the simulation and reality. In reality, some pallets are preliminarily stored in zone A throughout the day and transported to the other zones at night (compare description of the two-stage storage process in Section 3.1). The slightly different logic may cause overflows in zone A or corrupt the learned strategy of the DRL agent. The second open challenge is posed by arrivals of new goods types, as the observation space of the DRL agent is fixed and depends on the total number of goods types. Therefore, the introduction of a new type of goods makes a re-training necessary. A direction of future research will be the effective handling and re-training for new types of goods.

8. Conclusions

This paper presented a successful application of deep reinforcement learning (DRL) to the dynamic storage location assignment problem (DSLAP) using real-world data for training and testing. The trained DRL agent effectively reduces the transportation cost in the warehouse presented in this study by 6.3% compared to the currently used method. The presented approach may easily be transferred to other warehouse layouts and logics. It can therefore be concluded that DRL is a promising approach for DSLAP that should be considered as an assistance system or even automated system when looking for more efficient warehouse operation.

Author Contributions: Conceptualization: C.W.d.P., J.L.-P. and T.M.; methodology: C.W.d.P. and D.T.N.; software: D.T.N.; resources: J.L.-P.; writing—original draft preparation: C.W.d.P.; writing—review and editing: H.T. and T.M. All authors have read and agreed to the published version of the manuscript.

Funding: This research received no external funding.

Institutional Review Board Statement: Not applicable.

Informed Consent Statement: Not applicable.

Data Availability Statement: Restrictions apply to the availability of these data. Data was obtained from an anonymous company owning the mentioned warehouse and are available upon request from the authors with the permission of said company.

Conflicts of Interest: The authors declare no conflict of interest.

References

1. Tompkins, J.; White, J.; Bozer, Y.; Tanchoco, J.M. *Facilities Planning*, 4th ed.; John Wiley & Sons: New York, NY, USA, 2010; ISBN 0470444045.
2. Reyes, J.J.R.; Solano-Charris, E.L.; Montoya-Torres, J.R. The storage location assignment problem: A literature review. *Int. J. Ind. Eng. Comput.* **2019**, *10*, 199–224. [CrossRef]
3. Sutton, R.S.; Barto, A. *Reinforcement Learning: An Introduction*, 2nd ed.; The MIT Press: Cambridge, MA, USA, London, UK, 2018; ISBN 9780262039246.
4. Badia, A.P.; Piot, B.; Kapturowski, S.; Sprechmann, P.; Vitvitskyi, A.; Guo, D.; Blundell, C. Agent57: Outperforming the Atari Human Benchmark. In Proceedings of the 37th International Conference on Machine Learning, Vienna, Austria, 12–18 July 2020; Volume 37, pp. 507–5017.
5. Vinyals, O.; Babuschkin, I.; Czarnecki, W.M.; Mathieu, M.; Dudzik, A.; Chung, J.; Choi, D.H.; Powell, R.; Ewalds, T.; Georgiev, P.; et al. Grandmaster level in StarCraft II using multi-agent reinforcement learning. *Nature* **2019**, *575*, 350–354. [CrossRef]
6. Samsonov, V.; Kemmerling, M.; Paegert, M.; Lütticke, D.; Sauermann, F.; Gützlaff, A.; Schuh, G.; Meisen, T. Manufacturing Control in Job Shop Environments with Reinforcement Learning. In Proceedings of the 13th International Conference on Agents and Artificial Intelligence, Online streaming, 4–6 February 2021; Rocha, A.P., Steels, L., van den Herik, J., Eds.; Science and Technology Publications Lda: Sétubal, Portugal, 2021; pp. 589–597, ISBN 978-989-758-484-8.
7. van Ekeris, T.; Meyes, R.; Meisen, T. Discovering Heuristics and Metaheuristics for Job Shop Scheduling from Scratch via Deep Reinforcement Learning. In Proceedings of the Conference on Production Systems and Logistics, online, 10–11 August 2021; pp. 709–718. [CrossRef]
8. de Puiseau, C.W.; Meyes, R.; Meisen, T. On reliability of reinforcement learning based production scheduling systems: A comparative survey. *J. Intell. Manuf.* **2022**, *33*, 911–927. [CrossRef]
9. Samsonov, V.; Hicham, K.B.; Meisen, T. Reinforcement Learning in Manufacturing Control: Baselines, Challenges and Ways Forward. *Eng. Appl. Artif. Intell.* **2022**, *112*, 104868. [CrossRef]
10. Iklassov, Z.; Medvedev, D.; Solozabal, R.; Takac, M. Learning to generalize Dispatching rules on the Job Shop Scheduling. *arXiv* **2022**, arXiv:2206.04423.
11. Baer, S.; Turner, D.; Mohanty, P.K.; Samsonov, V.; Bakakeu, R.J.; Meisen, T. Multi Agent Deep Q-Network Approach for Online Job Shop Scheduling in Flexible Manufacturing. In Proceedings of International Conference on Manufacturing System and Multiple Machines, Tokyo, Japan, 17–18 November 2020.
12. Wu, W.; Zhou, W.; Lin, Y.; Xie, Y.; Jin, W. A hybrid metaheuristic algorithm for location inventory routing problem with time windows and fuel consumption. *Expert Syst. Appl.* **2021**, *166*, 114034. [CrossRef]
13. Kübler, P.; Glock, C.H.; Bauernhansl, T. A new iterative method for solving the joint dynamic storage location assignment, order batching and picker routing problem in manual picker-to-parts warehouses. *Comput. Ind. Eng.* **2020**, *147*, 106645. [CrossRef]

14. Trindade, M.A.M.; Sousa, P.S.A.; Moreira, M.R.A. Ramping up a heuristic procedure for storage location assignment problem with precedence constraints. *Flex. Serv. Manuf. J.* **2022**, *34*, 646–669. [CrossRef] [PubMed]
15. Zhang, G.; Shang, X.; Alawneh, F.; Yang, Y.; Nishi, T. Integrated production planning and warehouse storage assignment problem: An IoT assisted case. *Int. J. Prod. Econ.* **2021**, *234*, 108058. [CrossRef]
16. Li, M.L.; Wolf, E.; Wintz, D. Duration-of-Stay Storage Assignment under Uncertainty. In Proceedings of the International Conference on Learning Representations 2019, New Orleans, LA, USA, 6–9 May 2019.
17. Rimélé, A.; Grangier, P.; Gamache, M.; Gendreau, M.; Rousseau, L.-M. Supervised Learning and Tree Search for Real-Time Storage Allocation in Robotic Mobile Fulfillment Systems. *arXiv* **2021**, arXiv:2106.02450v1.
18. Berns, F.; Ramsdorf, T.; Beecks, C. Machine Learning for Storage Location Prediction in Industrial High Bay Warehouses. In Proceedings of the International Conference on Pattern Recognition, Virtual Event, 10–15 January 2019; Springer: Cham, Switzerland, 2021; pp. 650–661.
19. Kim, B.; Jeong, Y.; Shin, J.G. Spatial arrangement using deep reinforcement learning to minimise rearrangement in ship block stockyards. *Int. J. Prod. Res.* **2020**, *58*, 5062–5076. [CrossRef]
20. Rimélé, A.; Grangier, P.; Gamache, M.; Gendreau, M.; Rousseau, L.-M. E-commerce warehousing: Learning a storage policy. *arXiv* **2021**, arXiv:2101.08828v1.
21. Brockman, G.; Cheung, V.; Pettersson, L.; Schneider, J.; Schulman, J.; Tang, J.; Zaremba, W. OpenAI Gym. *arXiv* **2016**, arXiv:1606.01540v1.
22. Mnih, V.; Kavukcuoglu, K.; Silver, D.; Graves, A.; Antonoglou, I.; Wierstra, D.; Riedmiller, M. Playing Atari with Deep Reinforcement Learning. *arXiv* **2013**, arXiv:1312.5602v1.
23. Sutton, R.S.; McAllester, D.; Singh, S.; Mansour, Y. Policy Gradient Methods for Reinforcement Learning with Function Approximation. *Adv. Neural Inf. Process. Syst.* **1999**, *12*, 1057–1063.
24. Schulman, J.; Wolski, F.; Dhariwal, P.; Radford, A.; Klimov, O. Proximal Policy Optimization Algorithms. *arXiv* **2017**, arXiv:1707.06347v2.
25. Raffin, A.; Hill, A.; Gleave, A.; Kanervisto, A.; Ernestus, M.; Dormann, N. Stable-Baselines3: Reliable Reinforcement Learning Implementations. *J. Mach. Learn. Res.* **2021**, *22*, 1–8.

Article

Data Model Design to Support Data-Driven IT Governance Implementation

Vittoria Biagi [1,2,*] and Angela Russo [2]

1 Department of Mechanical and Aerospace Engineering, Sapienza University of Rome, Via Eudossiana, 18, 00184 Rome, Italy
2 FSTechnology, Piazza della Croce Rossa, 1, 00161 Rome, Italy
* Correspondence: vittoria.biagi@uniroma1.it

Abstract: Organizations must quickly adapt their processes to understand the dynamic nature of modern business environments. As highlighted in the literature, centralized governance supports decision-making and performance measurement processes in technology companies. For this reason, a reliable decision-making system with an integrated data model that enables the rapid collection and transformation of data stored in heterogeneous and different sources is needed. Therefore, this paper proposes the design of a data model to implement data-driven governance through a literature review of adopted approaches. The lack of a standardized procedure and a disconnection between theoretical frameworks and practical application has emerged. This paper documented the suggested approach following these steps: (i) mapping of monitoring requirements to the data structure, (ii) documentation of ER diagram design, and (iii) reporting dashboards used for monitoring and reporting. The paper helped fill the gaps highlighted in the literature by supporting the design and development of a DWH data model coupled with a BI system. The application prototype shows benefits for top management, particularly those responsible for governance and operations, especially for risk monitoring, audit compliance, communication, knowledge sharing on strategic areas of the company, and identification and implementation of performance improvements and optimizations.

Keywords: business intelligence; data model; data warehouse; enterprise system; IT governance; IT performance monitoring

Citation: Biagi, V.; Russo, A. Data Model Design to Support Data-Driven IT Governance Implementation. *Technologies* 2022, 10, 106. https://doi.org/10.3390/technologies10050106

Academic Editor: Mohammed Mahmoud

Received: 31 August 2022
Accepted: 4 October 2022
Published: 8 October 2022

Publisher's Note: MDPI stays neutral with regard to jurisdictional claims in published maps and institutional affiliations.

Copyright: © 2022 by the authors. Licensee MDPI, Basel, Switzerland. This article is an open access article distributed under the terms and conditions of the Creative Commons Attribution (CC BY) license (https://creativecommons.org/licenses/by/4.0/).

1. Introduction

In any organization, in order to achieve the best results, performance management must involve people at all levels of management. Performance management is one of the standard mechanisms for improving alignment between business unit/customer management and personnel [1].

In particular, performance management has been recognized as a crucial mechanism in information technology, although the literature is scarce in this field [2]. Information technology (IT) companies and high-tech companies belong to the category of technology companies (also known as tech companies). They provide technology products or services, such as electronics-based technology products, including activities related to digital electronics, software, and Internet-related services (e.g., e-commerce services; examples of tech company are Apple Inc., Samsung, Alphabet Inc., Meta, Intel, Microsoft, and Alibaba) [3]. In this dynamic business environment, the IT structure supports the flexible and effective use of technology systems and products to grow the business and improve cost efficiency. Therefore, centralized governance is needed to guide, coordinate, and support the business. IT governance has also been recognized as a structure that specifies decision rights and an accountability framework to encourage desirable behaviors [4]. Additionally, it is critical in providing strategic direction to ensure that goals are met, risks are properly managed, and company resources are used appropriately [5]. Researchers put their efforts into investigating IT governance, methods, techniques, and tools to support decision making and align

IT with business strategies and different frameworks. The Calder–Moir IT Governance Framework (Figure 1) was designed to help organizations by using these overlapping frameworks and standards and deploying the best-practice guide contained in ISO/IEC 38500. Calder argued that none of the international standards provide comprehensive guidance and that most standards have overlapping issues; therefore, he proposed the Calder–Moir IT Governance Framework [6]. The result is a series of proposals and plans that describe the characteristics of the business and IT, the expected performance, the changes needed to achieve that performance, and the resource implications [7].

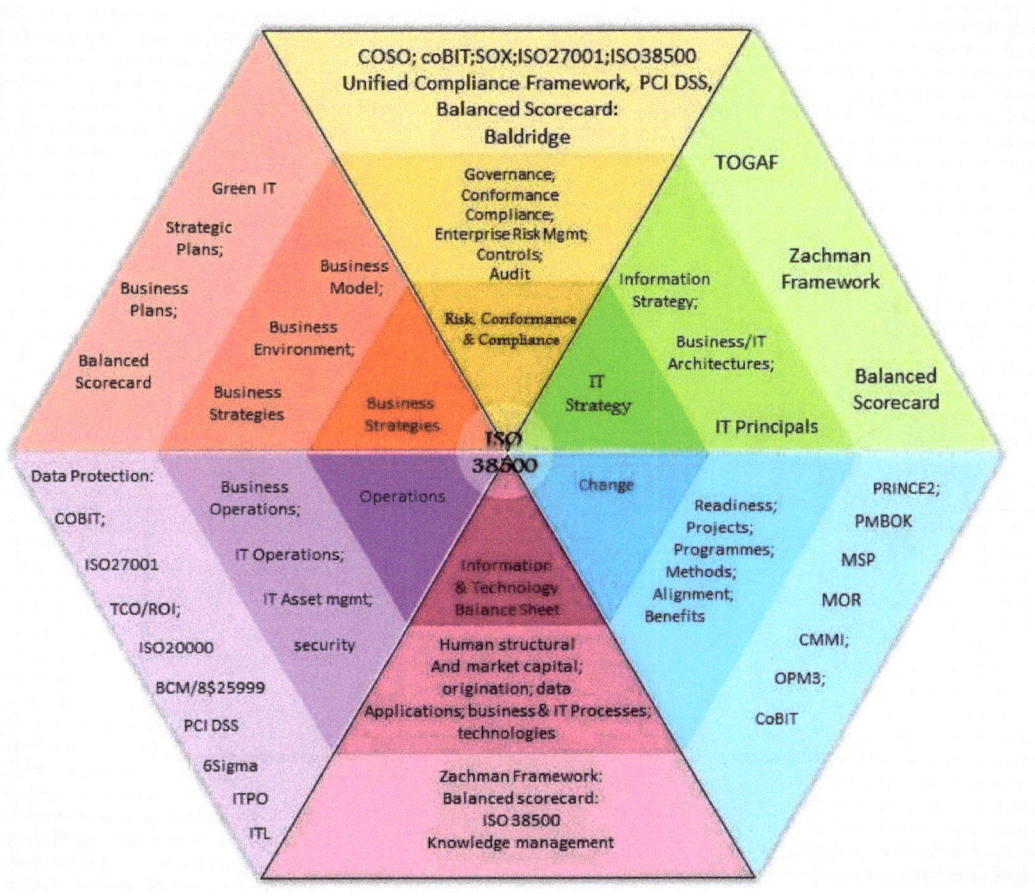

Figure 1. IT governance framework. The upper half covers the processes that determine directions, make plans and decisions, and establish constraints. The lower half covers processes that manage capabilities or develop new ones and use them to deliver products/services. Once the business strategies (red in figure), governance regimes, risk assessment, and controls have been developed (yellow in figure), IT works with the business to develop architectures and deliver plans based on those requirements (green in figure). The three layers into which the framework is divided, respectively, indicate the key issue for the board to consider (internal level), the executive management responsibilities (middle layer) and the issue related to IT practitioners (external layer) [7].

As outlined in the literature and by the Information Technology Governance Institute (ITGI), the domains of IT governance are IT strategic alignment, IT value delivery, IT risk management, IT resource management, and IT performance monitoring [8–10]. IT delivery value is enabled by IT strategic alignment with the business. Risk management is driven by embedding accountability in the enterprise; it needs to be supported by reliable measures to verify the results achieved (Figure 2).

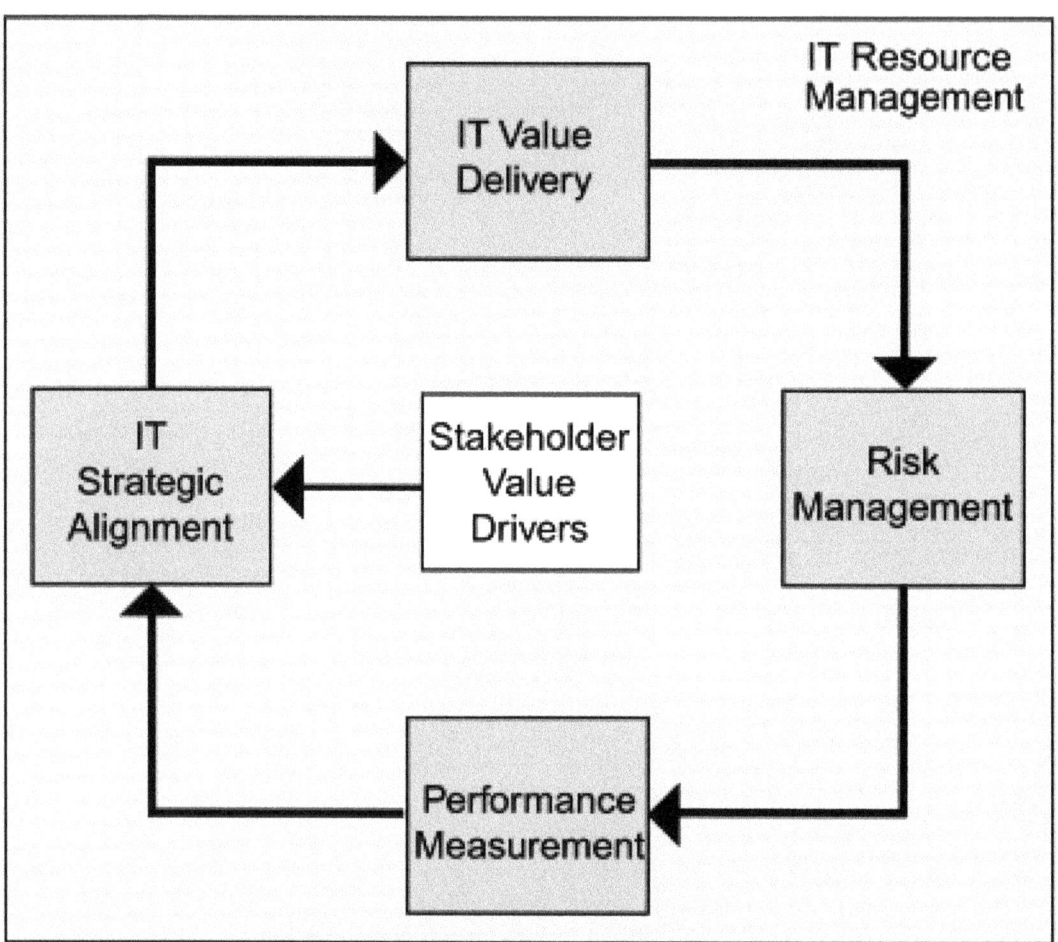

Figure 2. IT governance framework. The five areas of governance. The system follows the five areas driven by the stakeholders needs. The two outcomes (IT delivery and risk management) and three drivers (IT strategic alignment, resource management, and performance measurement) [9].

The performance measurement domain has been considered as one of the most important for increasing the organization's capabilities and the IT governance maturity [11]. Therefore, the implementation of an enterprise performance measuring system is an integral part of effective IT governance [12]. However, literature highlights a gap between theoretical frameworks and practices and states that, although hard governance (structures, procedures) attracts the attention of many, soft governance (behaviour, collaboration) could be crucial in bridging the gap [13–16]. Therefore, this research aimed to investigate the soft governance practices and contribute to designing a decisional support system to implement data-driven governance. The literature scouting outlined limitations in the implementation of governance practices. As such, the proposed approach intends to help bridge this gap. Starting from the previewed research work, it extends the area of monitoring, overcoming the main limitation by structuring a data model that includes not only project information but also data sources from other organizations, providing comprehensive and organized reporting, as a key element in guiding organizations in such an ever-changing environment [17]. Therefore, the research proposes a solution that enables information sharing as one of the missions of governance in organizations and facilitates monitoring of the identified critical governance area, overcoming the current limitations in governance [18]:

- siloed information management;
- non-standardized data extraction; and
- lack of report development techniques.

The proposed repository data model can support online analytical processing (OLAP) and make available the information needed for decision making, providing flexibility and autonomy to users in data analysis and reporting.

The proposed model was then tested on a case-study, FSTechnology, which is part of the Italian Ferrovie dello Stato Group. It is an Italian rail transportation company with about 83,000 employees. It has declared its intention to invest EUR 58 billion, EUR 6 billion of which is earmarked for innovation and technology, as stated in its 2019–2023 strategic plan. FSTechnology was born in 2019 and is a services company dedicated to technology and innovation initiatives in support of the parent group. It is a multi-sourcing integration company, and its market extends to rail, freight, infrastructure, bus, and services.

Therefore, it helped support the main needs for data-driven governance-monitoring by linking IT performance measurement with data-driven solutions. The main results obtained attested to the bridging of the gap that emerged. Its managerial implications have led to (i) the availability of critical information across the enterprise; (ii) a centralized visualization by which to monitor processes and implement process improvements; (iii) compliance verification activities; (iv) management support in data reporting (e.g., rapid and reliable reporting of critical information to the advisory board or to customers); (v) increased digitization through automation of daily manual tasks in updating data; (vi) improved contract and subcontract monitoring and formalization of new ones; (vii) optimization of financial area monitoring; (viii) scalability that enables rapid customization of reporting at any organizational level; and (ix) the ability to further integrate unstructured data from operations.

The remainder of the paper is organized as follows. Section 2 describes the state-of-the-art decision support system for data-driven governance and the data model of a data warehouse (DWH) coupled with a BI as one of the DSS systems. Section 3 outlines the methodology applied to design the data model and a description of the ER diagram, highlighting the main results, along with the BI reporting system developed for analysis. Section 4 reviews strengths and weaknesses of the proposed solution and managerial implications discussing the main obtained results, and finally, Section 5 summarizes the main contributions and limitations of this work, documenting the potential for future research.

2. Background—Literature Review
2.1. Performance Measurement

Performance measurement has been recognized as the key element in bringing value to the business through IT and increasing the level of IT maturity [19,20]. In addition, a CIO's role is to attest to where the business is and show the business intelligence dashboards representing the state of the organization and the metrics identified (e.g., showing the total cost of ownership (TCO) and service level performance) toward the use of business intelligence (BI) [21,22]. Therefore, the performance measurement domain helps the organization make an effective decision structure, especially regarding IT principles, infrastructure management, and investments [23]. This holds especially true in governance, wherein the focus on decisional problems is growing, pushing toward data-driven decision making [24]. The means of value creation has shifted from tangible to intangible assets, and the latter cannot be measured by using traditional financial measures. The first method proposed for organizations' performance measurement is the balance scorecard (BSC). It has four measurement perspectives: customer focus, process efficiency, and ability to learn and grow. Each perspective is designed to answer the question about how the organization operates. As such, organizations consider intangible items (e.g., level of customer satisfaction, streamlining of internal functions, creation of operational efficiencies, and developing staff skills). This allows long-term strategic goals to be linked with short-term actions through a single, more complete view of business operations. However, setting clear goals and measures is still a challenge and requires cooperation among different levels of governance within the company. Thus, BSC should include cause-and-effect relationships, which are difficult to implement [25]. Others have proposed the use of critical success factors (CSF) and key performance indicators (KPI) to monitor performance. Nowadays, the importance of data leads organizations to adopt business intelligence and analytics to uncover hidden information and accelerate organizational performance and innovation [26,27]. A performance measurement system (PMS) is defined as a system for assessing organizational performance in qualitative and quantitative terms through financial and non-financial indicators. The evaluated data are essential for making strategic decisions [28,29]. IT governance standards (proposed by ISO), repositories of best-practices and recommendations (e.g., ITIL, COBIT), methods (e.g., BSC) and models (e.g., capability maturity model integration (CMMI)), are widely used to reduce the complexity of decision making. However, the lack of a standardized measurement method leads to poor data consistency and practical implementation of performance monitoring [30]. Some studies have suggested that understanding the governance process, along with monitoring IT performance, is critical to the effective implementation of IT governance. Therefore, relational mechanisms, also known as the communication approach, along with knowledge sharing are effective supports in disseminating IT governance principles, policies, and decision outcomes to stakeholders [31]. Knowledge sharing is the provision of information and know-how to support the other person in collaborating to solve the problems, implement policies or procedures, or develop ideas [32]. A knowledge-sharing strategy has been recognized as a fundamental part of organizational strategy, as it enables adequate response to business needs and, consequently, the implementation of a long-term strategy [33].

Therefore, this study analysed the supporting methods and tools in performance measurement. Although the gap between IT and management may increase with this implementation, it is crucial to bridge the gap between a performance management system, business intelligence, and analytics, which must be integrated with each other [34]. The data warehouse (DWH) is a key element of a BI system, supporting data integration, storage, processing, analysis, and reporting [22].

Finally, such systems have been recognized as crucial company assets in several fields, such as: in the area of security incident analysis, where alerts and events from different Internet security sources are stored in a single data warehouse [35], or in the field of Earth observation, wherein the concept of a multidimensional data model has been used [36]. Other fields of application include health care, wherein a unified data framework has been proposed with the aim of simplifying the health information system infrastructure [37], and in manufacturing to improve the quality of productivity [38,39].

2.2. Decision Support System for a Data-Driven Governance Background

Since ancient times, the intelligence of decision-making has been recognized as crucial. Despite the amount of research in decision making, it still remains one of the biggest challenges [40]. Since the 1960s the topic of decision making has attracted the attention of academics and practitioners, when organisations implemented transaction-processing systems for analysing operations. Nevertheless, there is a gap in using analytics to their advantage. Later, decision support was combined with computers, which led to decision support systems (DSS) and executive support systems (ESS) [40]. In the 1990s, organizations began to realize the importance of a business intelligence, following the development of data warehousing [41,42], and online analytical processing (OLAP) [43]. Next, the complexity of data coming from different sources requires data integration and identification of KPIs to extract relevant information to support decision makers. The digitalization of decision making belongs to the governance domains along with performance measures (Figure 2); as such, decision support systems are information systems designed to enable these activities. Decision support systems refer to a field of research that includes the design and study of DSS application, clustered in five components [44–46]:

- Model driven;
- Data driven;
- Communication driven;
- Document driven; and
- Knowledge driven.

One of the most popular DSS tools is the balance score card (BSC), which integrates financial and non-financial indicators, as mentioned in Section 2.1. Later, the two creators (Kaplan and Norton) extended the tool to the strategy map (SM) [47] (both represented in the Business Strategy quadrant by Calder in Figure 1). The SM provides a cause-and-effect relationship among indicators. Others proposed activity-based costing/management or performance PRISM as a DSS system [47]. However, they require a great deal of human activity to implement. Digitalization allows one to collect a large amount of data, which companies use to develop strategies and make decisions. The development of IT enables these systems not only to reason about knowledge and provide detailed financial information, but also to predict future measures. They can be used to measure enterprise performance, to support decision makers in rapid evaluations of measured values and to predict future measures. Later, they were called retrieval-only DSS, executive information systems, OLAP systems and BI. A BI system is a data-driven DSS that provides support in querying a historical database and reports [44]. The greatest capability of data-driven DSS occurred in the early 1990s with the introduction of OLAP. The key element in the success of a data-driven DSS is ease of use and quick access to a large amount of accurate and organized multidimensional data [46].

DSSs are usually classified into three groups to support the identification of the most suitable one for the purpose [48]:

- Passive: This group does not suggest any decision but helps decision makers in the decision-making process; it is common in field operations in the organization.
- Active: This group recommends decisions and gives advice to the decision makers. It requires the active participation of managers or leaders in organizations to define gaps in processes or improvements in the organization.
- Cooperative: This is a framework designed for making decisions on behalf of the decision makers. These proposals are then fine-tuned and validated by decision makers.

In summary, a data-driven DSS represents a support in governance providing insights and analytics to estimate impacts of the different policy options [49]. It is, thus, a necessary IT tool for a technology company, to support strategic and operational decisions [50] and to enable activities of data-driven governance.

2.3. Data Model for DWH Coupled with a BI System for Data-Driven Governance

To adequately address the design of a data model, a literature review was conducted with the goal of finding the optimal solution for designing a data warehouse data model for BI purposes as a support for analysing and reporting crucial business information in a data-driven governance context. Both the development and management of a BI system have emerged as critical activities, in light of the demonstrated effectiveness of a business intelligence technology along with the data warehouse for decision-making process support [51,52].

The term business intelligence was coined in 1958 by Luhn and defined as: "the ability to apprehend the interrelationships of presented facts in such a way as to guide action towards a desired goal" [53]. This tool can transform data into information and, through human analysis, into knowledge [54].

The main question that a BI can answer is:

- What is happening now and why? In contrast, business analytics can answer the question:
- What will probably happen in the future? BI refers to immediate answer and the central elements are [50]:
- real-time data warehousing;
- detection of exceptions and anomalies;
- automatic learning and refining;
- seamless workflow; and
- data mining.

The BI system gathers data from a variety of sources, and the main differences between BI and big data are highlighted below [55] in Table 1:

Table 1. Main differences between BI and big data.

	BI	Big Data
Data Sources	Mostly internal	Mostly external
Data Types	Mostly structured	Unstructured
History	Essential	Less relevant
Users	Managers/Controller	Data scientist
Precision	Exact results	Approximate results
Privacy	Not critical	Critical
Control over data	Almost full control	Little or no control

The types of data come from the following sources:

- Unstructured: e.g., conversations, graphics, images, and movies.
- Structured: e.g., data coming from OLAP, data warehouse (DWH), data marts (DM), enterprise information system (EIS) or enterprise resource planning (ERP).

In summary, BI has been widely used to describe the process of gathering, analysing, and transforming large amounts of data into information for decision makers [40]. Although the use of big data is highly promoted today, standard relational databases are still essential [56]. The purpose of BI performance monitoring and control of an organization is to support many users; it should not be directed at solving a single business problem, but should support a group of users in different business decisions [57]. Therefore, difficulties occur both when an information cube (data warehouse) must support all levels of business, and when a single group of data must feed several BI tools, resulting in the loss of performance. When implementing a BI system, a trade-off between a bottom-up and top-down approach must be considered. Another key aspect is that the system must be connected and adhere to the processes of the organization to convey correct information. For this reason, the criticality of the data model design in developing a BI system emerges. Finally, business intelligence and analytics frameworks enable linking different business elements (organizational rules, KPIs, authorizations, and visualizations).

The data warehouse for BI purposes must ensure that data is available in the right form for analytical processing activities, such as OLAP, queries, reporting, and other decision support applications [58]. In addition, the design is highly dependent on both data sources and user needs [59]. Bill Inmon defined the DWH as follows: "A warehouse is a subject-oriented, integrated, time variant and non-volatile collection of data in support of management's decision-making process". Ralph Kimball defined it as follows: "A warehouse is a copy of transaction data specifically structured for query and analysis". A data warehouse is a large repository that collects data from internal databases, such as operational data, and databases outside the organization. Its main characteristics are that it is topic-driven, its data is stored in a single source, and that it is time varying and not volatile [41,60]. In summary, operational databases are different from data warehouses, so user queries have no impact on these systems. Furthermore, the integration of BI and DWH enables an organizational operational platform for decision making, ensuring the security of data access [51,61]. Maryska et al. proposed a DWH architecture based on a traditional BI solution, with the aim of integrating it into the enterprise architecture of any organization to support the implementation of cost allocation, profitability, and management within the analytics task performed [62]. Researchers propose using data integration and business analytics techniques to define a data governance model that measures data quality [5]. Although the design of DWH along with BI systems is a well-established practice, the literature on IT governance application is still poor.

To prepare a data warehouse for BI purposes, the data collected must be cleaned, integrated, and transformed. Integration includes such operations as identifying and resolving data conflicts and removing redundancies. At this stage, different types of data are stored while maintaining the same format throughout the extract transform load (ETL) process [60]. In an integrated architecture, the ETL layer enables improvements in data quality and consistency and the flow of information between systems [51]. Data quality has been classified into four dimensions: intrinsic, contextual, representational, and accessibility [63,64]. The repository containing the data can range from spreadsheet to mainframe systems, after data modelling a crucial part of ensuring data quality is ETL, which is a key component of the DWH. Therefore, proper design of this process is necessary for data integrity and quality improvement, as it refreshes the DWH with updated and added data in source systems since the last extraction [65]. Extraction and transformation are the same in both Kimball's and Inmon's approaches, whereas the loading process differs in that clean data are loaded directly into data marts and then into a central DWH. The literature recommends the use of Kimball's DWH design method in organizations where people operate in different departments/units and information is siloed [66]. Therefore, we adopt Kimball's approach to develop the model.

The data model typically defines the dataset for an application and supports the development of information systems by providing the definition and format of the data [67]. The literature states that there are no standard methods for implementing the conceptual model [67,68]; hence, the designer must choose the right data model based on the application. In addition, the common and main criteria needed to evaluate a data warehouse design methods are correctness, completeness, minimization, and comprehensibility [69].

To support the designer in obtaining a data warehouse data model, several approaches have been proposed. The main proposed methods, based on operational systems, can be grouped into [70] the structure-based method, known as a data-driven approach, and the process-based approach [22,71]. The former considers that the data sources available in operational systems influence the conceptual and logical design of the data warehouse. However, this approach highlights a lack of guidance in identifying the DWH model, a gap between the design and behavioural aspects of the system and a manual transformation required to obtain the model. The latter is aimed at designing a DWH that can provide the measurement of business performance. Therefore, it requires a deep understanding of business processes and their relationships, identifying the necessary data source. The main advantage is that it incorporates process performance measures into the process activities, giving those performing the process the opportunity to get an accurate picture of the business [72]. In this research, the structured-based approach was chosen, as explained in Section 3. The dimensional model design technique represents data in a standard framework and is based on the following principles: focus on the business, build an appropriate information infrastructure, provide meaningful increments [42]. The dimensional model consists of facts, which represent key tables and dimensions, indicating the details and features. The main model design techniques are [73] as follows:

- Star Schema: This is a simple model, which the dimension tables are directly related to the fact table. However, this model does not consider the necessary storage space and data normalization.
- Snowflake Schema: This model allows normalization of dimensions, and hierarchies are separated. This model has better maintenance agility by reducing the number of redundancies.

Other approaches proposed in the literature for modelling a data warehouse are multi-dimensional modelling (MDM) [42] and normalized modelling (data mart) [41]. The former is able to process data quickly and has advanced data warehouse features [50]; it is also used for decision support in BI [74,75]. It consists of fact tables and multi-dimensional tables [76]. Therefore, the MDM mainly addresses business process or transaction, and it is simple to design. The second, on the other hand, is used for data integration and redundancy reduction; often a combination of the two methods is applied to two-tier data model [77]. Researchers proposed the data vault model, which consists of using the many-to-many relationship of all entities at the beginning. This means representing the worst-case scenario at the initial stage, and it is easier to modify the architecture, if a user requirements change [57]. Moreover, another area of investigation is the optimization of a multi-dimensional data model by using a multi-criteria decision-making approach, in order to increase the flexibility of the data model for BI purposes [78]. However, the optimization problem is beyond the scope of this work. In addition, others have defined a multi-dimensional reference models to allow designers to adapt the model of a specific company and facilitate the design and development of a BI system solution [79].

3. Proposed Approach and Results

This section describes the proposed approach used to design and develop the data model and the resulting dashboards to support data-driven governance implementation. The data model of a DWH coupled with a BI system was designed according to the main steps outlined in the literature: (i) requirements analysis; (ii) data source analysis; (iii) data warehouse modelling; ETL process; and (iv) reporting [80,81]. This section describes the proposed approach and the main results obtained in contributing to a data-driven governance implementation.

3.1. Requirement Analysis

To adequately address business needs on reporting requirements, the first key step is to define the desires of end users [59,82]. The type of the data-driven decision-support system developed is both passive and active. Therefore, as explained in Section 2.2, it aims to help decision-makers in the decision-making process. Furthermore, the managers of organization have been involved in gap analysis and identification of the eventual process improvements. As such, the tool can suggest decisions and provide guidance to leaders and decision makers.

Therefore, in implementing data-driven governance, the macro functions the system must cover have been classified as [83,84]:

- monitoring and reporting of critical information;
- communication;
- knowledge sharing; and
- process improvement and optimization.

This classification was made through literature scouting and interviews with managers. To simplify the analysis, the governance needs were mapped and represented on the different DSS layers, as shown in Figure 3.

3.2. Data Sources Analysis

As discussed in Section 2.3, BI data are mostly from internal sources, and big data are mostly external (Table 1). In this research, the goal was to design a data model for a DWH coupled with a BI system to support decision-makers in the organization. Therefore, in this second phase, after defining the requirements, the necessary data sources were mapped. The data sources involved were the organizational transactional system, planning system and repositories, including Excel files and document repositories (e.g., Microsoft SharePoint), in which all company documents (e.g., policy, procedure, guidelines) were stored. At this stage of the work presented, big data were excluded. However, we believe that future developments could include the collection and analysis of big data from the operational area of organization.

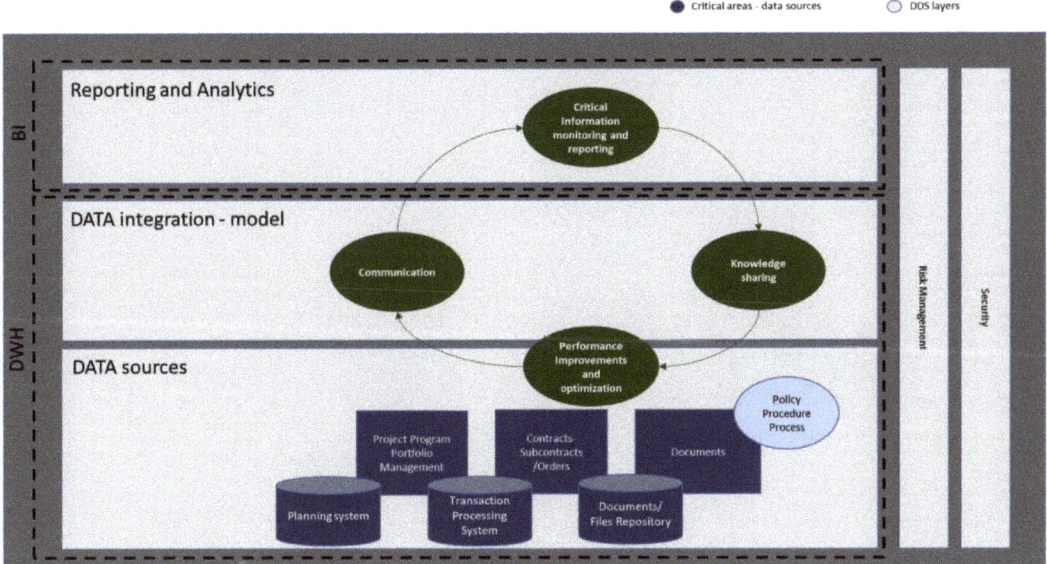

Figure 3. Data-driven governance framework for a performance monitoring domain. In grey are represented the DSS layers and in blue are the main data sources. The requirements in green have been mapped on the DSS layers.

3.3. Data Integration and Data Warehouse Modelling

DWH designers mainly use the entity-relationship (ER) model as the basis for the proposed solution [85]. In this research, we adopted an ER model to represent the data model with the cross-foot notation. The data model, whose architecture is represented in Figure 4, is made up of 25 tables. The model has been built to report the project information (as represented in the tables on the left side of the figure) and the contract information (reported on the right side of the figure). Note that the presented model is intended as a general data architecture to be used for a DWH coupled with a BI. The structure shows the relationships between the elements in tables and their cardinality. The zero cardinality is represented as a circle and the one cardinality as a bar. In addition, the cross-foot's notation allows us to specify either the mandatory or the optional cardinality. The link between projects information and contract information (table "Project-contract link") allows us to create reports giving a comprehensive view of the critical information, such as the relationship between the project progress and the new contracts signed or the expiring one. Moreover, including the table "System info", an overview of the technology context in relation to the ongoing projects can be represented and monitored. It was considered that the projects' information is updated four time per year and the key is the "ID project". Meanwhile, the data related to the "Final balance" and the "Order" tables are collected from the transactional system about six times per year, or when required.

3.4. Reporting and Analytics of Critical Information

Once the data have been organized in the data model represented in Figure 4, the analysis has been performed to support a data-driven governance decision support system. OLAP databases are suitable for efficient data analysis of a large amount of data, especially when multiple measures must be performed [86]. It permits the analyst and the domain experts to go deep into an investigation analysis [87]. Coupling OLAP systems with multidimensional representation of data allows analysts to inspect the data at different granularity; a query language can be used, such as MDX, SQL, or SPARQL, to perform the data querying [88]. In summary, this data structure allows representing both the details of the projects, contracts, and application/system information and to give an overview of the crucial company information.

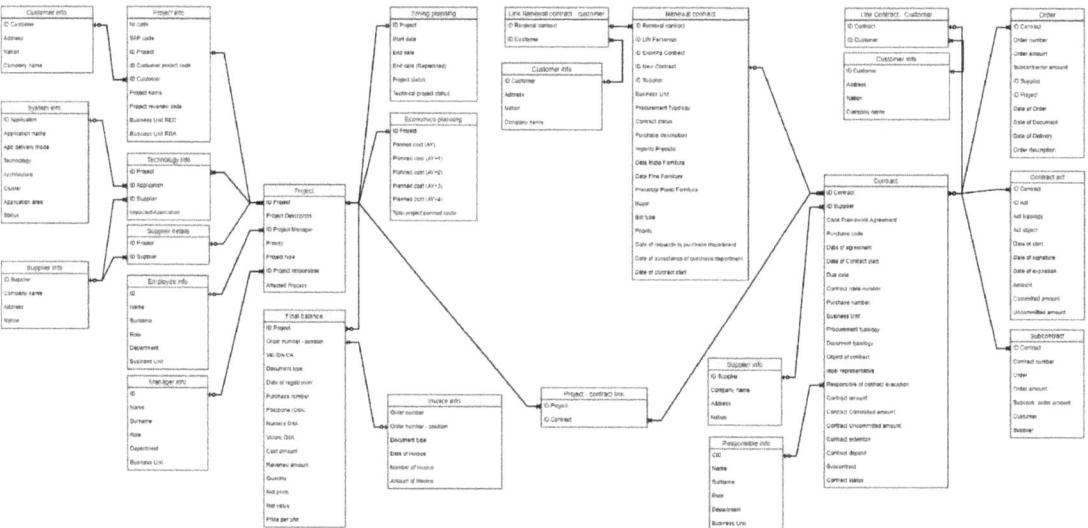

Figure 4. ER diagram data model design using the crow's foot notation. The open-source software used for the model design was draw.io (tables' elements name were manipulated and de-identified in order not to reveal the intellectual property of the units involved).

Once the crucial information to be monitored and the personnel involved in this process were identified, data visualization was implemented. Exemplary reporting is represented in Figures 5 and 6. The first provides an overview of the status of the contracts managed by operations, as a critical monitoring area to be integrated into a comprehensive enterprise performance monitoring system [89]. It informs the CEO, or the person responsible for auditing the organization's performance, about the type of procurement (tender or direct contract), the number of contracts signed, and the business unit responsible for managing them. It warns of the expiration date of contracts, enabling managers to make quick decisions if a contract reaches its due date or the maximum capacity. The table shows whether an action has already been taken by the operational manager (in the contract renewal status) or needs to be noticed urgently. Similarly, to be compliant with the audit activity, subcontracts need to be monitored. The speedometer graph shows the amount (in euros) of subcontracts compared to the total number of contracts in force. Finally, the labels return a quick overview of current contracts and their total amount. These are examples of the different KPIs that can be displayed with the information organized.

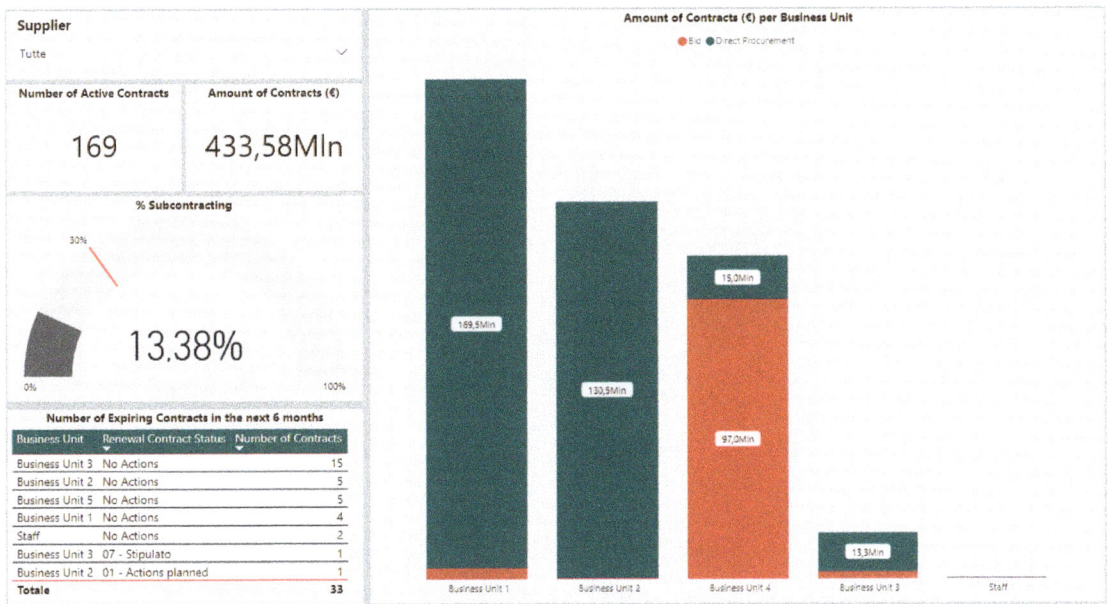

Figure 5. Contracts monitoring overview (quantitative data were manipulated and contracts' details de-identified in order not to reveal the intellectual property of the units involved). The percentage of subcontracting (30%) is the average value; by selecting the supplier and business unit this value will change according to agreed maximum subcontracting amount.

Additionally, this reporting system allows one to drill down on information details, as shown in Figure 6. Project timetables allow the management to monitor all the details of the project and its progress. This visualization also warns about time planning versus actual project status and economic trends. For example, the yellow indicator shows that the actual project costs are almost reaching the maximum total projected cost, attesting that the planned cost of the project may change. This is crucial information for the organization's spending forecast for the current and next year. Another warning represented (red in the figure) concerns the project's time plan. If it is out of time, it represents a critical issue, for example, for the organization's resource allocation. Linking the projects to the contract details (represented in the data model Figure 4 and described in Section 3.3) made it possible to view the current passive contract for project implementation. System/application details are embedded and attest to the technical details of the application or system developed. The service delivery mode (cloud or on premises), the programming languages, the application areas, and the application's cluster are needed information for both the responsible of the project execution or the program manager to verify the technical details of the project. These technical details are critical to provide an overview of the enterprise architecture, to monitor infrastructure spending costs or the level of technological innovation. The aforementioned information falls within the crucial domain of the governance monitoring [90]. Overall, a dedicated user interface was proposed to highlight the most critical information. In addition, reports were used by the management to indicate implemented actions or future critical actions to be taken. In the domain of a complex business environment, this solution represents a strategic tool to facilitate fast and fact-based decision making.

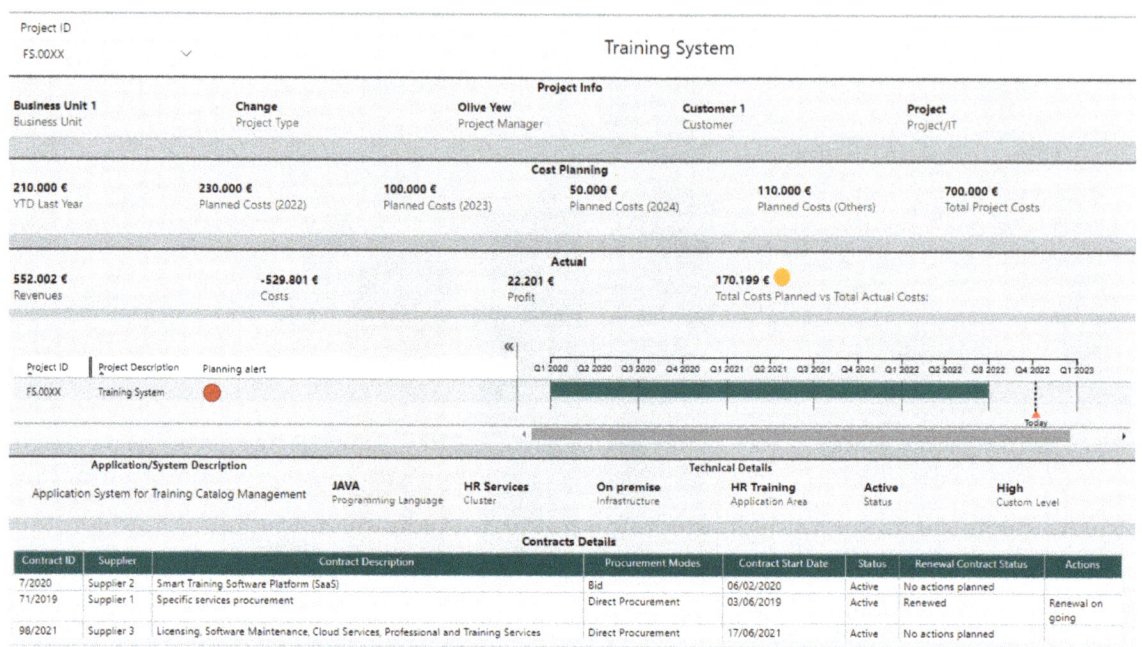

Figure 6. Project sheet (quantitative data were manipulated and the project's details de-identified in order not to reveal the intellectual property of the units involved). These data are crucial information for managers, who report to the responsible or for the manager accountable to the customer about the project's progress.

4. Discussion

As already demonstrated in the previous work [17], approaches for the implementation of a data-driven governance are scarce in the literature, requirements are only partial, and no IT tool is available [91]. In addition to previous work, this proposal extends monitoring and reporting to the entire area of the performance monitoring within the governance's domain. This work proposes an approach for developing a DWH coupled with a BI system to support centralized, data-driven organizational governance, attesting to it as a strategic business asset for structured analysis and reporting. This is through near real-time dashboarding available in a single location. The difficulties in requirement elicitation and identification are highlighted in the literature [57], especially in defining the need for the implementation of data driven governance. Therefore, this paper supports the design of a data model starting from structured data-driven governance' requirements, improving the lack of clear criteria.

Moreover, this research demonstrated the ability to access a large amount of accurate and organized multidimensional data to perform rapid and reliable supervising of critical information (e.g., in Figure 5), facilitate knowledge sharing, and be compliant with audit activities, as the crucial elements for a successful data-driven DSS [46]. The needs were defined by combining both the requirements of company managers interviewed and the documented requirements in the literature [92] with the purpose of meeting stakeholder's needs and current research evidence. Furthermore, companies struggle with siloed and fragmented data in both systems and processes [93]. Therefore, this solution extends to all organizations, and its scalability allows customized reporting at any organizational level; it is based primarily on a common repository that collects data from various organizational data sources, and its analyses were designed for the management. In summary, the system demonstrated the ability to meet the functionality requirements for data-driven governance implementation (Figure 3). That is: (i) performance monitoring and reporting critical information, which allows us to verify the expiring contracts status and the related subcontracts [94], as well as the technical infrastructure [95]; (ii) communication, as it allows us, through visualization, to understand projects and benefit management [96] and demonstrate earned value or show critical KPIs; in addition, the ability for involved staff to drill down into data, product portfolio reports, and contract status increases analytical capacity, and understanding of objectives and KPIs [97], along with the ability to demonstrate compliance with audit rules; (iii) knowledge sharing, the transactional, the planning system and the repository system concur to provide information, enabling knowledge transfer in a centralized place in the company; and (iv) process improvement and optimization, storing the data in one place and the fast data elicitation from multiple business units, which differ widely in terms of products, policies, and customers facilitate governance managers involved in the IT performance monitoring process to check the alignment of the current process with the operational execution of the work. Thus, they quickly identify and close gaps between the documented process and its actualization or eventually process improvement. This overcomes the constraints in governance of siloed information management, unstructured data extraction, and scarce report development techniques [18].

The reporting system is currently in use in the company to ensure dynamic and reliable data analysis by executives, middle-managers, and operators. The proposed approach can be applied in different contexts, following these building steps: (i) starting from the requirements analysis and mapping the needs onto the high-level block schema represented in Figure 3; (ii) identification and mapping the data sources needed to gather the information needed for the performance monitoring process in IT governance domain; (iii) designing the data model to identify the elements and their relationship along with the cardinality; and (iv) finally, the reporting should be tailored to the specific monitoring needs.

5. Conclusions

The current "data revolution" is not new in principle, as data processing has always been fundamental to the practices of public administration and governance. Nevertheless, new digital data technologies have enabled improved quality through data density, granularity, linked data, and machine learning. These improved qualities enable more encompassing monitoring, more sophisticated analyses, and forecasting, and thus, more efficient, and anticipatory government practices. The governance of organizations ultimately chooses whether and which of the competing formulated policies to implement. Therefore, data-driven governance can support these decision processes with insights and simulations based on predictive analytics to estimate impacts of the different policy options [49,98]. Thus, this work demonstrates that a data-driven decision support system is a necessary IT tool for a technology company, to support both operational and strategic decision making [50] and to enable knowledge sharing, communication, and process diagnosis, as a part of a data-driven governance. Nevertheless, the development and implementation of an IT governance framework is critical for modern businesses enterprise [99], along with the digitalization of the involved processes. Therefore, this work adds to the current literature by demonstrating that data-driven decision support systems support the entire decisional process, attesting that a data-driven governance is a key IT element for a technology company [49]. The paper aimed to document that DWH coupled with BI is becoming an increasingly important technology for organizations that operate in dynamic environments, attesting that data-driven governance improves the overall organization in seeking to gain insights from diverse data sources and big data to support decision making [81]. This paper demonstrated the importance of the design and the development of a decision support system for implementing the IT performance monitoring as one of the fourth governance domains (Figure 2) [9]. Key data-driven governance monitoring needs have been analysed, identified, and met with the system. The results of this work showed: (i) awareness of critical information across the enterprise; (ii) a unique point to monitor policies and processes to facilitate process improvements;

(iii) support the management in compliance verification activities and in data reporting (e.g., to the advisory board or to customers); (iv) decision-making process digitization through automation of daily manual tasks; (v) improved contract, subcontracts monitoring and early formalization of new one; (vi) optimization of financial area monitoring; (vii) scalability that enables rapid customization of reporting at any organizational level; and (viii) ability to further integrate unstructured data from operations. As such, this research calls for the implementation of data-driven solutions in governance and performance monitoring. It bridges the gap between performance measurement in IT governance and practical implementation. The scope of this research ranges from program and project portfolio, contract, subcontract, and order management as a crucial area of governance to be monitored, to KPI/SLA and accountability management, thus helping to increase the dynamism of the processes under study [100]. Further research is needed to improve the proposed approach, as to make decisions on behalf of decision-makers (belonging to the cooperative DSS category as described in Section 2.2), which then requires further validation by the decision-makers themselves [48]. Furthermore, the data elicitation problems should be improved. As such, recent studies have demonstrated the application of artificial neural networks to reduce the problem of missing data [101] and others have suggested the improvement of data requirement elicitation through a requirements-driven DW design methodology based on the e-pivot table [59]. Moreover, investigations are directed toward the possibility of resource allocation on projects [102] and the inclusion of unstructured data to build a comprehensive decision-making support system [76]. Finally, research in this direction is expected to support decision making through performance monitoring in such ever-changing environments.

Author Contributions: Conceptualization, V.B. and A.R.; methodology, V.B.; software, V.B.; validation, A.R.; formal analysis, V.B.; investigation, V.B.; data curation, V.B.; writing—original draft preparation, V.B.; writing—review and editing, A.R.; visualization V.B., supervision, A.R.; project administration, A.R.; funding acquisition A.R. All authors have read and agreed to the published version of the manuscript.

Funding: This research received no external funding.

Institutional Review Board Statement: Not applicable.

Informed Consent Statement: Not applicable.

Data Availability Statement: The data presented in this study are available within the article.

Acknowledgments: The authors wish to extend their full gratitude to all who assisted in conducting this research. In particular, we thank Lorenzo Sgambellone, who actively and proactively participated to the work in collaboration with FSTechnology.

Conflicts of Interest: The authors declare no conflict of interest.

References

1. Saetang, S.; Haider, A. CIO and CTO Nexus: Empowering Organizations with IT Governance. In Proceedings of the 2012 PICMET '12: Technology Management for Emerging Technologies, Vancouver, BC, Canada, 29 July–2 August 2012; pp. 3681–3691.
2. Herz, T.P.; Hamel, F.; Uebernickel, F.; Brenner, W. IT Governance Mechanisms in Multisourcing—A Business Group Perspective. In Proceedings of the 2012 45th Hawaii International Conference on System Sciences, Maui, HI, USA, 4–7 January 2012; pp. 5033–5042. [CrossRef]
3. Vargas-Hernández, J.G. Uber's Strategy as a Competitive Business Model of Sharing Economy. In *Sharing Economy and the Impact of Collaborative Consumption*; IGI Global: Hershey, PA, USA, 2020; p. 19.
4. Alaeddini, M.; Hashemi, S.A. Evaluating the Performance of IT Governance in Service-Oriented Enterprises. *Lect. Notes Inf. Syst. Organ.* **2019**, *30*, 323–333. [CrossRef]
5. Barrenechea, O.; Mendieta, A.; Armas, J.; Madrid, J.M. Data Governance Reference Model to Streamline the Supply Chain Process in SMEs. In Proceedings of the 2019 IEEE XXVI International Conference on Electronics, Electrical Engineering and Computing (INTERCON), Lima, Peru, 12–14 August 2019; pp. 8–11. [CrossRef]
6. Theron, H. Koornhof PGJ Bow to the King (IV)? A New Era for IT Governance in South Africa. In In Proceedings of the African Cyber Citizenship Conference 2016 (ACCC2016), Port Elizabeth, South Africa, 31 October–1 November 2016; pp. 161–173.
7. Calder, A. *The Calder-Moir It Governance Framework*; IT Governance: Ely, UK, 2008.

8. Miyamoto, M.; Kudo, S. Five Domains of Information Technology Governance in Japanese SMEs; An Empirical Study. In Proceedings of the 2013 International Conference on ICT Convergence (ICTC), Jeju, Korea, 14–16 October 2013; pp. 964–969. [CrossRef]
9. IT Governance Institute. *Board Briefing on IT Governance*; IT Governance: Ely, UK, 2003.
10. Lunardi, G.L.; Maçada, A.C.G.; Becker, J.L.; Van Grembergen, W. Antecedents of IT Governance Effectiveness: An Empirical Examination in Brazilian Firms. *J. Inf. Syst.* **2017**, *31*, 41–57. [CrossRef]
11. Elagha, H. The Use of Partial Least Squares Path Modeling in IT Governance Discipline. In Proceedings of the 2014 11th International Conference on Information Technology: New Generations, Las Vegas, NV, USA, 7–9 April 2014; pp. 624–626. [CrossRef]
12. Ferguson, C.; Green, P.; Vaswani, R.; Wu, G. Determinants of Effective Information Technology Governance. *Int. J. Audit.* **2013**, *17*, 75–99. [CrossRef]
13. Dietz, J.L.G.; Hoogervorst, J.A.P. The Principles of Enterprise Engineering. *Lect. Notes Bus. Inf. Process.* **2012**, *110*, 15–30. [CrossRef]
14. Smits, D.; Van Hillegersberg, J. The Continuing Mismatch between IT Governance Maturity Theory and Practice: A New Approach. *Procedia Comput. Sci.* **2018**, *138*, 549–560. [CrossRef]
15. Smits, D.; Van Hillegersberg, J. IT Governance Maturity: Developing a Maturity Model Using the Delphi Method. In Proceedings of the 2015 48th Hawaii International Conference on System Science, Kauai, HI, USA, 5–8 January 2015; pp. 4534–4543. [CrossRef]
16. Smits, D.; Van Hillegersberg, J. Evaluation of the Usability of a New ITG Instrument to Measure Hard and Soft Governance Maturity. *Int. J. Inf. Syst. Proj. Manag.* **2019**, *7*, 37–58. [CrossRef]
17. Biagi, V.; Patriarca, R.; Di Gravio, G. Business Intelligence for IT Governance of a Technology Company. *Data* **2022**, *7*, 2. [CrossRef]
18. Erasmus, W.; Marnewick, C. An IT Governance Framework for IS Portfolio Management. *Int. J. Manag. Proj. Bus.* **2020**, *14*, 721–742. [CrossRef]
19. Nan, S.S.; Gilbert, S. *Enterprise IT Governance, Business Value and Performance Measurement*; IGI Global: Hershey, PA, USA, 2011.
20. Alagha, H. Examining the Relationship between IT Governance Domains, Maturity, Mechanisms, and Performance: An Empirical Study toward a Conceptual Framework. In Proceedings of the 2013 10th International Conference on Information Technology: New Generations, Las Vegas, NV, USA, 15–17 April 2013; pp. 767–772. [CrossRef]
21. Gordon Hunter, M. The Chief Information Officer: A Review of the Role. *J. Inf. Inf. Technol. Organ.* **2010**, *5*, 125–143. [CrossRef]
22. Oliveira, E.; Sá, J.; Santos, M.Y. Process-Driven Data Analytics Supported by a Data Warehouse Model. *Int. J. Bus. Intell. Data Min.* **2017**, *12*, 383–405. [CrossRef]
23. Joshi, A.; Bollen, L.; Hassink, H. An Empirical Assessment of IT Governance Transparency: Evidence from Commercial Banking. *Inf. Syst. Manag.* **2013**, *30*, 116–136. [CrossRef]
24. Rajeshkumar, V.; Anandaraj, S.; Kavinkumar, V.; Elango, K.S. Analysis of Factors Influencing Formwork Material Selection in Construction Buildings. *Mater. Today Proc.* **2020**, *37*, 880–885. [CrossRef]
25. Fabac, R. Digital Balanced Scorecard System as a Supporting Strategy for Digital Transformation. *Sustainability* **2022**, *14*, 9690. [CrossRef]
26. Jain, S.; Sharma, S. Application of Data Warehouse in Decision Support and Business Intelligence System. In Proceedings of the 2018 Second International Conference on Green Computing and Internet of Things (ICGCIoT), Bangalore, India, 16–18 August 2018; pp. 231–234. [CrossRef]
27. Wixom, B.; Watson, H. The BI-Based Organization. *Int. J. Bus. Intell. Res.* **2010**, *1*, 13–28. [CrossRef]
28. Ensslin, S.R.; Rodrigues, K.T.; Junior, L.; Yoshiura, M. Organizational Performance Management and the 'Sustainability' of the Performance Evaluation System: A View Guided by the Integrative Review Sustainability Organizational Performance Management and the 'Sustainability' of the Performance Evaluation S. *Sustainability* **2022**, *14*, 11005. [CrossRef]
29. Franco-Santos, M.; Otley, D. Reviewing and Theorizing the Unintended Consequences of Performance Management Systems. *Int. J. Manag. Rev.* **2018**, *20*, 696–730. [CrossRef]
30. Hitz, C.; Schwer, K. The Role of It Governance in Digital Operating Models. *J. East. Eur. Cent. Asian Res.* **2018**, *5*, 61–79. [CrossRef]
31. Juiz, C.; Gomez, B. Delving Into the IT Governance-Management Communication Interface. *Int. J. Digit. Strateg. Gov. Bus. Transform.* **2021**, *11*, 1–37. [CrossRef]
32. Santos, V.; Goldman, A.; de Souza, C.R.B. Fostering Effective Inter-Team Knowledge Sharing in Agile Software Development. *Empir. Softw. Eng.* **2015**, *20*, 1006–1051. [CrossRef]
33. Levy, M.; Hadar, I.; Aviv, I. Agile-Based Education for Teaching an Agile Requirements Engineering Methodology for Knowledge Management. *Sustainability* **2021**, *13*, 2853. [CrossRef]
34. Abai, N.H.Z.; Yahaya, J.H.; Deraman, A. An Integrated Framework of Business Intelligence and Analytic with Performance Management System: A Conceptual Framework. In Proceedings of the 2015 Science and Information Conference (SAI), London, UK, 28–30 July 2015; pp. 452–456. [CrossRef]
35. Valladares, P.; Fuertes, W.; Tapia, F.; Toulkeridis, T.; Pérez, E. Dimensional Data Model for Early Alerts of Malicious Activities in a CSIRT. *Simul. Ser.* **2017**, *49*, 74–81. [CrossRef]
36. Nativi, S.; Mazzetti, P.; Craglia, M. A View-Based Model of Data-Cube to Support Big Earth Data Systems Interoperability. *Big Earth Data* **2017**, *1*, 75–99. [CrossRef]
37. Gamal, M.; Barakat, S.; Rezk, A. Integrated Document-Based Electronic Health Records Persistence Framework. *Int. J. Adv. Comput. Sci. Appl.* **2021**, *12*, 147–155. [CrossRef]

38. Neuböck, T.; Schrefl, M. Modelling Knowledge about Data Analysis Processes in Manufacturing. *IFAC PapersOnLine* **2015**, *28*, 277–282. [CrossRef]
39. Opresnik, D.; Fiasché, M.; Taisch, M.; Hirsch, M. An Evolving Fuzzy Inference System for Extraction of Rule Set for Planning a Product–Service Strategy. *Inf. Technol. Manag.* **2017**, *18*, 131–147. [CrossRef]
40. Shollo, A. Using Business Intelligence in IT Governance Decision Making. *IFIP Adv. Inf. Commun. Technol.* **2011**, *366*, 3–15. [CrossRef]
41. Inmon, W.H. Building the Data Warehouse. *Commun. ACM* **2005**, *41*, 52–60.
42. Kimball, R.; Ross, M. *The Data Warehouse Toolkit*; John Wiley & Sons: Chichester, UK, 2002.
43. Scholl, M.H.; Mansmann, S.; Golfarelli, M.; Rizzi, S. Visual Online Analytical Processing (OLAP). In *Encyclopedia of Database Systems*; Springer: New York, NY, USA, 2018; pp. 4517–4527.
44. Felsberger, A.; Oberegger, B.; Reiner, G. A Review of Decision Support Systems for Manufacturing Systems. *CEUR Workshop Proc.* **2017**, *1793*, 8.
45. Psarommatis, F.; Kiritsis, D. A Hybrid Decision Support System for Automating Decision Making in the Event of Defects in the Era of Zero Defect Manufacturing. *J. Ind. Inf. Integr.* **2022**, *26*, 100263. [CrossRef]
46. Abdullah, M.; Bahurmuz, N.; Alnajim, R.; Alshingiti, Z. Decision Making Using Document Driven Decision Support Systems. *Int. J. Data Sci.* **2020**, *5*, 168. [CrossRef]
47. Pirnay, L. Data-Driven Strategy Maps: A Hybrid Approach to Strategic and Performance Management Combining Hard Data and Experts' Knowledge. *CEUR Workshop Proc.* **2021**, *2906*, 59–68.
48. Alowaigl, A.A.; Al-Shqeerat, K.H.; Hadwan, M. A Multi-Criteria Assessment of Decision Support Systems in Educational Environments. *Indones. J. Electr. Eng. Comput. Sci.* **2021**, *22*, 985. [CrossRef]
49. Pohancenik, A. *Predictive Analytics and AI in Governance: Data-Driven Government in a Free Society-Artificial Intelligence, Big Data and Algorithmic Decision-Making in Government from a Liberal Perspective*; NEOS Lab: Viena, Austria, 2019; ISBN 9783200065550.
50. Zulkepli, F.S.; Ibrahim, R.; Bakri, A.; Zakaria, N.H.; Hamed, H.N.A.; Khalid, H.; Maarof, M.A. A Multi-Dimensional Database Model for Research Performance Analysis. *ARPN J. Eng. Appl. Sci.* **2015**, *10*, 17923–17929.
51. Ul Hassan, C.A.; Irfan, R.; Shah, M.A. Integrated Architecture of Data Warehouse with Business Intelligence Technologies. In Proceedings of the 2018 24th International Conference on Automation and Computing (ICAC), Newcastle Upon Tyne, UK, 6–7 September 2018; pp. 6–7. [CrossRef]
52. Janković, S.; Mladenović, S.; Mladenović, D.; Vesković, S.; Glavić, D. Schema on Read Modeling Approach as a Basis of Big Data Analytics Integration in EIS. *Enterp. Inf. Syst.* **2018**, *12*, 1180–1201. [CrossRef]
53. Luhn, H.P. A Business Intelligence System. *IBM J. Res. Dev.* **1958**, *2*, 314–319. [CrossRef]
54. Bank, M. Using Business Intelligence Capabilities to Improve the Quality of Decision-Making: A Case Study Of. *Int. J. Econ. Manag. Eng.* **2019**, *13*, 147–158.
55. Pedersen, T.B. *Managing Big Multidimensional Data*; Aalborg University: Aalborg, Denmark, 2013; pp. 3–6.
56. Němec, R. Assessment of Query Execution Performance Using Selected Business Intelligence Tools and Experimental Agile Oriented Data Modeling Approach. In Proceedings of the 2015 Federated Conference on Computer Science and Information Systems (FedCSIS), Lodz, Poland, 13–16 September 2015; Volume 5, pp. 1327–1333. [CrossRef]
57. Goede, R. Sustainable Business Intelligence Systems: Modelling for the Future. *Syst. Res. Behav. Sci.* **2021**, *38*, 685–695. [CrossRef]
58. Nakhal, A.A.J.; Patriarca, R.; Di Gravio, G.; Antonioni, G.; Paltrinieri, N. Investigating Occupational and Operational Industrial Safety Data through Business Intelligence and Machine Learning. *J. Loss Prev. Process Ind.* **2021**, *73*, 104608. [CrossRef]
59. Bimonte, S.; Antonelli, L.; Rizzi, S. Requirements-Driven Data Warehouse Design Based on Enhanced Pivot Tables. *Requir. Eng.* **2021**, *26*, 43–65. [CrossRef]
60. Tanphet, S.; Wanchai, P. Applying Business Intelligence Technology for Equipment Maintenance and Repair Plan of Telecommunications Services Provider. In Proceedings of the 2018 20th International Conference on Advanced Communication Technology (ICACT), Chuncheon, Korea, 11–14 February 2018; pp. 448–453. [CrossRef]
61. Singh, R.P.; Singh, K. Design and Research of Data Analysis System for Student Education Improvement (Case Study: Student Progression System in University). In Proceedings of the 2016 International Conference on Micro-Electronics and Telecommunication Engineering (ICMETE), Ghaziabad, India, 22–23 September 2016; pp. 508–512. [CrossRef]
62. Maryska, M.; Doucek, P. Reference Model of Cost Allocation and Profitability for Efficient Management of Corporate ICT. *Procedia Econ. Financ.* **2015**, *23*, 1009–1016. [CrossRef]
63. Souibgui, M.; Atigui, F.; Zammali, S.; Cherfi, S.; Yahia, S. Ben Data Quality in ETL Process: A Preliminary Study. *Procedia Comput. Sci.* **2019**, *159*, 676–687. [CrossRef]
64. Huaman, E. Steps to Knowledge Graphs Quality Assessment. *arXiv* **2022**, arXiv:2208.07779.
65. Dhaouadi, A.; Bousselmi, K.; Gammoudi, M.M.; Monnet, S.; Hammoudi, S. Data Warehousing Process Modeling from Classical Approaches to New Trends: Main Features and Comparisons. *Data* **2022**, *7*, 113. [CrossRef]
66. Moscoso-Zea, O.; Andres-Sampedro; Luján-Mora, S. Datawarehouse Design for Educational Data Mining. In Proceedings of the 2016 15th International Conference on Information Technology Based Higher Education and Training (ITHET), Istanbul, Turkey, 8–10 September 2016. [CrossRef]

67. Palanisamy, A.M.; Nataraj, R.V.; Sangeetha, S.; Sountharrajan, S. Virtual DataStack for Application Domains: Concepts, Challenges and Generation Techniques. In Proceedings of the 2020 3rd International Conference on Intelligent Sustainable Systems (ICISS), Thoothukudi, India, 3–5 December 2020; pp. 1314–1318. [CrossRef]
68. Macedo, H.D.; Oliveira, J.N. A Linear Algebra Approach to OLAP. *Form. Asp. Comput.* **2015**, *27*, 283–307. [CrossRef]
69. Takács, V.L.; Bubnó, K.; Ráthonyi, G.G.; Bába, É.B.; Szilágyi, R. Data Warehouse Hybrid Modeling Methodology. *Data Sci. J.* **2020**, *19*, 1–23. [CrossRef]
70. Santos, M.Y.; Oliveira e Sá, J. A Data Warehouse Model for Business Processes Data Analytics. In Proceedings of the International Conference on Computational Science and Its Applications, Beijing, China, 4–7 July 2016; Springer: Berlin/Heidelberg, Germany, 2016; pp. 241–256.
71. Kassem, G.; Turowski, K. Matching of Business Data in a Generic Business Process Warehousing. In Proceedings of the 2018 International Conference on Computational Science and Computational Intelligence (CSCI), Las Vegas, NV, USA, 12–14 December 2018; pp. 284–289. [CrossRef]
72. Sturm, A. Supporting Business Process Analysis via Data Warehousing Arnon. *J. Softw. Evol. Process* **2012**, *24*, 303–319. [CrossRef]
73. Borges, V.A.; Nogueira, B.M.; Barbosa, E.F. A Multidimensional Data Model for the Analysis of Learning Management Systems under Different Perspectives. In Proceedings of the 2016 IEEE Frontiers in Education Conference (FIE), Erie, PA, USA, 12–15 October 2016. [CrossRef]
74. Tyrychtr, J.; Brožek, J.; Vostrovský, V. Multidimensional Modelling from Open Data for Precision Agriculture. *Lect. Notes Bus. Inf. Process.* **2015**, *231*, 141–152. [CrossRef]
75. Nešetřil, K.; Šembera, J.; Nešetřil, K.; Šembera, J.; Intelligence, B.; Information, G. Business Intelligence and Geographic Information System for Hydrogeology. In Proceedings of the International Symposium on Environmental Software Systems, Wageningen, The Netherlands, 5–7 February 2018.
76. Patel, J. An Effective and Scalable Data Modeling for Enterprise Big Data Platform. In Proceedings of the 2019 IEEE International Conference on Big Data (Big Data), Los Angeles, CA, USA, 9–12 December 2019; pp. 2691–2697. [CrossRef]
77. Höpken, W.; Fuchs, M.; Keil, D.; Lexhagen, M. Business Intelligence for Cross-Process Knowledge Extraction at Tourism Destinations. *Inf. Technol. Tour.* **2015**, *15*, 101–130. [CrossRef]
78. Korelič, I.; Mirchevska, V.; Rajkovič, V.; Kljajić Borštnar, M.; Gams, M. Multiple-Criteria Approach to Optimisation of Multidimensional Data Models. *Informatica* **2015**, *26*, 283–312. [CrossRef]
79. Schuetz, C.G.; Neumayr, B.; Schrefl, M.; Neuböck, T. Reference Modeling for Data Analysis: The BIRD Approach. *Int. J. Coop. Inf. Syst.* **2016**, *25*, 1–46. [CrossRef]
80. Amin, M.M.; Sutrisman, A.; Dwitayanti, Y. Development of Star-Schema Model for Lecturer Performance in Research Activities. *Int. J. Adv. Comput. Sci. Appl.* **2021**, *12*, 74–80. [CrossRef]
81. Moscoso-Zea, O.; Paredes-Gualtor, J.; Luján-Mora, S. A Holistic View of Data Warehousing in Education. *IEEE Access* **2018**, *6*, 64659–64673. [CrossRef]
82. Muntean, M.; Dănăiață, D.; Hurbean, L.; Jude, C. A Business Intelligence & Analytics Framework for Clean and Affordable Energy Data Analysis. *Sustainability* **2021**, *13*, 638. [CrossRef]
83. Muszyńska, K.; Marx, S. Communication Management Practices in International Projects in Polish and German Higher Education Institutions. *Procedia Comput. Sci.* **2019**, *164*, 329–336. [CrossRef]
84. Levstek, A.; Pucihar, A.; Hovelja, T. Towards an Adaptive Strategic IT Governance Model for SMEs. *J. Theor. Appl. Electron. Commer. Res.* **2022**, *17*, 230–252. [CrossRef]
85. Huesemann, B.; Lechtenboerger, J.; Vossen, G. Conceptual Data Warehouse Design. *Data Wareh. Syst.* **2014**, *2000*, 89–119. [CrossRef]
86. Snider, D.; Morgan, J.D.; Schwartz, M.; Adkison, A.; Baptiste, D.J. An Online Analytical Processing Database for Environmental Water Quality Analytics. In Proceedings of the SoutheastCon 2018, St. Petersburg, FL, USA, 19–22 April 2018; pp. 18–22. [CrossRef]
87. Schütz, C.; Schausberger, S.; Kovacic, I.; Schrefl, M. Semantic OLAP Patterns: Elements of Reusable Business Analytics. In Proceedings of the OTM Confederated International Conferences "On the Move to Meaningful Internet Systems", Rhodes, Greece, 23–27 October 2017.
88. Hilal, M.; Schuetz, C.G.; Schrefl, M. Using Superimposed Multidimensional Schemas and OLAP Patterns for RDF Data Analysis. *Open Comput. Sci.* **2018**, *8*, 18–37. [CrossRef]
89. Chen, Y.; Wang, M.; Li, L. A Framework for the Contract Management System in Cloud-Based ERP for SMEs in the Construction Industry. In Proceedings of the International Conference on Construction and Real Estate Management 2019, Lyon, France, 2–4 August 2019; pp. 1–11. [CrossRef]
90. Veneberg, R.K.M.; Iacob, M.E.; Sinderen, M.J.V.; Bodenstaff, L. Enterprise Architecture Intelligence: Combining Enterprise Architecture and Operational Data. In Proceedings of the 2014 IEEE 18th International Enterprise Distributed Object Computing Conference, Ulm, Germany, 1–5 September 2014; pp. 22–31. [CrossRef]
91. Volden, G.H. Assessing Public Projects' Value for Money: An Empirical Study of the Usefulness of Cost-Benefit Analyses in Decision-Making. *Proj. Manag. J.* **2018**, 917–925. [CrossRef]
92. Sefair, J.A.; Méndez, C.Y.; Babat, O.; Medaglia, A.L.; Zuluaga, L.F. Linear Solution Schemes for Mean-SemiVariance Project Portfolio Selection Problems: An Application in the Oil and Gas Industry. *Omega* **2017**, *68*, 39–48. [CrossRef]

93. Hannila, H.; Kuula, S.; Harkonen, J.; Haapasalo, H. Digitalisation of a Company Decision-Making System: A Concept for Data-Driven and Fact-Based Product Portfolio Management. *J. Decis. Syst.* **2020**, *31*, 258–279. [CrossRef]
94. Bhimani, A.; Broedel Lopes, A.; de Aquino, A.C.B. Measurement Costs and Control in Outsourcing Relationships. *Int. J. Manag. Financ. Account.* **2017**, *8*, 296–318. [CrossRef]
95. Dumitriu, D.; Popescu, M.A.-M. Enterprise Architecture Framework Design in IT Management. *Procedia Manuf.* **2020**, *46*, 932–940. [CrossRef]
96. Baker, M.; Bourne, M. A Governance Framework for the Idea-to-Launch Process: Development and Application of a Governance Framework for New Product Development. *Res. Technol. Manag.* **2014**, *57*, 42–48. [CrossRef]
97. Tolonen, A.; Shahmarichatghieh, M.; Harkonen, J.; Haapasalo, H. Product Portfolio Management—Targets and Key Performance Indicators for Product Portfolio Renewal over Life Cycle. *Int. J. Prod. Econ.* **2015**, *170*, 468–477. [CrossRef]
98. Chugh, R.; Grandhi, S. Why Business Intelligence? *Int. J. E Entrepreneursh. Innov.* **2013**, *4*, 1–14. [CrossRef]
99. Pajić, A.; Pantelić, O.; Stanojević, B. Representing IT Performance Management as Metamodel. *Int. J. Comput. Commun. Control* **2014**, *9*, 758–767. [CrossRef]
100. Yigitbasioglu, O.M. Drivers of Management Accounting Adaptability: The Agility Lens. *J. Account. Organ. Chang.* **2017**, *13*, 262–281. [CrossRef]
101. Izonin, I.; Tkachenko, R.; Verhun, V.; Zub, K. An Approach towards Missing Data Management Using Improved GRNN-SGTM Ensemble Method. *Eng. Sci. Technol. Int. J.* **2021**, *24*, 749–759. [CrossRef]
102. Shen, X.; Guo, Y.; Li, A. Cooperative Coevolution with an Improved Resource Allocation for Large-Scale Multi-Objective Software Project Scheduling. *Appl. Soft Comput.* **2020**, *88*, 106059. [CrossRef]

Case Report

Business Intelligence's Self-Service Tools Evaluation

Jordina Orcajo Hernández [1] and Pau Fonseca i Casas [2,*]

[1] BarcelonaTech School of Mathematics and Statistics, Universitat Politècnica de Catalunya, C. Pau Gargallo 5, 08028 Barcelona, Spain
[2] BarcelonaTech Statistics and Operations Research Department, Universitat Politècnica de Catalunya, Jordi Girona 3-1, 08034 Barcelona, Spain
* Correspondence: pau@fib.upc.edu; Tel.: +34-934-01-7735

Abstract: The software selection process in the context of a big company is not an easy task. In the Business Intelligence area, this decision is critical, since the resources needed to implement the tool are huge and imply the participation of all organization actors. We propose to adopt the systemic quality model to perform a neutral comparison between four business intelligence self-service tools. To assess the quality, we consider eight characteristics and eighty-two metrics. We built a methodology to evaluate self-service BI tools, adapting the systemic quality model. As an example, we evaluated four tools that were selected from all business intelligence platforms, following a rigorous methodology. Through the assessment, we obtained two tools with the maximum quality level. To obtain the differences between them, we were more restrictive increasing the level of satisfaction. Finally, we got a unique tool with the maximum quality level, while the other one was rejected according to the rules established in the methodology. The methodology works well for this type of software, helping in the detailed analysis and neutral selection of the final software to be used for the implementation.

Keywords: business intelligence; self-service tools; systemic quality model; software selection

Citation: Orcajo Hernández, J.; Fonseca i Casas, P. Business Intelligence's Self-Service Tools Evaluation. *Technologies* **2022**, *10*, 92. https://doi.org/10.3390/technologies10040092

Academic Editor: Mohammed Mahmoud

Received: 11 July 2022
Accepted: 4 August 2022
Published: 10 August 2022

Publisher's Note: MDPI stays neutral with regard to jurisdictional claims in published maps and institutional affiliations.

Copyright: © 2022 by the authors. Licensee MDPI, Basel, Switzerland. This article is an open access article distributed under the terms and conditions of the Creative Commons Attribution (CC BY) license (https://creativecommons.org/licenses/by/4.0/).

1. Introduction

Business Intelligence (BI) is associated with a set of tools and techniques related to the transformation of raw data into meaningful and useful information for business analysis purposes [1,2]. BI technologies are capable of handling large amounts of unstructured data to help identify, develop and otherwise create new strategic business opportunities. One of the principal objectives of BI is to allow an easy interpretation of these large volumes of data. Specifically, self-service BI aims to improve the company's useful information use from their data. Self-service BI wants to allow workers to understand and analyze data without specialized expertise. In that sense, workers can make, faster and better decisions because the information is available and is not needed to wait for a specific reporting. Technical teams will be freed from the burden of satisfying end-user report requests, so they can focus their efforts on more strategic IT initiatives. There are many self-service BI tools in the market, and before recommending a particular one, an in-depth analysis of the available tools on the market should be conducted. The automation and systematization of the selection process of critical enterprise software such as enterprise resource planning (ERP) was studied by several authors (e.g., see [3]). Researchers attempted to rank several techniques and ERP alternatives in the process [4,5], as well as adapt existing methodologies using artificial neural networks to improve the decision process [6], use hybrid methodologies [7] or specify different scopes, for instance in the application to the management information system of a power plant [8] or supply chains [9]. In line with the definition of the BI tools, in [10] an in-depth analysis of existing challenges of business intelligence (BI) and a proposal for the new generation of tools are presented, with a focus on new data sources (e.g., social media) and including concepts like security and trust. In this context, social business intelligence requires integration with trusted external data [11].

Therefore, we need a method to be able to select or implement the appropriate information system that allows us to use this information in an appropriate manner in our organization.

In line with the implementation of an information system, an analysis of the problems related to its implementation and use can be reviewed in [12]. Moreover, some proposals for modeling information systems [13] and performing a functional safety assessment [14] can be useful for the modeling of the overall infrastructure. However, no attempts have been made to systematize the selection of BI tools in the context of a big corporation.

In software selection, the systemic quality model (SQMO) was proposed [15], providing successful implementation examples in other software areas (see [16,17]).

This work aims to build a comparative assessment of self-service BI tools, adapting a systemic quality model (SQMO) and applying the method to finally evaluate, in this case, four tools. Therefore, we focused on the development of a method that guides the selection process of BI tools. It must consider that the "best tool" concept is not applicable in this scope. For this reason, it is more usual to talk about an appropriate solution for a particular project.

2. BI Users

A rigorous evaluation should be conducted by several users to obtain trustworthy results. In particular, self-service BI tools, as data systems, usually have different user profiles and several users of each type should evaluate the tools from their particular point of view.

There are three different profiles of a user in data systems, according to [18].

Farmers: They access information predictably and repetitively. We could say that they have their parcel of information and they regularly cultivate and extract profit from this. They do not access a huge amount of data (because they do not leave the parcel) and they usually ask for aggregated data. These users usually use OLAP (online analytical processing) tools, which are focused on non-informatics users. They are simple and their main objective is data visualization. As farmers, there are employers, providers, and customers to whom the organization offers informational services. Currently, business intelligence, which promotes the use of these systems at all levels of the organization, allows business users to use data and information in business processes naturally, without having to leave their applications.

Explorer: Opposite to farmers, explorers have unpredictable and irregular access. They spend much time planning and preparing for their studies and when they have everything ready, they start to explore a lot of detailed information. They do not know exactly what they are looking for until they find it, and the results are not guaranteed in every case. However, sometimes they find something really interesting that improves the business. They are also known as power users. Thanks to big data, explorers have become data scientists. A data scientist must be able to extract information from large volumes of data according to a clear business objective and then present it in a simple way to non-expert users in the organization. Therefore, it consists of a cross profile with skills in computer science, mathematics, statistics, data mining, graphic design, data visualization, and usability.

Tourists: Typically, they entail a group of two or more people. On one side, there is a person with an overview of the company that comes up with the possibility of a study on a certain topic. On the other, there is a computer expert that knows the systems analysis of the company and is the manager who finds out if the study is feasible with the available data and tools. This team will access data without following any pattern and will rarely observe the same data twice. Therefore, their requirements cannot be known a priori. Tools used by tourists are browsers or search engines (to search both data and metadata) and the result of their work will be the projects carried out by *farmers* or *explorers*. In short, a tourist is a casual user of the information.

This project aims to develop a method of evaluation that should be applicable taking into consideration the different profiles of the tool. For example, if the tool will be used by *farmers* and *explorers*, some *farmer* and *explorer* users should evaluate the tool. After this evaluation, a mean is done with the results. In this paper, to illustrate the methodology used, the evaluation by an *explorer* user is shown.

To carry out an assessment, several steps should be followed. First of all, the evaluator responsible for preparing the assessment has to know the subject and propose a methodology adapted to the specific scope. The adaption implies choosing a set of interesting metrics that will be used in the evaluation. Users can advise the evaluator about interesting metrics and the evaluator has to design a questionnaire to include them, the questionnaire is presented on Appendix D. Next, the evaluator must send a questionnaire to the users to collect the opinions from experts in the area. Moreover, the evaluator has to provide every item required to perform the evaluation (questionnaires, data, applications, etc.). Finally, the questionnaires are collected and the assessment proceeds in line with the chosen methodology to evaluate the results.

3. Methodology, the Systemic Quality Model (SQMO)

The systemic quality model (SQMO) was proposed in 2001 by [15]. The application of the SQMO for software evaluations provided successful implementation examples, see Figure 1.

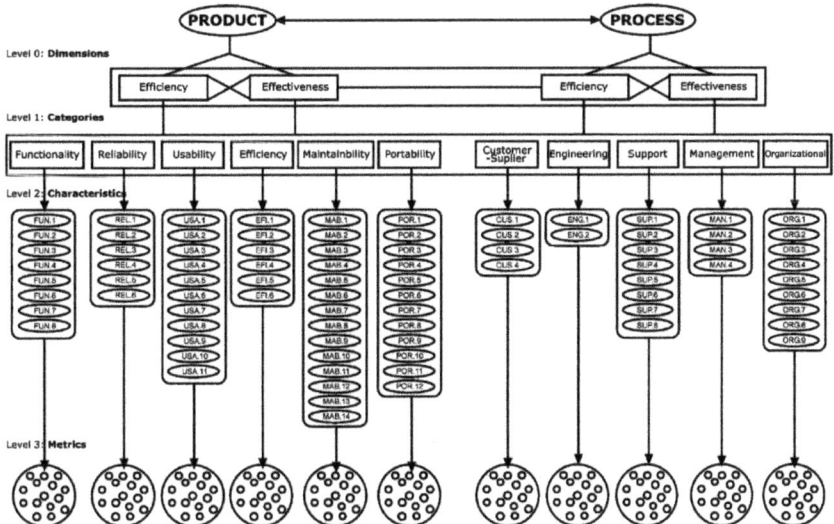

Figure 1. Diagram of the systemic quality model (SQMO) [16].

Until then, several models existed to evaluate product software and others to evaluate process software, but none with the capability to evaluate both aspects accurately. The SQMO can use either the *product* or the *process* sub-model or both. The first sub-model is designed to evaluate the developed software, while the second is designed to evaluate the development process of the software. From [15], the SQMO sub-models have different levels to assess software, see [16,17].

3.1. Level 0: Dimensions

There are two dimensions for each sub-model: *efficiency* and *effectiveness* for the *product* and *efficiency* and *effectiveness* for the *process*. *Effectiveness* is the capability of producing the required result, while *efficiency* is the capability to produce a specific result effectively with a minimum amount or quantity of waste, expense, or unnecessary effort.

3.2. Level 1: Categories

There are six elements corresponding to *product* and five corresponding to *process*. The categories for the *product* sub-model are presented in Table 1.

Table 1. SQMO product sub-model categories [16].

Category	Definition
Functionality (FUN)	Functionality is the capacity of the software product to provide functions that meet specific and implicit needs when software is used under specific conditions
Reliability (FIA)	Reliability is the capacity of a software product to maintain a specified level of performance when used under specific conditions
Usability (USA)	Usability is the capacity of the software product to be attractive, understood, learned, and used by the user under certain specific conditions
Efficiency (EFI)	Efficiency is the capacity of a software product to provide appropriate performance, relative to the number of resources used, under stated conditions
Maintainability (MAB)	Maintainability is the capacity of the software to be modified. Modifications can include corrections, improvements, or adaptations of the software to adjust to changes in the environment, in terms of the functional requirements and specifications
Portability (POR)	Portability is the capacity of the software product to be transferred from one environment to another

The categories for the *process* sub-model are presented in Table 2.

Table 2. SQMO process sub-model categories [16].

Category	Definition
Client-supplier (CUS)	Is made up of processes that have an impact on the client, support the development and transition of the software to the client, and give the correct operation and use of the software product or service
Engineering (ENG)	Consists of processes that directly specify, implement, or maintain the software product, its relation to the system, and documentation on it
Support (SUP)	Consists of processes that can be used by any of the processes (including support ones) at several levels of the acquisition life cycle
Management (MAN)	Consists of processes that contain practices of a generic nature that can be used by anyone managing any kind of project or process, within a primary life cycle
Organizational (ORG)	Contain processes that establish the organization's commercial goals and develop process, product, and resource goods (value) that will help the organization attain the goals set in the projects

3.3. Level 2: Characteristics

SQMO specifies that each category consists of a set of characteristics, which define the more important characteristics and features that must be satisfied to assure the software *product* and/or *process* quality. *Product* characteristics are specified in Table 3. and process characteristics in Table 4. They are defined more accurately in [17].

Table 3. Characteristics for product sub-model.

Category	Characteristics	
	Product Effectiveness	Product Efficiency
Functionality	Fit to purpose	Correctness
	Precision	Structured
	Interoperability	Encapsulated
	Security	Specified
Reliability	Maturity	Correctness
	Fault tolerance	Structured
	Recovery	Encapsulated

Table 3. *Cont.*

Category	Characteristics	
	Product Effectiveness	**Product Efficiency**
Usability	Ease of understanding	Complete
	Ease of learning	Consistent
	Graphical Interface	Effective
	Operability	Specified
	Conformity of standards	Documented
		Auto-descriptive
Efficiency	Execution performance	Effective
	Resource utilization	No redundant
		Direct
		Used
Maintainability	Analysis Capability	Attachment
	Ease of changing	Cohesion
	Stability	Encapsulated
	Testability	Software maturity
		Structure information
		Descriptive
		Correctness
		Structural
		Modularity
Portability	Adaptability	Consistent
	Installation capability	Parameterized
	Co-existence	Encapsulated
	Replacement capability	Cohesive
		Specified
		Documented
		Auto-descriptive
		No redundant
		Auditing
		Quality management
	Data Quality -both dimensions-	

Table 4. Characteristics for the process sub-model.

Category	Characteristics	
	Process Effectiveness	**Process Efficiency**
Customer–Supplier	Acquisition system or software product	Supply
	Requirement determination	Operation
Engineering	Development	Maintenance of software and systems Principio del formulario

Table 4. Cont.

Category	Characteristics	
	Process Effectiveness	**Process Efficiency**
Support	Quality assurance	Documentation
	Joint review	Configuration management
	Auditing	Verification
	Solving problems	Validation
		Joint review
		Auditing
		Solving problems
Management	Management	Management
	Quality management	Project management
	Risk management	Quality management
		Risk management
Organizational	Organizational alignment	Establishment of the process
	Management of change	Process evaluation
	Process improvement	Process improvement
	Measurement	HHRR management
	Reuse	Infrastructure

3.4. Level 3: Metrics

Each characteristic consists of a group of metrics to be evaluated. They are the evaluable attributes of the product and the process, and they are not agreed upon because they vary depending on each study case. Metrics are detailed in Appendix "Appendix A. The Metrics Used in the Selection Process".

3.5. Algorithm

The algorithm to measure the systematic quality by the SQMO, referenced in [15] is the following explained. First of all, the product software is measured, and then the development process.

3.6. Product Software

The first measured category must be always *functionality*. If the product does not meet the *functionality* category, the evaluation is ended. It is because the functional category identifies the software capability to fit the purpose for what it was built.

After that, a sub-model is adapted depending on the requirements. The algorithm suggests working with a maximum of three characteristics of the product (including *functionality*) because if more than three product features are selected, some might conflict. In this sense, [19] indicates that the satisfaction of quality attributes can have an effect, sometimes positive and sometimes negative, on meeting other quality attributes. The definition of satisfaction can vary depending on the case of use and it is not fixed by the methodology. In Section 6, this issue is discussed.

Finally, to measure the quality product of the software, Table 5 shows the quality levels related to the satisfied categories.

Once the evaluation of the product software has ended, recalling that only if the quality level is at least *basic*, the *development process* evaluation may start.

Table 5. Quality levels for the product software.

Functionality	Second Category	Third Category	Quality Level
Satisfied	No satisfied	No satisfied	Basic
Satisfied	Satisfied	No satisfied	Medium
Satisfied	No satisfied	Satisfied	Medium
Satisfied	Satisfied	Satisfied	Advanced

3.7. Development Process

To evaluate the *development process* there are four steps to follow. The algorithm used in the *development process* evaluation is fixed, unlike the *product software* evaluation. The steps are as follows: (i) determining the percentage of N/A (not applying) answers in the questionnaire for each category. If this percentage is greater than 11%, the application of the measuring instrument must be analyzed, and the algorithm stops. Otherwise, we continue with step 2; (ii) determining the percentage of N/K (not knowing) answers in the questionnaire for each category. If this percentage is greater than 15%, it shows that there is a high level of ignorance of the activities of the particular category. If the percentage is lower, we continue with step 3; (iii) determining the satisfaction level for each category (the definition of satisfaction can vary depending on the case of use and it is not fixed by the methodology; in Section 6, this issue is discussed); (iv) measuring the quality level of the process. The quality levels related to the satisfied categories in Table 6 are:

- *Basic level*: It is the minimum required level. Categories *customer-supplier* and *engineering* are satisfied.
- *Medium level*: In addition to the basic level categories satisfied, categories *support* and *management* are satisfied.
- *Advanced level*: All categories are satisfied.

Table 6. Quality levels for development process.

Quality Levels			Category Satisfied
Advanced	Medium	Basic	Customer–supplier
			Engineering
			Support
			Management
			Organizational

Finally, there must be a joint between the product quality measuring and the process quality measuring, to obtain systematic quality measuring. The systemic quality levels are proposed in Table 7.

Table 7. Systemic quality levels.

Product Quality Level	Process Quality Level	Systemic Quality Level
Basic	-	Null
Basic	Basic	Basic
Medium	-	Null
Medium	Basic	Basic
Advanced	-	Null
Advanced	Basic	Medium
Basic	Medium	Basic
Medium	Medium	Medium
Advanced	Medium	Medium
Basic	Advanced	Medium
Medium	Advanced	Medium
Advanced	Advanced	Advanced

This method of measurement is responsible for maintaining a balance between the sub-models (when they are both included in the model).

4. Adoption of the Systemic Quality Model (SQMO)

SQMO was selected as a reference because it is a complete approach influenced by many other models. First of all, it respects the concept of systemic total quality from [20]. It also considers the balance between the *process* and *product* sub-models proposed by [21]. These sub-models are based on the *product* and *process* quality models from [22] and [23], respectively. Moreover, the product quality categories are based on the work of [24] and the international standard ISO/IEC 9126 (JTC 1/SC 7, 1991). The process categories are extracted from the international standard ISO/IEC 15504 (ISO IEC/TR 15504-2, 1998).

Some authors [25] have pointed out that when characteristics are complex, they can be divided into a simpler set and a new level for sub-characteristics can be created. In this particular case, sub-characteristics were considered to gain clarity. To adapt the SQMO to each particular case, it should be decided which sub-model will be considered (*product*, *process*, or both), as well as which dimension (*efficiency* or/and *effectiveness*), which sub-characteristics, and which respective metrics. In the current evaluation, only the *product* sub-model of SQMO was considered. The *process* sub-model is excluded because we intend to evaluate the fully developed tools as future tools useful for the BI workforce. Moreover, only the *effectiveness* dimension is considered because special attention is focused on the evaluation of features observed during the execution. However, if one considers including the sub-model *process* or the *efficiency* dimension, there is an option to do so by following the steps explained above. Figure 2 reflects the adapted model used in the current evaluation.

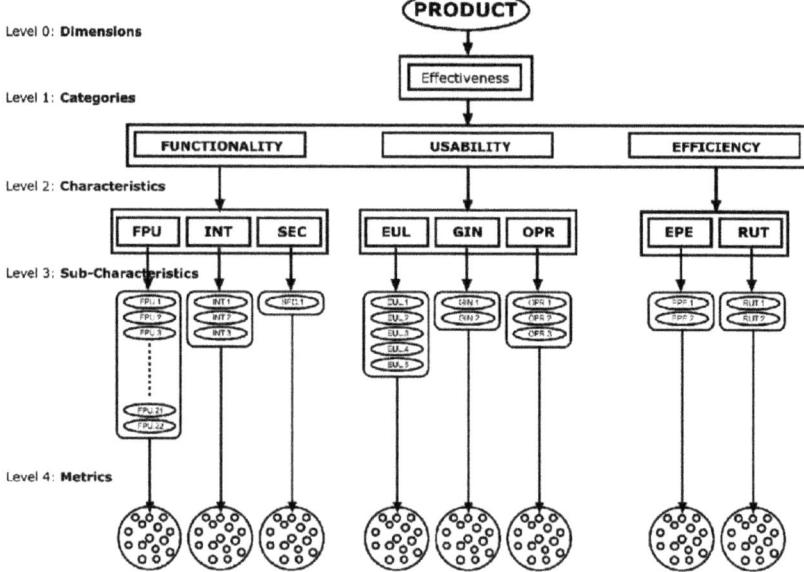

Figure 2. Diagram of the adapted systemic quality model [16].

Besides the *functionality* category, we choose *usability* because this type of tool (self-service BI tool) is focused on non-technical users and the difficulty of the product should be minimal. Moreover, it must be an attractive product because the success of the tool depends on the user's satisfaction. Finally, the *efficiency* category was chosen because the processor type, the hard disk space, and the minimum RAM required are all factors that determine the success of the tool's deployment. Self-service BI tools are popular thanks to their "working memory". Then, it is important to evaluate the minimum amount of memory required.

5. Scales of Measurement

In the current evaluation, all the evaluated metrics are ordinal variables because they have more than two categories and they can be ordered or ranked (see annex Appendix A. The Metrics Used in the Selection Process There are different types of scale measurement depending on the metric.

Type A of Scale Measurement

The following scale measures the metrics with a scale from 0 to 4 as follows:

- **0:** The application does not have the feature.
- **1:** The application matches the feature poorly or it does not strictly match the feature but it can obtain similar results.
- **2:** The application has the feature and matches the expectations, although it needs an extra corporative complement. This mark should also be assigned when the feature implies a manual job (e.g., typing code, clicking a button) and the metric requires an automatic job.
- **3:** The application has the feature and matches the expectations successfully without a complement.
- **4:** The application has the feature and presents advantages over others.

Even so, other metrics need to be measured specifically. Sub-type A.1 of scale measurement is assigned to binary metrics: We assign 0 values if the application does not have the feature, and 4 values if the application has it. We chose these values to be consistent with the rest of the measurement scales. Sub-type A.2 of scale measurement is assigned when the metric is measurable; we assign 4 to the application with a better result and a lower score than the others. As there are 4 values, the scale is from 4 to 1. Although, if some applications have the same value for a metric, the same score has to be assigned to them. To clarify the current scale measurement, we present an example of the metric *compilation speed* (see annex Appendix A.3. Efficiency Category). The *compilation speed* is measured with a scale from 1 to 4. We assign 1 value to the tools that require more time to compile, and 4 to the tool that requires a shorter time.

The official SQMO method involves a balance between all the characteristics because they have the same level of importance. However, sometimes, the user wants to give more importance to certain characteristics depending on his interests, and for that, we provided the following alternative, also used as a variant of SQMO. This alternative consists of assigning weights to the metrics. Therefore, the importance level of the metrics varies. We remark that weights must depend on each evaluation. However, we tried to assign weights generalizing, and based on our own experience, the weights were assigned considering the stakeholders of the company and experts' knowledge and information. Recalling that if the methodology is implemented in another use case, it can be modified. The used weights scale is the following:

- **0:** Not applicable to the organization.
- **1:** Possible feature or wish list item.
- **2:** Desired feature.
- **3:** Required or must-have feature.

Finally, final scores for sub-characteristics are computed using the weights assigned to the metrics. The final score of a sub-characteristic corresponds to the following formula:

$$score_{sub-characteristic\ i} = \frac{\sum_1^n v_j \times w_j}{\sum_j^n w_j} \quad (1)$$

where v_j is the value for the score assigned to metric j, while w_j is the weight for the corresponding metric. Moreover, n corresponds to the number of metrics in the sub-characteristic i. This adaption is applied when the importance level of the metrics is not the same for all metrics (see Table 8 as an example). In this way, we got a score for each sub-characteristic, considering the weights of metrics.

Table 8. Weights of metrics. The complete list is in the Appendix A.

Metric	Weight
Excel files	3
Plain text	3
Connecting to different data sources at the same time	2
Allow renaming fields	3
R connection	2
Geographic information	2
...	

6. The Concept of Satisfaction

The term satisfaction can vary depending on the case of use. The evaluator can assign a limit, for example, 50%, and a sentence that a feature is satisfied if its score is higher than 50% of the maximum score on the measuring scale. For example, as our metric measuring scale is from 0 to 4, a score is satisfactory if it is higher than 2. However, the evaluator can also sentence the limit to 3 and in this way, a score is satisfactory if it is higher than 3. Usually, assessments are done to determine which tools are better than others, supposing that all the evaluated tools satisfy the main parts of the features. When the evaluator is looking for a distinction between tools, this type of limit can be useful. This concept applies to our units of measurement, which are metrics, sub-characteristics, characteristics, and categories. Once the metrics are evaluated with their respective scales of measurement (A, A.1, A.2), the methodology used to determine the satisfaction score is as follows: metrics scores are normalized with a percentage. A metric is satisfied if its percentage score is higher or equal to the fixed limit (satisfaction limit). Sub-characteristics are measured by the number of metrics satisfied (satisfaction score). Then, a particular sub-characteristic is satisfied if the number of satisfied metrics is higher or equal to its fixed limit (satisfaction limit). As weights are added, the satisfaction score becomes as Equation (1), where

$$v_j = \begin{cases} 1, \text{ if the metric } j \text{ is satisfied,} \\ 0, \text{ if the metric } j \text{ is not satisfied} \end{cases}$$

and characteristics are measured by the number of satisfied sub-characteristics (satisfaction score). Then, a particular characteristic is satisfied if the amount of satisfied sub-characteristics is higher or equal to its fixed limit (satisfaction limit). Categories are measured by the number of satisfied characteristics (satisfaction score). Then, a particular category is satisfied if the number of satisfied characteristics is higher or equal than its fixed limit (satisfaction limit). In the current evaluation, we decide to use the following limits, to get distinctions between tools, see Table 9. The evaluator can decide to modify the levels, to find distinctions between tools, or to be more restrictive or unrestrictive.

Table 9. Satisfaction limits.

Limit for metric	50%
Limit for sub-characteristic	50%
Limit for characteristic	75%
Limit for category	75%

Sub-Characteristics and Metrics for Self-Service BI Tools Evaluation

In an evaluation, the most key step is to decide which characteristics must be evaluated. According to the SQMO schema, these characteristics are already agreed upon, but we have to establish the metrics related to each characteristic, see Figure 3.

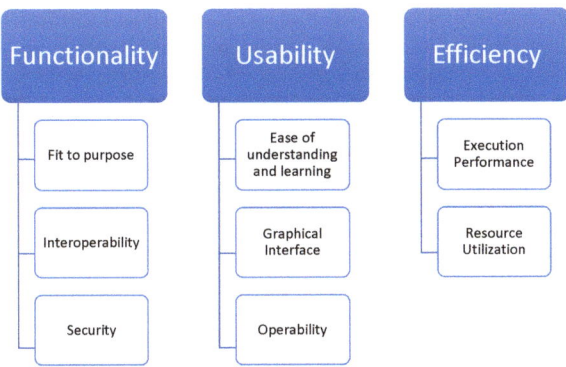

Figure 3. Characteristic schema for each category, according to [16].

With our experience in the BI department and after working with these types of tools, we feel confident to decide which particular topics should be checked from self-service BI software. For each of the three evaluable characteristics, the sub-characteristics are listed in Tables 10–12, their respective metrics can be found in the appendix "Appendix A. The Metrics Used in the Selection Process".

Table 10. Sub-characteristics for the functionality category, according to [17].

Functionality Category		
Fit for purpose	Interoperability	Security
Data loading	Languages	Security devices
Data model	Use project by third parts	
Fields relations	Languages	
Analysis	Data exchange	
Dashboard		
Reporting		

Table 11. Sub-characteristics for the usability category, according to [17].

Usability Category		
Ease of understanding and learning	Graphical interface	Operability
Learning time	Windows and mouse interface	Versatility
Browsing facilities	Display	
Terminology		
Help and documentation		
Support and training		

Table 12. Sub-characteristics for the efficiency category, according to [17].

Efficiency Category	
Execution performance	Resource utilization
Compilation speed	Hardware requirements
	Software requirements

7. Software Selection for the Evaluation

Before an evaluation, there must be a detailed selection of software that can be evaluated with the current evaluation model. Firstly, the area of application and the expected use of the software should be pre-established. The selection of software depends on this aspect because not every software is appropriate for every area. If the area of application is pre-established, the selected software will be according to it. Secondly, a new level of depth should be considered with more specifications about the tool functionality. It should consider the features that make the tool useful for what we want to do.

Finally, it is needed to perform the identification of the required attributes based on the particular aims of the organization that will use the tool. Some of these attributes must be mandatory and others must be non-mandatory. Mandatory attributes are those that must be met by the selected software, while non-mandatory attributes are those that will be evaluated, which are the metrics. This aspect takes a key role in the selection and in the evaluation.

Algorithm

Nowadays, there are many applications in the market related to business intelligence and because of that, deciding which applications should be included in an evaluation is a laborious task. Here we follow the methodology for selecting software proposed by Le Blanc [26]. In the first place, a long list of BI tools is elaborated (area of application). The next step is to reduce this to a medium list containing only tools that accomplish critical capabilities for business intelligence and analytics (the features that make the tool useful). Finally, a short list provided with the particular aims of the organization is built (required attributes).

The particular area of application is business intelligence. There are many platforms specialized in this area in the market. In this first step, we use Gartner as a data source for all business intelligence and analytics platforms in the market. Each year it edits and updates the report and inclusion criteria change depending on how the market changes, so it is a reference company. Therefore, we focus on those that have been mentioned in the report from Gartner Magic Quadrant for Business Intelligence and Analytics Platforms [27]. In this way, all the tools mentioned in the Magic Quadrant report of February 2015 (although Gartner, finally, has not evaluated them) compose the long list of sixty-three different platforms, which is shown in Table 13.

Table 13. The long list.

Adaptive Insights	Birst	DataRPM	FICO	Jedox	Oracle	Salesforce
Advizor Solutions	Bitam	Datawatch	GoodData	Kofax(Altosoft)	Palantir Technologies	Salient Management Company
AFS Technologies	Board International	Decisyon	IBM Cognos	L-3	Panorama	SAP
Alteryx	Centrifuge Systems	Dimensional Insight	iDashboards	LavaStorm Analytics	Pentaho	SAS (SAS Business Analytics)
Antivia	Chartio	Domo	Incorta	Logi Analytics	Platfora	Sisense
Arcplan	ClearStory Data	Dundas Data Visualization	InetSoft	Microsoft BI	Prognoz	Splunk
Automated Insgihts	DataHero	Eligotech	Infor	MicroStrategy.	Pyramid Analytics	Strategy Comapnio
BeyondCore	Datameer	eQ Technologic	Information Builder	Open Text (Actuate)	Qlik	SynerScope
Tableau	Targit	ThoughtSpot	Tibco Software	Yellowfin	Zoomdata	Zucche

To build the medium list we also base our selection on Gartner, in the Magic Quadrant report, where they choose the platforms to be evaluated if they satisfied particular capabilities that Gartner deems are critical to every business intelligence and analytics platform. In the Magic Quadrant report, Gartner chooses the platforms that satisfy 13 technique features and 3 non-techniques and they were classified into three categories: *enable*, *produce* and *consume*.

For *enable*, these features include:

- Functionality and modeling: Diverse source combination and analytical models' creation of user-defined measures, sets, groups, and hierarchies. Advanced capabilities can include semantic auto discovery, intelligent profiling, intelligent joins, data lineage, hierarchy generation, and data blending from varied data sources, including multi-structured data.
- Internal platform integration: To achieve a common look and feel, and install, query engine, shared metadata, and promo ability across all the components of the platform.
- BI platform administration: Capabilities that enable securing and administering users, scaling the platform, optimizing performance, and ensuring high availability and disaster recovery.
- Metadata management: Tools for enabling users to control the same systems-of-record semantic model and metadata. They should provide a robust and centralized way for administrators to search, capture, store, reuse, and publish metadata objects, such as dimensions, hierarchies, measures, performance metrics/KPIs, and report layout objects.
- Cloud deployment: Platform as a service and analytic application as service capabilities for building, deploying, and managing analytics in the cloud.
- Development and integration: The platform should provide a set of visual tools, programmatic and a development workbench for building dashboards, reports and also queries, and analysis.

For *produce*, these features include:

- Free-form interactive exploration: Enables the exploration of data through the manipulation of chart images; it must allow changing the color, brightness, size, and shape, and allow to include the motion of visual objects representing aspects of the dataset being analyzed.
- Analytic dashboards and content: The ability to create highly interactive dashboards and content with possibilities for visual exploration. Moreover, the inclusion of geospatial analytics to be consumed by others.
- IT-developed reporting and dashboards: Provides the capability to create highly formatted, print-ready, and interactive reports, with or without a previous parametrization. This includes the ability to publish multi objects, linked reports, and parameters with intuitive and interactive displays.
- Traditional styles of analysis: Ad hoc query that allows users to build their data queries, without relying on IT, to create a report. Specifically, the tools must have a reusable semantic layer that enables users to navigate available data sources, predefined metrics, hierarchies, and so on.

For *consume*, these features include:

- Mobile: Enables organizations in the development of mobile content and delivers it in a publishing and/or interactive mode.
- Collaboration and social integration: Enables users to share information, analysis, analytic content, and decisions via discussion threads, chat annotations, and storytelling.
- Embedded BI: Resources for modifying and creating analytic content, visualizations, and applications. Resources for embedding this analytic content into a business process and/or an application or portal.

Moreover, platforms had met other non-technical criteria. Generating at least $20 million in total BI-related software license revenue annually, or at least $17 million in total BI-related software license revenue annually, plus 15% year-over-year in new license growth. For vendors that also supply more transactional applications, it is necessary to analyze if its BI platform is used regularly by organizations that do not use its other transactional applications. Had a minimum of 35 customer survey responses from companies that use the vendor's BI platform in production.

With these added non-technical features, Gartner guarantees that at least 35 companies use each one of the tools. Moreover, it guarantees that companies that are growing year-over-year use these tools. The medium list obtained was composed of 24 platforms (see Table 14). Notice that this can change depending on the time of the analysis and the specific needs of the company.

Table 14. Medium list.

Alteryx	Information Builder	Panorama	SAP (SAP Lumira)
Birst	Logi Analytics	Pentaho	SAS (SAS Business Analytics)
Board International	Microsoft BI	Prognoz	Tableau
Datawatch	MicroStrategy. (MicroStrategy Visual Insight)	Pyramid Analytics	Targit
GoodData	Open Text (Actuate)	Qlik (QlikView)	Tibco Software
IBM Cognos	Oracle	Salient Management Company	Yellowfin

Finally, to build the short list we focus on the particular aims of our organization. The particular tools that we want to evaluate are self-service BI tools and which means that the business user should be able to analyze the information he wants and build his reports. In traditional tools, the user asks a technical team for the information he needs, and he orders how information has to be displayed the technical team prepares data and built the ordered reports. Against that, self-service tools are being imposed on others because the working methodology is changing from being driven by the business model to being driven by the data model. There are six [6] features that characterize the particular aims of the organization: *ease of use*, *ability to incorporate data sources*, *"intelligence" to interpret data models*, *analysis functions*, *integration with corporative systems*, and *support*.

Ease of use: These tools are designed to be used by non-technical people. It means that users do not need to spend much time learning how the tool works before doing basic analysis.

Ability to incorporate data sources, both corporative databases (Oracle, SAP, etc.) local information (basically Microsoft Excel®), and external databases (Twitter, etc.).

"Intelligence" to interpret correctly data models. As they are auto-service tools and they face many types of data models, without previous modeling by a technical team, the interpretation of the model from the tool must be the correct one. If it is not the correct one, it can be misleading. How easy is to discover that the data model is wrong and how easy is to arrange the data model, are also important points to consider.

Analysis functions: Besides the typical pie and bar graphs, they must incorporate other tools to get advanced analysis (integration in R, statistic routines ...) always remembering the easy use.

Possible integration with corporative systems and efficiency: Usually, the user will work with a huge volume of data and therefore the analysis cannot be on a local PC. Tools should have the option of a central server that accesses data and process them. Big companies need security when the server is incorporated into the corporative environment. Then, the role of an administrator in managing the user's access is key for big companies.

Support: In the case of an open-source tool being included in the larger list, it will not be considered in the medium list if it cannot offer instant customer support.

8. The Evaluated Software, the Short List

Finally, the short list is composed of eight platforms that can be evaluated with the adapted SQMO and they are nicked as software A, B, C, D, E, F, G, and H. See Figure 4 for a description of the process of list creation.

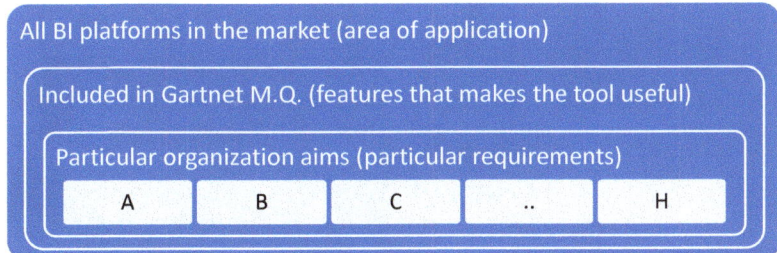

Figure 4. Schema for the selection process.

We describe next the evaluation of the four first tools from the short list, A, B, C, and D. For confidentiality reasons we are not going to provide the name of the short list, however, this does not have any impact on the description of the methodology used.

Data Used

To use and evaluate the applications, we needed a set of data and we decided to simulate it. The data set was simulated using R language and it was constructed by doing an emulation of a car insurance company database and using a relational structure. The structure of the dataset used can be consulted in Appendix C. The use of simulated data helps us in the testing of extreme cases.

9. Evaluation Results

Once metrics are chosen, weights are assigned to each metric, applications are selected and data are available, it is time to carry out the evaluation. The evaluation shown here is done only by one *explorer* user. However, an evaluation should be done by several users, representing all the different types of users. In particular, self-service BI tools, such as data systems, usually have different user profiles [28]. The same amount of each type of user should evaluate the tools, from their particular point of view. From the operative point of view, to store the scores, an excel sheet with the 82 metrics is built. It is where users complete the cells with the score for each one of the metrics. The sheet is built considering the weights, see annex Appendix B. Metrics Weights and the satisfaction scores (see Section 6). The sheet is replicated identically assigning a sheet to each application. Therefore, a total of four excel sheets are filled by users, see Appendix C. 0141220_Initial_Test. With the evaluation sheets, the user must score the metrics for the selected applications. Scoring the metrics is the key step to getting results about each of the applications in each of the three categories: *functionality*, *usability*, and *efficiency*. The four sheets, one for each application, and the same database must be offered to each of the users.

Results

Once time every metric has been evaluated it is time to get the results of the assessment. In the usual case that more than one user is being implied in the evaluation of the metrics, we recommend calculating a mean score for each metric. On the other hand, one of the bases of the methodology [17] is that if the *functionality* category is not satisfied, the evaluation is aborted and other categories are not evaluated. Because of that, the analysis starts with the satisfaction score of the *functionality* category. In the current evaluation, using the satisfaction limits mentioned in Table 9, the obtained satisfaction scores for *functionality* are shown in Figure 5.

With the adaption of the methodology, we sentence that a category is satisfied if 75% of its characteristics are satisfied. Applying that software, A does not satisfy the *functionality* category because it only satisfies 66.67% of the *functionality* characteristics. Then, the evaluation of software A is aborted.

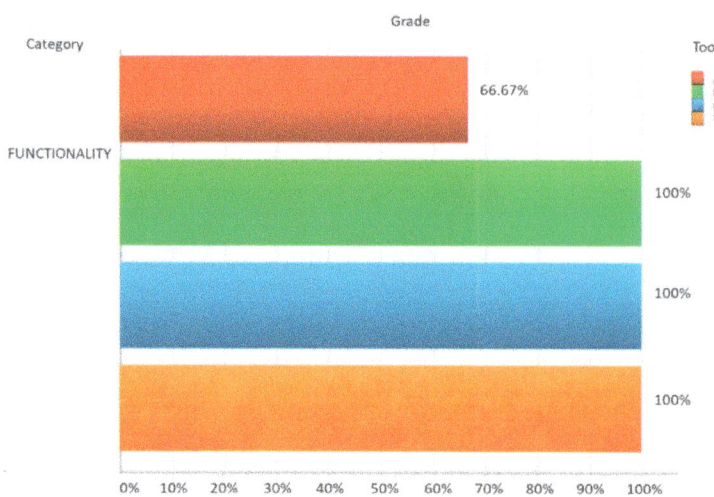

Figure 5. Results for the functionality category.

To know the reason software A does not satisfy the *functionality* category, an analysis of a deeper level helped us to know what the scores for each functional characteristic are. Functional characteristics are fit for purpose, interoperability, and security, and Figure 6. shows their respective satisfaction scores. We could see that the characteristic fit for purpose is not satisfied because only 66.67% of its sub-characteristics are satisfied. Particularly, the non-satisfied sub-characteristics are *field relations* and *reporting*.

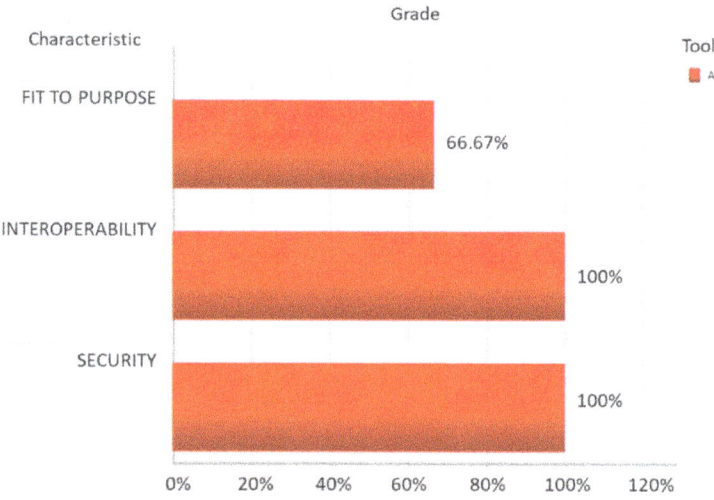

Figure 6. Functionality characteristics results, for tool A.

Software A does not satisfy the sub-characteristic Fields relations because it is not capable to alert about the presence of circular references (FFF1), and in fact, it does not skip them (FFF2). Moreover, it cannot directly relate a table to more than one table (FFF3). On the other hand, reporting sub-characteristics is not satisfied because software A does not have an option to build reports (FFR1), (FFR2), and (FFR3). Then, software A evaluation is aborted, and the evaluation continues with the three other tools. The other three tools satisfy the *usability* category in addition to functionality. Moreover, software B and D also satisfy the *efficiency* category, but C does not. Figure 7 shows the satisfaction score in each category.

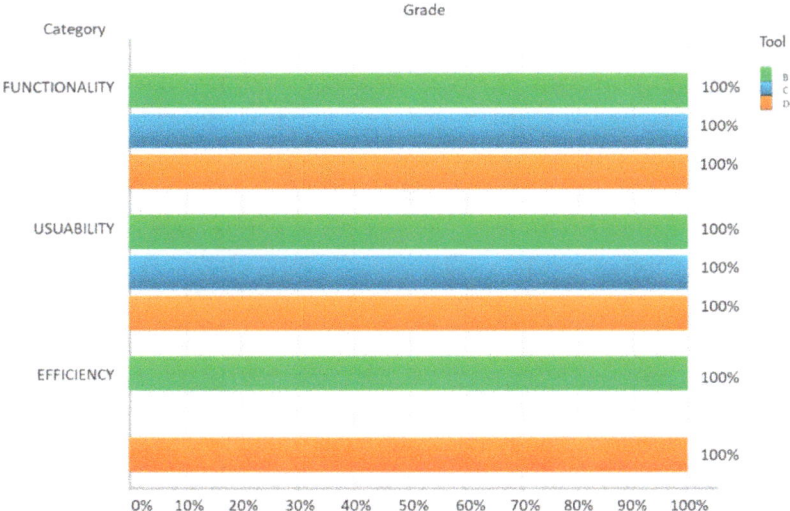

Figure 7. Category results.

Software C does not satisfy the efficiency category. It does not satisfy the characteristic *resource utilization*, as it is shown in Figure 8.

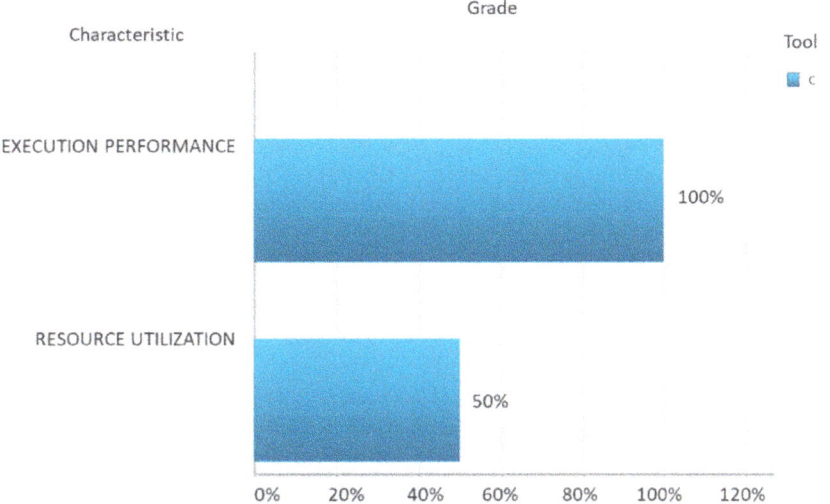

Figure 8. Resource utilization sub-characteristics results, for tool C.

Resource utilization characteristic has a satisfaction score of 50%, lower than the fixed limit of 75% hence it is considered as not satisfied. Only 50% of the *resource utilization* sub-characteristics are satisfied. In particular, Figure 9 shows the satisfaction scores for the corresponding sub-characteristic.

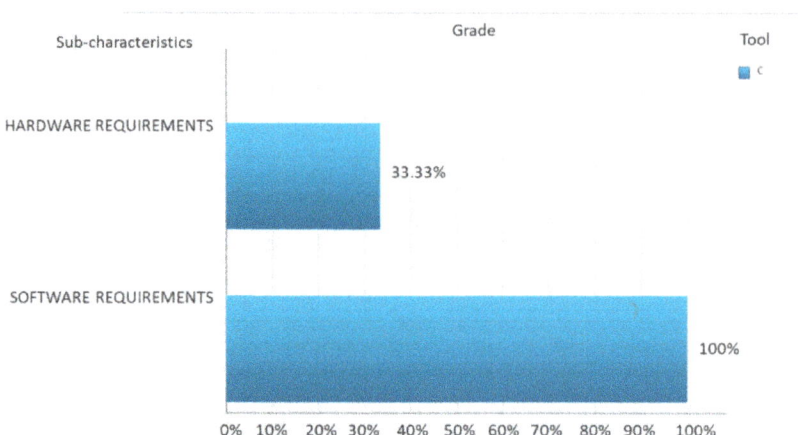

Figure 9. Efficiency characteristics results, for tool C.

Hardware requirements sub-characteristic is not satisfied with a 33.33% of satisfaction score because it is the tool that requires more disk space *(ERH3)* and additionally, software C cannot be installed in processors of 32 bits *(ERH1)*.

Finally, according to Table 5, the product quality levels of software B, C, and D are those defined in Table 15.

Table 15. Quality levels depend on satisfied categories.

Tool	Functionality	Usability	Efficiency	Quality Level
Software B	Satisfied	Satisfied	Satisfied	Advanced
Software C	Satisfied	Satisfied	No satisfied	Medium
Software D	Satisfied	Satisfied	Satisfied	Advanced

Then, software B and D offer an advanced quality level while software C has a medium quality level. To get differences between software B and software D, the fixed levels for satisfaction are increased, being more restrictive. Particularly, we use the following levels defined in Table 16.

Table 16. Satisfaction limits, for a second evaluation.

Limit for metric	50%
Limit for sub-characteristic	50%
Limit for characteristic	80%
Limit for category	75%

In this way, a characteristic becomes satisfied if only 80% of its sub-characteristics are satisfied. As it can be seen in Figure 10, only software D satisfies the *functionality* category, unlike software B, which does not, because only 66.67% of its functional characteristics are satisfied.

As is seen in Figure 11, software B does not satisfy the *functionality* category in this second evaluation because the *interoperability* characteristic is not satisfied it has a score of 75%, meaning that only the 75% of the *interoperability* sub-characteristics are satisfied.

It is because the *Portability* sub-characteristic is not satisfied, as a consequence of software B working only on one specific operating system *(F1P1)*, and it does not offer an available SaaS (software as a service) edition *(FIP2)*.

Then, software D reached an advanced quality level. It can be considered the most appropriate tool for the established requirements.

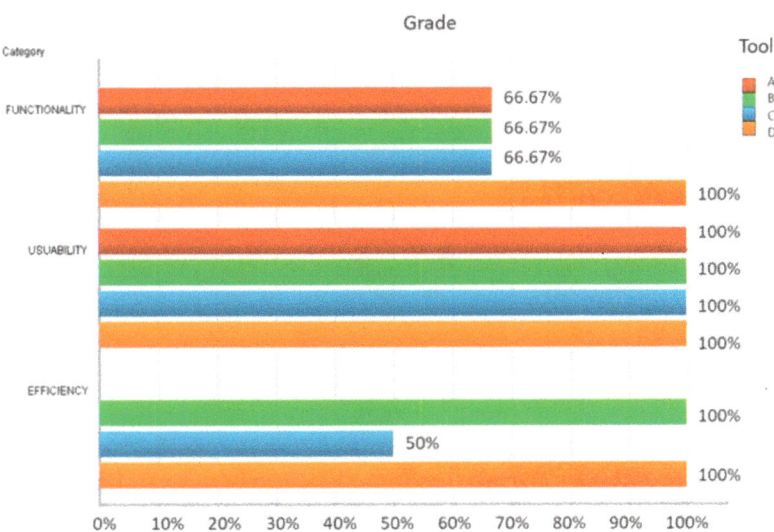

Figure 10. Category results, second evaluation.

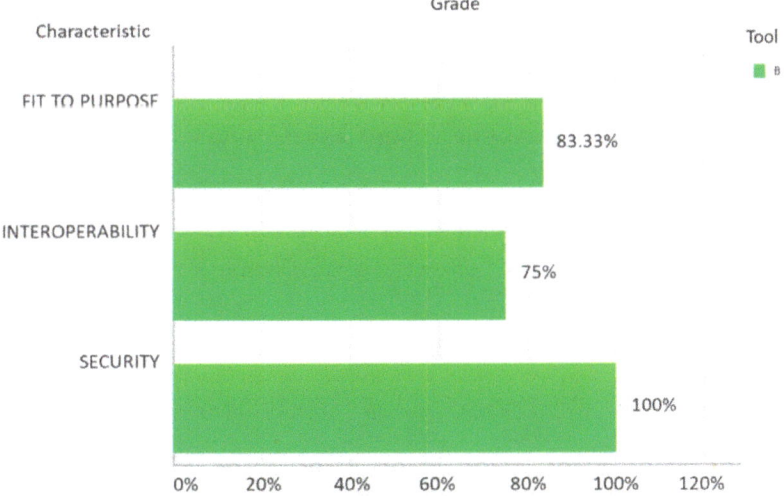

Figure 11. Characteristic results, for a second evaluation for tool B.

10. Conclusions

This project has the purpose of building an assessment of self-service BI tools, and evaluating, in particular, four tools (formerly named A, B, C, and D for confidentiality reasons). To build the assessment, an existing quality model is taken as a reference, the systemic quality model (SQMO) developed by the Universidad Simón Bolívar (Venezuela). We adapt it to our aims and then we establish the metrics.

While we are deciding how to measure the metrics, we realize that the cutoff of satisfaction might be subjective. That is why we evaluate with two different satisfaction limits. The first one established that a feature is satisfied if 75% of its sub-characteristics are met. The second one establishes that it is satisfied if 80% of its sub-characteristics are met. In both cases, the rest of the satisfaction limits keep constant. In the first scenario, we observe that tools B and D get an *advanced quality level*, unlike tool C, which gets a *medium quality level.* Tool C is rejected according to the rules established by SQMO. To obtain the differences between tools B and D, we perform the second evaluation being more restrictive in the satisfaction limit. The results are that tool D got an *advanced quality level* and tool C is rejected according to the rules established by SQMO.

The current limitations of the proposal lie in the limitations of the SQMO approach and the metrics selections. In its original form, it does not consider aspects like social or financial, being the original SQMO proposal strongly focused only on software technical specifications [29].

Therefore, depending on the organization, the forms must be adapted to include all those metrics needed to provide a good selection, being this a key aspect to consider depending on the area and the organization. The proposed adaptation of SQMO, with the metrics presented in this paper, can be used as a tool to perform a neutral evaluation of the different BI tools that currently exist in the market. This evaluation mitigates the existing risks in a critical implementation due to the time, resources, and personnel involved in these kinds of projects.

Author Contributions: Conceptualization, J.O.H. and P.F.i.C.; methodology, J.O.H. and P.F.i.C.; software, J.O.H.; validation, J.O.H. and P.F.i.C.; formal analysis, J.O.H. and P.F.i.C.; investigation, J.O.H. and P.F.i.C.; resources, J.O.H. and P.F.i.C.; data curation, J.O.H.; writing—original draft preparation, J.O.H. and P.F.i.C.; writing—review and editing, J.O.H. and P.F.i.C.; visualization, J.O.H. and P.F.i.C.; supervision, P.F.i.C.; project administration, J.O.H. and P.F.i.C.; funding acquisition, J.O.H. All authors have read and agreed to the published version of the manuscript.

Funding: This research received no external funding.

Institutional Review Board Statement: Not applicable.

Informed Consent Statement: Not applicable.

Data Availability Statement: Not applicable.

Conflicts of Interest: The authors declare no conflict of interest.

Appendix A. The Metrics Used in the Selection Process

This appendix includes the metrics used for the selection process for the different categories analyzed.

Appendix A.1. Functionality Category

Appendix A.1.1. Fit to Purpose Characteristic

This characteristic includes different metrics classified into five sub-characteristics: data loading, data model, field relations, analysis, dashboards, and reporting.

Data loading: This sub-characteristic includes various metrics to evaluate the loading process.

Direct connection to a data source (FFI1): It measures the possibility of a direct connection to data sources. There are some applications with integrated connector drivers (e.g., ODBC, JDBC, etc.) compatible with some databases, and the user does not need to install it to connect the application to the data source.

Big Data sources (FFI2): It measures the capability to connect to any Big Data source different from Hadoop.

Apache Hadoop (FFI3): It refers to the ability to connect to Hadoop infrastructure. This technology is used to manage large volumes of structured or non-structured data allowing fast access to data. Hadoop simply becomes one more data source and it is the most common way of storing big data.

Microsoft Access (FFI4): It evaluates the capability to connect to the Microsoft Access database.

Excel files (FFI5): It evaluates the capability to load data from Excel files.

From an Excel file, load data from all sheets at the same time (FFI6): It evaluates the capability to load data from all sheets at the same time. In some applications, the user must do the same data loading process for each one of the sheets, while other tools let the user choose which sheets he wishes to load and import them at the same time.

Cross-tabs *(FFI7)*: It measures the capability of loading data from cross-tabs in Excel files. Usually, applications need cross-tabs in a specific format and some of them have an excel complement to normalize the cross-tabs before importing them.

Plain text *(FFI8)*: It evaluates the capability of loading data from plain text files (.txt, .inf, .80, .dat, .tmp, .prv, .hlp, .htm., etc.).

Connecting to the different data sources at the same time *(FFI9)*: It evaluates the capability to connect the application to several data sources at the same time and to do cross-analysis between data from them.

Easy integration of many data sources *(FFI10)*: It evaluates how easy is for the user to integrate many data sources in the data analysis.

Showing data before the data loading *(FFI11)*: It evaluates the capability to show data before the data loading. Showing data can be useful for the user to understand how data are before loading them.

Determining data format *(FFI12)*: It evaluates the capability to show data formats *(integer, double, date, string...)* of the fields before the data loading. Some applications assign formats to fields automatically while some others let the user assign them before the loading. Determining data formats before the loading is the best choice but, in some applications, it can be done after the loading, and it is equally evaluated.

Determining data type *(FFI13)*: It evaluates the capability to show data types *(dimension, measure)* of the fields before the data loading. Some applications assign types to fields automatically, while some others let the user assign them before the loading. Depending on the application's terminology, data types can be attributes or dimensions and measured. Determining data types before the loading is the best choice but, in some applications, it can be done after the loading, and it is equally evaluated.

Allowing column filtering before the loading *(FFI14)*: It evaluates the capability to load only the columns that the user wants.

Allowing row filtering before the loading *(FFI5)*: It evaluates the capability to filter registers before loading them. Sometimes, the user does not want to analyze the whole dataset, and data filtering can be useful before loading them.

Automatic measures creation *(FFI16)*: The ability of the tool to automatically create some measures, possibly useful, from the already loaded data.

Allow renaming datasets *(FFI17)*: It evaluates the capability to assign a name to datasets that should be loaded in the application.

Allow renaming fields *(FFI18)*: It evaluates the capability to rename fields. It can be useful when the user has not named the fields in the database by himself and prefers to rename them with more appropriate names for the analysis. Renaming fields before the loading is the best choice but, in some applications, it can be done after the loading, and it is equally evaluated.

Data cleansing *(FFI19)*: It evaluates the capability of the applications to allow the user to clean data. For example, drop registers with null values or substitute particular values.

Data model: This sub-characteristic includes various sub-metrics to evaluate the modeling process for each tool.

The data model is done automatically *(FFD1)*: It refers to the capability of the applications to relate automatically tables. Some applications relate two tables if they have fields with the same name and structure, therefore, these applications model data automatically.

The done data model is the correct one *(FFD2)*: This metric evaluates the capability of applications to get relations between tables as the user wants it. In our particular case of 20141220_Initial_test data, the model is shown in Figure A1. If the user builds the data model manually, getting the desired model should be easy. While, if the model is done automatically, it can be more difficult depending on if the automatic model is the right one, or if there exists the possibility to modify the model by the user.

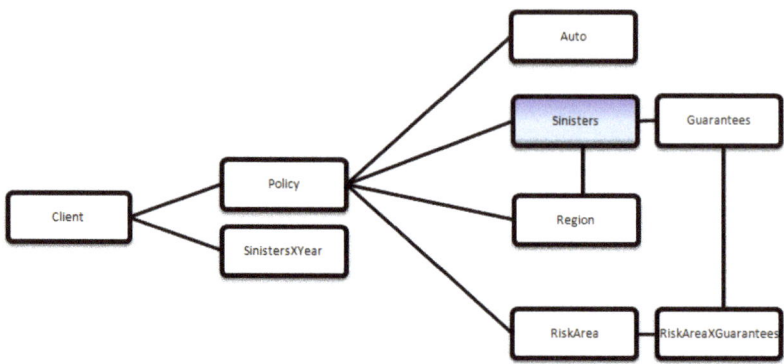

Figure A1. The correct data model for 20141220_Initial_test data.

The data model can be visualized (FFD3): This metric evaluates if a tool allows seeing the data model during the analysis. Visualizing the model during the analysis always lets the user check the relations between fields.

Field relations: This sub-characteristic includes several metrics related to the connections between fields when the data source is relational. To clarify some of the proposed metrics, the database 20141220_Initial_test is used with examples.

Alerting about circular references (FFF1): A circular reference exists when there are, at least, 3 tables related between them.

Figure A2 synthesizes the concept. For example, the user can desire to visualize Table A1; it represents particular policies and the regions where the policies have had an accident. *The policy table* is related to the *region table* by the field *code*, which refers to the identification code for the region where the policy is registered. *Region table* has other fields, additionally to *code*, as the name of the region. On the other hand, the *sinisters table* is also related to the *region table* by the field *code*, which refers to the code identification for the region where accidents occur.

Table A1. Circular reference.

Policy_id	Code of the Region	Region

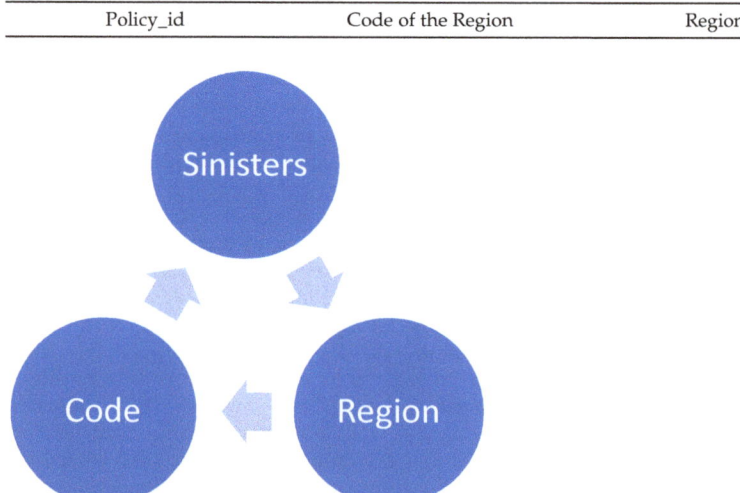

Figure A2. Circular reference.

In that particular case, some applications could show non-correct values for the *region* because of the ambiguity about which way to take to reach the *region table*. If it passes by the *policy table* then it shows regions where the policy is registered, but if it passes by the *sinister table*, it shows regions where accidents occur. This metric evaluates the capability of a tool to realize a circular reference and alert the user about it.

Skipping circular references (FFF2): This sub-characteristic evaluates the capability of the software to omit circular references.

The same table can be used several times (FFF3): It evaluates the capability of the application to use a table directly related to more than one table. For example, if there is a table with coordinates, it can be related to more than one table, for example, with two tables where in the first table there is a place of birth and in the second one there is a place of death. Some tools allow the to load just once the table and use it as many times as the user needs. Other tools require loading the table as many times as relations it will have.

Analysis: This sub-characteristic includes several metrics about the capabilities of the analysis.

Creating new measures based on previous measures (FFA1): All the applications analyzed must be able to create a measure based on already loaded measures. This sub-characteristic evaluates how easy is to build new measures based on loaded measures.

The creation of new measures based on dimensions (FFA2): This sub-characteristic evaluates how easy is to build new measures based on loaded dimensions.

Variety of functions (FFA3): It measures the diversity of functions offered by the application to build a new field. Applications can offer functions related to statistics, economics, mathematics, and also with strings and logic functions.

Descriptive statistics (FFA4): It refers to the possibility to analyze data statistically from a descriptive point of view. All the applications analyzed in that project can do descriptive statistics. Therefore, this metric evaluates the complexity of the descriptive statistic allowed in each program.

Predictive statistics (FFA5): It measures the ability to get indicators by predictive functions. It is not a common feature in self-service BI tools and because of that, the presence of few predictive methods will be positively evaluated.

R connection (FFA6): It evaluates the capability of applications to connect to R to get advanced analytical functions.

Geographic information (FFA7): This sub-characteristic measures the capability of displaying data on maps.

Time hierarchy (FFA8): It evaluates the capability of the application to create *time intelligence*. It consists in, from a particular date, creating other fields like a month, quarter, or year. These sets of fields are grouped in a hierarchy. Particularly, a time hierarchy. This metric evaluates the capability of the tool to create automatic time hierarchies.

Creating sets of data (FFA9): It evaluates the capability of a tool to create sets of data. During the analysis, the user can be interested in a deeper analysis of a set of registers. Some tools let to save these datasets and work with them.

Filtering data by an expression (FFA10): It evaluates the capability of a tool to filter data during the analysis by expression values.

Filtering data by a dimension (FFA11): It evaluates the capability of a tool to filter data during the analysis by dimension values.

Visual perspective linking (FFA12): It evaluates the capability to link multiple images, so a selection on one image shows related and relevant data in other images.

No null data specifications (FFA13): This metric evaluates if the applications have any requirements to the null values, for example, that null values must be noted as NULL, or just with a space or by contrary that the user can define how are the null values represented in the data source.

Considering nulls (FFA14): This metric measures if applications consider null values as another value. Considering null as another value might be useful because the user can visualize the behavior of null data and then detect a pattern for them. This metric also evaluates if null values are skipped from a calculated expression.

Variety of graphs (FFA15): It measures the diversity of graphs offered by the application.

Modifying graphs (FFA16): It measures the capability to modify the default setting of graphs. For example, if there is the possibility to change levels of a legend, change colors, change the shapes of markers... It is an important characteristic because sometimes it is the key to understanding a data pattern.

Huge amount of data (FFA17): It measures the capability to display a huge amount of data. Particularly, it measures the capability to display datasets without any data problems because of their size.

Data refresh (FFA18): It measures the capability to update data automatically. For example, if data are modified in the original file, some applications update automatically the data while in others the user must do it, manually.

Dashboard: This sub-characteristic includes several metrics to measure the capabilities of a tool relating to dashboards.

Dashboard exportation (FFD1): It evaluates the capability of the tool to export the dashboard to share with other people to visualize and interact with the results.

Templates (FFD2): It evaluates the capability to fix a schema dashboard or access templates to use it several times with different types of data. It is a useful feature to homogenize projects.

Free design (FFD3): It measures the ability to let the user build dashboards with total freedom. Some tools have limited options for building dashboards, while others let the user insert text, format it, insert images, etc.

Reporting: This sub-characteristic includes several metrics to measure reporting capabilities of a tool.

Reports exportation (FFR1): It evaluates the diversity of formats to export reports. Some formats are Excel spreadsheets, PDF files, HTML files, Flash files, the own tool format, etc.

Templates (FFR2): It evaluates the capability to fix a schema report or access templates to use it several times with different data. It is a useful feature to improve consistency when the user builds the same type of report periodically.

Free design (FFR3): It measures the ability to let the user build reports with total freedom. Some tools have limited options for building dashboards, while others let the user insert text, format it, insert images, etc.

Appendix A.1.2. Interoperability Characteristic

This characteristic includes several sub-characteristics to evaluate the capability of an application to work with other organizations and systems.

Languages: This sub-characteristic is composed of a metric, which evaluates the variety of languages displayable in the tool.

Languages displayed (FIL1): It evaluates the variety of displayed languages offered by the tool. In particular, it evaluates if the tool can be displayed in more than two languages or not.

Portability: This sub-characteristic is composed of three metrics, which evaluate the ability of a tool to be executed in different environments.

Operating systems (FIP1): This metric measures the variety of different operating systems compatible with the tool. In particular, it evaluates if the tool can work, at least, in two different operating systems.

SaaS/Web (FIP2): The acronym SaaS means Software as a Service. This metric evaluates if a tool offers access to projects via a web browser for hosting their deployments in the cloud.

Mobile (FIP3): It evaluates the possibility to have reports and dashboards available on the mobile device via a mobile app.

Use project by third parts: This sub-characteristic is composed of a unique metric, and it measures the capability of sharing and modifying projects by other people.

Using the project by a third party (FIU1): It evaluates the capability to share projects and modify them with other users.

Data exchange: This sub-characteristic is composed of metrics, which evaluate the data exportation when they have already been manipulated in the tool.

Exportation in .txt (FID1): It evaluates the capability of a tool to export data .txt.

Exportation in CSV (FID2): It evaluates the capability of a tool to export data in CSV format.

Exportation in HTML (FID3): It evaluates the capability of a tool to export data in HTML format.

Exportation in Excel file (FID4): It evaluates the capability of a tool to export data in Excel files.

Appendix A.1.3. Security Characteristic

This characteristic is composed of a unique sub-characteristic, which groups metrics about the security process.

Security devices: This sub-characteristic is composed of two metrics related to the protection of data.

Password protection (FSS1): It evaluates the capability to protect projects with a password.

Permissions (FSS2): It evaluates the capability to assign different permissions to different users.

Appendix A.2. Usability Category

Appendix A.2.1. Ease of Understanding and Learning Characteristic

This characteristic includes different sub-characteristics.

Learning time: This sub-characteristic includes only one metric.

Average learning time (UEL1): This metric measures the time spent by the user in learning the functionality of the tool.

Browsing facilities: This sub-characteristic evaluates how the user can browse inside the tool.

Consistency between icons in the toolbars and their actions (UEB1): This metric measures the capability of the tool to be consistent with its icons.

Displaying right-click menus (UEB2): This metric measures if the tool offers a displaying menu by right-clicking.

Terminology: This sub-characteristic evaluates if the terminology is consistent with the global business intelligence terminology.

Ease of understanding the terminology (UET1): This metric measure how easy is for the user to understand the terminology.

Help and documentation: This sub-characteristic is composed of metrics, which measure the help offered by the tool to a user when he has doubts about the functionality or management of the tool.

User guide quality (UEH1): This metric evaluates if the user guide is understandable. Highlighting that self-service tools are also offered for non-technical users.

User guide acquisition (UEH2): This metric measures the process to get to the user manual. For example, if it is free if it is difficult to find on the web, etc.

On-line help (UEH3): It measures the offering of online help.

Support and training: These sub-characteristics measure the quality and variety of the support offered by the tool.

Availability of tailor-made training courses (UES1): It measures if the tool offers training courses adapted to organizations, and it is positively measured if the course can be done in the organization.

Phone technical support (UES2): It measures if the tool offers a phone for technical support and the timetable of it.

Online support (UES3): It measures if the tool offers online support and if it is in life or not.

Availability of consulting services (UES4): It measures if the company offers consulting services.

Free formation (UES5): It evaluates if the platform offers free formation for users.

Community (UES6): It evaluates if there exists a community to ask for doubts or to share knowledge with other users.

Appendix A.2.2. Graphical Interface Characteristic

This characteristic evaluates the graphical interface of the tool.

Windows and mouse interface: This sub-characteristic evaluates the windows interface and the mouse functions.

Editing elements by double-clicking (UGW1): It measures if the tool offers editing elements by double-clicking.

Dragging and dropping elements (UGW2): It measures the capability of the tool in dragging and dropping elements.

Display: This sub-characteristic refers to a unique metric about the capability of editing the screen layout.

Editing the screen layout (UGD1): It measures the capability of a tool to edit the screen layout.

Appendix A.2.3. Operability Characteristic

This characteristic evaluates the ability of the tool to keep the system and the tool in reliable functioning conditions.

Versatility: This sub-characteristic evaluates the versatility of the tool.

Automatic update (UOV1): It measures if the tool is automatically updated when new versions appear.

Appendix A.3. Efficiency Category

Appendix A.3.1. Execution Performance Characteristic

This characteristic is composed of a sub-characteristic, which evaluates the execution performance of the tool.

Compilation speed: This sub-characteristic measures the compilation speed, and how fast the software builds a particular chart.

Compilation speed (EEC1): It measures the compilation speed. It is a very subjective measure because it depends on the machine where it is installed.

Appendix A.3.2. Resource Utilization Characteristic

This characteristic is composed of two (2) sub-characteristics, which evaluate the extra hardware and software requirements.

Hardware requirements: This sub-characteristic is composed of three metrics, which measure the vital hardware to run the tool.

CPU (processor type) (ERH1): This metric evaluates if the tool can be installed as much to ×86 processors as to ×64 processors.

Minimum RAM (ERH2): It measures the RAM needed in the way that maximum punctuation means it requires low memory while minimum punctuation means it needs much memory.

Hard disk space required (ERH3): It measures the hard disk space needed in the way that maximum punctuation means it requires low space while minimum punctuation means it needs much memory.

Software requirements: This sub-characteristic is composed of a unique metric, which measures if extra software is required to execute the tool.

Additional software requirements (ERS1): this metric evaluates if extra software is required to run the tool.

Appendix B. Metrics Weights

Table A2. Metric weights.

Metric	Weight
Direct connection to data sources	2
Bigdata sources	1
Apache Hadoop	1
Microsoft Access	2
Excel files	3
From an excel file, import all sheets at the same time	2
Cross-tabs	2
Plain text	3
Connecting to different data sources at the same time	2
Easy integration of many data sources	2
Visualizing data before the loading	2
Determining data format	2
Determining data type	2
Allowing column filtering before the loading	2
Allowing row filtering before the loading	2
Automatic measures creation	3
Allow renaming datasets	2
Allow renaming fields	3
Data cleansing	2
The data model is done automatically	2
The done data model is the correct one	2
The data model can be visualized	3
Alerting about circular references	3
Skipping with circular references	3
The same table can be used several times	2
Creating new measures based on previous measures	3
Creating new measures based on dimensions	3
Variety of functions	3
Descriptive statistics	2
Prediction functions	2
R connection	2
Geographic information	2
Time hierarchy	3
Creating sets of data	2
Filtering data by expression	3
Filtering data by dimension	3
Visual perspective linking	2
No null data specifications	2
Considering nulls	3

Appendix C. 0141220_Initial_Test

The created database, used to evaluate the applications, is called **20141220_Initial_test**. It is composed of nine tables forming a relational database, particularly a snowflake schema.

In Figure A3, it is showed the relational data model structure, where two tables are related by a common field (*foreign key*), which appears in both tables and which is shown in the figure, next to the type of relationship. The *fact table* is called *sinisters*, and the *dimension tables* are *client*, *policy*, *auto*, *region*, *SinistersXYear*, *risk area*, *guarantees*, and *GuaranteesXRiskArea*.

We decided to propose a relational database to realize how the evaluated self-service BI tools managed the relations between tables. Some of these tools built automatically the data model (the relations between tables), that is that the user loads tables, and the tool, by itself, relates tables. Hence, we wanted to know if this automatic modeling worked well or not.

Moreover, we wanted to evaluate if applications were capable to understand both types of relationships. The most common relationship is 1: n, and we were almost certain that applications support them. However, we doubted the support of n:m relationships. There was one of the evaluated tools, could not relate two tables by an n:m relationship.

Additionally, our model has a particularity. There are two circular references in *region* and *guarantees* fields. A circular reference exists when there are, at least, 3 tables related between them. For example, the *Region table* has information about the regions, and it has the name of all regions and their population. The *policy table* is connected to the *region table*, by the field *code*. This field corresponds to the code of the region where the policy is registered. On the other hand, the *sinisters table* is also connected to the *region table*, by the field *code*. However, this time, it corresponds to the code of the region where the accident had happened. Both relations have different meanings, but they are related to the same table. We added these circular references to know how the self-service applications managed them.

Skipping circular references can be done easily, by duplicating tables. We have loaded two tables identically equal to the *region table*, one is related to the *policy table* and the other one to the *sinisters table*. However, this action implies the use of more memory, and it is not recommended.

The fact that we decided to simulate a car's insurance company database is due to it is a common case of use in consultancy. Moreover, we were lucky to know an actuarial expert who offered us some information about the car's insurance area.

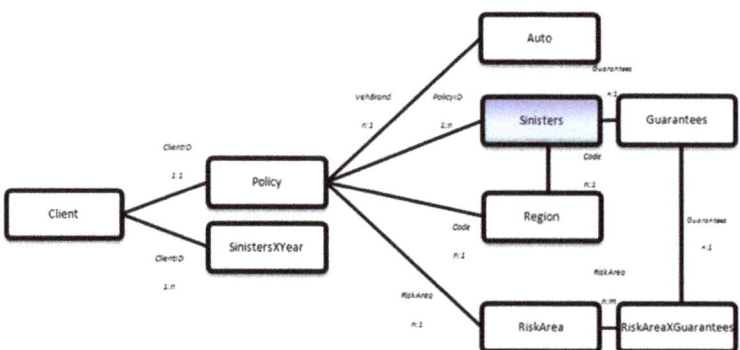

Figure A3. The data model for 20141220_Initial_test.

The main point of the work was not to do an accurate analysis of data. For this reason, the simulation was just a way of getting data and they cannot be considered real data, because the process to get them is just a rough approximation.

We obtained some data from two existing datasets of R. To not have to invent all data, although some fields were invented by us because they were not in the existing datasets. Some data were extracted from the *CASdatasets* package of R. It is composed of several actuarial datasets (originally for the "Computational Actuarial Science" book). Particularly, we extracted some data from *freMPL6* and *freMTPL2freq* datasets.

Moreover, to evaluate the analysis capabilities of the applications, data were simulated forcing patterns. In particular, geographical, and stationary patterns were imposed. In **20141220_Initial_test**, the amount of occurred car accidents in a region is proportional to the amount of population in it. However, in the months of July, August, and September, in the region of Granada, we force to have more accidents. Additionally, some people are forced to have more probability to have accidents than the main part of the population. They are a woman with ages between 40 and 45, a man with ages between 50 and 65, young people under 24, and beginners.

The database consists of 26000 policies. Each policy is identified by one client. There are 22 different variables, classified in tables.

Appendix C.1. Client Table

It consists of client characteristics. As a consequence, there are 26,000 clients, and this table has 26,000 rows. The variables inside are the followings:

- ClientID: Discrete variable with 26,000 different values from 1 to 26,000.
- Gender: Qualitative variable that can take the answers "Male" and "Female".
- Maristat: Qualitative variable that can take the answers "Others" and "Alone".
- CSP: Qualitative variable referenced to the social category known as CSP in France. It can take values as "CSP50". The classification of socio-professional categories (CSP) was conceived by INSEE in 1954. The objective was to categorize individuals according to their professional situation, taking account of several criteria: their profession, economic activity, qualification, hierarchical position and status.
- It included 9 main groups subdivided into 30 socio-professional categories.
- LicBeg: Date variable with 26,000 values between "5 September 1941" and "11 January 2009". It refers to the date when the client got the driver's license.
- *DrivBeg:* Date variable with 26,000 values between "25 January 1916" and "6 January 1991". It refers to the birth date client.

Appendix C.2. Auto Table

It consists of vehicle characteristics depending on its brand. As a consequence there are 11 different brands of vehicles, this table has 11 rows. The variables inside are the followings:

- *VehBrand*: Categorized numeric variable that refers to the vehicle brand. It takes 11 different values from {1, 2, 3, 4, 5, 6, 10, 11, 12, 13, 14}.
- *VehPow*: Categorized numeric variable that refers to the vehicle power. It takes 4 different values from {6, 7, 8, 9 }.
- *VehType*: Qualitative variable that refers to the vehicle type. There are 4 possible answers: "familiar", "compact", "sport" and "terrain".

Appendix C.3. Region Table

It shows the information about regions. There are 52 regions and therefore this table has 52 rows. Its variables are the followings:

- *Code:* Numeric variable which refers to a code for each region. For example, Zaragoza has the code 52, because it is the last region if they are ordered alphabetically.
- *Region*: Qualitative variable that refers to the Spain province(region) where the sinister happens. The answers can be: "Alava", "Albacete", "Alicante", "Almeria", "Asturias", "Avila", "Badajoz", "Barcelona", "Burgos", "Caceres", "Cadiz", "Cantabria", "Castellon", "Ciudad Real", "Cordoba", La Coruna", "Cuenca", "Gerona", "Granada", "Guadalajara", "Guipuzcoa", "Huelva", "Huesca", "Islas Baleares", "Jaen", "Leon", "Lerida", "Lugo", "Madrid", "Malaga", "Murcia", "Navarra", "Orense", "Palencia", "Palmas", "Pontevedra", "La Rioja", "Salamanca", "Segovia", "Sevilla", "Soria", "Tarragona", "Teruel", "Tenerife", "Toledo", "Valencia", "Valladolid", "Vizacaia", "Zamora", "Zaragoza", "Melilla" and "Ceuta".is a whole name of the region, in last example region should be "Zaragoza".
- *Population*: Discrete variable that refers to the population of the region where the car is declared.

Appendix C.4. Risk Area Table

It has the name of each type of the 5 Risk Area types. As there are 5 different Risk Areas there are 5 rows in this table. The variables inside are the following:
- *RiskArea*: Categorized variable meaning the type of insurance included in each policy, also known as the product. The categories are {1,2,3,4,5}.
- *RiskAreadesc*: Qualitative variable referring to the corresponding Risk Area name. They are "gold", "silver", "master", "plus" and "regular".

Appendix C.5. Guarantees Table

This table shows two variables. The name of different guarantees covered by the insurance company and their base cost. There are 8 different guarantees and therefore the table has 8 rows.
- *Guarantees:* Qualitative variable referring to guarantees with the following possible answers: "windows", "travelling", "driver insurance", "claims", "fire", "theft", "total loss", and "health assistant".
- *Base*: Discrete Variable refers to the cost covered by the insurance company. It has 8 different values: 50, 500, 100, 25, 1000, 20,000, 3000 and 300.

Appendix C.6. Risk X Guarantees Table

This table joins the Risk Area variable with the guarantees that it provides. This table has 29 rows because the Risk Area categorized by 1 has 8 guarantees, the 2 has 7 guarantees, the 3 has 6 guarantees, the 4 has 5 guarantees and the 5 has 3 guarantees.
- *RiskArea*: Categorized variable meaning the type of insurance included in each policy, also known as the product. The categories are {1,2,3,4,5}.
- *Guarantees*: Qualitative variable referring to guarantees provided by the Risk Area corresponding. The different answers are "windows", "travelling", "driver insurance", "claims", "fire", "theft", "total loss" and " health assistance".

Appendix C.7. Policy Table

It consists of policy characteristics. As a consequence, there are 26,000 different policies, and this table has 26,000 rows. Its variables are the followings:
- *PolicyID*: Discrete variable with 26,000 different values from 1 to 26,000.
- *ClientID*: Discrete variable with 26,000 different values from 1 to 26,000.
- *RecordBeg*: Date variable with 26,000 values between "1 January 2000" and "31 December 2010". It refers to the date when the policy is begun.
- *RecordEnd*: Date variable with 26,000 values between "1 January 2000" and "31 December 2010". It refers to the date when the policy is finished. In most cases, it has the value "1 January 9999", which means that the policy is still active.
- *VehBeg*: Date variable with 26,000 values between "26 January 1911" and "1 January 2011". It refers to the date when the vehicle was built.
- *VehBrand*: Categorized numeric variable that refers to the brand of the secured vehicle, by the policy. It takes 11 different values from {1, 2, 3, 4, 5, 6, 10, 11, 12, 13, 14}.
- *BonusMalus*: Discrete variable between 50 and 350: below 100 means bonus, above 100 means malus in France.
- *RiskArea*: Categorized variable meaning the type of insurance included in each policy, also known as the product. The categories are {1, 2, 3, 4, 5}.
- *Code:* Numeric variable which refers to the code of the region where the policy is registered.

Appendix C.8. SinistersXYear Table

It shows the number of sinister for each policy in each year, from 2000 to 2010. As there are 26,000 different policies, the table has 26,000 different rows. About the columns, it has one for each year, therefore there are 11 columns. The unique variable is *sinister*. It is evaluated for each policy and each year. Three is the maximum of sinister in one year, imposed in the simulation process.

Appendix C.9. Sinisters Table

This table shows information about the sinister of each policy. It has 196,235 rows. It is because in total, for all the policies there are 196,235 sinister. The variables inside are the followings:

- *PolicyID*: Discrete variable with 26,000 different values from 1 to 26,000. However, in the table, every policy is repeated as times as sinister has it in the total of 11 years.
- *RiskArea*: Categorized variable meaning the type of insurance included in each policy, also known as the product. The categories are {1,2,3,4,5}. As the *PolicyID*, it is repeated as times as the policy uses the risk area that has been included.
- *Guarantees*: Qualitative variable referring to a guarantee provided by the Risk Area corresponding and used in the sinister. The different answers are "windows", "travelling", "driver insurance", "claims", "fire", "theft", "total loss" and " health assistance".
- *Sinisterdate*: Date variable with values between "1 January 2000" and "31 December 2010". It refers to the date when the sinister happens.
- *Code:* Numeric variable which refers to the code of the region where the sinister happens.

The names of the variables explained above, Table A3, are the final names. During the simulation process, some variables were called different. In the simulation, some variables have been built two times with different lengths. To keep the consistency in the code, all different fields are called different. However, after the simulation, the names have been changed to let the user build connections between tables by a common field.

Table A3. Variables names in the data simulation.

Variable Name in Simulation	Table	Variable Name
VehBrand_N	*Policy*	VehBrand
RiskArea_N	*Policy*	RiskArea
Code_O	*Policy*	Code
V1, ... , V11	*SinistersXYear*	2000, ... , 2010
PolicyID_S	*Sinisters*	PolicyID
RiskArea_s	*Sinisters*	RiskArea
Guarantees_s	*Sinisters*	Guarantees
Code_S	*Sinisters*	Code

Appendix D. Questionnaires

This annex attaches one of the questionnaires, Table A4, that must be filled by the users implied in the evaluation. In our case, there are four questionnaires, one for each evaluated tool. They show the scores, according to the scale of measurement established in Section 5, for each metric. Moreover, according to the satisfaction limits established in Section 6 for the second evaluation, the satisfaction score is shown.

The column **M.S** refers to the scale of measurement established for each metric. The column **WEIGHTS** refers to the weights established for each metric in Section 5. The **COMPENSATED VALUE** refers to the product of the weight and the metric's score.

The **NORMALIZED VALUE** is the satisfaction score for the metric. While for sub-characteristics/characteristics/categories they are called simply **TOTAL**.

The columns called **INDICATOR** take values 1 or 0, depending on if the Metric/Sub-characteristic/Characteristic/Category is satisfied according to the satisfaction limit established in Section 6.

Table A4. Evaluation questionnaire for B tool.

Category	Characteristic	Subcharacteristic-Desc	Metric-Code	Metric	M.S	Value	Weight	Compensated Value	Normal. Value	Indicator Metric	Total Sub-Characteristic	Indicator Sub-Charac.	Total Characteristic	Indicator Charac	Total Category	Indicator Categ.
Functionality	Fit to Purpose	Data loading	FFI1	Direct connection to data sources	A	2	2	4	50.00%	1	82.50%	1	83.33%	1	66.67%	0
			FFI2	BigData sources	A	2	1	2	50.00%	1						
			FFI3	Apache Hadoop	A	2	1	2	50.00%	1						
			FFI4	Microsoft Access	A	2	2	4	50.00%	1						
			FFI5	Excel files	A	3	3	9	75.00%	1						
			FFI6	From an excel file, import all sheets at the same time	A	1	2	2	25.00%	0						
			FFI7	Cross-tabs	A	4	2	8	100.00%	1						
			FFI8	Plain text	A	3	3	9	75.00%	1						
			FFI9	Connecting to different data sources at the same time	A	3	2	6	75.00%	1						
			FFI10	Easy integration of many data sources	A	3	2	6	75.00%	1						
			FFI11	Visualizing data before the loading	A	1	2	2	25.00%	0						
			FFI12	Determining data format	A	3	2	6	75.00%	1						
			FFI13	Determining data type	A	4	2	8	100.00%	1						
			FFI14	Allowing column filtering before the loading	A	3	2	6	75.00%	1						
			FFI15	Allowing row filtering before the loading	A	2	2	4	50.00%	1						
			FFI16	Automatic measures creation	A	0	3	0	0.00%	0						
			FFI17	Allow renaming datasets	A	3	2	6	75.00%	1						
			FFI18	Allow renaming fields	A	3	3	9	75.00%	1						
			FFI19	Data cleansing	A	2	2	4	50.00%	1						

Table A4. Cont.

Category	Characteristic	Subcharacteristic-Desc	Metric-Code	Metric	M.S	Value	Weight	Compensated Value	Normal Value	Indicator_Metric	Total Sub-Characteristic	Indicator_Sub-Charac.	Total Characteristic	Indicator_Charac.	Total Category	Indicator_Categ.
		Data model	FFD1	The data model is done automatically	A	3	2	6	75.00%	1	100.00%	1				
			FFD2	The done data model is the correct one	A	2	2	4	50.00%	1						
			FFD3	The data model can be visualized	A	4	3	12	100.00%	1						
		Field relations	FFF1	Alerting about circular references	A	3	3	9	75.00%	1	75.00%	1				
			FFF2	Skipping with circular references	A	3	3	9	75.00%	1						
			FFF3	The same table can be used several times	A	0	2	0	0.00%	0						
		Analysis	FFA1	Creating new measures based on previous measures	A	3	3	9	75.00%	1	73.33%	1				
			FFA2	Creating new measures based on dimensions	A	3	3	9	75.00%	1						
			FFA3	Variety of functions	A	3	3	9	75.00%	1						
			FFA4	Descriptive statistics	A	3	2	6	75.00%	1						
			FFA5	Prediction functions	A	0	2	0	0.00%	0						
			FFA6	R connection	A	3	2	6	75.00%	1						
			FFA7	Geographic information	A	2	2	4	50.00%	1						
			FFA8	Time hierarchy	A	2	3	6	50.00%	1						
			FFA9	Creating sets of data	A	1	2	2	25.00%	0						
			FFA10	Filtering data by expression	A	1	3	3	25.00%	0						

Table A4. Cont.

Category	Characteristic	Subcharacteristic-Desc	Metric-Code	Metric	M.S	Value	Weight	Compensated Value	Normal. Value	Indicator Metric	Total Sub-Characteristic	Indicator Sub-Charac.	Total Characteristic	Indicator Charac.	Total Category	Indicator Categ.
	Interoperability		FFA11	Filtering data by dimension	A	1	3	3	25.00%	0						
			FFA12	Visual Perspective Linking	A	4	2	8	100.00%	1						
			FFA13	No Null data specifications	A.1	0	2	0	0.00%	0						
			FFA14	Considering nulls	A	4	3	12	100.00%	1						
			FFA15	Variety of graphs	A	3	3	9	75.00%	1						
			FFA16	Modify graphs	A	4	3	12	100.00%	1						
			FFA17	No limitations to displaying large amounts of data	A.1	4	2	8	100.00%	1						
			FFA18	Data refresh	A	2	2	4	50.00%	1						
		Dashboards	FFD1	Dashboards Exportation	A	3	3	9	75.00%	1						
			FFD2	Templates	A	0	2	0	0.00%	0	71.43%	1				
			FFD3	Free design	A	4	2	8	100.00%	1						
		Reporting	FFR1	Reports Exportation	A	3	3	9	75.00%	1						
			FFR2	Templates	A	0	2	0	0.00%	0	42.86%	0				
			FFR3	Free design	A	1	2	2	25.00%	0						
		Languages	FIL1	Languages displayed	A.1	4	2	8	100.00%	1	100.00%	1				
		Portability	FIP1	Operating Systems	A.1	0	2	0	0.00%	0						
			FIP2	SaaS/Web	A	1	1	1	25.00%	0	40.00%	0				
			FIP3	Mobile	A	3	2	6	75.00%	1						
		Using the project in third parts	FIU1	Using the project by third parts	A	3	2	6	75.00%	1	75.00%	1	75.00%	0		
		Data exchange	FID1	Exportation in txt	A	3	2	6	75.00%	1						
			FID2	Exportation in CSV	A	3	2	6	75.00%	1						
			FID3	Exportation in HTML	A	3	2	6	75.00%	1	100.00%	1				
			FID4	Exportation in Excel file	A	3	3	9	75.00%	1						

Table A4. Cont.

Category	Characteristic	Subcharacteristic-Desc	Metric-Code	Metric	M.S	Value	Weight	Compensated Value	Normal. Value	Indicator_Metric	Total Sub-Characteristic	Indicator_Sub-Charac.	Total Characteristic	Indicator_Charac	Total Category	Indicator_Categ.
Usability	Security	Security devices	FSS1	Password protection	A	3	3	9	75.00%	1	100.00%	1	100.00%	1		
			FSS2	Permissions	A	3	3	9	75.00%	1		1				
	Ease of Understanding and Learning	Learning time	UEL1	Average learning time	A.2	4	3	12	100.00%	1	100.00%	1				
		Browsing facilities	UEB1	Consistency between icons in the toolbars and their actions	A	3	3	9	75.00%	1	100.00%	1				
			UEB2	Displaying right-click menus	A	3	3	9	75.00%	1		1				
		Terminology	UET1	Ease of understanding the terminology	A	4	3	12	100.00%	1	100.00%	1				
		Help and documentation	UEH1	User guide quality	A.2	3	2	6	75.00%	1	100.00%	1	100.00%	1		
			UEH2	User guide acquisition	A	3	2	6	75.00%	1		1				
			UEH3	On-line documentation	A	3	2	6	75.00%	1		1				
		Support training	UES1	Availability of tailor-made training courses	A	3	2	6	75.00%	1	100.00%	1			100.00%	1
			UES2	Phone technical support	A	3	2	6	75.00%	1		1				
			UES3	Online support	A	3	2	6	75.00%	1		1				
			UES4	Availability of consulting services	A	3	2	6	75.00%	1		1				
			UES5	Free formation	A	3	2	6	75.00%	1		1				
			UES6	Community	A	3	2	6	75.00%	1		1				
	Graphical Interface Characteristic	Windows and mouse interface	UGW1	Editing elements by double-clicking	A	0	2	0	0.00%	0	50.00%	1	100.00%	1		
			UGW2	Dragging and dropping elements	A	3	2	6	75.00%	1						
		Display	UGD1	Editing the screen layout	A	3	2	6	75.00%	1	75.00%	1				
	Operability	Versatility	UOV1	Automatic update	A	2	2	4	50.00%	1	50.00%	1	100.00%	1		

Table A4. *Cont.*

Category	Characteristic	Subcharacteristic-Desc	Metric-Code	Metric	M.S	Value	Weight	Compensated Value	Normal. Value	Indicator_Metric	Total Sub-Characteristic	Indicator_Sub-Charac.	Total Characteristic	Indicator_Charac	Total Category	Indicator_Categ.
Efficiency	Execution Performance	Compilation speed	EEC1	Compilation Speed	A.2	4	2	8	100.00%	1	100.00%	1	100.00%	1	100.00%	1
	Resource Utilization	Hardware requirements	ERH1	CPU(processor type)	A.1	4	2	8	100.00%	1	100.00%	1	100.00%	1		
			ERH2	Minimum RAM	A.2	3	2	6	75.00%	1						
			ERH3	Hard disk space required	A.2	4	2	8	100.00%	1						
		Software requirements	ERS1	Additional software requirements	A	4	2	8	100.00%	1	100.00%	1				

References

1. Hass, K.B.; Lindbergh, L.; Vanderhorst, R.; Kiemski, K. *From Analyst to Leader: Elevating the Role of the Business Analyst Management Concepts*; Berrett-Koehler Publishers: Oakland, CA, USA, 2007; p. 152.
2. International Institute of Business Analysis. *The Guide to the Business Analysis Body of Knowledge TM*; International Institute of Business Analysis: London UK, 2012.
3. Pollock, N.; Williams, R. Technology choice and its performance: Towards a sociology of software package procurement. *Inf. Organ.* **2007**, *17*, 131–161. Available online: http://www.sciencedirect.com/science/article/pii/S147177270700022X (accessed on 9 July 2022). [CrossRef]
4. Zaidan, A.A.; Zaidan, B.B.; Hussain, M.; Haiqi, A.; Mat Kiah, M.L.; Abdulnabi, M. Multi-criteria analysis for OS-EMR software selection problem: A comparative study. *Decis. Support Syst.* **2015**, *78*, 15–27. Available online: http://linkinghub.elsevier.com/retrieve/pii/S0167923615001347 (accessed on 9 July 2022). [CrossRef]
5. Sudhaman, P.; Thangavel, C. Efficiency analysis of ERP projects—Software quality perspective. *Int. J. Proj. Manag.* **2015**, *33*, 961–970. Available online: http://linkinghub.elsevier.com/retrieve/pii/S0263786314001689 (accessed on 9 July 2022). [CrossRef]
6. Yazgan, H.R.; Boran, S.; Goztepe, K. An ERP software selection process with using artificial neural network based on analytic network process approach. *Expert. Syst. Appl.* **2009**, *36*, 9214–9222. Available online: http://www.sciencedirect.com/science/article/pii/S0957417408008877 (accessed on 9 July 2022). [CrossRef]
7. Gürbüz, T.; Alptekin, S.E.; Işıklar Alptekin, G. A hybrid MCDM me thodology for ERP selection problem with interacting criteria. *Decis. Support Syst.* **2012**, *54*, 206–214. Available online: http://linkinghub.elsevier.com/retrieve/pii/S0167923612001170 (accessed on 9 July 2022). [CrossRef]
8. Bao, T.; Liu, S. Quality evaluation and analysis for domain software: Application to management information system of power plant. *Inf. Softw. Technol.* **2016**, *78*, 53–65. Available online: http://linkinghub.elsevier.com/retrieve/pii/S0950584916300933 (accessed on 9 July 2022). [CrossRef]
9. Koh, S.C.L.; Gunasekaran, A.; Goodman, T. Drivers, barriers and critical success factors for ERPII implementation in supply chains: A critical analysis. *J. Strateg. Inf. Syst.* **2011**, *20*, 385–402. Available online: http://linkinghub.elsevier.com/retrieve/pii/S0963868711000400 (accessed on 9 July 2022). [CrossRef]
10. Abu Salih, B.; Wongthongtham, P.; Beheshti, S.M.R.; Zajabbari, B. Towards a Methodology for Social Business Intelligence in the Era of Big Social Data Incorporating Trust and Semantic Analysis. *Lect. Notes Electr. Eng.* **2019**, *520*, 519–527.
11. Wongthongtham, P.; Salih, B.A. Ontology and Trust based Data Warehouse in New Generation of Business Intelligence. *IEEE 13th Int. Conf. Ind. Inform.* **2015**, *Idc*, 476–483.
12. Arvidsson, V.; Holmström, J.; Lyytinen, K. Information systems use as strategy practice: A multi-dimensional view of strategic information system implementation and use. *J. Strateg. Inf. Syst.* **2014**, *23*, 45–61. Available online: http://linkinghub.elsevier.com/retrieve/pii/S0963868714000055 (accessed on 9 July 2022). [CrossRef]
13. Kovtun, V.; Izonin, I.; Gregus, M. The functional safety assessment of cyber-physical system operation process described by Markov chain. *Sci. Rep.* **2022**, *12*, 7089. Available online: https://doi.org/10.1038/s41598-022-11193-w (accessed on 9 July 2022). [CrossRef] [PubMed]
14. Kovtun, V.; Izonin, I.; Gregus, M. Model of Information System Communication in Aggressive Cyberspace: Reliability, Functional Safety, Economics. *IEEE Access* **2022**, *10*, 31494–31502. [CrossRef]
15. Mendoza, L.E.; Grimán, A.C.; Rojas, T. Algoritmo para la Evaluación de la Calidad Sistémica del Software. In Proceedings of the 2nd Ibero-American Symposium on Software Engineering and Knowledge Engineering, Salvador, Brasil, October 2002.
16. Rincon, G.; Alvarez, M.; Perez, M.; Hernandez, S. A discrete-event simulation and continuous software evaluation on a systemic quality model: An oil industry case. *Inf. Manag.* **2005**, *42*, 1051–1066. [CrossRef]
17. Mendoza, L.E.; Pérez, M.A.; Grimán, A.C. Prototipo de Modelo Sistémico de Calidad (MOSCA) del Software 2 Matriz de Calidad Global Sistémica. *Comput. Y Sist.* **2005**, *8*, 196–217.
18. Kirkwood, H.P. *Corporate Information Factory*; John Wiley & Sons: Hoboken, NJ, USA, 1998; Volume 22, pp. 94–95. Available online: http://search.proquest.com.bibl.proxy.hj.se/docview/199904146/abstract?accountid=11754 (accessed on 9 July 2022).
19. Bass, L.; Clements, P.; Kazman, R. *Software Architecture in Practice*; Addison-Wesley Professional: Boston, MA, USA, 2003; p. 528.
20. Callaos, N.; Callaos, B. Designing with Systemic Total Quality. *Educ. Technol.* **1993**, *34*, 12.
21. Humphrey, W.S. *Introduction to the Personal Software Process*; Addison-Wesley Professional: Boston, MA, USA, 1997.
22. Ortega, M.; Pérez, M.; Rojas, T. A Model for Software Product Quality with a Systemic Focus. *Int. Inst. Inform. Syst.* **2001**, 395–401.
23. Pérez, M.A.; Rojas, T.; Mendoza, L.E.; Grimán, A.C.; Procesos, D.; Bolívar, U.S. Systemic Quality Model for System Development Process: Case Study. In Proceedings of the AMCIS 2001, Boston, MA, USA, 3–5 August 2001; pp. 1–7.
24. Dromey, G. Cornering to Chimera. *IEEE Softw.* **1996**, *13*, 33–43. [CrossRef]
25. Kitchenman, B.A.; Jones, L. Evaluating software engineering methods and tool part 5: The influence of human factors. *ACM SIGSOFT Softw. Eng. Notes* **1997**, *22*, 13–15. [CrossRef]
26. Jelassi, T.; Le Blanc, L.A. DSS Software Selection: A multiple Criteria Decision Methodology. *Inf. Manag.* **1989**, *17*, 49–65.
27. Hostmann, B.; Oestreich, T.; Parenteau, J.; Sallam, R.; Schlegel, K.; Tapadinhas, J. Magic Quadrant for Business Intelligence and Analytics Platforms MicroStrategy Positioned in 'Leaders' Quadrant. 2013. Available online: http://www.microstrategy.com/about-us/analyst-reviews/gartner-magic-quadrant. (accessed on 9 July 2022).

28. Abelló Gamazo, A.; Samos Jiménez, J.; Curto Díaz, J. *La Factoría De Información Corporativa*; Universitat Oberta de Catalunya: Barcelona, Spain, 2014.
29. Rincon, G.; Perez, M. Discrete-event Simulation Software Decision Support in the Venezuelan Oil Industry. In Proceedings of the AMCIS 2004 Proceedings, New York, NY, USA, 22 August 2004. Available online: http://aisel.aisnet.org/amcis2004/7 (accessed on 9 July 2022).

Article

Rough-Set-Theory-Based Classification with Optimized *k*-Means Discretization

Teguh Handjojo Dwiputranto *, Noor Akhmad Setiawan and Teguh Bharata Adji

Department of Electrical and Information Engineering, Universitas Gadjah Mada, Yogyakarta 55281, Indonesia; noorwewe@ugm.ac.id (N.A.S.); adji@ugm.ac.id (T.B.A.)
* Correspondence: teguh.handjojo.d@mail.ugm.ac.id; Tel.: +62-822-8480-1480

Abstract: The discretization of continuous attributes in a dataset is an essential step before the Rough-Set-Theory (RST)-based classification process is applied. There are many methods for discretization, but not many of them have linked the RST instruments from the beginning of the discretization process. The objective of this research is to propose a method to improve the accuracy and reliability of the RST-based classifier model by involving RST instruments at the beginning of the discretization process. In the proposed method, a *k*-means-based discretization method optimized with a genetic algorithm (GA) was introduced. Four datasets taken from UCI were selected to test the performance of the proposed method. The evaluation of the proposed discretization technique for RST-based classification is performed by comparing it to other discretization methods, i.e., equal-frequency and entropy-based. The performance comparison among these methods is measured by the number of bins and rules generated and by its accuracy, precision, and recall. A Friedman test continued with post hoc analysis is also applied to measure the significance of the difference in performance. The experimental results indicate that, in general, the performance of the proposed discretization method is significantly better than the other compared methods.

Keywords: rough set theory; genetic algorithm; discretization; classification; data pre-processing

Citation: Dwiputranto, T.H.; Setiawan, N.A.; Adji, T.B. Rough-Set-Theory-Based Classification with Optimized *k*-Means Discretization. *Technologies* **2022**, *10*, 51. https://doi.org/10.3390/technologies10020051

Academic Editor: Mohammed Mahmoud

Received: 10 March 2022
Accepted: 6 April 2022
Published: 8 April 2022

Publisher's Note: MDPI stays neutral with regard to jurisdictional claims in published maps and institutional affiliations.

Copyright: © 2022 by the authors. Licensee MDPI, Basel, Switzerland. This article is an open access article distributed under the terms and conditions of the Creative Commons Attribution (CC BY) license (https://creativecommons.org/licenses/by/4.0/).

1. Introduction

Classification is one of the processes commonly completed by researchers in machine learning (ML). In general, the purpose of classification is to assign an object to one of the categories that has been predefined. Currently, there are various algorithms for classification, such as Decision Tree, Artificial Neural Network, Random Forest, Fuzzy Logic, and many more, including Rough Set Theory (RST). To obtain the best result, selecting the proper algorithm is crucial by considering not only the accuracy but also the cost of training, cost of testing, and cost of the implementation. Another important factor is whether the classification model needs to be built as a white or black box model. If a white box model is expected, a method such as Decision Tree, Fuzzy Logic, or RST can be applied because this method can produce transparent decision rules.

In a dataset that will be processed for classification, attributes that have continuous values are often found. Hence, the data of the attributes cannot be directly processed by a classifier that requires discrete data, such as RST. To be able to process the dataset, a discretization process should be carried out first.

Currently, there are many state-of-the-art methods for discretization, as reported in Refs. [1,2]. Based on this report, there are two main groups of discretization methods, i.e., supervised and unsupervised. This work also conducted a survey, finding that the popular methods for unsupervised discretization use an equal-width and equal-frequency base. The disadvantage of this unsupervised method is that we cannot be sure whether the discrete results are optimal since there is no feedback to measure the optimality of discrete results at the time of the process. To generate optimal discretized values, a supervised method should be applied. One of the popular methods for supervised discretization is entropy-based [1]. However, the next question is whether the entropy-based method will be suitable or not for RST-based classifiers.

This paper aims to improve the classification performance using the RST method on various datasets with continuous values obtained from UCI. The contribution of this study is to propose data pre-processing methods related to discretization before carrying out the classification process. The proposed method starts with applying k-means to discretize continuous value attributes, then optimizes them by using a genetic algorithm (GA) that involves one of the RST instruments, called the dependency coefficient, to maintain the quality of the dataset as the original after the implementation of the discrete process.

By involving one of the RST elements in the discretization process, it is expected that the discretization results will be suitable for the RST-based classifier. Thus, the novelty of the proposed method compared to other discretization processes is that the method is based on approximation quality with the expectation that it will give better results to be used by the RST-based classifier because the approximation is controlled by one of the RST elements from the beginning.

This paper is organized as follows: Section 2 explains the theoretical basis of the RST, which begins with the concept of approximation in the framework of rough sets, and then continues with an explanation of the basic notions and characteristics of the RST. Section 3 presents the need for discretization and its various techniques, especially those related to the proposed method. Section 4 describes the basic concepts of the proposed method and the algorithm in pseudo-code form. Section 5 presents the experimental framework, the datasets used, and other popular discretization methods. Section 6 describes the analysis of the experimental results, and this paper is concluded in Section 7.

2. Basic Notions

Before the detailed description of the method proposed in this article is discussed, a basic picture of RST that was first proposed by Zdzislaw Pawlak in 1982 will be given. This RST method is intended to classify and analyze imprecise, uncertain, or incomplete information and knowledge [3,4]. The underlying concept of the RST is the size approximation of the lower and upper sets. The approximation of the size of the lower subset is determined by the group of objects that are becoming members of the desired subset. Meanwhile, the size of the upper subset approximation is determined by the possible group of objects to become a member of the desired subset. Any subset defined or bordered by an upper–lower approximation is called a Rough Set [3]. Since it was proposed, RST has been used as a valuable tool for solving various problems, such as for imprecise or uncertain knowledge representation, knowledge analysis, quality measurement of the information available on the data pattern, data dependency and uncertainty analysis, and information reduction [5].

This RST approach also contributes to the artificial intelligence (AI) foundation, especially in machine learning, knowledge discovery, decision analysis, expert systems, inductive reasoning, and pattern recognition [3].

The rough sets approach has many advantages. Some of the most prominent advantages of applying RST are 6:

1. Efficient in finding hidden patterns in the dataset;
2. Able to identify difficult data relationships;
3. Able to reduce the amount of data to a minimum (data reduction);
4. Able to evaluate the level of significance of the data;
5. Able to produce a set of rules for transparent classification.

The following sub-sections will explain the basic and important philosophies associated with RST to be discussed based on Refs. [3,6–9].

2.1. Equivalent Relations

Let U be a non-empty set, whereas p, q, and r are elements of U. If R is a symbol of a relation so that pRq is a relation function between p and q, then R is said to be an equivalent relation when it meets three properties as follows:

1. Reflexive: pRp for all p in U;
2. Symmetric: if pRq, then qRp;
3. Transitive: if pRq and qRr, then pRr.
4. If x in U, then $Rx = \{y \in U : yRx\}$ is the equivalence class of x with respect to R.

2.2. Information System and Relationship Indiscernibility

Let $T = (U, A, Q, \rho)$ be an Information System (IS), where U is a set of non-empty objects called universe, A is a set of attributes, Q is the union among the attribute domains in A, and $\rho : U \times Q \to A$ is the description of the total function. For classification, the set of attributes, A, is divided into condition attributes denoted by CON and a decision attribute denoted by DEC. When the attributes of the information table have been divided into condition and decision attributes, then the table is called a decision table. The element of U can be called object, case, instance, or observation [10]. The attributes can be called features, variables, or characteristic conditions. If an attribute a is given, then: $a : U \to V_a$ for $a \in A$. V_a is called the set of values of a.

If $a \in A$, $P \subseteq A$, then an indiscernibility relation $IND(P)$ can be defined as: $IND(P) = \{(x,y) \in U \times U : \text{for all } a \in P, a(x) = a(y)\}$, or in the statement that the two objects are said to be indiscernible when the two objects are indistinguishable since they do not have sufficient differences in the set of attributes called P. The equivalence class of indiscernibility relation $IND(P)$ is denoted by $[X]_P$.

2.3. Lower Approximation Subset

Let $B \subseteq C$, where C is a set of condition attributes, and $X \subseteq U$; then, the B-lower approximation subset of X is the set of all elements of U that can be classified exactly as an element of X, and it is shown in Equation (1):

$$B_*(X) = \{x \in U : [X]_B \subseteq X\} \qquad (1)$$

2.4. Upper Approximation Subset

A B-upper approximation subset of X is the set of all elements of U that may be classified as elements of X, and this is shown in Equation (2):

$$B^*(X) = \{x \in U : [X]_B \cap X \neq \varnothing\} \qquad (2)$$

2.5. Boundary Region Subset

This subset contains a group of elements as defined in Equation (3). This set contains objects that, whether they belong to the X classification, cannot be determined exactly.

$$BN_B(X) = B^*(X) - B_*(X) \qquad (3)$$

2.6. Rough Set

A set obtained by the lower and upper approximations is called a rough set. When a rough set is found, then it must be $B^*(X) \neq B_*(X)$. Figure 1 illustrates each set that meets Equations (1)–(3).

2.7. Crisp Set

If $B^*(X) = B_*(X)$, then the set is called a crisp set.

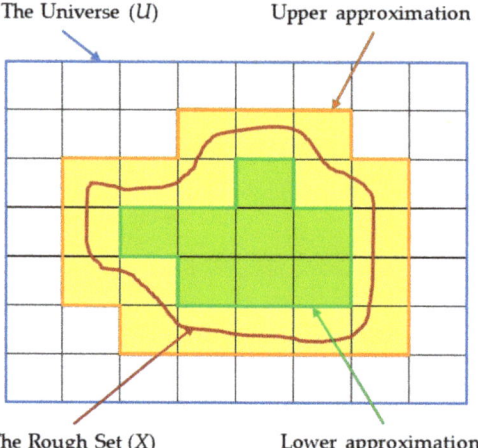

Figure 1. The illustration of rough set. The universe (U) is the union of all blocks. If the set (X) is represented by the red shape, then the lower approximation is the union of all green blocks, the upper approximation is the union of all green and yellow blocks, and the boundary region is the union of yellow blocks, while the union of all white blocks is called outside approximation.

2.8. Positive Region Subset

This is a set that has an object of the universal set U that can be classified or partitioned into certain classes of U/D using the set of attributes C, as shown in Equation (4).

$$POS_C(D) = \bigcup C_*(X), \tag{4}$$

where U/D is the partitioning of U based on the attribute values of D and $C_*(X)$ is the notation of lower approximation of the set X with respect to C. The positive region of the subset X belonging to the partition U/D is also called the lower approximation of the set X. The positive region of a decision attribute with respect to a subset C approximately represents the quality of C. The union of the positive and the boundary regions yields the upper approximation [7].

2.9. Dependency Coefficient

Let $T = (U, A, C, D)$ be a decision table. The dependency coefficient between attribute condition C and attribute decision D can be formulated as in Equation (5) as follows:

$$\gamma(C, D) = |POS_C(D)|/|U| \tag{5}$$

The value of the dependency coefficient is in the range from 0 to 1. This coefficient represents a portion of the objects that can be correctly classified against the total. If $\gamma = 1$, then D is completely related to C, if $0 < \gamma < 1$, then D is said to have partial relation on C, and if $\gamma = 0$, then D has no dependency to C. A decision table depends on the feature set condition when all values on the decision feature D can be uniquely determined by the condition attribute values.

2.10. Reduction of Attributes

As explained in Section 2.2., it is possible that two or more objects are indiscernible because they do not have enough different attribute values. In this case, it is necessary to make savings so that only one element of the equivalence class is required to represent the whole class. To be able to make savings, some additional notions are needed.

Let $T = (U, A)$ be an information system, $P \subseteq A$, and let $a \in P$. It can be said that a is dispensable in P if $IND_T(P) = IND_T(P - a)$; otherwise, a is indispensable in P. A set P is called independent if all of its attributes are indispensable.

Any subset P' of P is called a reduct of P if P' is independent and $IND_T(P') = IND_T(P)$.

Therefore, *reduct* is the minimal set of attributes without changing the classification results when using all attributes. In other words, the attributes not in *reduct* are considered redundant and have no effect on classification.

2.11. Discernibility Matrix and Function

Reducts have several properties, one of which is the validity of the relation, as shown in Equation (6). Let P be a subset of A. The *core* of P is the set off all indispensable attributes of P [10].

$$Core(P) = \bigcap Red(P), \tag{6}$$

where $Red(P)$ is the set of all *reducts* of P.

In order to easily calculate *reduct* and *core*, discernibility matrix can be used [10], which is defined as follows.

Let $T = (U, A)$ be an information system with n objects. The discernibility matrix of T is a symmetric $n \times n$ matrix with entries in c_{ij}, as given in Equation (7).

$$c_{ij} = \{a \in A | a(x_i) \neq a(x_j)\} \text{ for } i, j = 1, \ldots, n \tag{7}$$

A discernibility function f_T for an information system T is a Boolean function of m Boolean variables $a_1^*, \ldots, a_m^*$ (corresponding to the attribute $a_1, \ldots, a_m$), defined as follows:

$$f_T(a_1^*, \ldots, a_m^*) = \forall \left\{ \exists c_{ij}^* \middle| 1 \leq j \leq i \leq n, c_{ij} \neq \varnothing \right\}, \tag{8}$$

where $c_{ij} = \{a^* | a \in c_{ij}\}$.

3. Discretization

Discretization is one of the data preprocessing activity types performed in the preparation stage as well as data normalization, data cleaning, data integration, and so on. Often, data preprocessing needs to be performed to improve the efficiency in subsequent processes [11]. It is also needed to meet the requirements of the method or algorithm to be executed. The rough-set-theory-based method is one of the methods that requires data in the discrete form. Therefore, if the dataset to be processed is in continuous mode, then the discretization process is required.

There are several well-known discretization techniques that can be categorized based on how the discretization process is carried out. When it is carried out by referring to the labels that have been provided in the dataset, then it is called supervised discretization, while, if the label is not available, then it is categorized as unsupervised discretization [11].

Discretization by binning is one of the discretization techniques based on a specified number of bins. If the dataset has a label, then the number of bins for discretization can be determined for as many as the number of classes on the label, while, for a dataset with no label, an unsupervised technique, such as clustering, should be applied.

3.1. k-Means

Cluster analysis or clustering is one of the most popular methods for discretization. This technique can be used to discretize a numeric attribute, A, by dividing the values of A into several clusters [11]. This experiment applies the *k*-means method to discretize the numeric attributes of the dataset.

k-means is a centroid-based method. Assume A is one of the numeric attributes of a dataset D. Partitioning can be performed on the A attribute into k clusters, $C_1, C_2, \ldots, C_k$, where $C_i \subset A$ and $C_i \cap C_j = \varnothing$ for $(1 \leq i, j \leq k)$. In *k*-means, the centroid, c_i, of a cluster C_i is the center point that is defined as the mean of the points assigned to the cluster. The difference between a point, p_n, and its centroid, c_i, is measured using a distance function, $dist(p_n, c_i)$. The most popular formula to measure the distance is by using the Euclidean distance formula, as shown by Equation (9).

$$dist(x,y) = \sqrt{\sum_{i=1}^{n}(x_i - y_i)^2} \qquad (9)$$

Because k-means is one of the unsupervised techniques, then the value of k is not known and it is usually defined through trial and error iteratively to find the optimum value. To automate this trial-and-error process, an optimization technique should be applied. There are many optimization techniques available, but this experiment employs genetic algorithm (GA) technique to find the optimum value for k.

In this experiment, k is optimum if the value is as minimal as possible without losing the quality of the information of the dataset. This experiment uses $\gamma(C, D)$ function, as shown in Equation (5).

3.2. Genetic Algorithm

Genetic algorithm (GA) is an algorithm inspired by biological phenomena, namely the process of genetic evolution from the creation of a population that consists of some individuals who later experience genetic evolution. There are three genetic processes that occur, i.e., selection, crossover, and mutation, to obtain new individuals who are expected to be stronger or fitter during the next cycle selection process [12]. Figure 2 shows GA's operational processes. Figure 3 illustrates the crossover process.

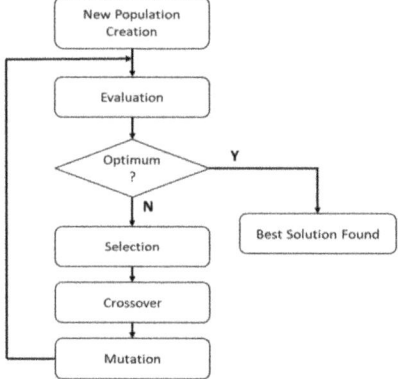

Figure 2. Genetic algorithm process flow.

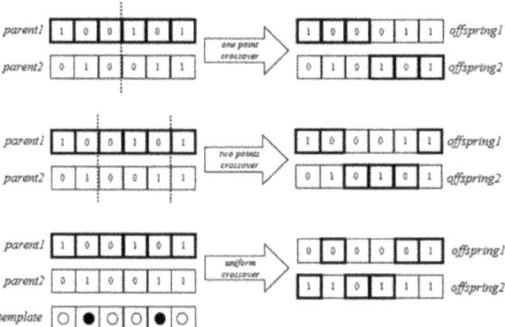

Figure 3. Illustration of some crossover-type processes.

4. Proposed Method

The concept of the proposed method for the discretization in this experiment is the integration of RST, k-means, and GA. An RST is used to measure the dependency coefficient, which can be used to define the approximation quality. Therefore, the transformed dataset after the discretization process will not decrease the quality of the information from the original dataset. To measure the approximation quality, the formula of RST dependency coefficient, $\gamma(C, D)$, as shown in Equation (5), is applied.

Further, k-means is applied to cluster continuum data attributes. The result is the number of bins or clusters of the attributes. The bins are then transformed into discrete values. The GA function is used to minimize the number of bins or clusters of every attribute, which, at the same time, must meet the constraint in which the value of $\gamma(C, D)$ is equal to 1 or any value that is targeted. Minimizing the number of bins is expected to generate the most optimum number of RST rules, which make the classification process become more efficient. The following algorithm of the proposed method is developed to find the most optimal discretization scenario of an Information System.

As shown on the *pseudo-code*, the algorithm of the proposed method begins with reading the training dataset to construct a table called $T = (U, A, V, f)$, where U is a set of objects, A is a set of the attributes, V is a set of values of the attributes, and f is a function of the relationship between the object and the attributes. This table is then transformed into a decision table, called $DT = (U, C, D, v, f)$, where C is the condition attribute set and D is the decision attribute set that satisfies $C \cup D = A$.

After the dataset is loaded, the process continues with the setting of the GA process, starting from the number of chromosomes, which is associated with the number of attributes, and followed by the number of genes for each chromosome, which is associated with the number of centroids or bins of the respective attribute. After the setting of the GA parameters is completed, it continues by executing the GA processes based on Figures 2 and 3. The objective function of the GA is to minimize the number of bins for each attribute with a certain value of $\gamma(C, D)$ as the constraint.

The end of the GA iteration contains the process to convert the chromosome values into the attribute bin values. When the maximum iteration is achieved, then the bin values of each attribute are considered optimum and then are used to discretize the condition of attribute values.

5. Experimental Setup

In this section, the test results of the proposed algorithm are compared with two popular discretization algorithms, namely *equal-frequency*, which is processed using unsupervised learning, and *entropy-based*, which uses supervised learning.

Four datasets downloaded from the UCI data repository with details of the properties owned by each dataset shown in Table 1 are selected. Those datasets are:

1. iris;
2. ecoli;
3. wine;
4. banknote.

Table 1. Descriptions of the tested datasets in this research.

Properties	Datasets			
	iris	ecoli	wine	banknote
# of examples	150	271	178	1370
# of classes	3	8	3	2
# of condition attributes	4	7	13	4

The proposed algorithm was tested on four datasets and compared with two discretization methods, namely *equal-frequency* and *entropy-based*. Figure 4 shows the flow of the research.

In the initial step, a *k*-fold mechanism with $k = 5$ is applied to each dataset so that a ratio of 80:20 is obtained, where 80% of the data are used for the training and 20% for testing. The *k*-fold approach is applied to ensure that every record in the dataset becomes either a training or test dataset. With the application of *k*-fold, it is expected that the results of testing the algorithm can be more reliable. Each fold of each dataset is then discretized using three tested methods, namely: *equal-frequency* (EQFREQ), *entropy-based* (ENTROPY), and the proposed method, which is based on genetic algorithm and rough set theory (GARST).

Discretization with the EQFREQ and ENTROPY methods was concluded on the Rosetta software ver. 1.4.41. Meanwhile, the proposed method was developed by using Python 3.8 based on Algorithm 1.

Algorithm 1. *Pseudo-code* of proposed method.

Input: A dataset in the form of Table $T = (U, A, V, f)$
Output: Optimum numbers of bins for each condition attribute in the form of discretized table $DiscT = (U, C, D, V_c \text{ disc}, f)$
Create decision table $DT = (U, C, D, V, f) = convert\_to\_DT(T)$, where $C \cup D = A$;
Introduce integer variable $maxK = 10$ or any integer value;
Introduce scalar and vector variables *genBit, numChrom, popSize, max Generation, constraintGA,*
   Chromosome, Individu, Fitness, Parents, Offsprings, New Pop for the GA processes;
$genBit \leftarrow integer\_to\_bineary(maxK)$; $numChrom \leftarrow cardinality(C)$;
$popSize \leftarrow 30$ or any integer value;
$maxGeneration \leftarrow 50$ or any integer value;
for $indv \leftarrow 1$ **to** $popSize$ **do**
  for $chr \leftarrow 1$ **to** $numChrom$ **do**
    $Chromosome[chr] \leftarrow binary\_random(genBit)$;
  end
$Individu[indv] \leftarrow [Chromosome[numChrom]]$;
end
$constraintGA \leftarrow 0.8$ or any real value between 0.0 and 1.0;
Introduce vector variables *Bins, Discr_V,* γCD for the RST processes;
for $generation \leftarrow 1$ **to** $maxGeneration$ **do**
  for $indv \leftarrow 1$ **to** $popSize$ **do**
    for $chr \leftarrow 1$ **to** $numChrom$ **do**
$Bins[chr] = KMeans(C[chr], binary\_to\_integer(Individu[chr]))$;
End
for $c \leftarrow 1$ **to** $cardinality$ **do**
  $Discr\_V[c] \leftarrow discretize(V[c], Bins[c])$;
  $\gamma CD[indvc] \leftarrow calc\_\gamma CD(Discr\_V[c], V[dc])$ by referring to Eq. 2.5;
  if $\gamma CD[indvc] \geq constraintGA$ **then**
    $Fitness[indv] \leftarrow sum\_cardinality(Bins[1], \ldots, Bins[numChrom])$
  else $Fitness[indv] \leftarrow very\_big\_vaule$;
End
End
$Parents \leftarrow select\_the\_most\_fit(Individu[1], \ldots, Individu[popSize])$ to create parents; the
   Individu have smaller *Fitness* value will have chance to be selected as a parent;
$Offsprings \leftarrow crossover(Parents)$ to create *Offsprings*;
$NewPop \leftarrow mutate(Offsprings)$;
Run $transform(NewPop)$ to create new list of *Individu* in the form of
$[Individu[1], \ldots, Individu[popSize]]$;
end
return $DiscT = (U, C, D, V, disc, f)$

After the 5-fold datasets have been discretized, each fold is reduced and then rules generation is performed using the Rosetta software. The *reduct* process is carried out using the RST method based on a discernibility matrix, and rule generation using the application of Boolean algebra to the built discernibility matrix, as described in Section 2. This process is repeated five times for each dataset due to the application of 5-fold.

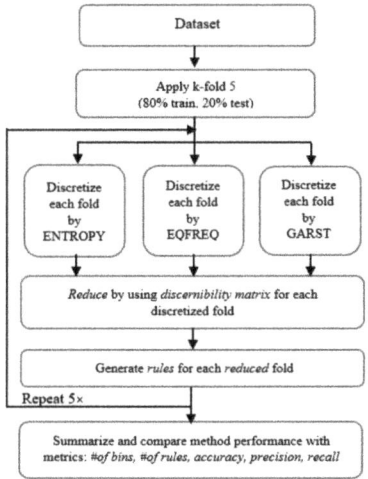

Figure 4. Flow of the research.

The final step of this experiment is to compare the performance of the three methods. The measuring instruments used in the experiment and their explanations are listed in Table 2.

Table 2. Metrics to measure the performance.

Measurement Unit	Objective	Remarks
# of bins	An integer value that indicates the number of bins resulting from discretization.	The smaller this value, the better the performance of the discretization method because the dataset resulting from the discretization becomes simpler.
# of rules	An integer value that indicates the number of rules generated by RST after the *reduct* process.	The smaller this number indicates the better performance of the discretization method because the smaller number of rules makes it easier to understand and more transparent.
Accuracy	Provides a measure of how many samples were correctly predicted by a classifier compared to the total number of samples.	This metric is applied to measure the overall performance.
Precision	Provides a measurement of how many samples are correctly predicted for a particular class. This is the TP ratio of a given class to the number of samples predicted as this class, in other words, the total number of TP and FP.	This metric is applied to measure the class-by-class performance of a method.
Recall	Provides a measurement of how many samples are correctly predicted in a given class.	This metric also measures the class-by-class performance of a model.

To ensure that there is a difference in performance between the three tested methods, the statistical Friedman test method was applied to this experiment. The Friedman test is a statistical measuring tool used to determine whether there is a statistically significant difference in the average value of three or more groups [13]. If the *p*-value of the Friedman test is less than 0.05, then there is a significant difference. The post hoc test was used as a continuation of the Friedman test to determine which group had a significant difference compared to the other groups.

6. Results and Discussion

After the entire process is completed, the last step is to review the performance of each discretization method. Table 3 shows the performance comparison of the discretization methods of the *equal-frequency* (EQFREQ), *entropy-based* (ENTROPY), and genetic algorithm and rough set theory (GARST) proposed in this paper.

Table 3. Number of bins and rules generated by each method.

		iris		ecoli		wine		banknote	
		# of bins	# of rules	# of bins	# of rules	# of bins	# of rules	# of bins	# of rules
ENTROPY	Fold-1	20	49	42	104	143	3952	501	2941
	Fold-2	20	60	36	107	152	4874	296	341
	Fold-3	21	83	32	137	155	6892	454	1364
	Fold-4	21	87	45	116	164	8366	564	2760
	Fold-5	21	102	43	118	167	9394	498	1423
	Average	*20.6*	*76.2*	*39.6*	**116.4**	*156.2*	*6695.6*	*462.6*	*1765.8*
	Max	*21*	*102*	*45*	*137*	*167*	*9394*	*564*	*2941*
	Min	*20*	*49*	*32*	*104*	*143*	*3952*	*296*	*341*
	StdDev	*0.4899*	*19.1353*	*4.8415*	*11.5689*	*8.6116*	*2047.2293*	*90.3761*	*967.3199*
EQFREQ	Fold-1	20	186	27	401	65	50473	20	158
	Fold-2	20	192	27	218	65	48770	20	149
	Fold-3	20	220	27	214	65	49921	20	154
	Fold-4	20	135	27	215	65	49929	20	157
	Fold-5	20	186	27	211	65	51401	20	151
	Average	*20*	*183.8*	*27*	*251.8*	*65*	*50098.8*	*20*	*153.8*
	Max	*20*	*220*	*27*	*401*	*65*	*51401*	*20*	*158*
	Min	*20*	*135*	*27*	*211*	*65*	*48770*	*20*	*149*
	StdDev	*0.0000*	*27.4547*	*0.0000*	*74.6335*	*0.0000*	*855.7926*	*0.0000*	*3.4293*
GARST	Fold-1	17	39	31	164	46	2527	17	55
	Fold-2	11	54	29	277	23	2995	13	36
	Fold-3	13	21	28	154	43	5212	13	73
	Fold-4	16	25	29	136	45	10319	15	88
	Fold-5	11	53	30	134	46	5734	13	65
	Average	**13.6**	**38.4**	*29.4*	*173*	**40.6**	*5357.4*	**14.2**	**63.4**
	Max	*17*	*54*	*31*	*277*	*46*	*10319*	*17*	*88*
	Min	*11*	*21*	*28*	*134*	*23*	*2527*	*13*	*36*
	StdDev	*2.4980*	*13.7055*	*1.0198*	*53.1940*	*8.8679*	*2770.2903*	*1.6000*	*17.4425*

Compared to the performance of the EQFREQ and ENTROPY discretization methods, it is confirmed that the proposed method (GARST) has a better performance, showing the smallest number of the generated bins and rules across three datasets, namely *iris*, *wine*, and *banknote*. The ENTROPY method indicates a better performance for the *ecoli* dataset, demonstrated by the smallest number of bins; however, the GARST method is still superior because it succeeded in generating the smallest number of rules in all the datasets, including *ecoli*.

Table 4 shows the test results that are presented in statistical measures, namely average and standard deviation. From this table, it can be seen that the GARST method has the highest average *accuracy*, *precision*, and *recall*, and has competitive values for standard deviation.

Table 4. The *accuracy*, *precision*, and *recall* of each method.

		iris			ecoli			wine			banknote		
		Acc (%)	Avg Prec	Avg Recall	Acc (%)	Avg Prec	Avg Recall	Acc (%)	Avg Prec	Avg Recall	Acc (%)	Avg Prec	Avg Recall
ENTROPY	Fold-1	96.67	0.97	0.95	29.85	0.18	0.21	38.89	0.42	0.41	74.40	0.74	0.74
	Fold-2	93.33	0.93	0.93	34.33	0.27	0.33	50.00	0.50	0.51	99.54	0.81	0.81
	Fold-3	96.67	0.97	0.97	26.87	0.42	0.40	41.67	0.38	0.40	99.89	0.84	0.84
	Fold-4	93.33	0.94	0.94	20.90	0.24	0.19	50.00	0.44	0.47	99.88	0.65	0.65
	Fold-5	93.33	0.95	0.95	25.37	0.23	0.20	49.65	0.51	0.49	99.96	0.83	0.82
	Global Avg	94.67	**0.95**	0.95	27.46	0.27	0.27	46.04	0.45	0.46	94.73	0.77	0.77
	Max	96.67	0.97	0.97	34.33	0.42	0.40	50.00	0.51	0.51	99.96	0.84	0.84
	Min	93.33	0.93	0.93	20.90	0.18	0.19	38.89	0.38	0.40	74.40	0.65	0.65
	StdDev	1.63	0.02	0.01	4.49	0.08	0.08	4.79	0.05	0.04	10.17	0.07	0.07
EQFREQ	Fold-1	53.33	0.62	0.54	50.75	0.40	0.34	52.78	0.54	0.53	91.20	0.74	0.74
	Fold-2	93.33	0.93	0.94	35.82	0.28	0.19	52.78	0.59	0.46	97.58	0.81	0.81
	Fold-3	100.00	1.00	1.00	29.85	0.35	0.19	41.67	0.27	0.42	99.94	0.90	0.90
	Fold-4	83.33	0.84	0.85	25.37	0.31	0.13	50.00	0.66	0.53	99.98	0.93	0.93
	Fold-5	83.33	0.81	0.83	32.84	0.37	0.23	47.57	0.65	0.53	99.97	0.87	0.87
	Global Avg	82.67	0.84	0.83	34.93	0.34	0.22	48.96	0.54	0.49	97.73	0.85	0.85
	Max	100.00	1.00	1.00	50.75	0.40	0.34	52.78	0.66	0.53	99.98	0.93	0.93
	Min	53.33	0.62	0.54	25.37	0.28	0.13	41.67	0.27	0.42	91.20	0.74	0.74
	StdDev	15.97	0.13	0.16	8.63	0.04	0.07	4.13	0.14	0.05	3.39	0.07	0.07
GARST	Fold-1	100.00	1.00	1.00	52.24	0.46	0.35	83.33	0.84	0.84	96.80	0.97	0.97
	Fold-2	96.67	0.96	0.97	49.25	0.23	0.25	88.89	0.91	0.88	99.86	0.94	0.94
	Fold-3	90.00	0.90	0.90	43.28	0.40	0.24	69.44	0.69	0.66	99.96	0.93	0.93
	Fold-4	93.33	0.94	0.94	55.22	0.40	0.32	66.67	0.77	0.69	99.99	0.97	0.98
	Fold-5	96.67	0.97	0.97	56.72	0.42	0.38	68.06	0.76	0.72	99.99	0.94	0.94
	Global Avg	**95.33**	**0.95**	**0.96**	**51.34**	**0.38**	**0.31**	**75.28**	**0.79**	**0.76**	**99.32**	**0.95**	**0.95**
	Max	100.00	1.00	1.00	56.72	0.46	0.38	88.89	0.91	0.88	99.99	0.97	0.98
	Min	90.00	0.90	0.90	43.28	0.23	0.24	66.67	0.69	0.66	96.80	0.93	0.93
	StdDev	3.40	0.03	0.03	4.78	0.08	0.05	9.06	0.07	0.09	1.26	0.02	0.02

Figure 5 describes the distribution of the accuracy values for each test. From this figure, it can be seen that the GARST method produces consistent accuracy values, although it is not always superior. Thus, it can be concluded that the GARST method is generally proven to have a superior performance in terms of accuracy and reliability, as measured by precision and recall, compared to the other two methods.

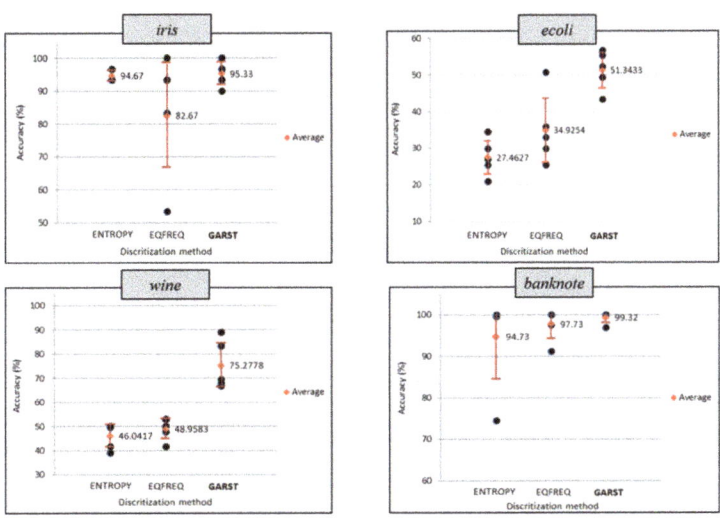

Figure 5. Plots showing the distribution of accuracy values.

According to non-parametric statistical testing, namely the Friedman test, as shown in Table 5, the *p*-value obtained is smaller than 0.05, so it can be concluded that there is a significant difference between the three methods. Meanwhile, from the post hoc test results, as shown in Table 6, the *p*-values of ENTROPY vs. GARST and EQFREQ vs. GARST are all less than 0.05, so it can be concluded that the GARST method is a method that has a significant difference compared to the other two methods.

Table 5. The results of Friedman test for the accuracy.

Dataset	Discretization Methods		
	ENTROPY	EQFREQ	GARST
iris	96.67	53.33	100.00
	93.33	93.33	96.67
	96.67	100.00	90.00
	93.33	83.33	93.33
	93.33	83.33	96.67
ecoli	29.85	50.75	52.24
	34.33	35.82	49.25
	26.87	29.85	43.28
	20.90	25.37	55.22
	25.37	32.84	56.72
wine	38.89	52.78	83.33
	50.00	52.78	88.89
	41.67	41.67	69.44
	50.00	50.00	66.67
	49.65	47.57	68.06
banknote	74.40	91.20	96.80
	99.54	97.58	99.86
	99.89	99.94	99.96
	99.88	99.98	99.99
	99.96	99.97	99.99
Friedman Test Result	*p-value*	0.000003224	

Table 6. The results of post hoc test.

Method	ENTROPY	EQFREQ	GARST
ENTROPY	1.000	0.556	**0.001**
EQFREQ	0.556	1.000	**0.001**
GARST	**0.001**	**0.001**	1.000

7. Conclusions

A method to improve the accuracy and reliability of the RST-based classifier model has been proposed by involving the RST instruments at the beginning of the discretization process. This method uses a *k*-means-based discretization method optimized with a genetic algorithm (GA). As a result, the method was proven not to sacrifice the degree of information quality from the dataset and the performance was quite competitive compared to the popular *state-of-the-art* methods, namely *equal-frequency* and *entropy-based*. Moreover, the proposed discretization method based on k-means optimized by GA and using one of the rough set theory instruments has proven to be effective for use in the RST classifier.

The test of the discretization method proposed in this study uses four datasets that have different profiles in the 5-fold scenario, and the results were tested by using Friedman and post hoc tests; therefore, it can be concluded that the proposed method should be effective for discretization purposes to any dataset, especially for the RST-based classification cases. The disadvantage of this proposed method is an unstable speed during discrete processes, especially in the optimization of the number of bins. This is due to the application of a heuristic approach by GA.

Author Contributions: Writing—review & editing, T.H.D., N.A.S. and T.B.A. All authors have read and agreed to the published version of the manuscript.

Funding: This research received no external funding.

Institutional Review Board Statement: Not applicable.

Informed Consent Statement: Not applicable.

Data Availability Statement: All the datasets used in this study were taken from the UCI public data repository.

Conflicts of Interest: The authors declare no conflict of interest.

References

1. Garcia, S.; Luengo, J.; Sáez, J.A.; Lopez, V.; Herrera, F. A Survey of Discretization Techniques: Taxonomy and Empirical Analysis in Supervised Learning. *IEEE Trans. Knowl. Data Eng.* **2013**, *25*, 29–37. [CrossRef]
2. Dash, R.; Paramguru, R.L.; Dash, R. Comparative Analysis of Supervised and Unsupervised Discretization Techniques. *Int. J. Adv. Sci. Technol.* **2011**, *2*, 29–37.
3. Pawlak, Z. Rough Set. *Int. J. Comput. Inf. Sci.* **1982**, *11*, 341–356. [CrossRef]
4. Pawlak, Z. Rough Sets, Rough Relations and Rough Functions. *Fundam. Inform.* **1996**, *27*, 103–108. [CrossRef]
5. Pawlak, Z. Information Systems Theoretical Foundations. *Inf. Syst.* **1981**, *6*, 205–218. [CrossRef]
6. Kalaivani, R.; Suresh, M.V.; Srinivasan, A. Study of Rough Sets Theory and It's Application Over Various Fields. *J. Appl. Sci. Eng.* **2017**, *3*, 447–455.
7. Pawlak, Z.; Skowron, A. Rudiments of Rough Sets. *Inf. Sci.* **2007**, *177*, 3–27. [CrossRef]
8. Czerniak, J. Evolutionary Approach to Data Discretization for Rough Sets Theory. *Fundam. Inform.* **2009**, *92*, 43–61. [CrossRef]
9. Pawlak, Z.; Skowron, A. Rough Membership Functions: A tool for reasoning with uncertainty. *Algebraic Methods Log. Comput. Sci.* **1993**, *28*, 135–150. [CrossRef]
10. Suraj, Z. An Introduction to Rough Set Theory and Its Applications A tutorial. In Proceedings of the ICENCO'2004, Cairo, Egypt, 27–30 December 2004.
11. Han, J.; Kamber, M.; Pei, J. *Data Mining*, 3rd ed.; Morgan Kaufmann Publishers: Burlington, MA, USA; Elsevier Inc.: Amsterdam, The Netherlands, 2012.
12. Vincent, P.; Cunha Sergio, G.; Jang, J.; Kang, I.M.; Park, J.; Kim, H.; Lee, M.; Bae, J.H. Application of Genetic Algorithm for More Efficient Multi-Layer Thickness Optimization in Solar Cells. *Energies* **2020**, *13*, 1726. [CrossRef]
13. Riffenburgh, R.H.; Gillen, D.L. *Statistics in Medicine*, 4th ed.; Academic Press: Cambridge, MA, USA; Elsevier Inc.: Amsterdam, The Netherlands, 2020.

Review

Big Data in Biodiversity Science: A Framework for Engagement

Tendai Musvuugwa [1], Muxe Gladmond Dlomu [1] and Adekunle Adebowale [2,*]

[1] Department of Biological and Agricultural Sciences, Sol Plaatje University, Private Bag X5008, Kimberley 8300, South Africa; tendai.musvuugwa@spu.ac.za (T.M.); dlomumuxe@gmail.com (M.G.D.)
[2] Department of Botany, Rhodes University, Grahamstown 6140, South Africa
* Correspondence: strychnos009@gmail.com

Abstract: Despite best efforts, the loss of biodiversity has continued at a pace that constitutes a major threat to the efficient functioning of ecosystems. Curbing the loss of biodiversity and assessing its local and global trends requires a vast amount of datasets from a variety of sources. Although the means for generating, aggregating and analyzing big datasets to inform policies are now within the reach of the scientific community, the data-driven nature of a complex multidisciplinary field such as biodiversity science necessitates an overarching framework for engagement. In this review, we propose such a schematic based on the life cycle of data to interrogate the science. The framework considers data generation and collection, storage and curation, access and analysis and, finally, communication as distinct yet interdependent themes for engaging biodiversity science for the purpose of making evidenced-based decisions. We summarize historical developments in each theme, including the challenges and prospects, and offer some recommendations based on best practices.

Keywords: big data; biodiversity; data curation; data generation; cyber infrastructure; data access; science communication

Citation: Musvuugwa, T.; Dlomu, M.G.; Adebowale, A. Big Data in Biodiversity Science: A Framework for Engagement. *Technologies* **2021**, *9*, 60. https://doi.org/10.3390/technologies9030060

Academic Editors: Mohammed Mahmoud and Pedro Antonio Gutiérrez

Received: 15 June 2021
Accepted: 28 July 2021
Published: 17 August 2021

Publisher's Note: MDPI stays neutral with regard to jurisdictional claims in published maps and institutional affiliations.

Copyright: © 2021 by the authors. Licensee MDPI, Basel, Switzerland. This article is an open access article distributed under the terms and conditions of the Creative Commons Attribution (CC BY) license (https://creativecommons.org/licenses/by/4.0/).

1. Introduction

Biodiversity refers to the variety of genes, species and ecosystems of life on Earth, and is the source of many essential goods and services (e.g., food, timber, medicine, nutrient recycling, crop pollination) that support human well-being and quality of life [1]. Despite several international treaties, efforts and commitments to curb its loss, biodiversity continues to decline at a rate above species discovery rate, largely due to anthropogenic factors [2]. To assess the status and trends (local and global) in biodiversity requires a vast amount of relevant information on the distribution and abundance of different species across varying spatial and temporal scales [3]. In other words, relevant data need to be collected, collated, and analyzed.

The last two and half decades have witnessed an exponential increase in the generation and analysis of data in virtually all domains of human engagement such that the term 'big data' was coined to distinguish the data explosion era from what went on before [4,5]. Scholz (2017) [6] tracked the origin of the term to the 1960s and 1970s and summarized its appearances in documents from the US Congress publications to various academic and non-academic works spanning a period from 1961 through to 1979. These early usages had little bearing on how it is conceived today. In its more contemporary form, several authors, for example, [5,7], have traced the emergence of the term from the world of commerce, whose main interest in big data was, and still is, driven by the need to monitor and improve performance. The concept has since spread to several areas of endeavor including, but not limited to, the healthcare industry, the agricultural industry, the education industry, the media sector, governance, the banking and finance sector, astronomy, climate change and biodiversity management. As with concepts of such diverse application, and to which several distinct domains can lay claim, there is no universally satisfactory definition of big data. However, there is a consensus as to the key elements of its essence: big data is characterized by the three Vs of huge volume, high velocity and diverse variety [5,8]. The volume component refers to the size of data generated, considered in petabytes or higher units of data; the velocity component suggests a rate of generation that is real-time or nearly so, thereby contributing to the huge volume; and the variety indicates a mixture of structured, semi-structured and unstructured pieces of information [4,9]. Two other possible Vs, veracity and variability, are sometimes included and are addressed in various forms later in this paper.

Within the context of biodiversity, big data is defined as a "techno-political tool to manage the distribution of biological species", and as "the intensive data accumulation of digitized information on biodiversity, corresponding to a spatial and temporal description of species distribution" [10]. While these rather similar definitions are limited in their scope, because they ignore some other aspects embedded in biodiversity [1], the first part, nevertheless, provides a historical anchor for situating the deliberate integration of big data and biodiversity within a techno-political agenda. This agenda, which could be viewed in simple terms as the implementation of policy supported by an evidence base, started in the mid-1960s [11], much in the tradition of the data-intensive research of the physical sciences (e.g., The Manhattan Project). Big data is central to biodiversity science because, at its barebone level, biodiversity involves species and their distributions across space and time. For instance, 36.5% of global plant species are considered as "exceedingly rare" [12], suggesting a need for conservation planning to, at least, take such metrics into account. In this paper, we assume the view that Biodiversity Big Data (BBD), as a concept, encompasses a cyclical scheme that involves the generation, curation, processing, analysis and communication of biodiversity information, at huge volumes and diverse varieties, with the purpose of making an informed decision for biodiversity management.

The emergence of big data (BD) as a discipline has raised some philosophical questions, challenging established ways of knowing in the various domains of knowledge, including biodiversity science. Some advocates of BD [13,14] have been quick to declare the end of theory; oppose the need for model building or hypothesis formulation as the sheer size of available data and the power of data analytics allow for pattern detection and the emergence of new insights independent of human bias. This view has been robustly contested in the BD literature, and is shown to be based on fallacious thinking, whilst recognizing the inherent potential of analyzing vast amount of data. Kitchin (2013) [4] and others [5,12,15,16] have shown that BD, however exhaustive, is still representational (a sample) and is therefore subject to the vagaries of sampling bias. Data collection and analysis are shaped by the theories underpinning the systems of collection and the algorithms of analytics. The emergent patterns are, thus, not free of human bias as they are interpreted within frameworks. In addition, there is the real possibility of random correlations between variables with no underlying causal linkage. Succi and Coveney (2019) [17] suggest that the pattern recognition power of BD analysis could provide a basis for further engaging theories in making sense of the patterns that would be otherwise undiscernible to the human mind. One application of BD raised in the work [17], and which is relevant to biodiversity science, is its ability to handle some of the sensitive aspects of non-linearity or chaos found in many complex systems [18]; a concept that underlies spatio-temporal organization and weather events and is best encapsulated by the popular phrase 'the butterfly effect'.

In addressing "the datafication of biodiversity" [10], it was convincingly demonstrated that the process of transforming ecological and other records of living forms into biodiversity data not only changes the nature of the information, it also corresponds to a politically-driven shift in priorities for ecological research from local concerns to a global outlook, resulting in the birth of global biodiversity. The key element was to underpin sustainability policy with a strong evidence base. They highlighted the positive role played by the creation of the global biodiversity information facility (GBIF)—one of the largest biodiversity databases in the world—in bridging the divide between science and politics for the global good. The aim was to facilitate the translation of good science to good government policy [19]. While this datafication process provided one approach to viewing the global environmental landscape and developing some of the tools for effective monitoring, it nevertheless came at the expense of biological context. As argued by Bowker (2000) [20], BBD production often results in the loss of ecological meaning as species become disconnected from their ecological context in the process of achieving uniformity and compatibility of data format in a single database. This poses a peculiar danger of database creation becoming an end in itself [20]. A similar line of reasoning was extended further by detailing how the real-world ecological niche of various organisms, captured by numerous information records, are reduced to a two-dimensional world of "rows and columns" [10], thereby creating an artificial data niche detached from the biophysical realities of the organisms supposedly represented. This is what was construed as the datafication of ecological records [10].

The discourse around the emergence of BD in biodiversity would be incomplete without consideration for the infrastructures that make it possible to generate, store and analyze BD. These infrastructures vary from instruments capable of recording tens of petabytes of information (e.g., radio-telescopes) to next-generation sequencers for sequencing whole genomes (about 3 billion nucleotide base-pairs in one human being for instance), to remote sensing devices for collecting a vast amount of environmental data. In addition to these are the rapidly increasing computer storage capabilities, including storing in the cloud, increasing computational power of PCs, coupled with innovations in statistical computing that allow new ways to analyze and visualize BD.

In this review, we adopt the life cycle of data as a framework to interrogate four main objectives, which are to (1): summarize the current state of BBD under each theme of the scheme, (2) identify opportunities for innovation/collaboration, (3) identify challenges, and (4) propose recommendations to drive best practices in the business of BBD. Figure 1 presents a schematic of the life cycle of biodiversity data as applied in this paper. Starting from data acquisition/generation, we track the journey of BBD and associated events through storage/curation, data access, data processing and analysis, and finally communication and decision making. An important point to note in all this is the reusable nature of BBD to address diverse questions relevant to the field. In treating each theme, we attempt to track practices from the past, through to the present, and where possible anticipate the direction for the foreseeable future.

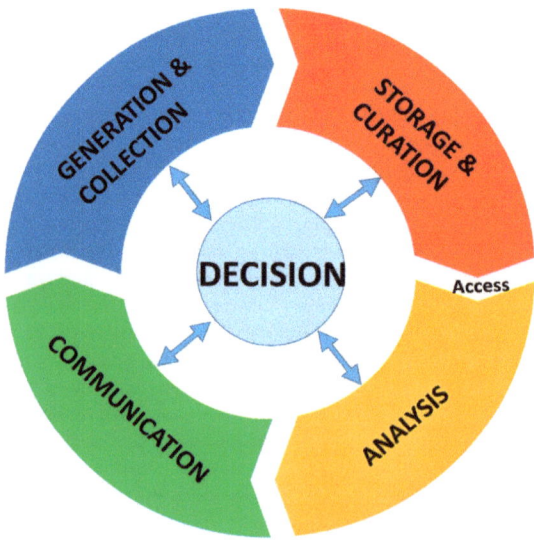

Figure 1. Schematic framework of data life cycle for engaging biodiversity science.

2. Data Generation and Collection

Biodiversity data generation and collection encompasses the various procedures, technologies and methodologies deployed to create and collate biodiversity-relevant datasets for subsequent use in the data value chain. The collation, integration and analysis of massive datasets has grown rapidly with advances in enabling technologies and infrastructures on the one hand, and the need for regional and global scale ecological assessment and monitoring on the other. It could be argued that the need for big biodiversity data collection and the technologies to achieve such ends have mutually enhanced each other in their sophistication. The importance of BBD collection is underscored by widely acknowledged pressures on biodiversity through loss and habitat degradation, the need to plug data gaps and to develop efficient monitoring initiatives aimed at informing scientists, conservation managers and the general public on the state of global biodiversity [21,22]. Furthermore, the possibility of coupling biodiversity metrics with the sustainability agenda adds robustness to ecological forecasting, whilst providing near real-time status of the environment [23,24].

2.1. Types of Biodiversity Data and History of Their Collection and Collation

Measuring biodiversity is a difficult undertaking due to the complex nature of biodiversity itself [25]. Depending on the questions of interest and the spatial and temporal scale of reference, biodiversity data types can vary from the taxonomic, the biogeographic to functional traits [26], and include molecular data (e.g., DNA sequences), species occurrence data, remotely sensed data of various forms (e.g., vegetation cover from satellite imagery) [27]. Traditionally, biodiversity data were collected without much standardization and were usually based on limited observations with little thought to notions of repeatability and statistical powers [25]. Often, data were captured in spreadsheets, small disaggregated local databases with little or no interoperability [27] or presented as volumes of floras and checklists sitting on library shelves. However, the last few decades have witnessed a progressive shift from the traditional methods. Data may now be generated and collected through automated instrumentations; static datasets sitting in bookshelves and as physical specimens in museums are now being digitized and made available online; databases and related infrastructures are being developed with an interoperability outlook for data aggregation on a grand scale [28,29].

Biodiversity monitoring, which requires repeated measurement of the same set of parameters over time, and the capacity to automate such process has meant that previous data collection and integration practices would inevitably be disrupted by novel approaches. The new approaches, which includes DNA sequence data generation, remotely sensed environmental data, aggregation of ecological data, integration, and mobilization of species occurrence databases across geographical boundaries, have all evolved hand-in-hand with developments in computer processing powers. A class of biodiversity data made readily accessible by the new approaches are metadata. Their value in biodiversity conservation is only just being recognized and appreciated. These are especially relevant in the taxonomic domain and may include such details as the names of specimen collectors, other locations where voucher materials are stored and date of collection, among others. With regards to museum and herbaria collections, metadata are being used to map a time series of phenological and other important biological events to track biodiversity responses to climate change [30]. They are also providing insight into how biodiversity datasets are being utilized.

2.2. Sources and Repositories of Big Biodiversity Data

Taking the species as a convenient unit of biodiversity, information regarding its taxonomy, distribution range, genetic diversity, population structure, community and ecosystem functions, and its adaptability to the abiotic components of the landscape all become relevant sources of biodiversity data for the species. Collecting such information on one individual carries little significance. However, when such data are scaled to thousands or even millions of individuals, across taxonomic categories and spatial and temporal scales, the outcomes are inevitably big data on which important biodiversity decisions could be based [31]. Although continuously acquiring new data is ideal, this is not always possible due to time and monetary constraints, thus leading to the use of existing datasets housed as collections in museums and herbaria, or published literature and other online platforms of private individuals, governments and NGOs [32].

A number of studies have highlighted the potential of biodiversity collections and their associated metadata held in museums and herbaria to improve biodiversity management plans for example, Reference [30]. The digitization of these collections is still in its early phase. Some reports suggest an estimate of less than 10% of collections in museums and herbaria are available in digital form [33]. Given that there are well over a billion specimens in thousands of collections around the world [34], even a modest number of 5% digitized records constitutes an impressive source of data for biodiversity assessment for generating robust predictive models.

Data repositories can serve dual purposes in biodiversity research: they act as storage platforms (both physical and digital) for data until required for use; they also serve as sources of data to be mobilized and integrated with other compatible platforms for a more in-depth analysis. While there are many online repositories of biodiversity data (see Appendix A Table A1), two, in particular, provide good illustrations of the volume of data available. The GenBank is a genetic sequence database of the National Institutes of Health based in the United States of America [35] and is part of the International Nucleotide Sequence Database Collaboration. Its current release version 242.0 (https://www.ncbi.nlm.nih.gov/genbank/statistics/, accessed on 10 May 2021) has 12.27 trillion nucleotide bases if one includes whole genome data, and well over 2 billion sequences. The numbers keep growing daily. The Global Biodiversity Information Facility (GBIF) is an international network and research infrastructure with a focus on providing free and open access biodiversity data to everyone. The platform currently holds nearly 1.7 billion occurrence records from about 60,000 datasets from across the globe (https://www.gbif.org/, accessed on 10 May 2021). The taxonomic breadth, genetic depth and geographic/ecological scale of data coverage represented by these two, and other similar repositories, has placed enormous amount of information within the reach of biodiversity researchers.

A last, but not the least, source of data collection is through citizen science. Citizen science initiatives involve enlisting members of the public to gather information, which is then pooled for analysis [36,37]. Advances in the development of smart mobile technology has further made data collection through this approach more amenable to biodiversity research [38]. Several citizen science drives around the globe, sometimes in the form of bioblitz, continue to contribute data to the large scale monitoring of biodiversity. The monitoring of charismatic taxa such as birds has benefited, in particular, from the efforts of citizen scientists spread all over the world. Finally, the development of online platforms (e.g., iNaturalist; Flickr and some social media) where amateurs and experts alike can readily interact and contribute data such as geotagged images of organisms, for screening and identification as needed, is a further data resource relevant to biodiversity. For a list of other potential data sources applicable to biodiversity, including their perceived strength and weaknesses, see an excellent summary in [31].

2.3. Data Collection Planning

From the Data Information Knowledge Wisdom (DIKW) hierarchy [39,40], it is clear that data are the foundation for information, knowledge and ultimately wise decision-making. The planning processes leading to data generation and collection are therefore important for quality assurance of the data and for achieving the goal of the undertaking. Although opportunistic data collection has its place and may not be discounted in biodiversity research [41], it is well recognized that deliberate planning, resulting in the systematic generation and collection of data, is the more sustainable approach. This is particularly so because data collection is expensive, and good quality datasets may be reused either independently or by integration with other types of data. Proper planning prior to data collection can help to identify current data gaps and needs relevant for the achievement of specified biodiversity outcomes. This way, scarce resources can be deployed efficiently, further reducing the cost of data collection.

Because good biodiversity datasets are akin to a gift that keeps on giving, quality assurance measures to ensure accuracy and reliability are necessary components of the data collection plan. In summary, a good data generation/collection plan would include preliminary analysis to identify data needs; identifying goals the data would be contributing towards achieving; defining the steps needed to achieve these goals; and finally selecting the tools and methods best suited to acquire the information or extract the data [31].

2.4. Opportunities in Data Collection

Data generation results in a large amount of information on biodiversity that can be accessed for use by almost anyone where access is free. This is desirable in situations where data collection is not feasible, for example, due to financial and time constraints or where one needs to use data collected over a period of many years. The rate at which data is generated has greatly increased with improvements in technology. In some cases, huge amounts of data can be produced within a short space of time as it is no longer done manually. A very good example is the Square Kilometer Array (SKA) project being co-hosted by Australia and South Africa, in which large amounts of astronomical data with a wide array of applications can be amassed within a short space of time.

2.5. Challenges in Data Collection

As shown above, data are the basis of science. However, the new scale of collection and synthesis requires a new way of collecting and storing data—with a longer-term view in mind. In some cases, there is little to no training given to data collectors, which results in errors during data collection. This can be the case when data are collected through citizen science efforts where members may not be well trained, for example when one is not able to distinguish between species. This can lead to inaccuracies during data entry resulting in data not being fit-for-purpose. Quality assurance is thus a major challenge to data collection playing out through the skill level of the data collector and the reviewers.

There are situations where there is lack of proper guidelines and procedures to be adhered to when data is collected for certain groups of species or for a given data platform. This leaves each data collector to use their own methods to gather data, which creates huge inconsistences. Some collectors gather data in a biased manner, prioritizing certain areas over others, opportunistically choosing places where they expect to find what they are looking for, or areas easier to navigate. This creates problems for example, when one needs to use that data for comparison purposes, or when the data has been collected using different methods that lack consistency.

Biodiversity data generation can be very time consuming, expensive and labor intensive for one to gather enough data that can be analyzed and confidently used for decision making purposes. Data collection requires good funding, which is often highly competitive and inadequate for the need. This is a bigger challenge in developing countries, which are usually the habitats to many biodiversity hotspots. Thus, the areas in need of biodiversity data are also the most impoverished leading to an asymmetry in the potential and actual amount of data generated from such areas. The data gap has a ripple effect on the quality of research-driven conservation and allied decisions in such regions of the world.

2.6. Recommendations in Data Collection

There is a need to ensure that adequate and relevant training is given to data collectors to improve the accuracy and reliability of the collected data. Although it is being done, the quality assurance of data could be improved by developing protocols to guide the data collection process in order to promote consistency and accuracy. Newly generated data could be routinely evaluated for accuracy based on well-set criteria before approval and storage. Currently, there are efforts in place to channel funding towards generation of biodiversity data in developing countries. However, more still needs to be done in this regard to reduce the asymmetry in potential and actual data generated and collected.

3. Data Storage and Curation

There are several types of platforms, some physical and some digital, on which big data on biodiversity is stored and curated. Some of these storage platforms include DNA barcoding databases, image libraries, natural history museums and herbaria, species interaction databases, government departments databases, non-governmental organization databases as well as trait information databases among many others [28,42,43]. Specific examples of the above data platforms include The Open Tree of Life (blog.opentreeoflife.org, GenBank), Barcode of Life Data System (BOLD), Global Biodiversity Information Facility (GBIF; gbif.org), Integrated Digitized Biocollections (iDigBio) [33,44], The Atlas of Living Australia, and various Natural History collections from museums around the world (some of these are listed in Appendix A Table A1). Knowledge of such storage databases is essential for those who utilize the stored data as well as those who generate the data. It is useful to know what these databases are, what kind of biodiversity information they store and the magnitude of data they hold. It will also be of interest to take a closer look at how these databases and methods of storage have evolved over time. Stored big data on biodiversity have been widely used for research purposes, resulting in well-informed decisions on the conservation of biodiversity. To sustainably support excellent research, it is ideal that such data be stored in a well-organized manner [28]. Storage of big data should be done in a credible manner, which ensures that a universally accepted standard is maintained in curating and archiving the data. A great example to achieve this will be the use of a taxonomic framework. There are even increased calls from the scientific community for data aggregators and servers to use tools that enable improved data quality storage at source level [45].

For the most part, biological data have been stored as large and complex datasets that have proven to be very challenging when it comes to the use of such datasets. Some of these storage platforms have, however, evolved over time and went through many developments and improvements to keep up with changing technology and needs of the user communities. Natural History Museums and Herbaria from different parts of the world constitute a reservoir of big data on biodiversity, some of which has been collected, curated and stored for hundreds of years. This has been one of the major biodiversity data storage methods used historically but is also still useful today for many researchers. Examples of such repositories include the Royal Botanic Garden Kew, The Netherlands National Herbarium and several other Natural History Museums located around the world. Invaluable data in these museums and herbaria were largely inaccessible to many interested parties in the past because researchers had to physically visit the respective repositories. However, with the advances in digitizing museum collections, a lot of rich data are being generated from historical specimens, and these are now within the reach of anyone with internet access [29]. The advantage of this system is that digitalized data not only have information on the distribution of species, but also form a connection with other relevant biological data for the species such as phylogenetic and DNA information. For example, in the United States, Integrated Digitized Biocollections (iDigBio) [33,44], which is one of the databases housing big data on biodiversity, serves as the national center for the digitization of biodiversity collections and other related data [29]. Having such data online makes them more accessible compared to being confined to physical specimens only available in museums. Given the pace at which museums are moving their collections online for better accessibility and the values being derived from such efforts, it is expected that virtual museums are here to stay as they complementarily extend the reaches of the physical collections to audiences beyond the physical confinement of the museums themselves. A recent estimate from 3400 global herbaria (Index Herbariorum), indicates there are about 350,000 plant species, and well over 350 million specimens [46,47]. This is a rich biodiversity minefield of stored big data, whose full potential can be explored if the data is fully digitized and if suitable software platforms are developed to integrate and analyze them.

Clearly, digitization is playing a big role in how data is stored, not only in the conversion of museum and herbaria records as explained above, but also on most other data storage platforms. With the current wave of the fourth industrial revolution, digitally migrating data provides a means of rendering them more accessible to the community. Inevitably, there has been an increase in the volume of data digitally stored and curated. Parallel to the increase in digitally stored data are initiatives that encourage data storage platforms, which store similar kind of data to build collaborations to improve the data quantity and quality through pooling databases rather than having small stand-alone databases that address the same problems [28]. Building standard protocols on data storage and curation that ensure high accuracy, consistency and reliability seems then to be the focus going into the future. Combining data from different sources into one database may require ontological adjustments to ensure harmonization of the information from the different collections into a common platform.

The volume of data on the different platforms has significantly increased over time. The rate at which data are collected and stored has increased considerably in the last decade, in particular. For example, there has been a quantum increase in the amount of molecular data stored in nucleotide sequence repositories such as GenBank and Barcode of Life Data System (BOLD). These databases store billions of DNA sequence data and relevant metadata, including specimen images (for BOLD) on different species. The recent initiative of targeting for sequencing well-curated and identified specimens in natural history museum collections has proven to be one of the ways to quickly generate large amounts of genetic data for storage on these platforms [48]. This is advantageous because it then creates a link between the DNA sequences stored on GenBank for example, to the specimen stored in some natural history museum [48]. As a whole, the advances and changes that have occurred in DNA barcoding, metabarcoding and genomic technology over time have led to the rapid growth of the databases holding such data. These techniques are expected to continue evolving with further improvements. Similar data growths are being witnessed in other storage databases besides those for DNA data. For example, one of the goals of the iDigBio project is to digitize close to a billion specimens housed in various museums and herbaria in the United States. This is more than the current specimen records on the site [29].

We cannot discuss the changes of biodiversity big data curation without acknowledging the role played by cyber infrastructure (CI) development. In the past decade or so there has been significant development and improvement in technological advances especially in computer infrastructure. The development of powerful tools in line with improving cyber infrastructure (CI) has helped to create the space for the storage of high volume of data with minimal problems. The changes brought about by current developments and improvements in cyber infrastructure have seen some of the big data platforms storing and curating data in such a way that data can be linked to the relevant analytical tools. This then ensures a quick and efficient use of data, which is important for evolutionary biologists, taxonomists, ecologists and other biodiversity data users. For example, The Open Tree of Life database is continuously improving and evolving with shifts in the types of questions asked by researchers making it an important tool for evolutionary biology [29]. There is no doubt that technological advances in CI help to facilitate new and innovative research using the stored data, ensuring a successful future in biodiversity research and conservation. The biodiversity community will continue to benefit from the advances in CI development.

3.1. Opportunities in Data Storage and Curation

Linkages between some of the big data sites such as Open Tree of Life and iDigBio together with relevant cyber infrastructure and several other tools, for example the BiotaPhy project, allows researchers to address different evolutionary questions very quickly [29]. The different types of data allow integrative research on biodiversity which in turn gives a starting point for evaluating the effects of environmental problems such as invasive species and the impacts of climate change. With the right infrastructure and improved analytical methods, it is possible to combine genetic, morphological, and other trait data from big datasets to undertake a comprehensive set of analyses. For example, Map of Life, is an e-infrastructure tool that uses data from GBIF records to spatially connect point data with layers of conservation reserves and geographical ranges. Therefore, when integrated with good e-infrastructure, big data can be analyzed to facilitate quick and informed decision making [28].

3.2. Challenges in Data Storage and Curation

Although progress has been made in the development of analytical tools and cyber infrastructure for handling big data, there is still room for further improvement. Some big data are not readily available. In other cases, the data entry and retrieval formats are difficult to understand, thus putting off potential users.

Often, there are some inconsistencies in how data is curated, especially when it involves citizen scientists who may lack the technical skills to correctly identify the biota, for instance, or are unable to distinguish between nomenclatural synonyms. All these lead to data inaccuracy. Storage of data can be very expensive especially when it comes to the maintenance of stored data and the upgrading of the systems where the data is stored. In cases where physical collections are converted to digital formats, they lose part of their ecological meaning since some relevant ecological information is exclusively found in the physical records rather than on databases [10].

The constant evolution of data storage platforms comes with the challenges of having to develop or keep modifying dependent analytical tools. In some cases, due to the differences in data types and standards, it can be challenging to integrate different datasets into a single analysis workflow [28]. At the same time, the community that utilizes such platforms must keep up with these changes and upskill for the technical competencies required to navigate the system.

3.3. Recommendations in Data Storage and Curation

Although big data platforms such as the Global Biodiversity Information Facility have gone a long way in serving the scientific community on different levels, there is still room for improvement to maintain the reliability, credibility and accuracy of data found on such platforms. For example, many of the GBIF's occurrence records of over 1.7 billion specimens are not represented by voucher specimens [29], thus indicating a need to develop validation tools for this platform. Whilst we recognize the value of a georeferenced information for a specimen in making conservation decisions, having a standardized framework for data storage and curation will improve the accuracy and reliability of data stored on the different databases. Putting in place systems that check for consistency between new data and already existing data on storage platforms as well as detecting any outliers to minimize errors are other ways that can be deployed to improve existing systems.

4. Access to Biodiversity Data

The accessibility of biodiversity data from the different big databases can be classified at different levels, namely: unrestricted; restricted for confidentiality purposes; require permission to access; or require formal acknowledgement first [49]. It is vital to promote free and open use of this data for many good reasons. However, ready access to data is not always easy or possible [32], and historically there has been a generic culture of not sharing science data [50]. If a database includes information on locations of threatened or rare species, then accessibility to such data may be restricted for the purpose of protecting such species [49]. Some restrictions are put in place to generate money from those who will be granted access after payment. In some cases, custodians of the data restrict accessibility to protect ownership of the data especially for research purposes, while some are reluctant to share due to lack of incentives, rewards or other forms of recognition [32].

A review of the Australian ERIN database found that 51% of data on the database were confidential data, restricted data or data requiring permission for accessibility, while 49% were freely accessible [51]. Access to biological data is more restricted relative to other biodiversity-related data types, for example, environmental data [32]. Although efforts are underway to digitize collections in natural history museums and herbaria, a significant amount of taxonomic data on plants still exist as physical specimens and in paper copies rather than in a readily accessible digital format [52]. Until recently, accessibility to data in natural history museums has mostly been limited to curators, taxonomists, and researchers in biosystematics. With the expectation of the continuous increase of digitization of natural history collections, constraints to accessibility of specimen data are expected to decrease [53].

The increase in threatened habitats, which may get worse in the coming decades if current projections are anything to go by, and the challenges of climate change are some the reasons for data accessibility to be more open. Research undertaken with such data can inform better decision for the protection of biodiversity. Restricting access to biodiversity data can end up being one of the limitations to achieving global conservation goals.

On a brighter note, it is encouraging that calls have been made and several concepts are being developed to promote the freeing up of data and encourage data sharing. This has resulted in open access data sharing concept being widely adopted and declared as best professional practice [47]. This is made easier in the current era, where digitization is being embraced, and global access to the internet is becoming the norm [53]. The Rio Convention of 1992 has been instrumental in the progress towards the free and open access of science data [52], resulting in big data platforms such as GBIF adopting and implementing this approach [47]. The expected trend in coming years is that more databases will go the open-source route.

Two major projects, summarized below, highlight the value of data sharing (through collaboration) and open access biodiversity data. The PREDICTS project [54] was built by collating freely shared data from a large collection of quality assured empirical studies across biodiversity science and integrating the massive dataset with remotely sensed climatic data. One of the main goals of the project is to provide a better understanding of the impact of biodiversity loss on ecosystem functions and services. The project, which is dynamic as it continues to incorporate more relevant data, has developed its own database now being used to generate high quality models for understanding human impacts in relation to various land use practices across the globe. The other project [55] investigated global tree species distributions by combining data from five aggregators of the occurrence data, including GBIF. The project distilled the big dataset into categories of data quality and used high quality records to generate robust model of tree species distribution. The work also shows geographical areas of data gap and the need for data quality improvement processes. Without ready access to BD, the idea of implementing projects of this magnitude would not have taken off in the first place.

4.1. Opportunities in Access to Biodiversity Data

Data access can help promote and accelerate the development of innovative solutions in biodiversity management. Open data can increase knowledge creation using existing knowledge base through research. It can also increase and encourage collaboration among several stakeholders at different levels, from those who collect the data, those who utilize it for research and to those who use the results of the research to make decisions and formulate policies that are biodiversity related. This promotes the sharing of data, reusing data and improving data quality by users who now have vested interest in good data they can always access. On a large scale, multidisciplinary and interdisciplinary research collaborations can be built for mutually leveraging each other for greater efficiency and accelerated development to benefit all aspects of the biodiversity enterprise.

4.2. Challenges in Access to Biodiversity Data

Some datasets are behind paywall, rendering such data inaccessible to organizations and individuals without the financial resources. Even for those who could pay, ethical and perhaps idealistic considerations (e.g., why should anyone pay to access data generated through publicly funded research?) may prevent them from accessing the data. Another challenge to data access is the difficulty in locating some data repositories. This is easily underestimated by developers of data platforms and those who deposit data there. If websites and data platforms are not published and the links widely circulated to the public, locating the repositories becomes a major hurdle to data access even if the datasets are freely available. In some cases where a data platform is well-known, there are no clear and easy-to-follow guidelines on how to access the datasets of interest. With respect to data housed in physical museums or herbaria, access is automatically limited to those who can be in the physical space, thus locking out those who are unable to afford the logistical cost of visiting the repository.

Another barrier to data access is tied to the behavior of some data creators in hoarding their data or prevent access for a specified period. While the accessibility to data is desirable, these behaviors are understandable from the perspectives of the data creators to promote proper attribution on the one hand, and to avoid being scooped on important insights from their data on the other. By and large, inaccessible data constitutes a body of information that is not widely available for many interested parties to use.

4.3. Recommendations in Access to Biodiversity Data

Although it is now being widely discussed in scientific circles, there is need for more ways to acknowledge and incentivize data creators. Protocols can be developed and widely promoted on the issues of acknowledging the owners of the data we utilize. The current practice of floating scientific journals dedicated to the publication of raw data and containing links to where they are stored is a good starting point to encourage data sharing. It is equally helpful to accelerate the mobilization of data into online repositories. Researchers and organizations involved in generating data should be encouraged to have parallel digital curation for all data collected and stored as hardcopy. This would minimize the struggle with accessing data stored either on disparate local computers, or in museums thousands of kilometers away from the end user. Data that is available in digital form is much easier to access as such data are just a click away.

5. Data Analysis

The goal of data collection endeavors is to derive value from datasets to guide decision making and necessary action plan. Deriving such value is at the heart of data analytics, which has become a big industry on its own. Any set of data, however big, is meaningless until and unless insight is extracted from it through an appropriate set of analyses. The need to manipulate large datasets in biodiversity science across various platforms has spawned the relatively young discipline of biodiversity informatics [56]. Here, we adopt the broad scope that analysis should encompass a set of "[w]ell-governed interoperable e-infrastructure, and workflows should support biodiversity discovery and documentation, environmental monitoring, reporting and decision making, as well as the capacity to run fundamental scientific modelling experiments to build understanding of biodiversity evolution, biogeography, and dynamics in a changing world" [28]. This view resonates with the four ideals of data analytics, which are description, explanation, prediction and prescription [57]. However, as a starting point for biodiversity data analysis, datasets need to be prepared to render them into useable and compatible formats for the required set of analyses. These pre-analytics steps involve data selection from a variety of sources, pre-processing to remove/reduce noise, dimension reduction through transformations, and finally enrichment by combining with other complementary datasets to provide better insight into the questions at hand [5,58].

Given the disaggregated and complex nature of many biodiversity datasets, the disparities in scale of observations and the variation in sampling techniques and differing research purposes, a major challenge facing BBD analysis is the mobilization and integration of these datasets into a coherent whole that is fit-for-purpose [29,59]. Relevant to the integration step is the development of cyber infrastructures, biodiversity analytical platforms and synergistic automated workflows to afford researchers the time to focus on doing their science. Recent developments in biodiversity informatics are largely encouraging as the acquisition of such integration facilities are gradually being prioritized, and the potential they hold for solving real-life biodiversity problems is being demonstrated by various case studies [26,54,55].

Some of the tools available for undertaking robust large scale biodiversity analysis include Lifemapper, which uses species occurrence records (available online) to produce distribution maps and makes prediction of habitat suitability for any given species based on the occurrence records [60]; BiotaPhy works on similar principles as Lifemapper [61]; Infomap bioregions and SpeciesGeoCoder [62] use species distributions data to assess both current and historical spatial groupings of taxa that could be important for conservation decision making [63], and ancestral area reconstruction; SUPERSMART [64] is a platform for assembling molecular and fossil data, and inferring robust time-calibrated phylogeny for any group of taxa. All these tools have the potential for hypothesis-driven research in historical biogeography, conservation, and systematics. Soltis et al. (2016) [29] offered a summary of other big data analytical tools in biodiversity, and detailed potential workflows for cross-linking them to address several big questions in biodiversity science. A recent and still ongoing advancement in biodiversity is the development of an analytical framework to interface primary biodiversity observations, indicators and assessment possibilities [65]. The Essential Biodiversity Variables (EBVs) framework [66], as it is referred to as, is a coordinated means to quantify biodiversity dynamics on a global scale, reducing the complexity of biodiversity into a list of priority measurements [67]. The framework is theory-driven rather than data-driven, helping to strengthen the information basis of biodiversity reporting to guide policy instruments [65]. The concept of EBVs is already finding application in monitoring both the populations of single species or their aggregates at multiple spatial scales of relevance to diverse research questions and associated decision-making [3].

A major debate at the core of big data analysis, especially of biodiversity, is the pre-eminence ascribed to the pattern-recognition powers of algorithms, usually to the abandonment of hypothesis testing and theory formulation. However, "[f]raming the issue of Big Data in terms of oppositions, that is, deduction versus induction, hypothesis-driven versus data-driven or human versus machine, misses the point that both strategies are necessary and can complement each other" [68]. Pattern detection capabilities driven by machine learning, artificial intelligence and related algorithms, can be the basis of fine-tuning research questions, hypothesis testing and new theory development. While it is important to put powerful analytical tools within the reach of researchers, meaningful data analysis still requires a clear circumscription of problems to which the analytical method is tailored, and for which the dataset is well suited.

The development of big data analysis in biodiversity, or any field for that matter, has a very young history, tied to the development of powerful computers and algorithms to match. More recent developments in the use of biodiversity big data, which have resulted in the emergence of new data sources and cyber infrastructure for organizing and integrating large biological datasets, have prompted the improvement of big data analytics [29]. Equally, historically, before the development of e-infrastructure data aggregators and servers, scientists have been striving to improve the techniques needed to analyze big data [45]. Although there are limitations in the currently available infrastructures for biodiversity big data analysis, the prospects of developing appropriate solutions are encouraging [69].

5.1. Challenges and Opportunities in BBD Analytics

The challenges of BBD analytics summarized here focus on the scientific side of big data rather than the financial resources for procuring the required infrastructures. Regardless of the power of analytics and the size of the data, the quality of insight derivable from any analysis is a function of the fitness of the dataset(s) for the questions of interest, all other things being equal. There are clear limits to what analytics can discern from poor quality datasets or the wrong use of datasets. In addition, it has been shown that an abundance of data for a particular purpose does not necessarily translate to more knowledge, as the data may be unstructured, such as those collated from citizen science initiatives and remote sensing technologies [70]. Despite the massive number of biodiversity datasets at our disposal, now more than at any other time in history, there are some inevitable shortfalls in our knowledge base, resulting in trade-offs between generalities and uncertainty, thus constraining the value derivable from available big data [55,71]. The reality about data gaps is that while we can reduce them to answer certain questions [72], we can never truly fill them all due to logistical and financial constraints. Closely linked to the wrong application of analytical method is the issue of technical expertise to analyze BBD meaningfully. The development of many open access biodiversity analytical platforms is making automated analysis relatively easy [29]. Nevertheless, there are significantly more opportunities to analyze large datasets than the volume of analyses being undertaken suggesting, among other possibilities, that a limited number of people possesses the skill set required to utilize currently available workflows [73]. It is equally plausible that the human factor of reluctance to embrace change is at play [59], given the disruptive nature of big data and its associated analytical tools. Finally, with an increasing number of data aggregator facilities, and the dynamic nature of BBD that keeps getting bigger, compatibility among platforms is a potential problem that could slow down development.

These challenges notwithstanding, the analysis of BBD presents opportunities to foster collaborative engagements across the various domains of biodiversity, used to operating within their disciplinary silos. It also opens avenues for technological innovations. Most of the key infrastructural components, both in terms of hardware and software, are already available [28]. The complexities of biodiversity science and the need for solutions beyond the capabilities of any singular organization or discipline is, rightly, leading to coordinated efforts on a global scale in providing a systems-level response to the biodiversity crisis.

5.2. Recommendations in BBD Analytics

To ensure quality analyses that can help with effective decision making and policy formation, data quality control processes must be in place. Human capacity development to use existing technologies [59], and regular upskilling due to a rapidly changing analytical landscape is vital. There is also an urgent need for the development of purpose-specific rankings of datasets and improved analytical models that account for data gaps [70].

6. Communicating Biodiversity Science to Inform Policy Formulation

The currently accepted view of science communication is that of an ongoing dialogue where science interacts with the public and other stakeholders in a multi-way stream of engagement [74]. This contrasts with the deficit model of science communication which supposes that provision of facts is sufficient for decision making and behavioral change [75]. Indeed, the consensus is that people's interpretation of science is influenced by their culture, ethics and other filters independent of the scientific fact at hand [76,77]. Given this background, it is little surprising that our increased knowledge of biodiversity is not on par with biodiversity policy guidelines and decisions.

Globally, biodiversity loss continues unabated, especially in ecologically valuable areas [78]. This is despite our wealth of knowledge accumulated from massive datasets, thus supporting the perception that insight from biodiversity science is underutilized in policy formulation [79]. A review of the literature at the interface of science communication and policy identified the linear model of science–policy interaction as a major impediment in translating good science into sound policy [80]. The model assumes that science and policy belong in separate domains and are treated as such, with science purportedly providing accurate answers to well-defined questions of policy makers. Available evidence, however, suggests that policy formulation is a much more nuanced process and is influenced by several considerations, of which scientific merit is but a fraction [80].

A cursory survey of how biodiversity research findings are being communicated indicates that most outputs are published in peer-reviewed science journals or technical books and volumes, automatically restricting the audience to fellow scientists. Added to this, the majority of science journals are locked behind pay walls, thus further limiting access to biodiversity research even among practitioners [81]. Several other discoveries are presented in learned conferences, which are largely gatherings of experts in the field. These communication practices amount to preaching to the biodiversity choir. Many policy makers are non-scientists whose understanding of biodiversity is shaped by readily accessible pieces (with their sensational and misconstrued headlines) in the popular media and not from scientific journals. For knowledge to shift mind-sets, therefore, the onus is on scientists to device effective means of conveying their hard-won findings to policy makers. Recent developments around the communication of biodiversity research recognize this need, and several calls-to-action have been issued to give effective communication a prominent role [82,83]. Tested strategies that have been proposed and are being deployed to bridge the communication divide include deliberately targeting categories of stakeholders outside the ivory towers with relevant information [82,84]. The media is of particular interest here because of the critical role they play in framing issues, and their power for influencing the direction of public policy. Legagneux et al. (2018) [85] highlighted the role of non-scientists in drawing global attention to climate change crisis through massive media coverage and involvement of global public figures to champion the cause. However, whether enough is being done by the protagonists of biodiversity science to close the gap between the science and its communication to influence policy remains an open question. In summary, for biodiversity science communication to achieve its goals, it might need to borrow from advances in communication and apply it as a developmental tool. It must view communication as an ongoing process of reciprocal interchange of views and opinions between the science and the public [74,86].

6.1. Challenges and Opportunities in Biodiversity Science Communication

Biodiversity science is widely recognized as complex and its communication to lay audience is no less. This, combined with the fact that many scientists are not trained in science communication and have, therefore, never thoughtfully entertained the prospect of breaking down their research to the non-scientist. Another factor that can muddle the communication waters between biodiversity science and stakeholders is a lack of understanding, on the part of the public, of the bounded uncertainties inherent in many biodiversity research, leading to unrealistic expectations of what science can deliver. Furthermore, biodiversity scientists (as are all scientists), are not always neutral parties on a particular policy issue. They sometimes hold biased views on which side they advocate for policy-wise; at other times, they operate under considerable political pressures. One other barrier to effectively communicating about biodiversity is the problem of assessing, in quantitative terms, the value of biodiversity. This is because not all values derivable from biodiversity (e.g., aesthetics) can be readily translated into quantitative formats [79,87].

The challenges present opportunities to develop, test and implement strategies for effectively conveying the key messages of science to stakeholders. For instance, development of inter-disciplinary studies at the interface of science and policy might create a unique category of professionals straddling both worlds comfortably to drive necessary policy transformations and biodiversity agendas.

6.2. Recommendations in Biodiversity Science Communication

Scientists should adapt scientific communication methods to other people's world view and form partnerships with non-scientists including the media to minimize miscommunications. Involvement of well-known global figures as biodiversity champions will go a long way to get the public and could potentially promote positive media coverage. There should also be a management of expectations as to the extent of the contribution that science can really make to wise biodiversity decision-making process [88].

7. Synthesis and Conclusions

The continuous loss of biodiversity affects ecosystem functioning, of which we are a part. To stem the tide, evidence-based decision-making processes should become the normative mode of operation. This is only possible on the back of adequate and quality data that is well analyzed and accurately interpreted. This review presents the data life cycle as an umbrella framework for critically engaging the subject of big data in biodiversity science with the goal of making informed decisions in biodiversity management. Although we present the framework in what appears to be a logical flow starting from data generation, through storage, to analysis and finally to communication, any of the themes could, arguably, be a starting point for engagement depending on context. The themes and associated sub-themes are all interlinked and dependent on each, and not necessarily in the neat order we have arranged them. Data collection could be informed by the analysis of previously available datasets, which may identify specific data gaps. In turn, data analysis is underpinned by access to some sets of data in the first place. For informed policy decisions on biodiversity issues, the insight gained through analysis must be effectively communicated to stakeholders and policy makers. Infrastructural developments to drive innovative data collection, the storage of massive datasets and the performance of relevant analyses are critical to the smooth operation of the scheme. The interlinked nature of the scheme suggests that there will be some element of redundancies for quality assurance. As summarized in Figure 2, such overlaps are reflected in the similarity of challenges and opportunities across some themes.

	Generation & Collection	**Storage, Access & Curation**	**Analysis**	**Communication**
Challenges	Errors and inaccuracies in data (poor quality data). Biased data collection resulting in data gaps for some taxa or regions. Time consuming, expensive, and labour intensive. Incompatible data formats and platforms	Lack of access to some datasets. Prohibitive cost of accessing the physical spaces housing biodiversity data and associated specimens. Financial cost of storage; some data behind paywall. Inconsistencies of style and format.	Inappropriate analysis due to the ease of point-and-click tools. Scarcity of experts in big data analysis with a sound grasp of biodiversity. Incompatibilities among platforms.	Miscommunication (by the scientist) and misunderstanding (sometimes by the public). Quantitative assessment of the value of biodiversity. Biased view of the proponents of biodiversity science. Political pressure.
Opportunities	Interdisciplinary collaborations. Development of infrastructures for data aggregation. Automated collection of high-volume data in some domain.	Innovative solution through integration of different datasets. One-point stop to access, integrate and analyse several datasets. Reusable data. Research leveraging through multidisciplinary collaboration.	Development of intelligent algorithms for big data analysis. Rapid decision based on robust data analysis. Development of system-level solution. Multidisciplinary collaboration.	Test of effective communication strategies. Development of professionals to straddle the science-policy interface.
Recommendations	Adequate training for data collectors. Development of data collection protocols to promote consistency and improve accuracy.	Development of data validation tools. Standardized format of storage and curation of data of similar type. Creative ways to incentivise data owners.	Training of biodiversity researchers to use available tools. Development of improved analytical models.	Provision of regular science communication training to scientists. Recruitment of well-known figures as biodiversity advocates.

Figure 2. Summary of challenges and opportunities across BBD themes.

The cyclic nature of the scheme also connotes the potential reusability of biodiversity data. Indeed, this is a necessity due to the historical element inherent to biodiversity datasets, and the logistical and financial constraints of data collection. Because biodiversity scientists are usually directly involved in every theme of the scheme except, perhaps, for the policy formulation and decision-making phase, the need for deliberate constructive engagement between scientists and policy makers becomes non-negotiable. A good starting point for such engagement is the recognition by both sets of players that they belong in the same domain, even if their roles are different. Critical to those roles is good quality big data and what can be done with it.

Author Contributions: Conceptualization, A.A. and T.M.; Theme definition, A.A., T.M. and M.G.D.; Literature search and compilation, T.M. and M.G.D.; Writing—original draft preparation, T.M. and A.A.; Writing—review and editing, A.A., T.M., M.G.D.; Visualization, A.A.; Project administration, A.A.; Funding acquisition, T.M. All authors have read and agreed to the published version of the manuscript.

Funding: This research was funded by ABSA Bank, grant number 11112019 and The APC was funded by ABSA Bank.

Acknowledgments: The authors thank Guy Midgley for reading through and offering helpful suggestions on an earlier draft of the manuscript.

Conflicts of Interest: The authors declare no conflict of interest. The funders had no role in the design of the study; in the collection, analyses, or interpretation of data; in the writing of the manuscript, or in the decision to publish the results.

Appendix A

Table A1. Examples of notable biodiversity big data platforms.

Platform/Site	Type of Data	Number of Records	Reference/Website
GenBank	Nucleotide sequences and their protein translations	>2 billion sequence records	www.ncbi.nlm.nih.gov/genbank/, accessed on 10 May 2021
Barcode of Life Data System (BOLD)	DNA barcode sequences	>6 million DNA barcode sequences from over 542,000 species.	http://barcodinglife.org/, accessed on 8 April 2021
Global Biodiversity Information Facility (GBIF)	Specimen-based and observational data on localities	>1.6 billion records	gbif.org, accessed on 8 April 2021
Integrated Digitized Biocollections (iDigBio)	Digitized neontological and paleontological biodiversity collections and associated media and metadata, specimen location	>70 million specimen records	www.idigbio.org, accessed on 8 April 2021
The Atlas of Living Australia	Collaborative, digital and open infrastructure that pulls together Australian biodiversity data from multiple sources, making it accessible and reusable	>67 million records	https://www.ala.org.au/about-ala/, accessed on 7 April 2021
The Open Tree of Life	Phylogenetic data and genealogical tree connection for all of Earth's >2.3 million named species	>2.3 million of earth's named species	blog.opentreeoflife.org, accessed on 10 April 2021
Chinese Virtual Herbarium	Records from the flora of China	>3 million records	http://www.cvh.org.cn/, accessed on 10 April 2021
Digitized herbarium of the Museum National d'Histoire Naturelle (MNHN) in Paris	Collection of vascular plants	>5 million records	https://science.mnhn.fr/institution/mnhn/collection/p/item/search, accessed on 10 April 2021
Australia's Virtual Herbarium	Specimen records of plants, algae and fungi	>7 million records	http://avh.chah.org.au/, accessed on 10 April 2021

Table A1. Cont.

Platform/Site	Type of Data	Number of Records	Reference/Website
Institutos Nacionals de Ciencia e Tecnologia e Herbario Virtual da Flora e Dos Fungos	Digitized specimen records	>5 million records	http://inct.florabrasil.net/, accessed on 14 March 2021
Canadensys	Digitized specimen and occurrence records especially for plants, insects, and fungi	About 3 million records	https://community.canadensys.net/, accessed on 20 November 2020
JACQ Virtual Herbarium	Digitized specimen records	>5.5 million specimens	http://herbarium.univie.ac.at/database/index.php, accessed on 20 November 2020
LUOMUS	Digitized botanical and mycological collections	>9 million specimens and sample lots	www.luomus.fi/en/botanical-andmycological-collections, accessed on 23 November 2020
Encyclopedia of Life Trait Bank	Trait data records for different taxa	>11 million records for over 330 attributes for more than 1.7 million taxa	www.eol.org/traitbank, accessed on 30 October 2020
TRY Plant Trait Database	Trait record data for plant species	>5.6 million trait records from more than 100,000 plant species	www.try-db.org, accessed on 20 November 2020
GloBI (Global Biotic Interactions)	Species interaction data	>1.3 million interactions for over 113,000 distinct taxa	www.globalbioticinteractions.org/about.html, accessed on 20 November 2020
Catalogue of Life	World's most comprehensive and authoritative index of known species of animals, plants, fungi and micro-organisms	1,829,672 living and 38,145 extinct species	www.catalogueoflife.org, accessed on 23 November 2020
International Barcode of Life (iBOL),	Use of sequence diversity, standardized gene regions as a tool for identifying known species and discovering new ones	>5 million georeferenced records	www.ibol.org, accessed on 10 April 2021
Australian Environmental Resources Information Network (ERIN),	Environmental information and data		https://www.environment.gov.au/about-us/environmental-information-data/erin, accessed on 10 April 2021
UK Biological Records Centre (BRC),	Focus on UK terrestrial and freshwater species records	Unknown	https://www.brc.ac.uk/, accessed on 10 April 2021
US Gap Analysis Project	Species, land cover and protected areas database of the United States	Unknown	https://www.usgs.gov/core-science-systems/science-analytics-and-synthesis/gap, accessed on 10 April 2021
Index Herbariorum	Herbaria serving species of bryophytes, ferns, lycopods, gymnosperms, and angiosperms	3400 herbaria with 350,000 species and 350 million specimens	sweetgum.nybg.org/science/ih/, accessed on 11 April 2021
National Biodiversity Network Gateway	Collects, sorts, analyses, and disseminates data for biodiversity in the United Kingdom	>127 million species records	http://data.nbn.org.uk/, accessed on 11 April 2021
Biodiversity Data Centre	Data and information on species, habitat types and sites of interest in Europe	Unknown	http://www.eea.europa.eu/themes/biodiversity/dc, accessed on 10 April 2021

References

1. Rands, M.R.W.; Adams, W.M.; Bennun, L.; Butchart, S.H.M.; Clements, A.; Coomes, D.; Entwistle, A.; Hodge, I.; Kapos, V.; Scharlemann, J.P.W. Biodiversity conservation: Challenges beyond 2010. *Science* **2010**, *329*, 1298–1303. [CrossRef]
2. Dietz, S.; Adger, W.N. Economic growth, biodiversity loss and conservation effort. *J. Environ. Manag.* **2003**, *68*, 23–35. [CrossRef]
3. Jetz, W.; McGeoch, M.A.; Guralnick, R.; Ferrier, S.; Beck, J.; Costello, M.J.; Fernandez, M.; Geller, G.N.; Keil, P.; Merow, C.; et al. Essential biodiversity variables for mapping and monitoring species populations. *Nat. Ecol. Evol.* **2019**, *3*, 539–551. [CrossRef] [PubMed]

4. Kitchin, R. Big data and human geography: Opportunities, challenges and risks. *Dialogues Hum. Geogr.* **2013**, *3*, 262–267. [CrossRef]
5. Kitchin, R. Big Data, new epistemologies and paradigm shifts. *Big Data Soc.* **2014**, *1*, 2053951714528481. [CrossRef]
6. Scholz, T.M. *Big Data in Organizations and the Role of Human Resource Management*; Peter Lang International Academic Publishers: New York, NY, USA, 2017.
7. Diebold, F.X. A Personal Perspective on the Origin(s) and Development of 'Big Data': The Phenomenon, the Term, and the Discipline, Second Version (26 November 2012). PIER Working Paper No. 13-003. Available online: https://ssrn.com/abstract=2202843 (accessed on 5 May 2021).
8. Swan, M. Philosophy of big data: Expanding the human-data relation with big data science services. In Proceedings of the 2015 IEEE First International Conference on Big Data Computing Service and Applications 2015, Redwood City, CA, USA, 30 March–2 April 2015; pp. 468–477.
9. Boyd, D.; Crawford, K. Critical questions for big data: Provocations for a cultural, technological, and scholarly phenomenon. Information. *Commun. Soc.* **2012**, *15*, 662–679. [CrossRef]
10. Devictor, V.; Bensaude-Vincent, B. From ecological records to big data: The invention of global biodiversity. *Hist. Philos. Life Sci.* **2016**, *38*, 1–23. [CrossRef] [PubMed]
11. Aronova, E.; Baker, K.S.; Oreskes, N. Big science and big data in biology: From the international geophysical year through the international biological program to the long term ecological research (LTER) Network, 1957—Present. *Hist. Stud. Nat. Sci.* **2010**, *40*, 183–224. [CrossRef]
12. Enquest, J.B.; Feng, X.; Boyle, B.; Maitner, B.; Newman, E.A.; Jørgensen, P.M.; Roehrdanz, P.R.; Thiers, B.M.; Burger, J.R.; Corlett, R.T.; et al. The commonness of rarity: Global and future distribution of rarity across land plants. *Sci. Adv.* **2019**, *5*, eaaz0414. [CrossRef]
13. Anderson, C. The end of theory: The data deluge makes the scientific method obsolete. *Wired Mag.* **2008**, *16*, 7–16. [CrossRef]
14. Prensky, M.H. Sapiens digital: From digital immigrants and digital natives to digital wisdom. *Innov. J. Online Educ.* **2009**, *5*, EJ834248.
15. Amin, A.; Thrift, N. *Cities: Reimagining the Urban*; Polity Press: Cambridge, UK, 2002; p. 192.
16. Crawford, K. The hidden biases in big data. *Harv. Bus. Rev.* **2013**, *1*, 814.
17. Succi, S.; Coveney, P.V. Big data: The end of the scientific method? *Philos. Trans. R. Soc. A* **2019**, *377*, 20180145. [CrossRef]
18. Bond, W.J.; Maze, K.; Desmet, P. Fire life histories and the seeds of chaos. *Ecoscience* **1995**, *2*, 252–260. [CrossRef]
19. Kelmelis, J.A.; Snow, M. *Proceedings of the US Geological Survey Global Change Research Forum*; US Government Printing Office: Washington, DC, USA, 1993.
20. Bowker, G.C. Biodiversity datadiversity. *Soc. Stud. Sci.* **2000**, *30*, 643–683. [CrossRef]
21. Tittensor, D.P.; Walpole, M.; Hill, S.L.L.; Boyce, D.G.; Britten, G.L.; Burgess, N.D.; Butchart, S.H.M.; Leadley, P.W.; Regan, E.C.; Alkemade, R. A mid-term analysis of progress toward international biodiversity targets. *Science* **2014**, *346*, 241–244. [CrossRef] [PubMed]
22. Proença, V.; Martin, L.J.; Pereira, H.M.; Fernandez, M.; McRae, L.; Belnap, J.; Böhm, M.; Brummitt, N.; García-Moreno, J.; Gregory, R.D. Global biodiversity monitoring: From data sources to essential biodiversity variables. *Biol. Conserv.* **2017**, *213*, 256–263. [CrossRef]
23. Chen, I.-C.; Hill, J.K.; Ohlemüller, R.; Roy, D.B.; Thomas, C.D. Rapid range shifts of species associated with high levels of climate warming. *Science* **2011**, *333*, 1024–1026. [CrossRef]
24. Runting, R.K.; Phinn, S.; Xie, Z.; Venter, O.; Watson, J.E.M. Opportunities for big data in conservation and sustainability. *Nat. Commun.* **2020**, *11*, 2003. [CrossRef]
25. Archaux, F. On methods of biodiversity data collection and monitoring. *Sci. Eaux Territ.* **2011**, *3*, 70–74.
26. König, C.; Weigelt, P.; Schrader, J.; Taylor, A.; Kattge, J.; Kreft, H. Biodiversity data integration—The significance of data resolution and domain. *PLoS Biol.* **2019**, *17*, e3000183. [CrossRef]
27. Diepenbroek, M.; Glöckner, F.O.; Grobe, P.; Güntsch, A.; Huber, R.; König-Ries, B.; Kostadinov, I.; Nieschulze, J.; Seeger, B.; Tolksdorf, R.; et al. *Towards an Integrated Biodiversity and Ecological Research Data Management and Archiving Platform: The German Federation for the Curation of Biological Data (GFBio)*, Informatik, Bonn, Germany; Plödereder, E., Grunske, L., Schneider, E., Ull, D., Eds.; Gesellschaft für Informatik e.V.: Bonn, Germany, 2014; pp. 1711–1721.
28. La Salle, J.; Williams, K.J.; Moritz, C. Biodiversity analysis in the digital era. *Philos. Trans. R. Soc. B Biol. Sci.* **2016**, *371*, 20150337. [CrossRef]
29. Soltis, D.E.; Soltis, P.S. Mobilizing and integrating big data in studies of spatial and phylogenetic patterns of biodiversity. *Plant Divers.* **2016**, *38*, 264–270. [CrossRef] [PubMed]
30. Heberling, M.; McDonough MacKenzie, C.; Fridley, J.D.; Kalisz, S.; Primack, R. Phenological mismatch with trees reduces wildflower carbon budgets. *Ecol. Lett.* **2019**, *22*, 616–623. [CrossRef] [PubMed]
31. BID-REX. *Better Data, Better Decisions: Increasing the Impact of Biodivesity Information. Technical Report of Phase 1 of the Project BID-REX—From Biodiversity Data to Decisions: Enhancing Natural Value through Improved Regional Development Policies*; Interreg Europe; Forest Sciences Centre of Catalonia: Catalonia, Spain, 2019.
32. Williams, P.H.; Margules, C.R.; Hilbert, D.W. Data requirements and data sources for biodiversity priority area selection. *J. Biosci.* **2002**, *27*, 327–338. [CrossRef]

33. Page, L.M.; MacFadden, B.J.; Fortes, J.A.; Soltis, P.S.; Riccardi, G. Digitization of biodiversity collections reveals biggest data on biodiversity. *BioScience* **2015**, *65*, 841–842. [CrossRef]
34. Beaman, R.S.; Cellinese, N. Mass digitization of scientific collections: New opportunities to transform the use of biological specimens and underwrite biodiversity science. *ZooKeys* **2012**, *209*, 7–17. [CrossRef] [PubMed]
35. Benson, B.W.; McIntosh, A.S.; Maddocks, D.; Herring, S.A.; Raftery, M.; Dvořák, J. What are the most effective risk-reduction strategies in sport concussion? *Br. J. Sports Med.* **2013**, *47*, 321–326. [CrossRef]
36. Bhattacharjee, Y. Citizen scientists supplement work of Cornell researchers. *Science* **2005**, *308*, 1402–1403. [CrossRef]
37. Bonney, R.; Cooper, C.B.; Dickinson, J.; Kelling, S.; Phillips, T.; Rosenberg, K.V.; Shirk, J. Citizen science: A developing tool for expanding science knowledge and scientific literacy. *BioScience* **2009**, *59*, 977–984. [CrossRef]
38. Pocock, M.J.O.; Roy, H.E.; August, T.; Kuria, A.; Barasa, F.; Bett, J.; Githiru, M.; Kairo, J.; Kimani, J.; Kinuthia, W. Developing the global potential of citizen science: Assessing opportunities that benefit people, society and the environment in East Africa. *J. Appl. Ecol.* **2019**, *56*, 274–281. [CrossRef]
39. Ackoff, R.L. From data to wisdom. *J. Appl. Syst. Anal.* **1989**, *16*, 3–9.
40. Bellinger, G.; Castro, D.; Mills, A. Data, Information, Knowledge, and Wisdom. Available online: http://www.Systems-thinking.org/dikw/dikw.htm (accessed on 15 January 2021).
41. Chandler, M.; See, L.; Buesching, C.D.; Cousins, J.A.; Gillies, C.; Kays, R.W.; Newman, C.; Pereira, H.M.; Tiago, P. Involving citizen scientists in biodiversity observation. In *The GEO Handbook on Biodiversity Observation Networks*; Walters, M., Scholes, R., Eds.; Springer: Cham, Swizerland, 2017; pp. 211–237.
42. Kattge, J.; Diaz, S.; Lavorel, S.; Prentice, I.C.; Leadley, P.; Bönisch, G.; Garnier, E.; Westoby, M.; Reich, P.B.; Wright, I.J.; et al. TRY–a global database of plant traits. *Glob. Chang. Biol.* **2011**, *17*, 2905–2935. [CrossRef]
43. Parr, C.S.; Schulz, K.S.; Hammock, J.; Wilson, N.; Leary, P.; Rice, J.; Corrigan, R.J., Jr. TraitBank: Practical semantics for organism attribute data. *Semant. Web* **2016**, *7*, 577–588. [CrossRef]
44. Matsunaga, A.; Thompson, A.; Figueiredo, R.J.; Germain-Aubrey, C.C.; Collins, M.; Beaman, R.S.; MacFadden, B.J.; Riccardi, G.; Soltis, P.S.; Page, L.M. A computational-and storage-cloud for integration of biodiversity collections. In Proceedings of the 2013 IEEE 9th International Conference on E-Science 2013, Beijing, China, 22–25 October 2013; pp. 78–87.
45. Constable, H.; Guralnick, R.; Wieczorek, J.; Spencer, C.; Peterson, A.T.; Committee, V.S. VertNet: A new model for biodiversity data sharing. *PLoS Biol.* **2010**, *8*, e1000309. [CrossRef]
46. Paton, A.J. From Working List to Online Flora of All Known Plants—Looking Forward with Hindsight1. *Ann. Mo. Bot. Gard.* **2013**, *99*, 206–213. [CrossRef]
47. Huettmann, F.; Ickert-Bond, S.M. On open access, data mining and plant conservation in the Circumpolar North with an online data example of the Herbarium, University of Alaska Museum of the North. *Arct. Sci.* **2018**, *4*, 433–470. [CrossRef]
48. Hebert, P.D.; DeWaard, J.R.; Zakharov, E.V.; Prosser, S.W.; Sones, J.E.; McKeown, J.T.; Mantle, B.; La Salle, J. A DNA 'Barcode Blitz': Rapid digitization and sequencing of a natural history collection. *PLoS ONE* **2013**, *8*, e68535. [CrossRef] [PubMed]
49. Gibbons, D.W.; Reid, J.B.; Chapman, R.A. *The New Atlas of Breeding Birds in Britain and Ireland: 1988–1991 (T. & AD Poyser)*; Academic Press: London, UK, 1994.
50. Carlson, D.J. IPY 2007–2008: Where threads of the double helix and sputnik intertwine. In *Protection of the Three Poles*; Huettmann, F., Ed.; Springer: Tokyo, Japan, 2012; pp. 35–50.
51. Austin, M.P.; Meyers, J.A.; Doherty, M.D. *Modelling of Landscape Patterns and Processes Using Biological Data. Sub Project 2: Predictive Models for Landscape Patterns and Processes*; CSIRO Division of Wildlife and Ecology: Canberra, Australia, 1994.
52. Huettmann, F. On the relevance and moral impediment of digital data management, data sharing, and public open access and open source code in (tropical) research: The Rio convention revisited towards mega science and best professional research practices. In *Central American Biodiversity*; Huettmann, F., Ed.; Springer: New York, NY, USA, 2015; pp. 391–417.
53. Lacey, E.A.; Hammond, T.T.; Walsh, R.E.; Bell, K.C.; Edwards, S.V.; Ellwood, E.R.; Guralnick, R.; Ickert-Bond, S.M.; Mast, A.R.; McCormack, J.E.; et al. Climate change, collections and the classroom: Using big data to tackle big problems. *Evol. Educ. Outreach* **2017**, *10*, 1–13. [CrossRef]
54. Hudson, L.N.; Newbold, T.; Contu, S.; Hill, S.L.; Lysenko, I.; De Palma, A.; Phillips, H.R.; Senior, R.A.; Bennett, D.J.; Booth, H.; et al. The PREDICTS database: A global database of how local terrestrial biodiversity responds to human impacts. *Ecol. Evol.* **2014**, *4*, 4701–4735. [CrossRef]
55. Serra-Diaz, J.M.; Enquist, B.J.; Maitner, B.; Merow, C.; Svenning, J.-C. Big data of tree species distributions: How big and how good? *For. Ecosyst.* **2017**, *4*, 1–12. [CrossRef]
56. Peterson, A.T.; Knapp, S.; Guralnick, R.; Soberón, J.; Holder, M.T. The big questions for biodiversity informatics. *Syst. Biodivers.* **2010**, *8*, 159–168. [CrossRef]
57. Minelli, M.; Chambers, M.; Dhiraj, A. *Big Data, Big Analytics: Emerging Business Intelligence and ANALYTIC Trends for Today's Businesses*, 1st ed.; John Wiley & Sons: Hoboken, NJ, USA, 2013.
58. Han, J.; Pei, J.; Kamber, M. *Data Mining: Concepts and Techniques*, 3rd ed.; Elsevier: Waltham, MA, USA, 2011.
59. Hardisty, A.; Roberts, D. A decadal view of biodiversity informatics: Challenges and priorities. *BMC Ecol.* **2013**, *13*, 16. [CrossRef] [PubMed]
60. Cavner, J.A.; Stewart, A.M.; Grady, C.J.; Beach, J.H. An innovative Web Processing Services based GIS architecture for global biogeographic analyses of species distributions. *OSGeo J.* **2012**, *10*, 15–59.

61. Allen, J.M.; Folk, R.A.; Soltis, P.S.; Soltis, D.E.; Guralnick, R.P. Biodiversity synthesis across the green branches of the tree of life. *Nat. Plants* **2019**, *5*, 11–13. [CrossRef] [PubMed]
62. Töpel, M.; Zizka, A.; Calió, M.F.; Scharn, R.; Silvestro, D.; Antonelli, A. SpeciesGeoCoder: Fast categorization of species occurrences for analyses of biodiversity, biogeography, ecology, and evolution. *Syst. Biol.* **2017**, *66*, 145–151. [CrossRef] [PubMed]
63. Edler, D.; Guedes, T.; Zizka, A.; Rosvall, M.; Antonelli, A. Infomap bioregions: Interactive mapping of biogeographical regions from species distributions. *Syst. Biol.* **2017**, *66*, 197–204. [CrossRef]
64. Antonelli, A.; Hettling, H.; Condamine, F.L.; Vos, K.; Nilsson, R.H.; Sanderson, M.J.; Sauquet, H.; Scharn, R.; Silvestro, D.; Töpel, M. Toward a self-updating platform for estimating rates of speciation and migration, ages, and relationships of taxa. *Syst. Biol.* **2017**, *66*, 152–166. [CrossRef]
65. Geijzendorffer, I.R.; Regan, E.C.; Pereira, H.M.; Brotons, L.; Brummitt, N.; Gavish, Y.; Haase, P.; Martin, C.S.; Mihoub, J.B.; Secades, C.; et al. Bridging the gap between biodiversity data and policy reporting needs: An Essential Biodiversity Variables perspective. *J. Appl. Ecol.* **2016**, *53*, 1341–1350. [CrossRef]
66. Pereira, H.M.; Ferrier, S.; Walters, M.; Geller, G.N.; Jongman, R.H.G.; Scholes, R.J.; Bruford, M.W.; Brummitt, N.; Butchart, S.H.M.; Cardoso, A.C. Essential biodiversity variables. *Science* **2013**, *339*, 277–278. [CrossRef]
67. Brummitt, N.; Regan, E.C.; Weatherdon, L.V.; Martin, C.S.; Geijzendorffer, I.R.; Rocchini, D.; Gavish, Y.; Haase, P.; Marsh, C.J.; Schmeller, D.S. Taking stock of nature: Essential biodiversity variables explained. *Biol. Conserv.* **2017**, *213*, 252–255. [CrossRef]
68. Mazzocchi, F. Could Big Data be the end of theory in science? A few remarks on the epistemology of data-driven science. *EMBO Rep.* **2015**, *16*, 1250–1255. [CrossRef]
69. Li, R.; Qian, L.; Sun, H. Current progress and future prospects in phylofloristics. *Plant Divers.* **2018**, *40*, 141–146. [CrossRef]
70. Bayraktarov, E.; Ehmke, G.; O'connor, J.; Burns, E.L.; Nguyen, H.A.; McRae, L.; Possingham, H.P.; Lindenmayer, D.B. Do big unstructured biodiversity data mean more knowledge? *Front. Ecol. Evol.* **2019**, *6*, 239. [CrossRef]
71. Hortal, J.; de Bello, F.; Diniz-Filho, J.A.F.; Lewinsohn, T.M.; Lobo, J.M.; Ladle, R.J. Seven shortfalls that beset large-scale knowledge of biodiversity. *Annu. Rev. Ecol. Evol. Syst.* **2015**, *46*, 523–549. [CrossRef]
72. Kindsvater, H.K.; Dulvy, N.K.; Horswill, C.; Juan-Jordá, M.J.; Mangel, M.; Matthiopoulos, J. Overcoming the data crisis in biodiversity conservation. *Trends Ecol. Evol.* **2018**, *33*, 676–688. [CrossRef] [PubMed]
73. Brooks, T.M.; Akçakaya, H.R.; Burgess, N.D.; Butchart, S.H.M.; Hilton-Taylor, C.; Hoffmann, M.; Juffe-Bignoli, D.; Kingston, N.; MacSharry, B.; Parr, M. Analysing biodiversity and conservation knowledge products to support regional environmental assessments. *Sci. Data* **2016**, *3*, 160007. [CrossRef] [PubMed]
74. Scheufele, D.A. Science communication as political communication. *Proc. Natl. Acad. Sci. USA* **2014**, *111*, 13585–13592. [CrossRef] [PubMed]
75. Limson, J. Engaging the Public in Scientific Research: Models, Prospects and Challenges from the Perspective of Scientists. In *Science Communication in South Africa: Reflections on Current Issues*; Weingart, P., Joubert, M., Falade, B., Eds.; African Minds: Cape Town, South Africa, 2019; pp. 19–44.
76. Scrimshaw, S.C. Science, health, and cultural literacy in a rapidly changing communications landscape. *Proc. Natl. Acad. Sci. USA* **2019**, *116*, 7650–7655. [CrossRef]
77. National Academies of Sciences, Engineering, and Medicine. *The Health Effects of Cannabis and Cannabinoids: The Current State of Evidence and Recommendations for Research*; National Academies Press: Washington, DC, USA, 2017.
78. Convention of Biological Diversity. Biodiversity and the 2030 agenda for sustainable development. *Tech. Note* **2020**, 1–28.
79. Spierenburg, M. Getting the message across biodiversity science and policy interfaces–A review. *GAIA-Ecol. Perspect. Sci. Soc.* **2012**, *21*, 125–134. [CrossRef]
80. Young, J.C.; Waylen, K.A.; Sarkki, S.; Albon, S.; Bainbridge, I.; Balian, E.; Davidson, J.; Edwards, D.; Fairley, R.; Margerison, C. Improving the science-policy dialogue to meet the challenges of biodiversity conservation: Having conversations rather than talking at one-another. *Biodivers. Conserv.* **2014**, *23*, 387–404. [CrossRef]
81. Gossa, C.; Fisher, M.; Milner-Gulland, E.J. The research–implementation gap: How practitioners and researchers from developing countries perceive the role of peer-reviewed literature in conservation science. *Oryx* **2015**, *49*, 80–87. [CrossRef]
82. Bickford, D.; Posa, M.R.C.; Qie, L.; Campos-Arceiz, A.; Kudavidanage, E.P. Science communication for biodiversity conservation. *Biol. Conserv.* **2012**, *151*, 74–76. [CrossRef]
83. Curtis, D.J.; Reid, N.; Ballard, G. Communicating ecology through art: What scientists think. *Ecol. Soc.* **2012**, *17*, 3. [CrossRef]
84. Novacek, M.J. Engaging the public in biodiversity issues. *Proc. Natl. Acad. Sci. USA* **2008**, *105*, 11571–11578. [CrossRef]
85. Legagneux, P.; Casajus, N.; Cazelles, K.; Chevallier, C.; Chevrinais, M.; Guéry, L.; Jacquet, C.; Jaffré, M.; Naud, M.-J.; Noisette, F. Our house is burning: Discrepancy in climate change vs. biodiversity coverage in the media as compared to scientific literature. *Front. Ecol. Evol.* **2018**, *5*, 175. [CrossRef]
86. Davies, S.R. Constructing communication: Talking to scientists about talking to the public. *Sci. Commun.* **2008**, *29*, 413–434. [CrossRef]
87. Schaich, H.; Bieling, C.; Plieninger, T. Linking ecosystem services with cultural landscape research. *Gaia-Ecol. Perspect. Sci. Soc.* **2010**, *19*, 269–277. [CrossRef]
88. Koetz, T.; Farrell, K.N.; Bridgewater, P. Building better science-policy interfaces for international environmental governance: Assessing potential within the Intergovernmental Platform for Biodiversity and Ecosystem Services. *Int. Environ. Agreem. Politics Law Econ.* **2012**, *12*, 1–21. [CrossRef]

Article

A Novel Ensemble Machine Learning Approach for Bioarchaeological Sex Prediction

Evan Muzzall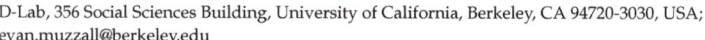

D-Lab, 356 Social Sciences Building, University of California, Berkeley, CA 94720-3030, USA; evan.muzzall@berkeley.edu

Abstract: I present a novel machine learning approach to predict sex in the bioarchaeological record. Eighteen cranial interlandmark distances and five maxillary dental metric distances were recorded from n = 420 human skeletons from the necropolises at Alfedena (600–400 BCE) and Campovalano (750–200 BCE and 9–11th Centuries CE) in central Italy. A generalized low rank model (GLRM) was used to impute missing data and Area under the Curve—Receiver Operating Characteristic (AUC-ROC) with 20-fold stratified cross-validation was used to evaluate predictive performance of eight machine learning algorithms on different subsets of the data. Additional perspectives such as this one show strong potential for sex prediction in bioarchaeological and forensic anthropological contexts. Furthermore, GLRMs have the potential to handle missing data in ways previously unexplored in the discipline. Although results of this study look promising (highest AUC-ROC = 0.9722 for predicting binary male/female sex), the main limitation is that the sexes of the individuals included were not known but were estimated using standard macroscopic bioarchaeological methods. However, future research should apply this machine learning approach to known-sex reference samples in order to better understand its value, along with the more general contributions that machine learning can make to the reconstruction of past human lifeways.

Keywords: SuperLearner ensemble machine learning; cross-validation; generalized low rank model; bioarchaeology; sex prediction; central Italy

Citation: Muzzall, E. A Novel Ensemble Machine Learning Approach for Bioarchaeological Sex Prediction. *Technologies* **2021**, *9*, 23. https://doi.org/10.3390/technologies9020023

Academic Editors: Mohammed Mahmoud and Manoj Gupta

Received: 15 March 2021
Accepted: 30 March 2021
Published: 1 April 2021

Publisher's Note: MDPI stays neutral with regard to jurisdictional claims in published maps and institutional affiliations.

Copyright: © 2021 by the author. Licensee MDPI, Basel, Switzerland. This article is an open access article distributed under the terms and conditions of the Creative Commons Attribution (CC BY) license (https://creativecommons.org/licenses/by/4.0/).

1. Introduction

Accurate sex prediction of archaeological skeletal remains is a fundamental step for reconstructing biological and demographic profiles of past humans. After an archaeological site is surveyed and excavated and unknown human remains are identified, documented, and recovered, the sex and age of deceased individuals are commonly estimated using macroscopic methods of the pelvis, skull, and teeth [1–3]. However, because female and male biological maturation rates differ [4,5], sex misidentification can lead to data recording bias and depreciated interpretability. After sex has been macroscopically estimated and with the assistance of other biological and archaeological contextual information, the identities and lifeways of the deceased can be reconstructed in bioarchaeological contexts. However, traditional macroscopic sex estimation methods possess varying degrees of accuracy [6–11]. For example, the pelvis and cranium might provide conflicting sex estimation results even within the same individual. This process is further complicated by other aspects, particularly of age, as tooth crown calcification and eruption and bone epiphyseal fusion are useful until early adulthood when 3rd molars erupt and bony ossification centers fuse skeletal elements into their final, united shapes. Pelvic, cranial suture, and sternal rib end methods are used to predict age in individuals through later stages of adulthood, albeit with wider margins of error.

Craniometric dimensions are frequently used as proxies for genetic relatedness of past humans due to their potentially heritable nature and correlations with neutral and adaptive genetic variation and selection [12–20]. In the absence of genetic information, these methods are used to approximate the genetic and evolutionary relationships of past humans [21], thus making accurate sex classification an integral first step in the reconstruction of other biological and demographic parameters. Hence, further examinations of sex correlations with other lines of evidence such as burial location, material culture, musculoskeletal stress markers, health, diet, disease, trauma prevalence, and biological relatedness will be skewed if sex is first misclassified.

Machine learning is slowly gaining a foothold in bioarchaeology and forensic anthropology despite our discipline's deep ties to statistics and computational research for investigation of large quantitative datasets. Cunningham's [22] pioneering machine learning social anthropological work for rule-based kinship structure detection set a high bar for anthropologists of all subdisciplines to aspire. However, her work remains largely unrecognized even though it exemplifies the types of problem-and-dataset-driven questions faced by bioarchaeologists. This discrepancy persists despite the promise for bioarchaeological machine learning applications for predicting sex, age, ancestry, body mass, and stature in forensic anthropology, radiography, and anatomy [23–31]. Even less bioarchaeological research has focused on missing data imputation [32].

Therefore, more examples are needed to better contextualize our methodological understandings of sex estimation techniques. This research is an extension of Muzzall et al. (2017) [33], which improved sex prediction accuracy of the William W. Howells Worldwide Craniometric Dataset and provided another example of the strong potential for machine learning to assist in sex prediction in bioarchaeological contexts. Here, I use a generalized low rank model to impute large amounts of missing data for a stratified cross-validated supervised ensemble machine learning approach. This framework consists of eight algorithms total and is fit to cranial interlandmark and dental metric distances to predict binary sex from six pelvic and cranially estimated samples at Alfedena (600–400 BCE) and Campovalano (750–200 BCE and 9–11th Centuries CE) in central Italy.

Italy is home to one of the most colossal bioarchaeological contexts on Earth and represents humans' deep history throughout the region. Its central Mediterranean location, deep temporal breadth, and geological and environmental diversities have been influential in shaping the genetic, morphological, and cultural histories of the region [34–39]. Humans here developed some of the richest and most divergent forms of social interaction through worship, architecture, iconography and writing, and empires that persisted for long periods of time and across the globe via trade, warfare, and colonization. Central Italy was a particular crossroads between Africa and Europe and the Near East and Iberia and was home to many chiefdoms and nation-states that contained both shared and varied forms of settlement patterns, social and burial organization, material cultures, mortuary behaviors, and skeletal-dental morphologies. As a result, Italy's bioarchaeological record provides a space to experiment with new methodologies for sex prediction.

2. Materials and Methods

2.1. Dataset

The dataset consists of metric cranial and dental data from $n = 240$ males and $n = 180$ females from central Italy: four locations from the Iron Age necropolis at Alfedena (600–400 BCE), the Iron Age graveyard at Campovalano (750–200 BCE), and the Medieval cemetery at Campovalano (9–11th Centuries CE) (Table 1). The ground truth sexes of these individuals were not known due to their antiquity and were estimated using standard macroscopic methods found in [1] by the original archaeologists [40,41] and by the author.

Table 1. Location, time period, and sex distributions for males and females from Central Italy used in this study.

Location	Time Period	Male	Female
Alfedena Arboreto	600–400 BCE	9	10
Alfedena Campo Consolino	600–400 BCE	61	19
Alfedena Scavi Mariani	600–400 BCE	37	28
Alfedena Sergi Museum	600–400 BCE	19	13
Campovalano Iron Age	750–200 BCE	89	77
Campovalano St. Peter	9–11th C. CE	25	33
Total		240	180

Cranial metric data were collected from twelve standard anatomical landmarks: four from the face, four from the cranial vault, and four from the cranial base (Table 2). This produced a total of eighteen cranial interlandmark distances, six from each of the four landmarks from the three cranial regions.

Table 2. Cranial anatomical landmarks used in this study. The four landmarks from each of the three regions produced eighteen total interlandmark distances—six for each region [1].

Face	Definition
Nasion (n)	The intersection of the naso-frontal suture in the midsagittal plane
Prosthion (pr)	The location of the anteriorly located portion of the anterior surface of the alveolar process at the most anterior point of the alveolar process
Right frontomalare orbitale (fmorR)	The location where the zygomaticofrontal suture intersects the orbital margin
Left zygomaxillare (zymL)	The most inferior and anterior location on the zygomaticomaxillary suture
Vault	
Bregma (b)	The landmark where the sagittal and coronal sutures meet in the midsagittal plane. In cases where the sagittal suture deflects laterally, an estimation must be made of the location in the midsagittal plane
Lambda (l)	The landmark where the left and right lambdoidal sutures intersect the sagittal suture. The landmark must be estimated when the suture intersection is obliterated, or where strongly serrated sutures are present
Right Asterion (astR)	The juncture of the lambdoid, parietomastoid, and occipitomastoid sutures
Left Frontotemporale (ftL)	The most medial and anterior point on the superior temporal line on the frontal bone
Base	
Nasion (n)	The intersection of the naso-frontal suture in the midsagittal plane
Basion (ba)	The inner border where the anterior portion of the foramen magnum is intersected by the midsagittal plane
Hormion (h)	The juncture of the sphenoid and vomer bones in the midsagittal plane
Left Porion (poL)	The most superior point on the external margin of the external auditory meatus

Dental metric data consisted of maximum mesiodistal dimensions of the right (or left-substituted when the right antimere was missing) maxillary canine (XC) and buccolingual breadths of the right mesial (P3) and distal (P4) premolars and first (M1) and second (M2) molars [42]. Thus, six different subsets of the data were used: (1) six metrics from the face, (2) six from the vault, (3) six from the base, (4) eighteen from the cranium (the combined face, vault, and base metrics), (5) five from the dentition, and (6) twenty-three from the total combined cranial and dental data. Tukey boxplots are used to illustrate sex differences in these metrics.

2.2. Missing Data

Missing data were prevalent from all areas of measurement and proportions of missing values for the face, vault, base, and dentition are shown in Table 3. A generalized low rank model (GLRM) was used to impute the missing values. GLRMs function as an extension of principal component analysis (PCA) for low rank matrix tabular dataset approximation, by

> "approximating a data set as a product of two low dimensional factors by minimizing an objective function. The objective will consist of a loss function on the approximation error together with regularization of the low dimensional factors. With these extensions of PCA, the resulting low rank representation of the data set still produces a low dimensional embedding of the data set, as in PCA" [43] (p. 3)

Table 3. Percentage of missing data for each variable.

Bony Region	Measurement	Proportion Missing Male	Proportion Missing Female
Face	n_pr	63	67
	n_fmorR	54	58
	n_zymL	57	65
	pr_fmorR	63	68
	pr_zymL	63	69
	fmorR_zymL	63	71
Vault	b_l	38	47
	b_astR	38	46
	b_ftL	42	51
	l_astR	37	44
	l_ftL	44	54
	astR_ftL	46	54
Base	n_ba	61	66
	n_h	63	68
	n_poL	53	61
	ba_h	65	69
	ba_poL	57	62
	h_poL	61	66
Dentition	XC	59	69
	P3	53	63
	P4	50	66
	M1	49	46
	M2	53	53

A generalized low rank model is essentially an unsupervised approach for data completion that uses clustering of known data in reduced dimensional space. The advantage of this data-adaptive approach to reconstruct missingness in the skeletal and dental remains instead of column mean, median, or k-nearest neighbor imputation is that it effectively uses clustering of features to impute the missing data, which makes sense given that the missingness of the data arises directly from missingness in the skeletal remains themselves. Missingness indicators were also added as columns to the dataset to indicate exactly where missing and imputed data were located. These columns also functioned as predictor variables in the machine learning models to see if the location of missing data was related to sex prediction ability.

2.3. Ensemble Machine Learning

Machine learning is defined as "a vast set tools for understanding data" [44] (p. 1). It originated as a combination of computer science and statistics, but its greatest strength is its breadth of research application [45,46]. Early examples stem from the social and cognitive sciences that attempted to predict and imitate human behavior [47–49]. In this research I use a supervised classification machine learning approach because the goal is to predict a categorical outcome (predict male sex from binary male/female options) using the craniodental features as predictor variables.

Ensembles are useful supervised machine learning methods because they optimize predictor accuracy through combinations of a suite of less accurate models [50]. They are preferred to fitting single algorithms for prediction because classification performance of single algorithms might differ due to variance (sensitivity to differences in the training data), algorithmic bias (erroneous assumptions about the relationships between the selected algorithm and the data), and/or algorithmic hyperparameter settings (pre-defined options that are selected before model training). The SuperLearner approach [51,52] is an algorithm that uses cross-validation [53] to estimate the performance of several machine learning models, and/or the same algorithm(s) with different hyperparameter settings. It then produces an optimal weighted average of those models (an "ensemble model"), using external cross-validation. This method is as accurate asymptotically as any single best-performing algorithm. I fit the eight algorithms (five constituent algorithms, the weighted SuperLearner ensemble, the benchmark mean of the Y outcome variable, and the resulting "DiscreteSL" single best performing algorithm/combination of algorithms) to predict binary sex classification for each of the six subsets of the data described above as the predictors: the face, vault, base, combined cranial regions, dentition, and combined craniodental data. In this sense, SuperLearner is essentially stacked/blended learning where the SuperLearner ensemble algorithm provides the ideal combinations of base learners by utilizing weighted combinations to provide asymptotically optimal learner configurations across algorithms and different subsets of the data.

Besides the SuperLearner approach, there are other ways to utilize machine learning ensembles. For example, the random forest algorithm is in itself an ensemble—it is "random" because it is based on individual bootstrap-aggregated (a sampling with replacement model averaging technique for variance reduction) decision trees and also because each individual tree uses a subset of predictor variables at each decision split (instead of using all predictors like a regular decision tree does); it is a "forest" because many trees are grown. The predictions based on each of these trees in the forest is then applied to the out-of-bag samples—holdout data not included in the training process of each tree—to evaluate performance and provide error estimates. The outcome variable is then predicted based on the majority vote of class labels for all the trees in the case of classification, or the prediction average across all trees in the case of regression. Bagging and boosting can be used to improve the performance of a variety of other algorithms as well. The eight different algorithms used in this study are defined in Table 4.

Table 4. Definitions of the eight machine learning algorithms used in this research.

Algorithm	Description	Reference
Logistic regression	Logistic regression models the relationships between the outcome variable (male/female sex) and the predictor variables. It computes the probability that the Y variable (sex) belongs to one of the two binary classes.	Dobson, 1990 [54]
Lasso	Lasso (least absolute shrinkage and selection operator) is a form of penalized regression (L1) that produces a sparse solution to remove predictor variables from the model that are not related to the outcome.	Friedman et al.,. 2010 [55]
Decision tree	A decision tree is a relatively simple tree-based method that gauges the probability of classifying the outcome based on the predictor variables before splitting a given decision node a certain number of times until there are no longer enough observations to split.	Breiman et al., 1984 [56]
Ranger (random forest)	Ranger is a decorrelated random forest ensemble classifier method that uses the average of multiple bootstrapped decision tree models for classification. Unlike single decision tree models that use all predictors at each split, random forests use only a random subsample of the total predictors for each split in each tree.	Breiman, 2001 [57]; Wright and Ziegler, 2017 [58]
Xgboost	A gradient boosted tree is another tree-based method that fits a tree to the residuals of the previous tree in succession. It downweights easily predicted cases but upweights those that it cannot predict. This continues over many iterations so that weak trees are "boosted" into strong ones.	Freund and Schapire, 1999 [59]; Chen et al.,. 2019 [60]
SuperLearner	The SuperLearner algorithm is an optimal weighted ensemble average that improves predictor construction and is flexible in that it can perform well on different data distributions and protects against overfitting through external cross-validation. Individual algorithm weights can be investigated to see which ones contribute most to the ensemble.	van der Laan et al., 2007 [51]; Kennedy, 2017 [61]
Mean of Y	The mean of Y (dependent variable) is the benchmark algorithm based only on the mean. This is a very simple prediction so the more complex algorithms should perform better than this one. It should not be the best single-performing algorithm and should have a low weight in the weighted-average ensemble. If it is the best performing algorithm something is likely wrong.	Polley and van der Laan, 2010 [52]
DiscreteSL	The discrete SuperLearner is the single best performing algorithm(s) as identified by the SuperLearner. Alternatively, this might also correspond to the combination of best performing algorithms at different cross-validation folds, in which case the DiscreteSL AUC-ROC will not be identical to that of a single algorithm.	Polley and van der Laan, 2010 [52]

2.4. Evaluating Model Performance

Stratified 20-fold cross-validated Area Under the Curve—Receiver Operating Characteristic (AUC-ROC) was used to evaluate the performance of the individual algorithms while an external/nested 20-fold cross-validation layer was used to estimate performance on the blended SuperLearner ensemble model via a separate holdout sample [61,62].

Stratified k-fold cross-validation is a process that divides the data into equally sized portions and trains a model on k-1 portions of the data so that the model can learn the relationship between male/female sex outcomes and the various craniodental predictor variables. The one holdout portion is used for testing purposes (but not for fitting the SuperLearner) and this process is repeated k times. I chose 20 folds, so each algorithm was trained on 19 portions of the data (95%) and tested on the one holdout (5%). This process was repeated twenty times, with the holdout set rotated each time. This process allows every data point to be in the test set once. This also produces standard errors for the performance of each algorithm that can be compared to the SuperLearner average.

The receiver operator characteristic curve itself represents the probability that a binary outcome (male or female predicted sex, in this case) is correctly classified [63] while the AUC-ROC provides the degree of separability for the sexes that the model achieves. The receiver operator characteristic curve models the sensitivity (true positive rate) versus specificity (true negative rate) at various thresholds along the receiver operator characteristic curve. Maximization of AUC-ROC is ideal, which ranges from zero (no predictive ability) to 0.5 (equivalent to random guessing) to 1.0 (perfect prediction). AUC-ROC is more useful for prediction of imbalanced classes and to prevent overfitting of a single class compared to simple classification accuracy.

Instead of fitting the models separately and looking at the performance (lowest risk), algorithms should be fit simultaneously. Risk is the average loss function used here and measures how far off the prediction was for a given observation and is calculated by nonnegative least squares error; the lower the risk the fewer errors were made by the model. SuperLearner also identifies which single algorithm (or combination of algorithms) is best (the "DiscreteSL" discrete winner), in addition to calculating the weighted average of the ensemble itself. Coefficient weights can be viewed to see each algorithm's contribution to this weighted ensemble average. Analysis was conducted in R version 3.6.2 and the ck37r, SuperLearner, and ggplot2 packages [64–66].

3. Results

Results indicate that ensemble machine learning has strong potential for sex prediction and yielded AUC-ROC values greater than 0.90 for the cranial metric data and ~0.74 for the dental metric data. Males are larger than females in all dimensions as shown by the Tukey boxplots in Figures 1 and 2 although distributions for the sexes overlap considerably.

AUC-ROC performance for each algorithm along with their standard errors and confidence intervals are shown in Table 5. The combined craniodental data had the highest AUC-ROC with 0.9722, followed by the combined cranial (0.9644), face (0.9426), vault (0.9116), base (0.9060), and dentition (0.7421). Expectedly, the mean of Y is the worst performing algorithm in all cases (AUC-ROC = 0.500 for each). The SuperLearner algorithm has the highest AUC-ROC for all six bony regions while ranger is a close second for the face, vault, base, cranial, and combined craniodental data. Logistic regression, lasso, and ranger are all close seconds for the dental data.

Additionally, the single best algorithm (or combination of algorithms)—the DiscreteSL—was the ranger random forest algorithm for all 20 cross-validation folds for the face, base, combined cranial data, and combined craniodental data. However, for the vault, ranger was the best performing algorithm 19 times and the decision tree algorithm once. For the dental data, logistic regression was the best performing algorithm 14 times, lasso 4 times, and ranger twice—this algorithmic confusion could be related to the considerably lower AUC-ROC for the dentition compared to any of the cranial data.

The SuperLearner weight distributions show which of the individual algorithms contributed most to the ensemble (Table 6). For the combined craniodental data, lasso contributed a coefficient of 0.4522, indicating that it contributed this percentage to the SuperLearner ensemble. This was followed by lesser contributes from the ranger algorithm (0.1734), xgboost (0.1700), logistic regression (0.1319), and decision tree (0.0726). For cranial data, ranger contributed a coefficient of 0.4610, followed by lesser contributions from logistic regression (0.1940), lasso (0.1411), decision tree (0.1267), and xgboost (0.0772). Contributions to the face stem mostly from ranger (0.4634) and logistic regression (0.4193), for the vault from ranger (0.5004) and decision tree (0.3234), and for the base from ranger (0.8878). For the dentition, contributions stem mostly from logistic regression (0.5591) and ranger (0.3582).

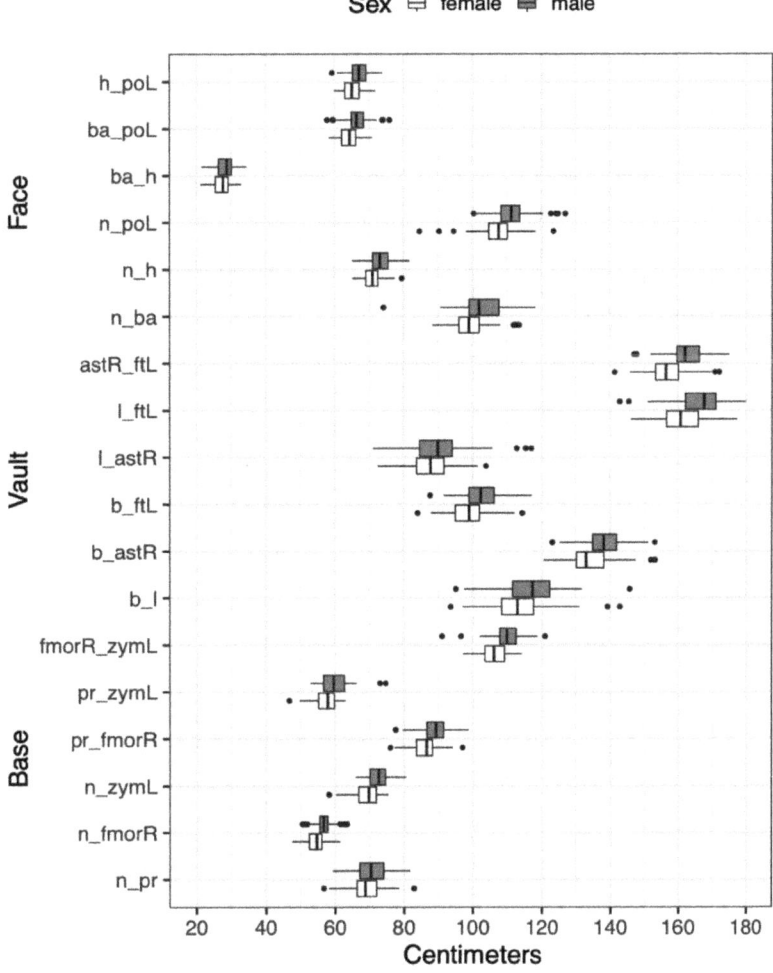

Figure 1. Distributions of raw cranial data for males and females. Cranial landmark abbreviations are defined in Table 2.

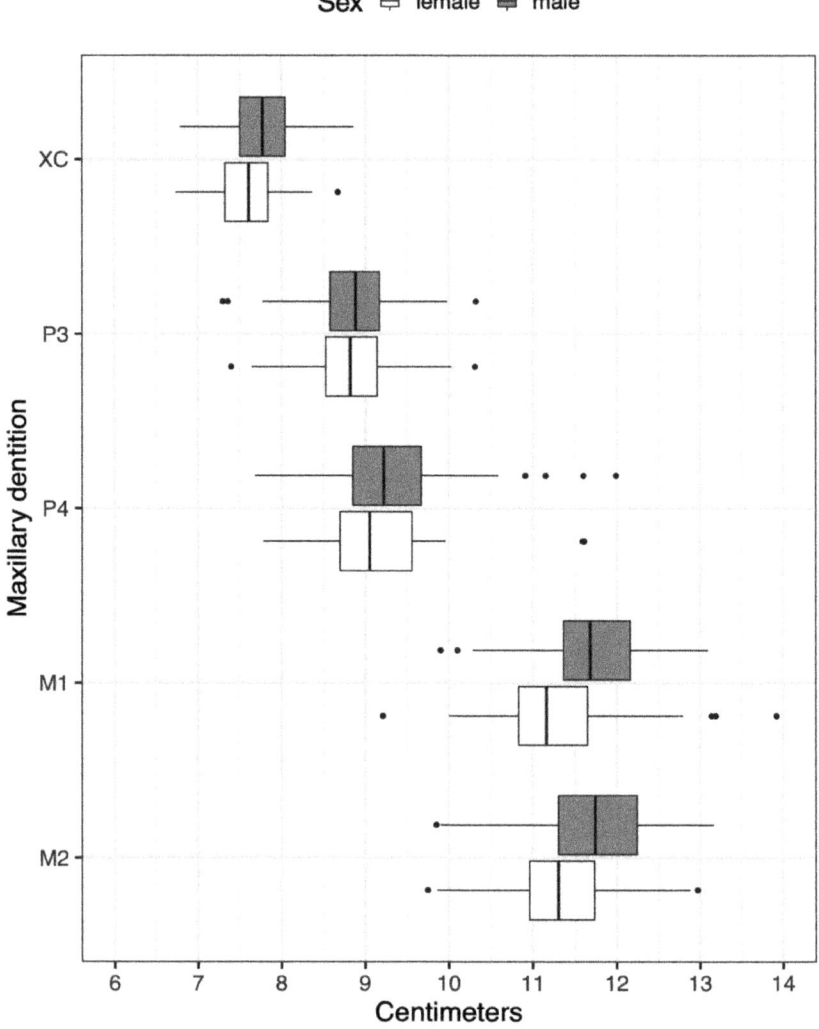

Figure 2. Distributions of raw dental data for males and females. Dental distance abbreviations are defined in Section 2.1.

Table 5. Cross-validated AUC-ROC statistics for the six different measurement regions. 0.5 is the equivalent of random guessing; 1 means perfect prediction.

Bony Region	Algorithm	AUC-ROC	Standard Error	Confidence Interval (Lower)	Confidence Interval (Upper)
Face	Mean of Y	0.5000	0.0493	0.4034	0.5966
	Decision tree	0.8069	0.0259	0.7562	0.8577
	Xgboost	0.8998	0.0152	0.8701	0.9295
	Lasso	0.9042	0.0161	0.8727	0.9357
	Logistic regression	0.9088	0.0157	0.8781	0.9395
	Ranger	0.9306	0.0122	0.9066	0.9545
	DiscreteSL	0.9306	0.0122	0.9066	0.9545
	SuperLearner	0.9426	0.0111	0.9208	0.9644
Vault	Mean of Y	0.5000	0.0493	0.4034	0.5966
	Logistic regression	0.8458	0.0200	0.8067	0.8850
	Lasso	0.8486	0.0198	0.8099	0.8873
	Xgboost	0.8690	0.0188	0.8322	0.9058
	Decision tree	0.8998	0.0218	0.8570	0.9425
	DiscreteSL	0.9030	0.0164	0.8709	0.9351
	Ranger	0.9065	0.0158	0.8756	0.9374
	SuperLearner	0.9116	0.0147	0.8827	0.9404
Base	Mean of Y	0.5000	0.0493	0.4034	0.5966
	Logistic regression	0.7667	0.0238	0.7201	0.8132
	Lasso	0.7685	0.0238	0.7219	0.8152
	Decision tree	0.7986	0.0248	0.7500	0.8472
	Xgboost	0.8646	0.0177	0.8298	0.8993
	Ranger	0.9051	0.0146	0.8764	0.9338
	DiscreteSL	0.9051	0.0146	0.8764	0.9338
	SuperLearner	0.9060	0.0146	0.8774	0.9347
Cranial	Mean of Y	0.5000	0.0493	0.4034	0.5966
	Decision tree	0.9125	0.0189	0.8754	0.9496
	Lasso	0.9236	0.0138	0.8966	0.9506
	Logistic regression	0.9282	0.0128	0.9032	0.9533
	Xgboost	0.9306	0.0128	0.9054	0.9557
	Ranger	0.9519	0.0103	0.9317	0.9720
	DiscreteSL	0.9519	0.0103	0.9317	0.9720
	SuperLearner	0.9644	0.0084	0.9480	0.9807
Dental	Mean of Y	0.5000	0.0493	0.4034	0.5966
	Decision tree	0.6537	0.0280	0.5989	0.7086
	Xgboost	0.6551	0.0270	0.6021	0.7081
	Ranger	0.7171	0.0250	0.6680	0.7662
	DiscreteSL	0.7213	0.0256	0.6711	0.7715
	Lasso	0.7412	0.0250	0.6921	0.7903
	Logistic regression	0.7417	0.0252	0.6924	0.7910
	SuperLearner	0.7421	0.0248	0.6935	0.7908
Combined craniodental	Mean of Y	0.5000	0.0493	0.4034	0.5966
	Decision tree	0.9060	0.0196	0.8675	0.9445
	Xgboost	0.9375	0.0116	0.9148	0.9602
	Logistic regression	0.9426	0.0111	0.9209	0.9643
	Lasso	0.9528	0.0104	0.9324	0.9731
	Ranger	0.9549	0.0100	0.9353	0.9745
	DiscreteSL	0.9549	0.0100	0.9353	0.9745
	SuperLearner	0.9722	0.0070	0.9585	0.9860

Table 6. Algorithm weight contributions to the SuperLearner ensembles.

Bony Region	Algorithm	Mean (Contribution to Ensemble)	Standard Deviation	Min	Max
Face	Ranger	0.4634	0.1058	0.2389	0.6044
	Logistic regression	0.4193	0.0373	0.3262	0.4779
	Xgboost	0.1159	0.0928	0.0000	0.3199
	Lasso	0.0013	0.0059	0.0000	0.0263
	Decision tree	0.0001	0.0004	0.0000	0.0017
	Mean of Y	0.0000	0.0000	0.0000	0.0000
Vault	Ranger	0.5004	0.1205	0.1910	0.7078
	Decision tree	0.3234	0.0935	0.1591	0.5442
	Logistic regression	0.1412	0.0520	0.0556	0.2234
	Xgboost	0.0350	0.0561	0.0000	0.1483
	Mean of Y	0.0000	0.0000	0.0000	0.0000
	Lasso	0.0000	0.0000	0.0000	0.0000
Base	Ranger	0.8878	0.0701	0.7068	0.9811
	Logistic regression	0.0758	0.0259	0.0189	0.1264
	Xgboost	0.0364	0.0590	0.0000	0.2168
	Mean of Y	0.0000	0.0000	0.0000	0.0000
	Lasso	0.0000	0.0000	0.0000	0.0000
	Decision tree	0.0000	0.0000	0.0000	0.0000
Crania	Ranger	0.4610	0.1162	0.2750	0.6789
	Logistic regression	0.1940	0.0859	0.0299	0.3193
	Lasso	0.1411	0.0753	0.0380	0.2882
	Decision tree	0.1267	0.1028	0.0000	0.3101
	Xgboost	0.0772	0.0826	0.0000	0.2452
	Mean of Y	0.0000	0.0000	0.0000	0.0000
Dental	Logistic regression	0.5591	0.0608	0.4472	0.6747
	Ranger	0.3582	0.0953	0.1797	0.5286
	Decision tree	0.0747	0.0719	0.0000	0.2339
	Xgboost	0.0080	0.0160	0.0000	0.0573
	Mean of Y	0.0000	0.0000	0.0000	0.0000
	Lasso	0.0000	0.0000	0.0000	0.0000
Combined craniodental	Lasso	0.4522	0.0918	0.2598	0.6602
	Ranger	0.1734	0.1048	0.0000	0.3853
	Xgboost	0.1700	0.0739	0.0416	0.2906
	Logistic regression	0.1319	0.0892	0.0000	0.3308
	Decision tree	0.0726	0.0755	0.0000	0.1891
	Mean of Y	0.0000	0.0000	0.0000	0.0000

4. Discussion

AUC-ROC of this SuperLearner ensemble machine learning framework demonstrates strong potential for cranial sex prediction of archaeological human skeletal remains in this particular central Italian context. An important potential contribution of this research is that it reframes the problem of sex estimation as a predictive one and does not rely on assumptions of p-values, traditional hypothesis testing, or causal inference approaches. Instead, the focus was on model performance, standard errors, and confidence intervals. Additionally, the goal here was not to optimize any algorithms for maximum predictive accuracy, but to instead provide a gentle overview of the process and to stimulate the reader into thinking about how this approach could be applied in their own research contexts. This method can also potentially be employed in the field to help resolve disagreements between experts or for indeterminate remains.

Results also support previous research that ensemble machine learning has strong potential for sex prediction in the bioarchaeological record [33]. Although the actual ground truth (in the binary sense; sex and gender are more dynamic than this in reality) male/female sexes of the individuals included in this study were not known, results support previous research that indicates contrasts between male and female morphological and burial patterns in central Italy during the Iron Age [39–41]. Among the three different cranial regions, the face had the highest AUC-ROC values, followed by the vault and base. This could provide further support for the utility of the face for population reconstruction despite its greater environmental plasticity compared to the base and vault due to sensory functions of sight, smell, and taste [67].

Of particular interest were the general size differences between males and females. Despite their overlapping measurement distributions—and if the modeling process was strongly influenced by size alone—it would be reasonable to expect that the dentition would have had higher AUC-ROC values similar to those of the cranial data. Whether or not the antimeric substitution of left teeth for right teeth in the absence of a right-side tooth and/or the sheer amount of missingness influenced the much lower dental AUC-ROC is unknown. More cranial-dental comparisons are necessary to evaluate the reliability of the dentition in this framework.

The ensembles themselves can be strengthened by including a greater diversity of algorithms and customizing them with varying hyperparameters (pre-training settings) to find the most accurate and best performing tunings [68]. Other considerations can be more thoroughly incorporated as well, such as different confusion matrix derivations to evaluate performance, such as precision and recall to further highlight class imbalance problems, balanced estimator constructions, false discovery rate, and F1 score. Negative log-likelihood could also be used as the optimizer instead of nonnegative least squares. Other algorithms and methods also might be more appropriate—only a few algorithms with default settings were incorporated in this project but many others can be included in the ensemble (e.g., Bayesian additive regression trees [69]). Features could be screened to identify more interpretable models and custom algorithms can be included to the researcher's exact specifications (see Kennedy, 2017 [61] for the R walkthrough). Moreover, deep learning—a subdiscipline of machine learning that utilizes multi-layered artificial neural networks for modeling, predicting, inferring, and understanding data—might be even more useful [70]. When dataset sizes and the number of algorithms exceed personal compute potential, the software packages for analyses mentioned in this research have instructions to be run in parallel across multiple cores on a single computer or across multiple machines in cluster or remote settings. Perhaps of great interest to the bioarchaeologist, variable importance information can be extracted from various algorithms to see which cranial and dental dimensions have the highest weights for sex classification.

It is critical to note that due to the antiquity of the samples included in this research, the ground truth sexes of the individuals included were estimated macroscopically using pelvic and skull traits. As a result, future researchers should consider implementing this or similar frameworks using known-sex reference skeletal collections from the Hamann-Todd Osteological Collection (housed at the Cleveland Museum of Natural History), the Robert J. Terry Anatomical Skeletal Collection (Smithsonian Institution, National Museum of Natural History), or the 21st Century Identified Skeletal Collection (University of Coimbra, Portugal). However, my goal was not to concretely establish this ensemble machine learning method in any dogmatic way, but to instead onboard the reader to the basic concepts and their application in bioarchaeology. This study is merely a demonstration of the methods and an advertisement of the potential for generalized low rank imputation and ensemble machine learning processes in bioarchaeological and forensic contexts. Known-sex references samples should be a prerequisite for confirmation of methods presented here, and larger sample sizes might also be important. Cadaver samples and skeletal collections such as those mentioned above would be particularly useful for these procedures. Furthermore, I encourage future researchers to examine the effects that different missing data handling methods (listwise deletion, mean, median, k-nearest neighbor, bootstrap, expectation-maximization, multiple imputation, GLRMs, etc.) have on error estimates in cases of sex prediction in the bioarchaeological record.

Ensemble machine learning techniques should be considered as part of the bioarchaeologist's toolkit as an additional method for comparison to macroscopic interrogations of the skeleton and dentition that we rely upon for reconstruction of the biological profiles of past humans. These techniques can potentially assist not only in bioarchaeological reconstructions, but also in forensic applications for identification of missing persons and perhaps even to material, faunal, and floral assemblages as well as mortuary studies and settlement organization. Furthermore, GLRMs warrant further exploration and should be considered by bioarchaeologists as a potentially strong data preprocessing tool when faced with missing data and analytical techniques that require full datasets for computation. Social scientists in general would benefit from updating their instrumentation with cross-validated ensemble machine learning techniques when research requires an outcome to be predicted.

Funding: This research received no external funding.

Institutional Review Board Statement: Not applicable.

Informed Consent Statement: Not applicable.

Data Availability Statement: Data and code are not publicly available because they are considered property of the Soprintendenza Archeologia d'Abruzzo and represent the heritage of Italian people, culture, and history. However, the R walkthrough for applying SuperLearner to your own data can be found in reference [61].

Acknowledgments: I thank Chris J. Kennedy, Aniket Kesari, Alfredo Coppa, the Soprintendenza Archeologia d'Abruzzo, and the staffs from the Museo Antropologia de "Giuseppe Sergi"—Sapienza, Museo Paludi di Celano, Museo Archeologico Nazionale d'Abruzzo di Chieti, and Museo di Archeologico Nazionale di Campli. Patrick M. Muzzall and three anonymous reviewers provided comments that improved the quality of this manuscript.

Conflicts of Interest: The author declares no conflict of interest.

References

1. Buikstra, J.E.; Ubelaker, D.H. *Standards for Data Collection from Human Skeletal Remains*; Arkansas Archaeological Survey: Fayetteville, AR, USA, 1994.
2. Garvin, H.M.; Ruff, C.B. Sexual dimorphism in skeletal browridge and chin morphologies determined using a new quantitative method. *Am. J. Phys. Anthr.* **2012**, *147*, 661–670. [CrossRef]
3. Krishan, K.; Chatterjee, P.M.; Kanchan, T.; Kaur, S.; Baryah, N.; Singh, R.K. A review of sex estimation techniques during examination of skeletal remains in forensic anthropology casework. *Forensic Sci. Int.* **2016**, *261*, e1–e165. [CrossRef]
4. Slemenda, C.W.; Reister, T.K.; Hui, S.L.; Miller, J.Z.; Christian, J.C.; Johnston, C.C. Inluences on skeletal mineralization in children and adolescents: Evidence for varying effects of sexual maturation and physical activity. *J. Pediatr.* **1994**, *125*, 201–207. [CrossRef]
5. Wang, Y. Is Obesity Associated with Early Sexual Maturation? A Comparison of the Association in American Boys Versus Girls. *Pediatrics* **2002**, *110*, 903–910. [CrossRef]
6. Weiss, K.M. On the systematic bias in skeletal sexing. *Am. J. Phys. Anthr.* **1972**, *37*, 239–249. [CrossRef]
7. Sutter, R.C. Nonmetric Subadult Skeletal Sexing Traits: I. A Blind Test of the Accuracy of Eight Previously Proposed Methods Using Prehistoric Known-Sex Mummies from Northern Chile. *J. Forensic Sci.* **2003**, *48*, 927–935. [CrossRef] [PubMed]
8. Konigsberg, L.W.; Algee-Hewitt, B.F.B.; Steadman, D.W. Estimation and evidence in forensic anthropology: Sex and race. *Am. J. Phys. Anthr.* **2009**, *139*, 77–90. [CrossRef]
9. Jackes, M. Representativeness and bias in archaeological skeletal samples. In *Social Bioarchaeology*; Agarwal, S.C., Glencross, B.A., Eds.; Wiley-Blackwell: West Sussex, UK, 2011; pp. 107–145.
10. Sierp, I.; Henneberg, M. The Difficulty of Sexing Skeletons from Unknown Populations. *J. Anthr.* **2015**, *2015*. [CrossRef]
11. Irurita Olivares, J.; Alemán Aguilera, I. Validation of the sex estimation method elaborated by Schutkowski in the Granada Osteological Collection of identified infant and young children: Analysis of the controversy between the different ways of analyzing and interpreting the results. *Int. J. Leg. Med.* **2016**, *130*, 1623–1632. [CrossRef]
12. Sjøvold, T. A report on the heritability of some cranial measurements and non-metric traits. In *Multivariate Statistical Methods in Physical Anthropology*; Van Vark, G.H., Howells, W.W., Eds.; Reidel Publishing Company: Dordrecht, The Netherlands, 1984; pp. 223–246.
13. Devor, E.J. Transmission of human cranial dimensions. *J. Craniofac. Genet. Dev. Biol.* **1987**, *7*, 95–106.
14. Roseman, C.C. Detecting interregionally diversifying natural selection on modern human cranial form by using matched molecular and morphometric data. *Proc. Natl. Acad. Sci. USA* **2004**, *101*, 12824–12829. [CrossRef]
15. Roseman, C.C.; Weaver, T.D. Multivariate apportionment of global human craniometric diversity. *Am. J. Phys. Anthr.* **2004**, *125*, 257–263. [CrossRef]
16. Carson, E.A. Maximum likelihood estimation of human craniometric heritabilities. *Am. J. Phys. Anthr.* **2006**, *131*, 169–180. [CrossRef] [PubMed]

17. Witherspoon, D.J.; Wooding, S.; Rogers, A.R.; Marchani, E.E.; Watkins, W.S.; Batzer, M.A.; Jorde, L.B. Genetic similarities within and between human populations. *Genetics* **2007**, *176*, 351–359. [CrossRef]
18. Martínez-Abadías, N.; Esparza, M.; Sjøvold, T.; González-José, R.; Santos, M.; Hernández, M. Heritability of human cranial dimensions: Comparing the evolvability of different cranial regions. *J. Anat.* **2009**, *214*, 19–35. [CrossRef] [PubMed]
19. Strauss, A.; Hubbe, M. Craniometric Similarities Within and between Human Populations in Comparison with Neutral Genetic Markers. *Hum. Biol.* **2010**, *82*, 315–330. [CrossRef] [PubMed]
20. Herrera, B.; Hanihara, T.; Godde, K. Comparability of multiple data types from the Bering Strait region: Cranial and dental metrics and nonmetrics, mtDNA, and Y-Chromosome DNA. *Am. J. Phys. Anthr.* **2014**, *54*, 334–348. [CrossRef] [PubMed]
21. Buikstra, J.E.; Frankenberg, S.R.; Konigsberg, L.W. Skeletal biological distance studies in American Physical Anthropology: Recent trends. *Am. J. Phys. Anthr.* **1990**, *82*, 1–7. [CrossRef]
22. Cunningham, S.J. Machine learning applications in anthropology: Automated discovery over kinship structures. *Comput. Humanit.* **1996**, *30*, 401–406. [CrossRef]
23. Bell, S.; Jantz, R. Neural network classification of skeletal remains. In *Archaeological Inormatics: Pushing the Envelope*; Burenhult, G., Ed.; Archaeopress: Oxford, UK, 2001; pp. 205–212.
24. Hefner, J.T.; Ousley, S.D. Statistical Classification Methods for Estimating Ancestry Using Morphoscopic Traits. *J. Forensic Sci.* **2014**, *59*, 883–890. [CrossRef]
25. Czibula, G.; Ionescu, V.S.; Miholca, D.L.; Mircea, I.G. Machine learning-based approaches for predicting stature from archaeological skeletal remains using long bone lengths. *J. Archaeol. Sci.* **2016**, *69*, 85–99. [CrossRef]
26. Ionescu, V.S.; Teletin, M.; Voiculescu, E.M. Machine learning techniques for age at death estimation from long bone lengths. In Proceedings of the 2016 IEEE 11th International Symposium on Applied Computational Intelligence and Inormatics (SACI), Timisoara, Romania, 12–14 May 2016; pp. 457–462.
27. Ionescu, V.S.; Czibula, G.; Teletin, M. Supervised Learning Techniques for Body Mass Estimation in Bioarchaeology. In *Soft Computing Applications—Advances in Intelligent Systems and Computing 634*; Balas, V., Jain, L., Balas, M., Eds.; Springer: Berlin/Heidelberg, Germany, 2018.
28. Miholca, D.L.; Czibula, G.; Mircea, I.G.; Czibula, I.G. Machine learning based approaches for sex identification in bioarchaeology. In Proceedings of the 18th International Symposium on Symbolic and Numeric Algorithms for Scientific Computing (SYNASC), Timişoara, Romania, 24–27 September 2016; pp. 311–314.
29. Pink, C.M. Forensic Ancestry Assessment Using Cranial Nonmetric Traits Traditionally Applied to Biological Distance Studies. In *Biological Distance Analysis–Forensic and Bioarchaeological Perspectives*; Pilloud, M.A., Hefner, J.T., Eds.; Academic Press: San Diego, CA, USA, 2016; pp. 213–230.
30. Porto, F.P.; Lima, L.N.C.; Flores, M.R.P.; Valsecchi, A.; Ibanez, O.; Palhares, C.E.M.; de Barros Vidal, F. Automatic cephalometric landmarks detection on frontal faces: An approach based on supervised learning techniques. *Digit. Investig.* **2019**, *30*, 108–116. [CrossRef]
31. Ortiz, A.G.; Costa, C.; Silva, R.H.A.; Biazevic, M.G.H.; Michel-Crosato, E. Sex estimation: Anatomical references on panoramic radiographs using machine learning. *Forensic Imaging* **2020**, *20*, 200356. [CrossRef]
32. Kenyhercz, M.W.; Passalacqua, N.V. Missing Data Imputation Methods and Their Performance with Biodistance Analyses. In *Biological Distance Analysis–Forensic and Bioarchaeological Perspectives*; Pilloud, M.A., Hefner, J.T., Eds.; Academic Press: San Diego, CA, USA, 2016; pp. 181–194.
33. Muzzall, E.; Kennedy, C.J.; Culich, A. Ensemble Machine Learning for Sex Prediction of a Worldwide Craniometric Dataset, Poster Presented at the Berkeley Institute for Data Science Data Science Faire. Available online: https://github.com/EastBayEv/Ensemble-machine-learning-for-sex-prediction-of-a-worldwide-craniometric-dataset (accessed on 7 July 2020).
34. Scozzari, R.; Cruciani, F.; Pangrazio, A.; Santolamazza, P.; Vona, G.; Moral, P.; Latini, V.; Varesi, L.; Memmi, M.M.; Romano, V.; et al. Human Y-chromosome variation in the Western Mediterranean area: Implications for the peopling of the region. *Hum. Immunol.* **2001**, *62*, 871–884. [CrossRef]
35. Coppa, A.; Cucina, A.; Lucci, M.; Mancinelli, D.; Vargiu, R. Origins and spread of agriculture in Italy: A nonmetric dental analysis. *Am. J. Phys. Anthr.* **2007**, *133*, 918–930. [CrossRef]
36. Muttoni, G.; Scardia, G.; Kent, D.V.; Swisher, C.C.; Manzi, G. Pleistocene magnetochronology of early hominin sites at Ceprano and Fontana Ranuccio, Italy. *Earth Planet Sci. Lett.* **2009**, *286*, 255–268. [CrossRef]
37. Fu, Q.; Rudan, P.; Pääbo, S.; Krause, J. Complete Mitochondrial Genomes Reveal Neolithic Expansion into Europe. *PLoS ONE* **2012**, *7*, e32473. [CrossRef]
38. Ghirotto, S.; Tassi, F.; Fumagalli, E.; Colonna, V.; Sandionigi, A.; Lari, M.; Vai, S.; Petiti, E.; Corti, G.; Rizzi, E.; et al. Origins and Evolution of the Etruscans' mtDNA. *PLoS ONE* **2013**, *8*, e55519. [CrossRef] [PubMed]
39. Muzzall, E.; Coppa, A. Temporal and Spatial Biological Kinship Variation at Campovalano and Alfedena in Iron Age Central Italy. In *Bioarcheology of Frontiers and Borderlands*; Tica, C., Martin, D.L., Eds.; University Press of Florida: Gainesville, FL, USA, 2019; pp. 107–132.
40. Coppa, A.; Macchiarelli, R. The maxillary dentition of the Iron-Age population of Alfedena (Middle-Adriatic Area, Italy). *J. Hum. Evol.* **1982**, *11*, 219–235. [CrossRef]
41. Bondioli, L.; Corruccini, R.S.; Macchiarelli, R. Familial segregation in the Iron Age community of Alfedena, Abruzzo, Italy, based on osteodental trait analysis. *Am. J. Phys. Anthr.* **1986**, *71*, 393–400. [CrossRef]

42. Hillson, S.; FitzGerald, C.; Flinn, H. Alternative dental measurements: Proposals and relationships with other measurements. *Am. J. Phys. Anthr.* **2006**, *126*, 413–426. [CrossRef]
43. Udell, M.; Horn, C.; Zadeh, R.; Boyd, S. Generalized Low Rank Models. *Found. Trends Mach. Learn.* **2016**, *9*, 1–118. [CrossRef]
44. James, G.; Witten, D.; Hastie, T.; Tibshirani, R. *An Introduction to Statistical Learning: With Applications in R.*; Springer: New York, NY, USA, 2013.
45. Breiman, L. Statistical Modeling: The Two Cultures. *Stat. Sci.* **2001**, *16*, 199–231. [CrossRef]
46. Welling, M. *Are ML and Statistics Complimentary? Roundtable Discussion at the 6th IMS-ISBA Meeting on Data Science in the Next 50 Years*; University of Amsterdam: Amsterdam, The Netherlands, 2015.
47. Turing, A.M. Computing Machinery and Intelligence. *Mind* **1950**, *59*, 433–460. [CrossRef]
48. Rosenblatt, F. The perceptron: A probabilistic model for information storage and organization in the brain. *Psychol. Rev.* **1958**, *65*, 386–408. [CrossRef]
49. Samuel, A.L. Some Studies in Machine Learning Using the Game of Checkers. *IBM J. Res. Dev.* **1959**, *3*, 207–226. [CrossRef]
50. Dietterich, T.G. Ensemble methods in machine learning. In *Lecture Notes in Computer Science 1857*; Goos, G., Hartmanis, J., van Leeuwen, J., Eds.; Springer: Berlin/Heidelberg, Germany, 2000; pp. 1–15.
51. Van der Laan, M.J.; Polley, E.C.; Hubbard, A.E. Super Learner. *Stat. Appl. Genet. Mol. Biol.* **2007**, *6*, 1–21. [CrossRef] [PubMed]
52. Polley, E.C.; van der Laan, M.J. Super Learner in Prediction, UC Berkeley Division of Biostatistics Working Paper Series Paper 266. Available online: https://biostats.bepress.com/ucbbiostat/paper266 (accessed on 8 September 2020).
53. Efron, B.; Gong, G. A Leisurely Look at the Bootstrap, the Jackknife, and Cross-Validation. *Am. Stat.* **1982**, *37*, 36–48. [CrossRef]
54. Dobson, A.J. *An Introduction to Generalized Linear Models*; Chapman and Hall: London, UK, 1990.
55. Friedman, J.; Hastie, T.; Tibshirani, R. Regularization Paths for Generalized Linear Models via Coordinate Descent. *J. Stat. Softw.* **2010**, *33*, 1–22. [CrossRef]
56. Breiman, L.; Friedman, J.; Olshen, R.; Stone, C. *Classification and Regression Trees*; Wadsworth: Belmont, CA, USA, 1984.
57. Breiman, L. Random Forests. *Mach. Learn.* **2001**, *45*, 5–32. [CrossRef]
58. Wright, N.; Ziegler, A. ranger: A fast implementation of random forests for high dimensional data in C++ and R. *J. Stat. Softw.* **2017**, *77*, 1–17. [CrossRef]
59. Freund, Y.; Schapire, R.E. A Short Introduction to Boosting. *J. Jpn. Soc. Art. Int.* **1999**, *14*, 1–14.
60. Chen, T.; He, T.; Benesty, M.; Khotilovich, V.; Tang, Y.; Cho, H.; Chen, K.; Mitchell, R.; Cano, I.; Zhou, T.; et al. Xgboost: Extreme Gradient Boosting, R Package, 2019, Version 0.90.0.2. Available online: https://CRAN.R-project.org/package=xgboost (accessed on 26 September 2020).
61. Kennedy, C. Guide to SuperLearner. 2017. Available online: https://cran.r-project.org/web/packages/SuperLearner/vignettes/Guide-to-SuperLearner.html (accessed on 26 September 2020).
62. Lantz, B. *Machine Learning with R.*; Packt Publishing: Birmingham, UK, 2015.
63. Hanley, J.A.; McNeil, B.J. The meaning and use of the area under a receiver operating characteristic (ROC) curve. *Radiology* **1982**, *143*, 29–36. [CrossRef]
64. Wickham, H. *Ggplot2: Elegant Graphics for Data Analysis*; Springer: New York, NY, USA, 2016.
65. Polley, E.; LeDell, E.; Kennedy, C.; van der Laan, M. SuperLearner: Super Learner Prediction, R Package Version 2.0-26. 2019. Available online: https://CRAN.R-project.org/package=SuperLearner (accessed on 21 November 2020).
66. Kennedy, C. Ck37r: Chris Kennedy's R Toolkit, R Package Version 1.0.3. 2020. Available online: https://github.com/ck37/ck37r (accessed on 10 March 2020).
67. Taubadel, N.V.C. Revisiting the homoiology hypothesis: The impact of phenotypic plasticity on the reconstruction of human population history from craniometric data. *J. Hum. Evol.* **2009**, *57*, 179–190. [CrossRef]
68. Bergstra, J.; Bengio, Y. Random Search for Hyper-Parameter Optimization. *J. Mach. Learn. Res.* **2012**, *13*, 281–305.
69. Chipman, H.A.; George, E.I.; McCulloch, R.E. BART: Bayesian additive regression trees. *Ann. Appl. Stat.* **2010**, *1*, 266–298. [CrossRef]
70. Chollet, F.; Allaire, J.J. *Deep Learning with R.*; Manning: New York, NY, USA, 2017.

MDPI
St. Alban-Anlage 66
4052 Basel
Switzerland
www.mdpi.com

Technologies Editorial Office
E-mail: technologies@mdpi.com
www.mdpi.com/journal/technologies

Disclaimer/Publisher's Note: The statements, opinions and data contained in all publications are solely those of the individual author(s) and contributor(s) and not of MDPI and/or the editor(s). MDPI and/or the editor(s) disclaim responsibility for any injury to people or property resulting from any ideas, methods, instructions or products referred to in the content.

www.ingramcontent.com/pod-product-compliance
Lightning Source LLC
LaVergne TN
LVHW070426100526
838202LV00014B/1539